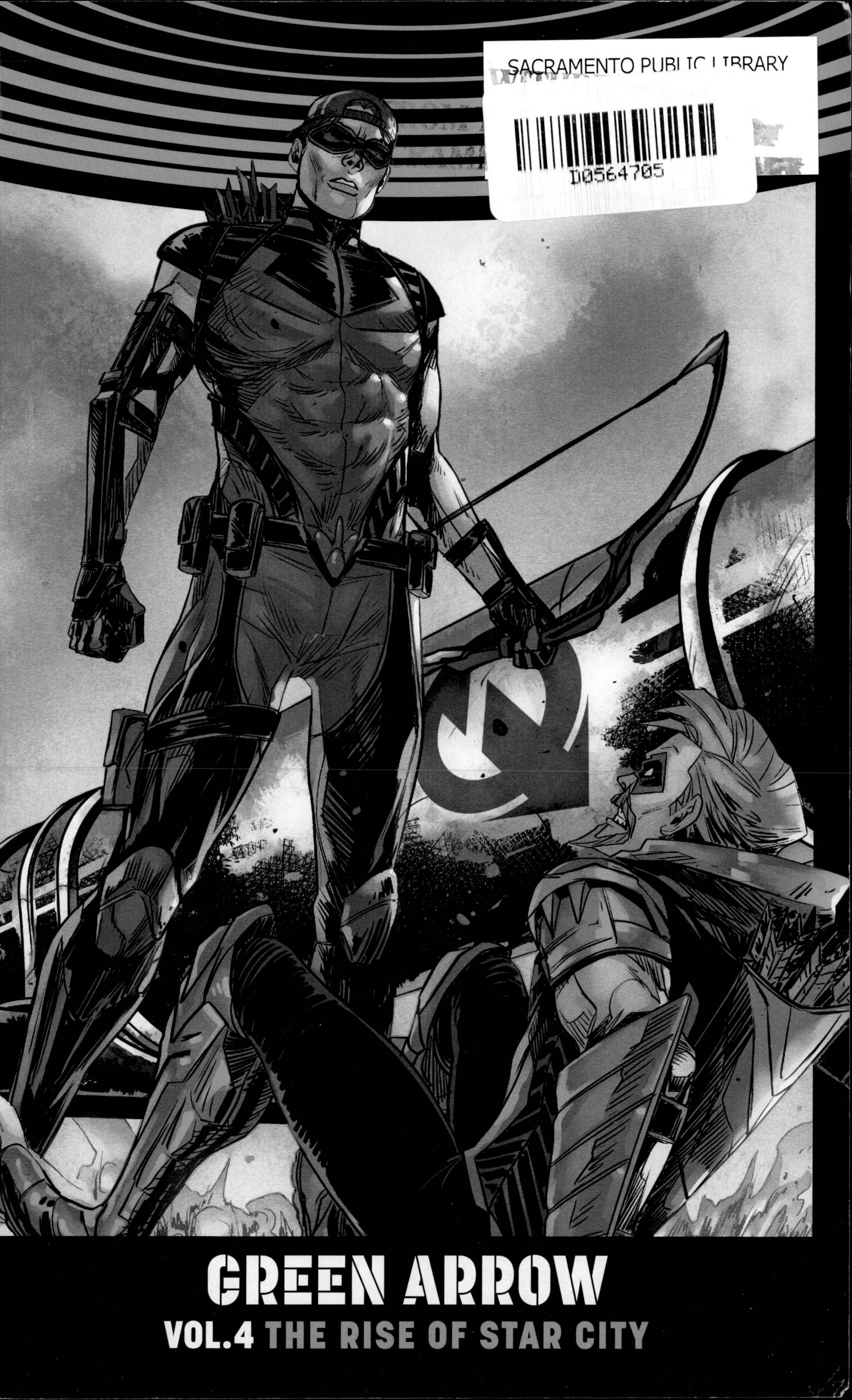

GREEN ARROW

VOL.4 THE RISE OF STAR CITY

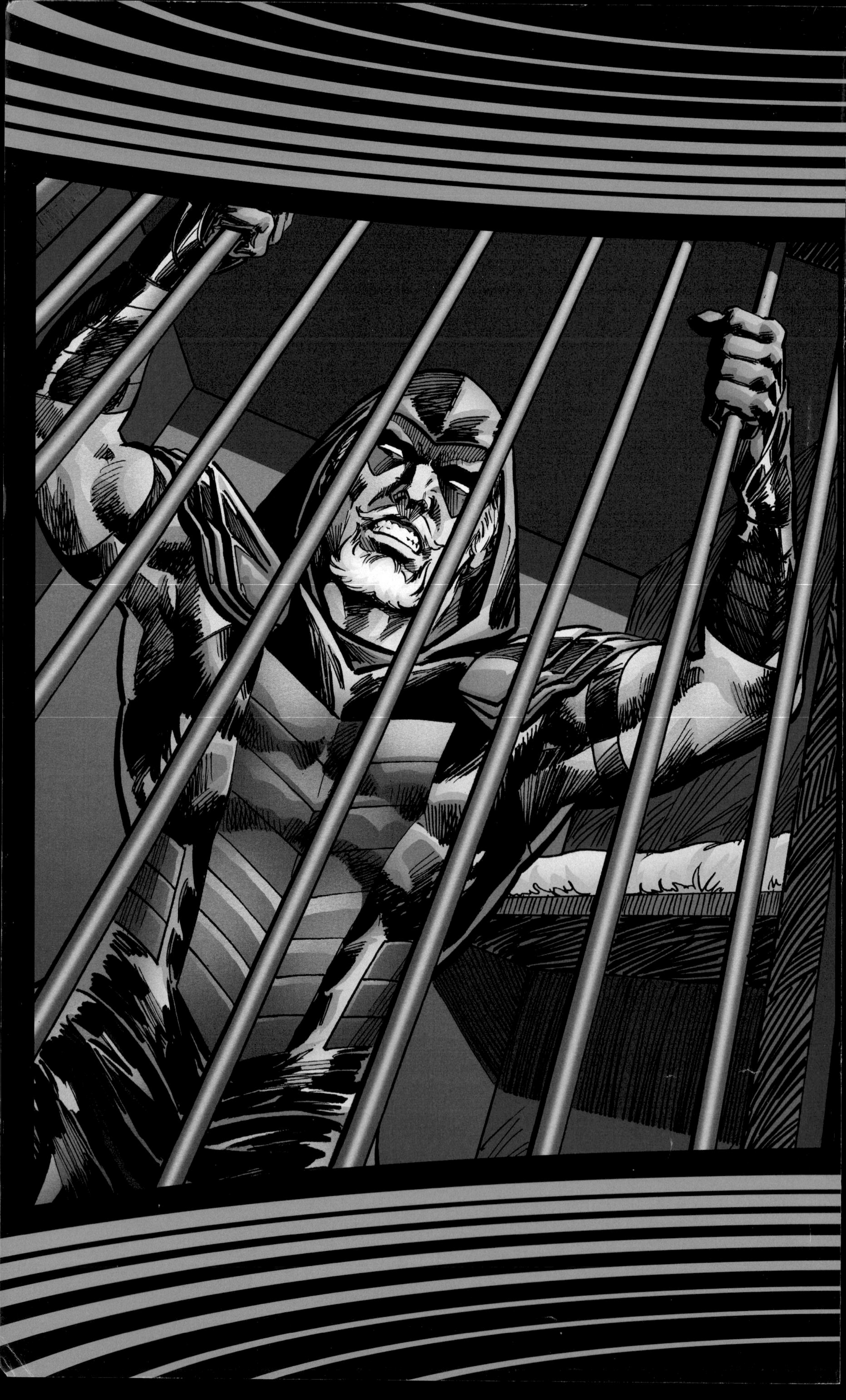

GREEN ARROW
VOL.4 THE RISE OF STAR CITY

BENJAMIN PERCY
writer

JUAN FERREYRA * ELEONORA CARLINI
MIRKA ANDOLFO * OTTO SCHMIDT
artists

JUAN FERREYRA * ARIF PRIANTO
HI-FI * OTTO SCHMIDT
colorists

NATE PIEKOS OF BLAMBOT®
letterer

JUAN FERREYRA
collection cover artist

ANDY KHOURI Editor - Original Series ✳ **HARVEY RICHARDS** Associate Editor - Original Series
JEB WOODARD Group Editor - Collected Editions ✳ **ERIKA ROTHBERG** Editor - Collected Edition
STEVE COOK Design Director - Books ✳ **MONIQUE NARBONETA** Publication Design

BOB HARRAS Senior VP - Editor-in-Chief, DC Comics
PAT McCALLUM Executive Editor, DC Comics

DIANE NELSON President ✳ **DAN DiDIO** Publisher ✳ **JIM LEE** Publisher ✳ **GEOFF JOHNS** President & Chief Creative Officer
AMIT DESAI Executive VP - Business & Marketing Strategy, Direct to Consumer & Global Franchise Management
SAM ADES Senior VP & General Manager, Digital Services ✳ **BOBBIE CHASE** VP & Executive Editor, Young Reader & Talent Development
MARK CHIARELLO Senior VP - Art, Design & Collected Editions ✳ **JOHN CUNNINGHAM** Senior VP - Sales & Trade Marketing
ANNE DePIES Senior VP - Business Strategy, Finance & Administration ✳ **DON FALLETTI** VP - Manufacturing Operations
LAWRENCE GANEM VP - Editorial Administration & Talent Relations ✳ **ALISON GILL** Senior VP - Manufacturing & Operations
HANK KANALZ Senior VP - Editorial Strategy & Administration ✳ **JAY KOGAN** VP - Legal Affairs ✳ **JACK MAHAN** VP - Business Affairs
NICK J. NAPOLITANO VP - Manufacturing Administration ✳ **EDDIE SCANNELL** VP - Consumer Marketing
COURTNEY SIMMONS Senior VP - Publicity & Communications ✳ **JIM (SKI) SOKOLOWSKI** VP - Comic Book Specialty Sales & Trade Marketing
NANCY SPEARS VP - Mass, Book, Digital Sales & Trade Marketing ✳ **MICHELE R. WELLS** VP - Content Strategy

GREEN ARROW VOLUME 4: THE RISE OF STAR CITY

DC Comics, 2900 West Alameda Ave., Burbank, CA 91505.
Printed by LSC Communications, Kendallville, IN, USA. 11/3/17. First Printing.
ISBN: 978-1-4012-7454-2

Library of Congress Cataloging-in-Publication Data is available.

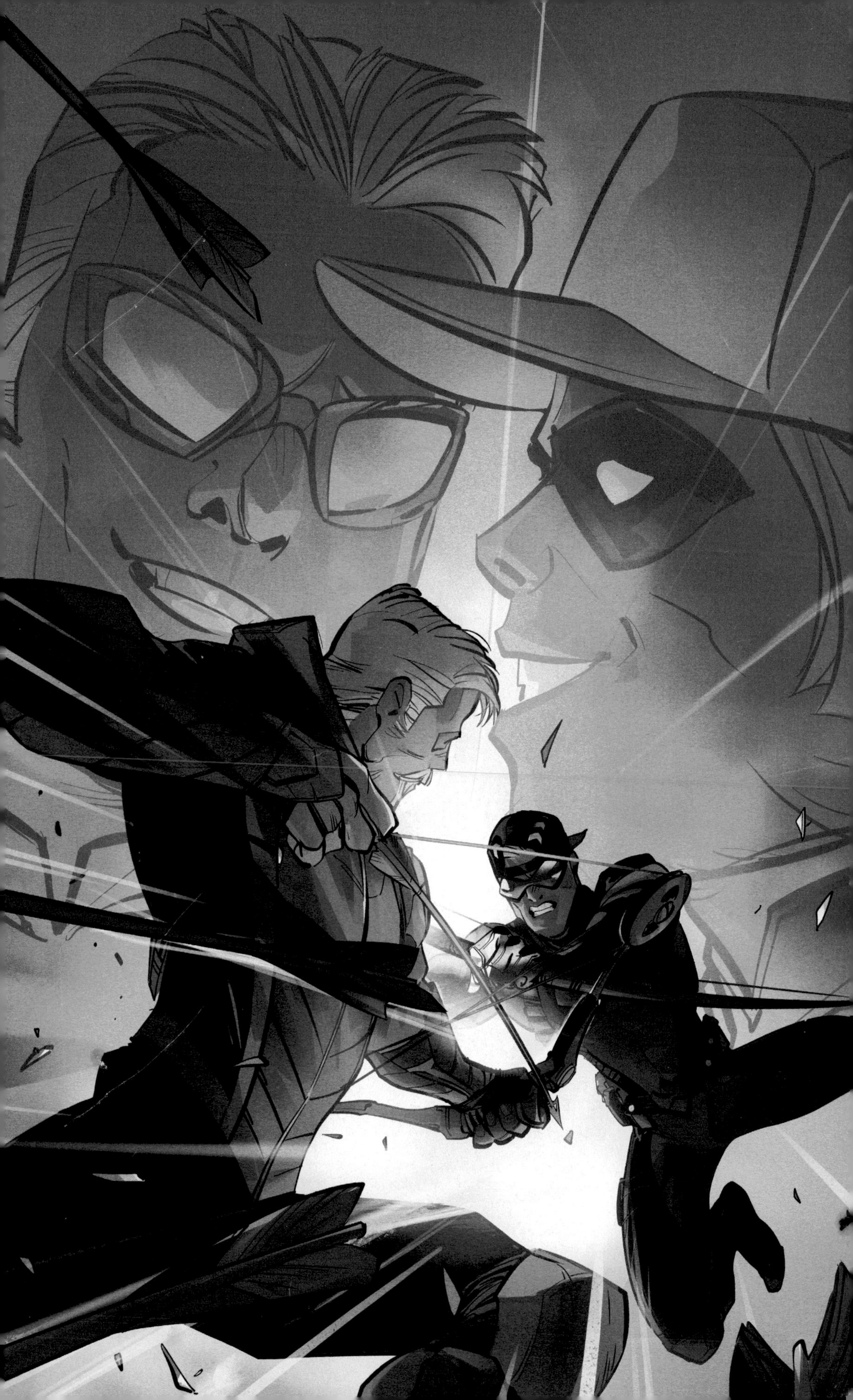

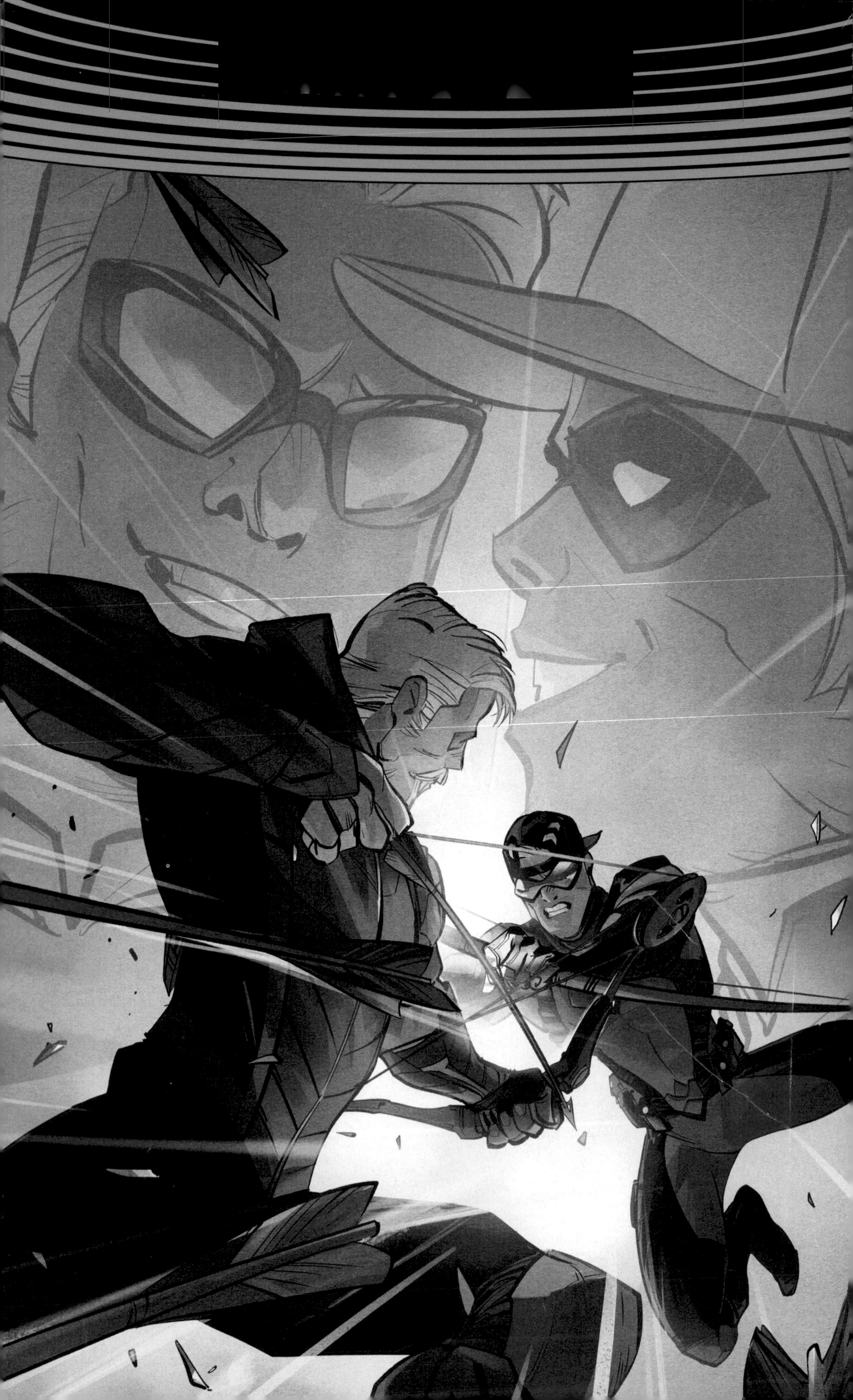

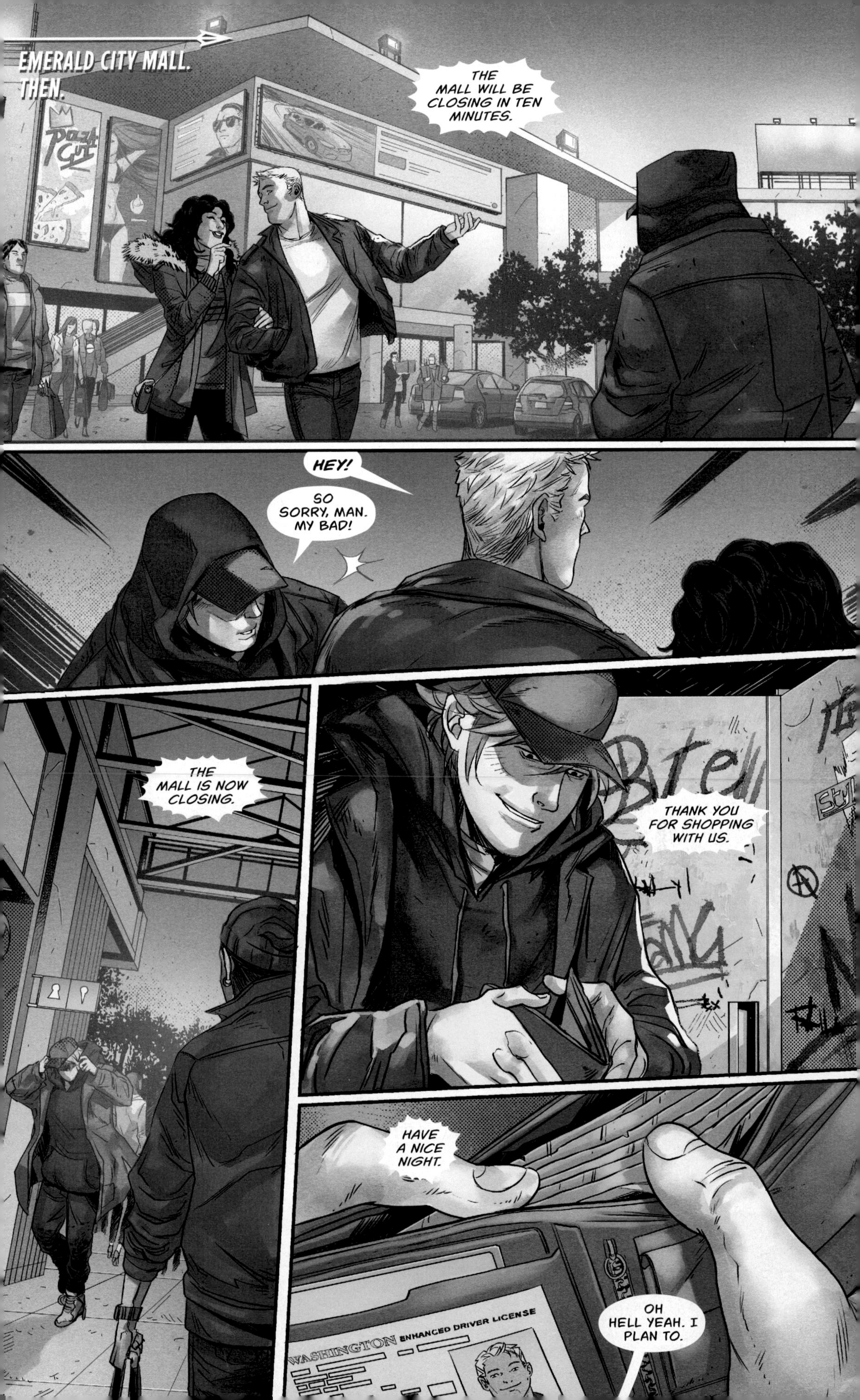
EMERALD CITY MALL.
THEN.
THE MALL WILL BE CLOSING IN TEN MINUTES.
HEY!
SO SORRY, MAN. MY BAD!
THE MALL IS NOW CLOSING.
THANK YOU FOR SHOPPING WITH US.
HAVE A NICE NIGHT.
OH HELL YEAH. I PLAN TO.
WASHINGTON ENHANCED DRIVER LICENSE

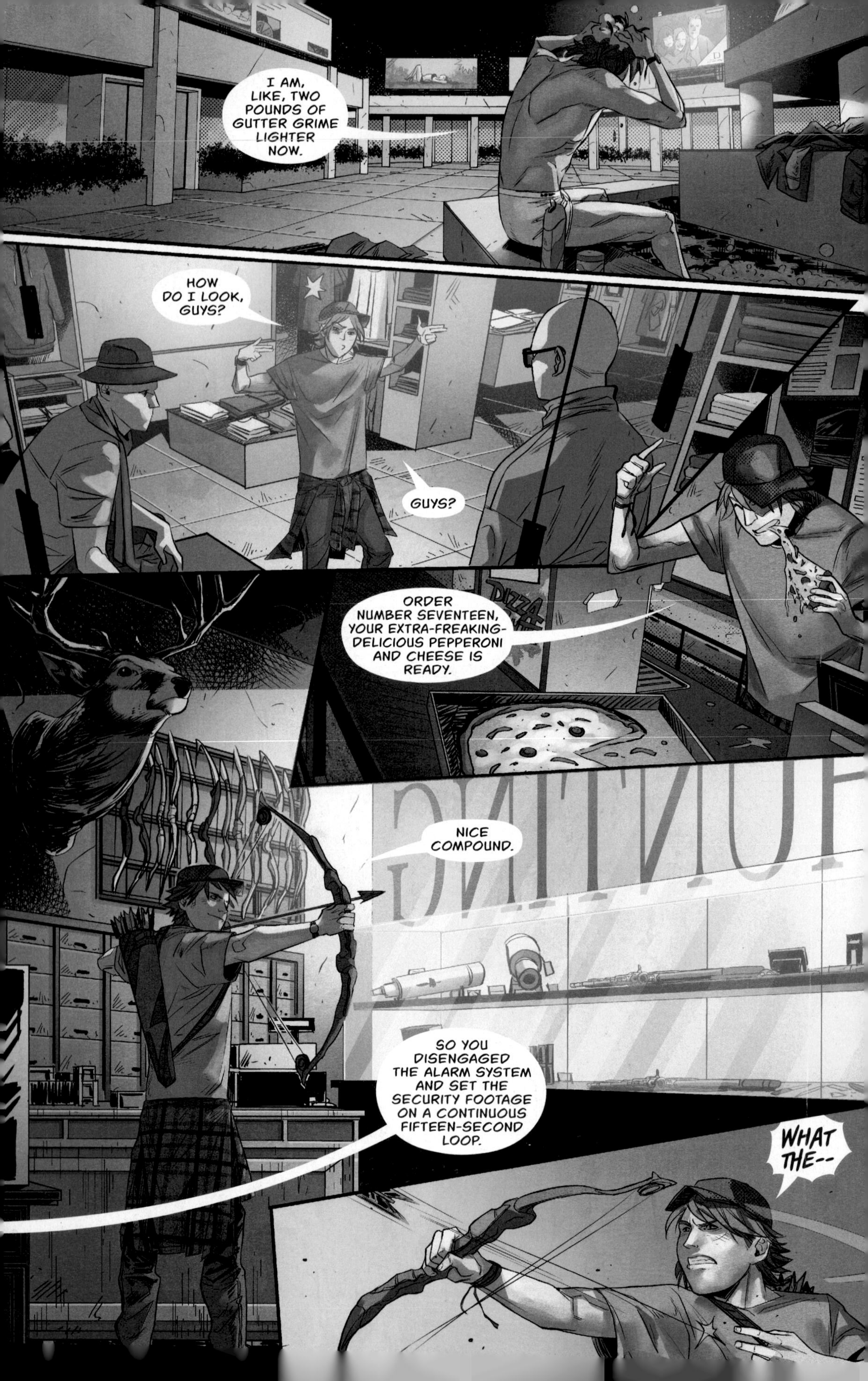

I AM, LIKE, TWO POUNDS OF GUTTER GRIME LIGHTER NOW.
HOW DO I LOOK, GUYS?
GUYS?
ORDER NUMBER SEVENTEEN, YOUR EXTRA-FREAKING-DELICIOUS PEPPERONI AND CHEESE IS READY.
NICE COMPOUND.
SO YOU DISENGAGED THE ALARM SYSTEM AND SET THE SECURITY FOOTAGE ON A CONTINUOUS FIFTEEN-SECOND LOOP.
WHAT THE--

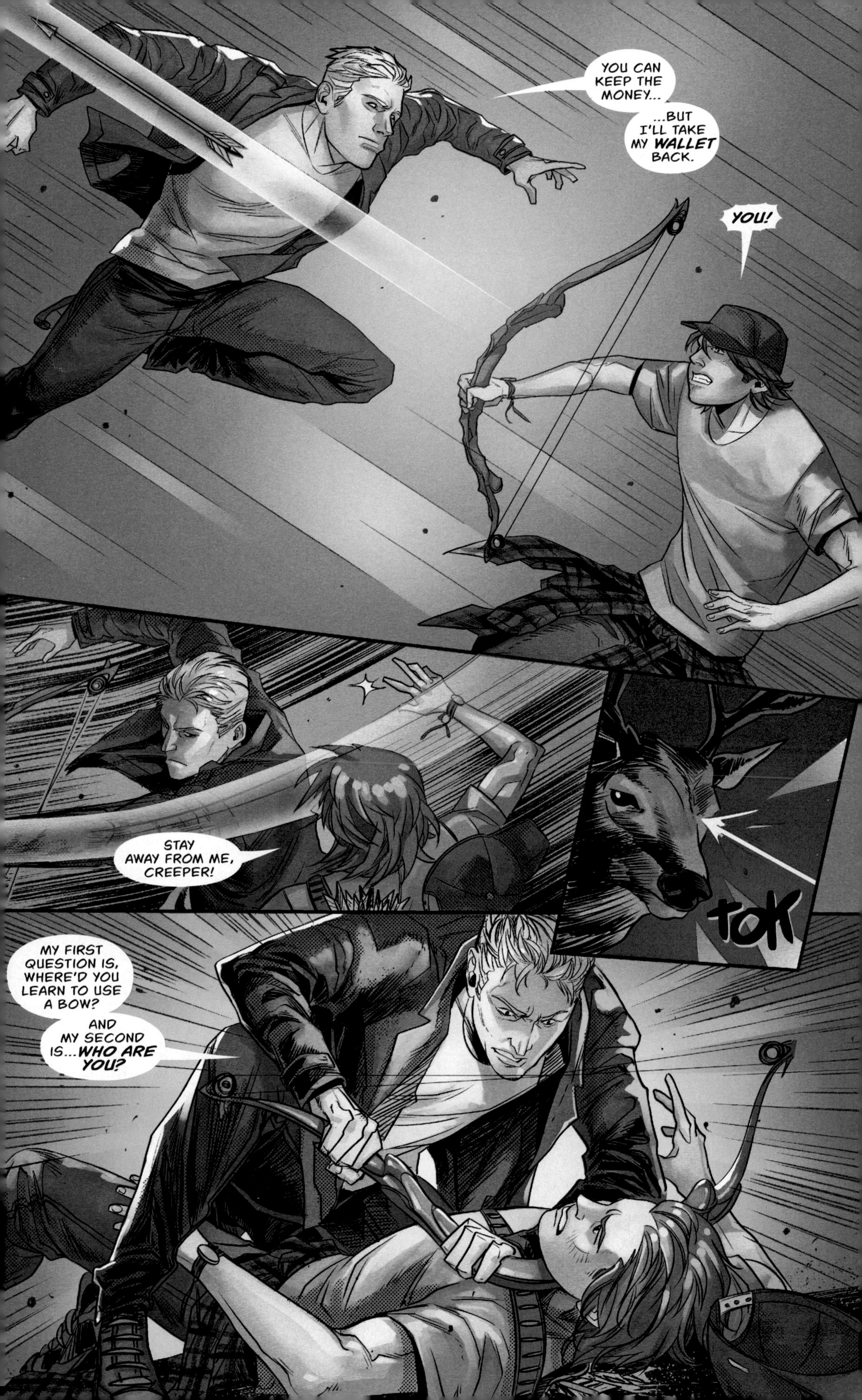
YOU CAN KEEP THE MONEY...
...BUT I'LL TAKE MY WALLET BACK.
YOU!
STAY AWAY FROM ME, CREEPER!
TOK
MY FIRST QUESTION IS, WHERE'D YOU LEARN TO USE A BOW?
AND MY SECOND IS...WHO ARE YOU?

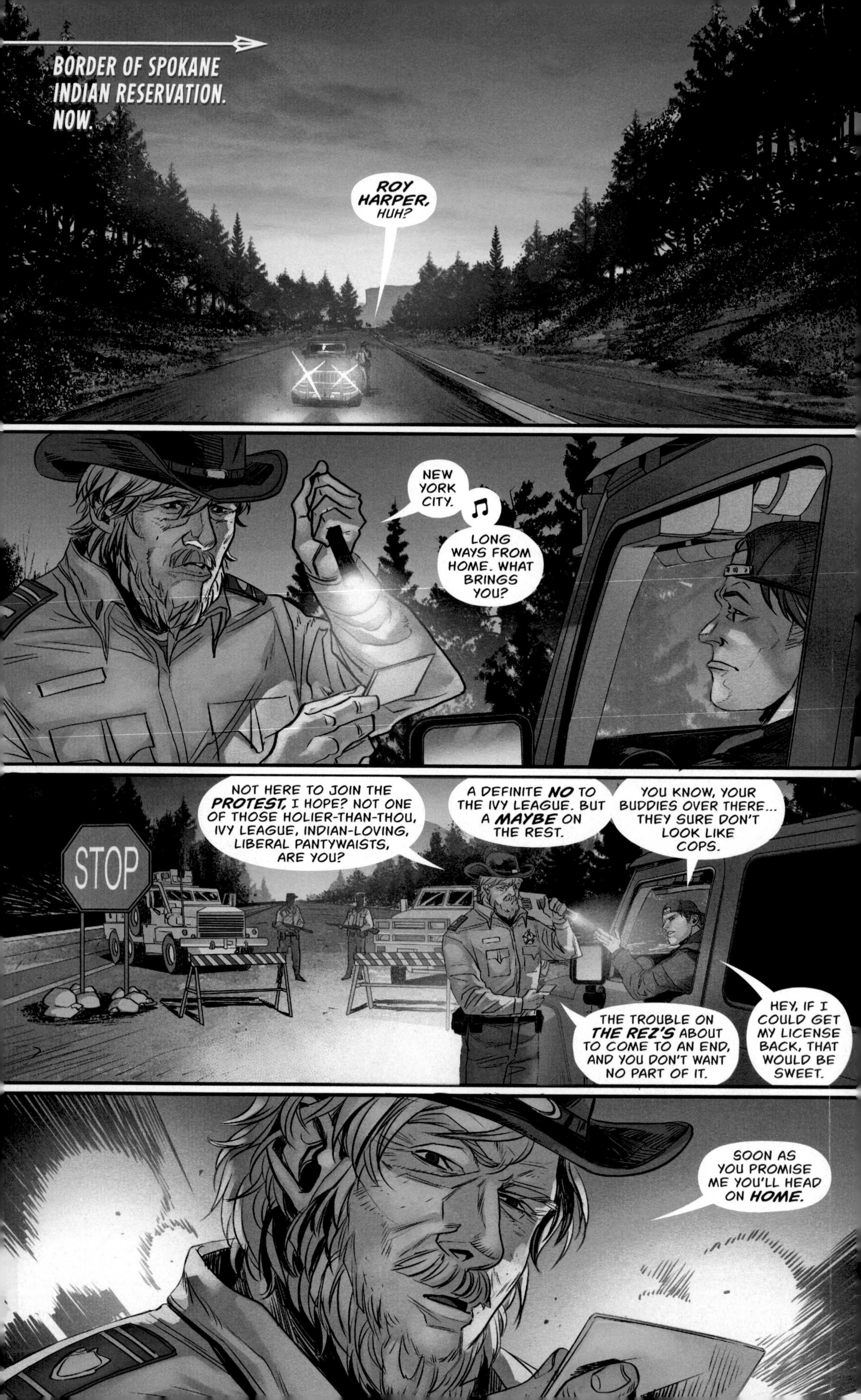
BORDER OF SPOKANE INDIAN RESERVATION. NOW.
ROY HARPER, HUH?
NEW YORK CITY.
♫
LONG WAYS FROM HOME. WHAT BRINGS YOU?
NOT HERE TO JOIN THE PROTEST, I HOPE? NOT ONE OF THOSE HOLIER-THAN-THOU, IVY LEAGUE, INDIAN-LOVING, LIBERAL PANTYWAISTS, ARE YOU?
A DEFINITE NO TO THE IVY LEAGUE. BUT A MAYBE ON THE REST.
YOU KNOW, YOUR BUDDIES OVER THERE... THEY SURE DON'T LOOK LIKE COPS.
STOP
THE TROUBLE ON THE REZ'S ABOUT TO COME TO AN END, AND YOU DON'T WANT NO PART OF IT.
HEY, IF I COULD GET MY LICENSE BACK, THAT WOULD BE SWEET.
SOON AS YOU PROMISE ME YOU'LL HEAD ON HOME.

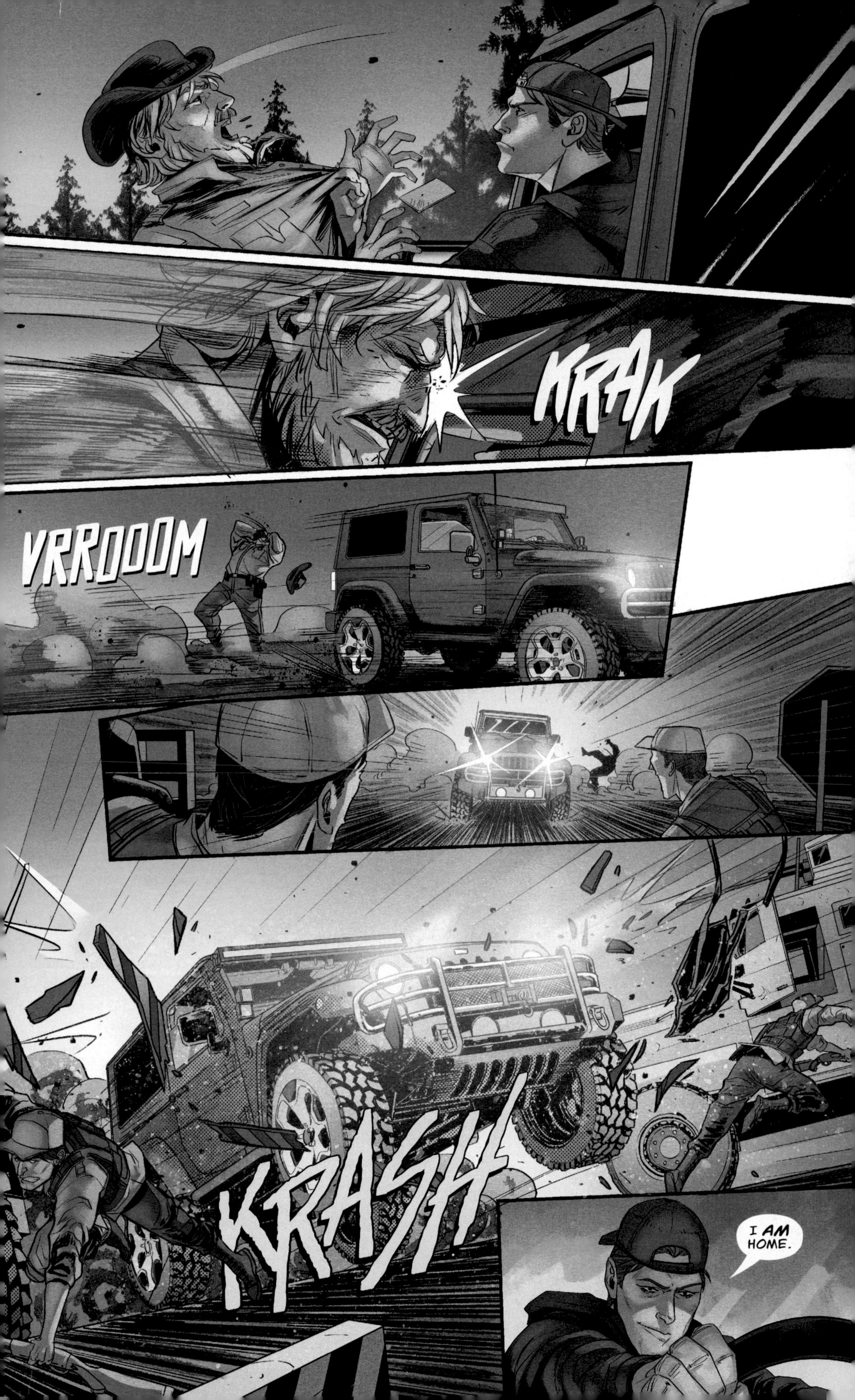
KRAK
VRROOOM
KRASH
I AM HOME.

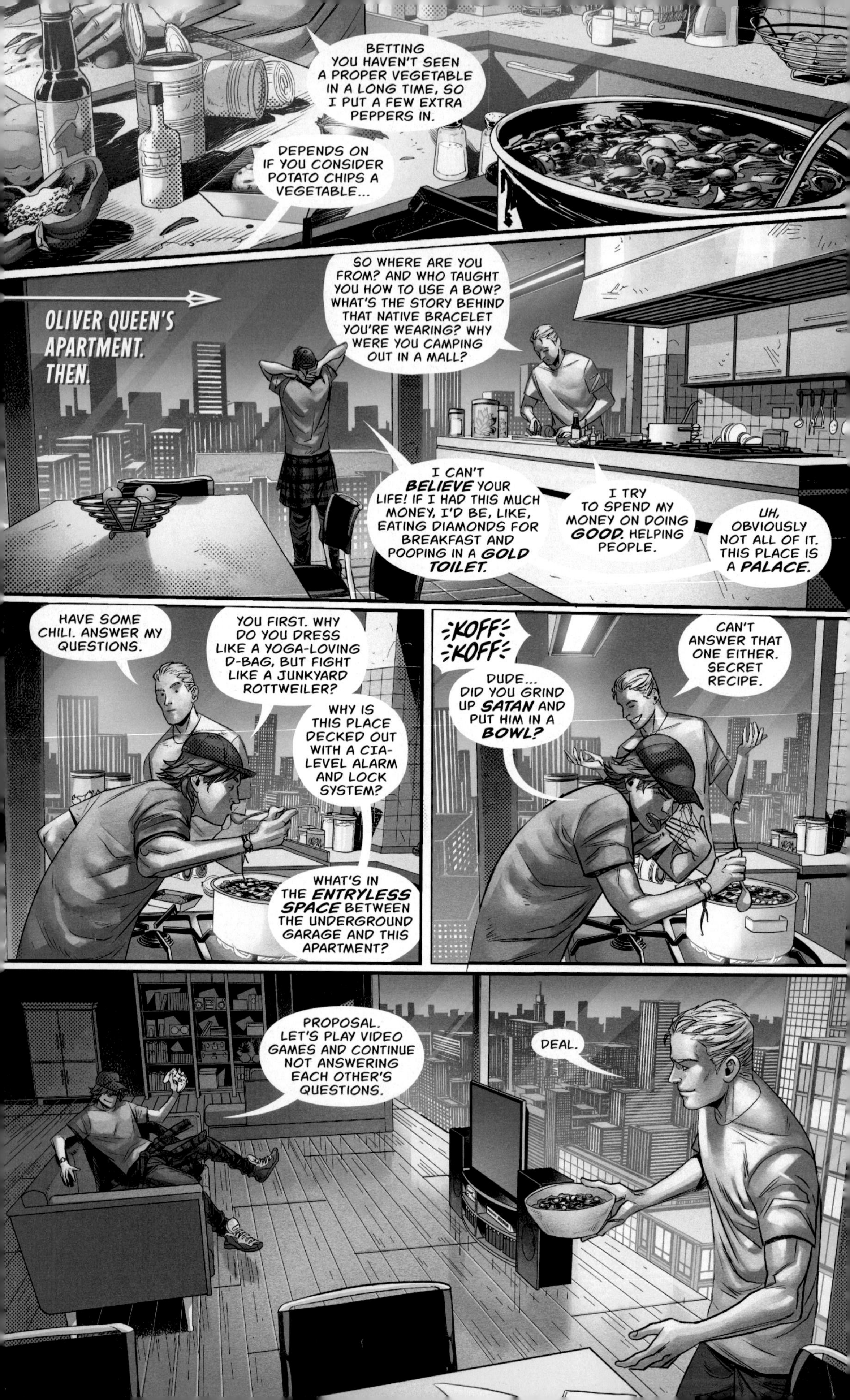
BETTING YOU HAVEN'T SEEN A PROPER VEGETABLE IN A LONG TIME, SO I PUT A FEW EXTRA PEPPERS IN.
DEPENDS ON IF YOU CONSIDER POTATO CHIPS A VEGETABLE...
OLIVER QUEEN'S APARTMENT. THEN.
SO WHERE ARE YOU FROM? AND WHO TAUGHT YOU HOW TO USE A BOW? WHAT'S THE STORY BEHIND THAT NATIVE BRACELET YOU'RE WEARING? WHY WERE YOU CAMPING OUT IN A MALL?
I CAN'T BELIEVE YOUR LIFE! IF I HAD THIS MUCH MONEY, I'D BE, LIKE, EATING DIAMONDS FOR BREAKFAST AND POOPING IN A GOLD TOILET.
I TRY TO SPEND MY MONEY ON DOING GOOD. HELPING PEOPLE.
UH, OBVIOUSLY NOT ALL OF IT. THIS PLACE IS A PALACE.
HAVE SOME CHILI. ANSWER MY QUESTIONS.
YOU FIRST. WHY DO YOU DRESS LIKE A YOGA-LOVING D-BAG, BUT FIGHT LIKE A JUNKYARD ROTTWEILER?
WHY IS THIS PLACE DECKED OUT WITH A CIA-LEVEL ALARM AND LOCK SYSTEM?
WHAT'S IN THE ENTRYLESS SPACE BETWEEN THE UNDERGROUND GARAGE AND THIS APARTMENT?
KOFF KOFF
DUDE... DID YOU GRIND UP SATAN AND PUT HIM IN A BOWL?
CAN'T ANSWER THAT ONE EITHER. SECRET RECIPE.
PROPOSAL. LET'S PLAY VIDEO GAMES AND CONTINUE NOT ANSWERING EACH OTHER'S QUESTIONS.
DEAL.

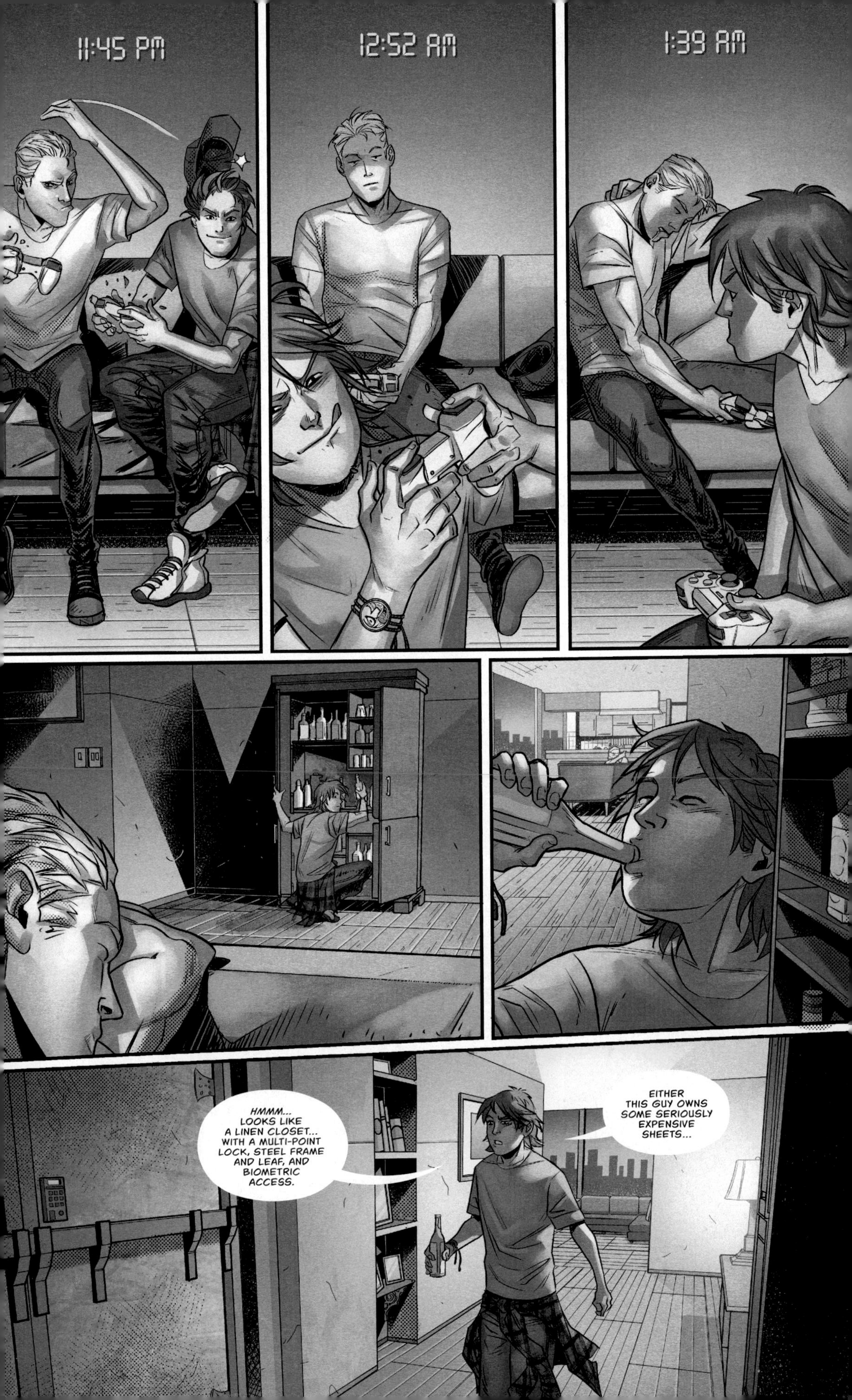
11:45 PM
12:52 AM
1:39 AM
HMMM... LOOKS LIKE A LINEN CLOSET... WITH A MULTI-POINT LOCK, STEEL FRAME AND LEAF, AND BIOMETRIC ACCESS.
EITHER THIS GUY OWNS SOME SERIOUSLY EXPENSIVE SHEETS...

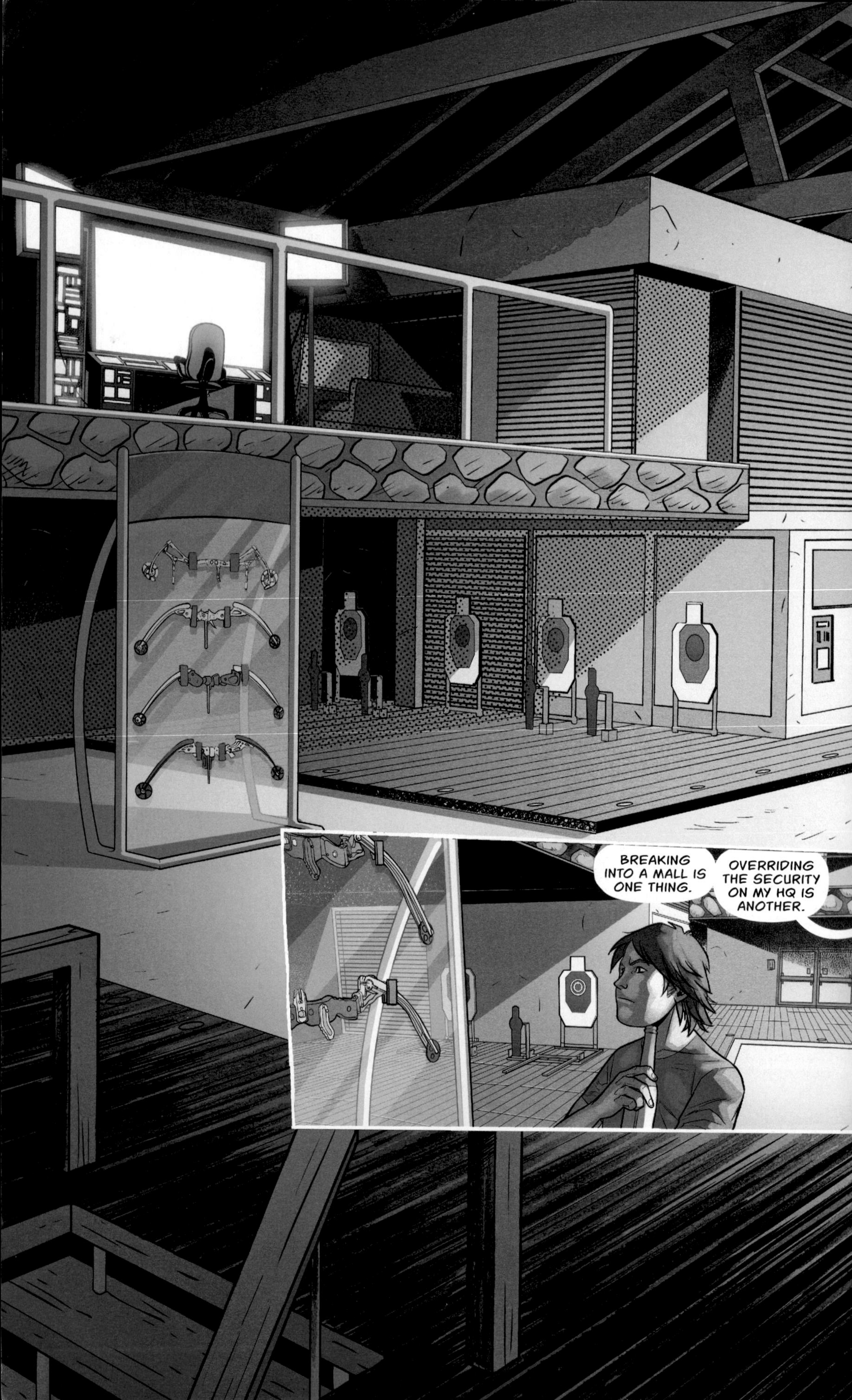
BREAKING INTO A MALL IS ONE THING.
OVERRIDING THE SECURITY ON MY HQ IS ANOTHER.

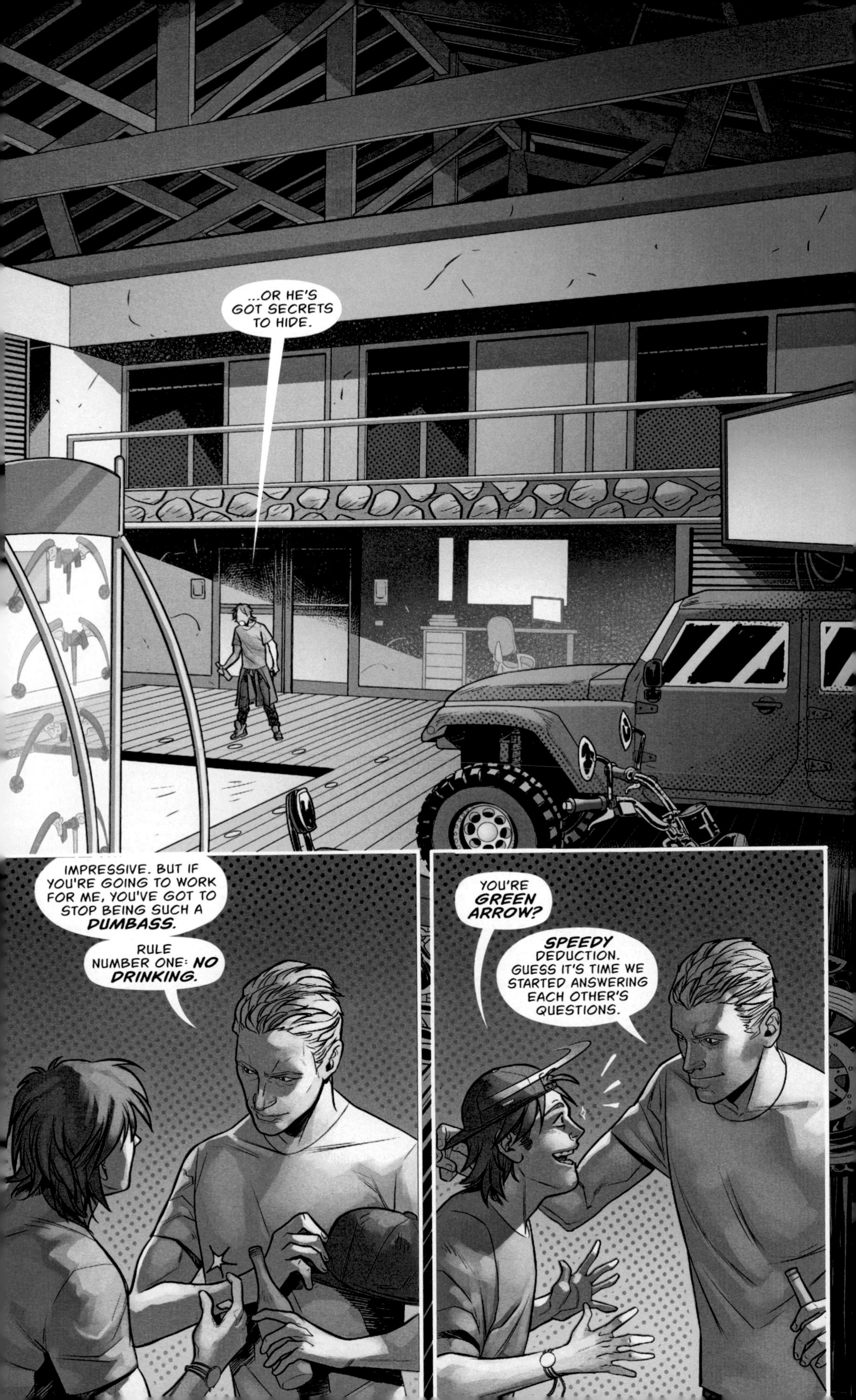
...OR HE'S GOT SECRETS TO HIDE.
IMPRESSIVE. BUT IF YOU'RE GOING TO WORK FOR ME, YOU'VE GOT TO STOP BEING SUCH A DUMBASS.
RULE NUMBER ONE: NO DRINKING.
YOU'RE GREEN ARROW?
SPEEDY DEDUCTION. GUESS IT'S TIME WE STARTED ANSWERING EACH OTHER'S QUESTIONS.

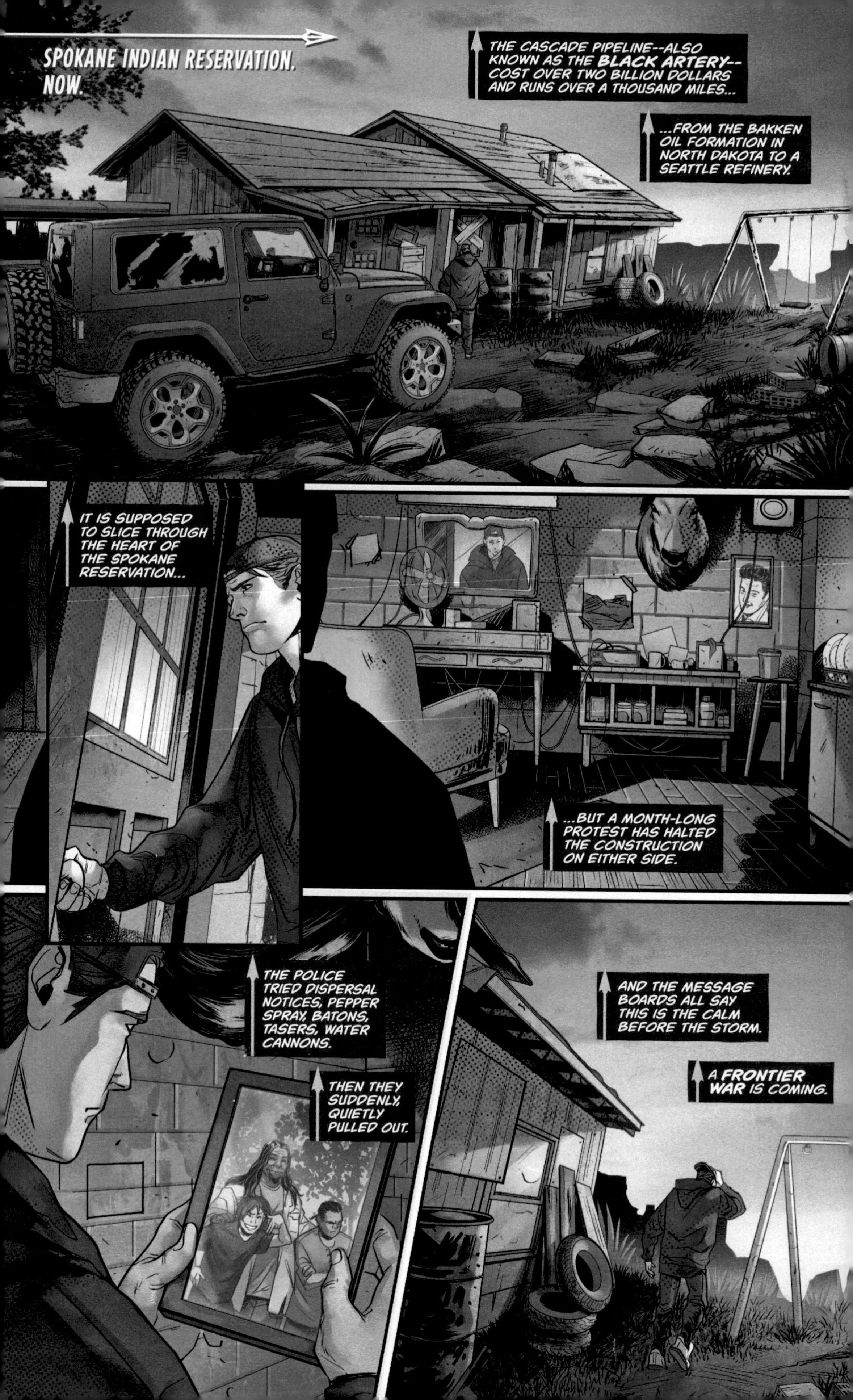
SPOKANE INDIAN RESERVATION. NOW.
THE CASCADE PIPELINE--ALSO KNOWN AS THE BLACK ARTERY--COST OVER TWO BILLION DOLLARS AND RUNS OVER A THOUSAND MILES...
...FROM THE BAKKEN OIL FORMATION IN NORTH DAKOTA TO A SEATTLE REFINERY.
IT IS SUPPOSED TO SLICE THROUGH THE HEART OF THE SPOKANE RESERVATION...
...BUT A MONTH-LONG PROTEST HAS HALTED THE CONSTRUCTION ON EITHER SIDE.
THE POLICE TRIED DISPERSAL NOTICES, PEPPER SPRAY, BATONS, TASERS, WATER CANNONS.
THEN THEY SUDDENLY, QUIETLY PULLED OUT.
AND THE MESSAGE BOARDS ALL SAY THIS IS THE CALM BEFORE THE STORM.
A FRONTIER WAR IS COMING.

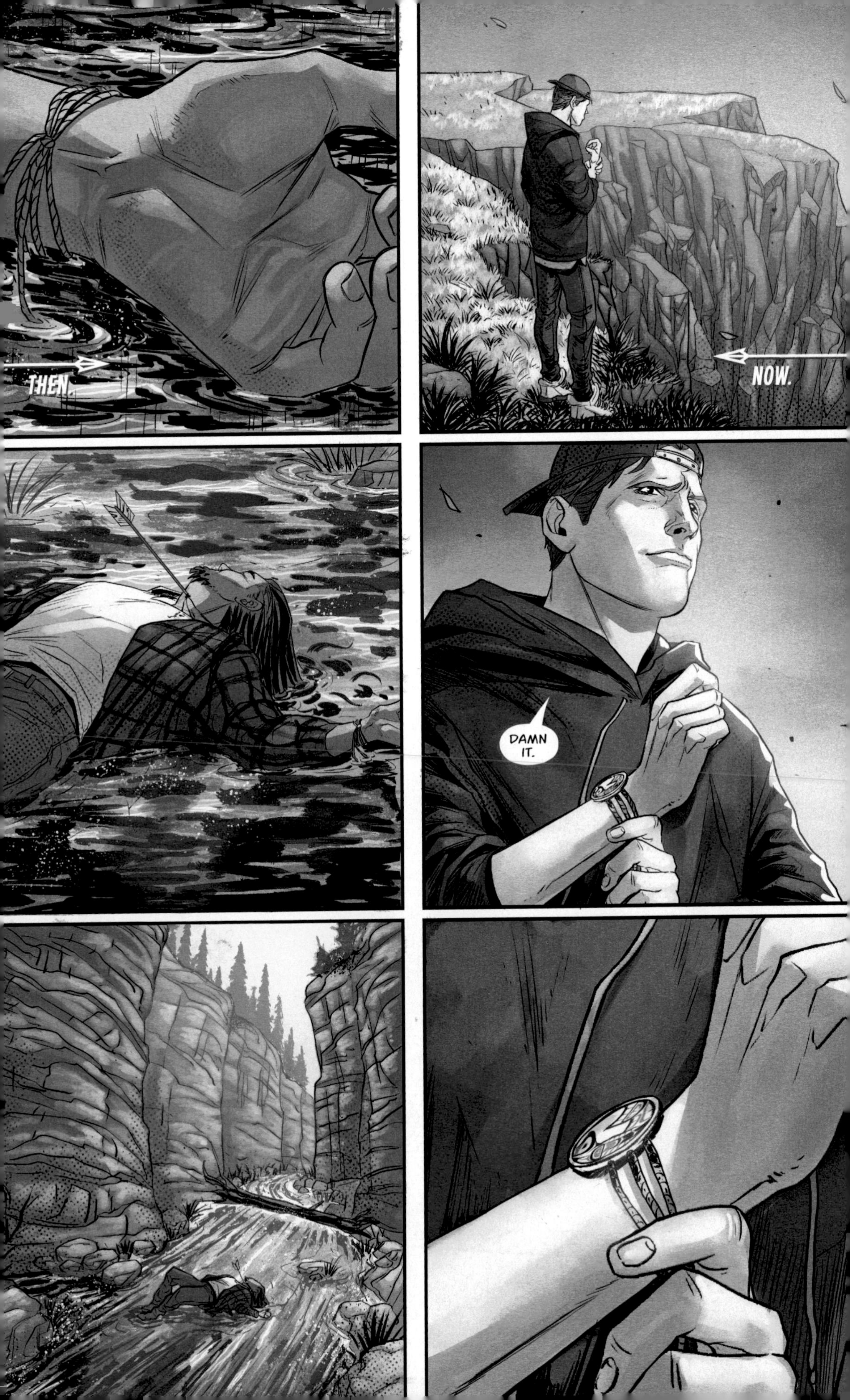
THEN.
NOW.
DAMN IT.

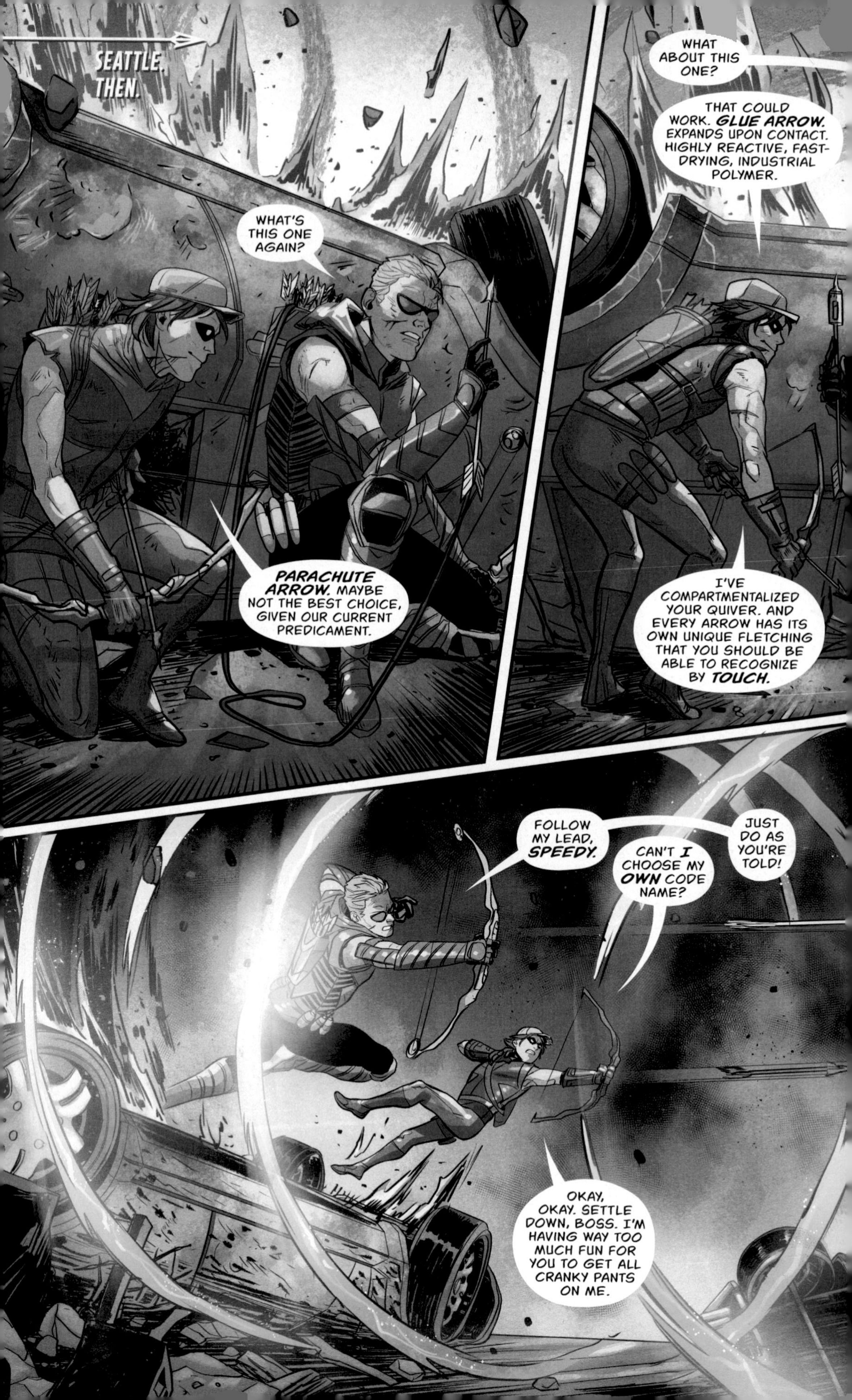
SEATTLE.
THEN.
WHAT'S THIS ONE AGAIN?
PARACHUTE ARROW. MAYBE NOT THE BEST CHOICE, GIVEN OUR CURRENT PREDICAMENT.
WHAT ABOUT THIS ONE?
THAT COULD WORK. GLUE ARROW. EXPANDS UPON CONTACT. HIGHLY REACTIVE, FAST-DRYING, INDUSTRIAL POLYMER.
I'VE COMPARTMENTALIZED YOUR QUIVER. AND EVERY ARROW HAS ITS OWN UNIQUE FLETCHING THAT YOU SHOULD BE ABLE TO RECOGNIZE BY TOUCH.
FOLLOW MY LEAD, SPEEDY.
CAN'T I CHOOSE MY OWN CODE NAME?
JUST DO AS YOU'RE TOLD!
OKAY, OKAY. SETTLE DOWN, BOSS. I'M HAVING WAY TOO MUCH FUN FOR YOU TO GET ALL CRANKY PANTS ON ME.

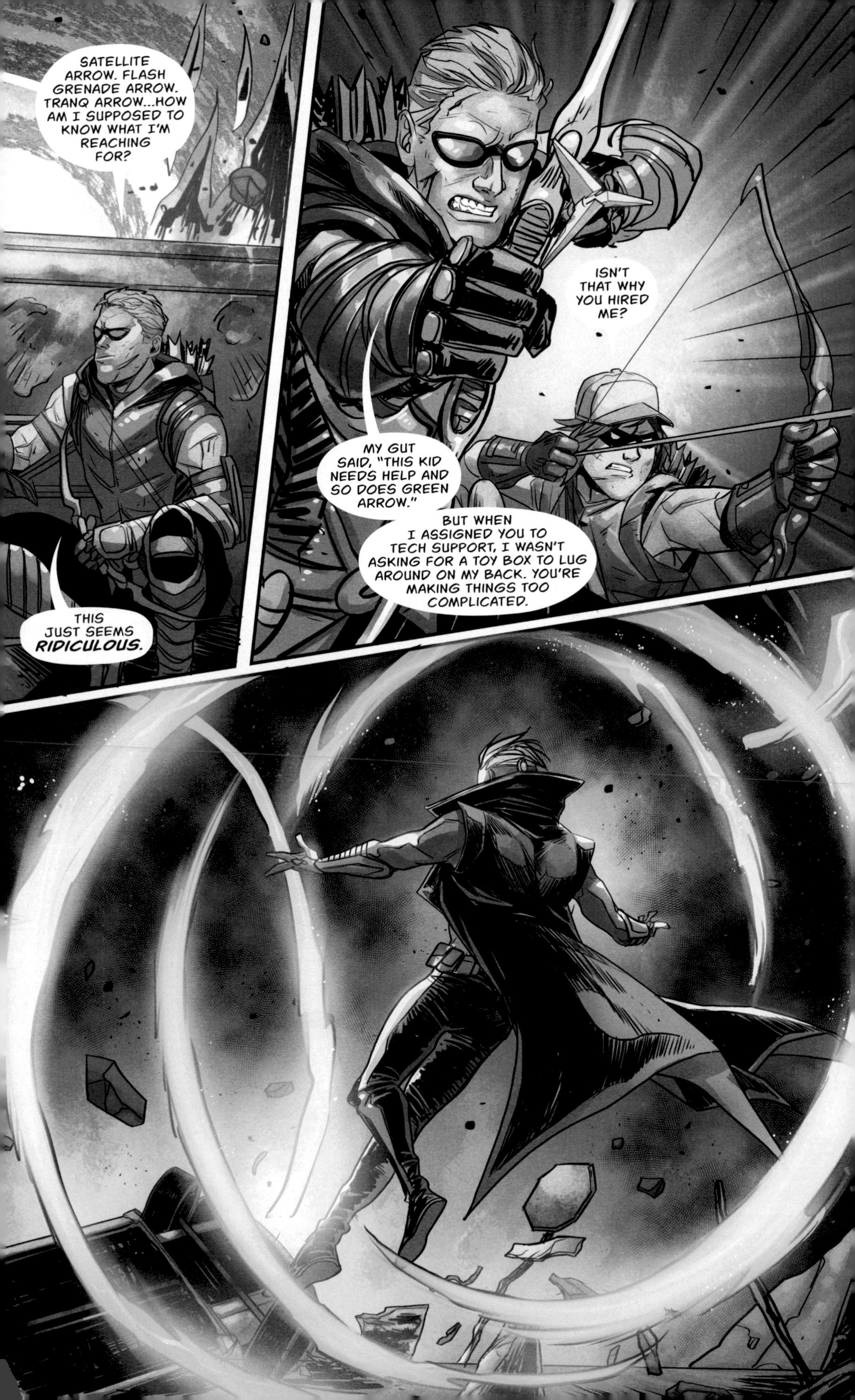

SATELLITE ARROW. FLASH GRENADE ARROW. TRANQ ARROW...HOW AM I SUPPOSED TO KNOW WHAT I'M REACHING FOR?
ISN'T THAT WHY YOU HIRED ME?
MY GUT SAID, "THIS KID NEEDS HELP AND SO DOES GREEN ARROW."
BUT WHEN I ASSIGNED YOU TO TECH SUPPORT, I WASN'T ASKING FOR A TOY BOX TO LUG AROUND ON MY BACK. YOU'RE MAKING THINGS TOO COMPLICATED.
THIS JUST SEEMS RIDICULOUS.

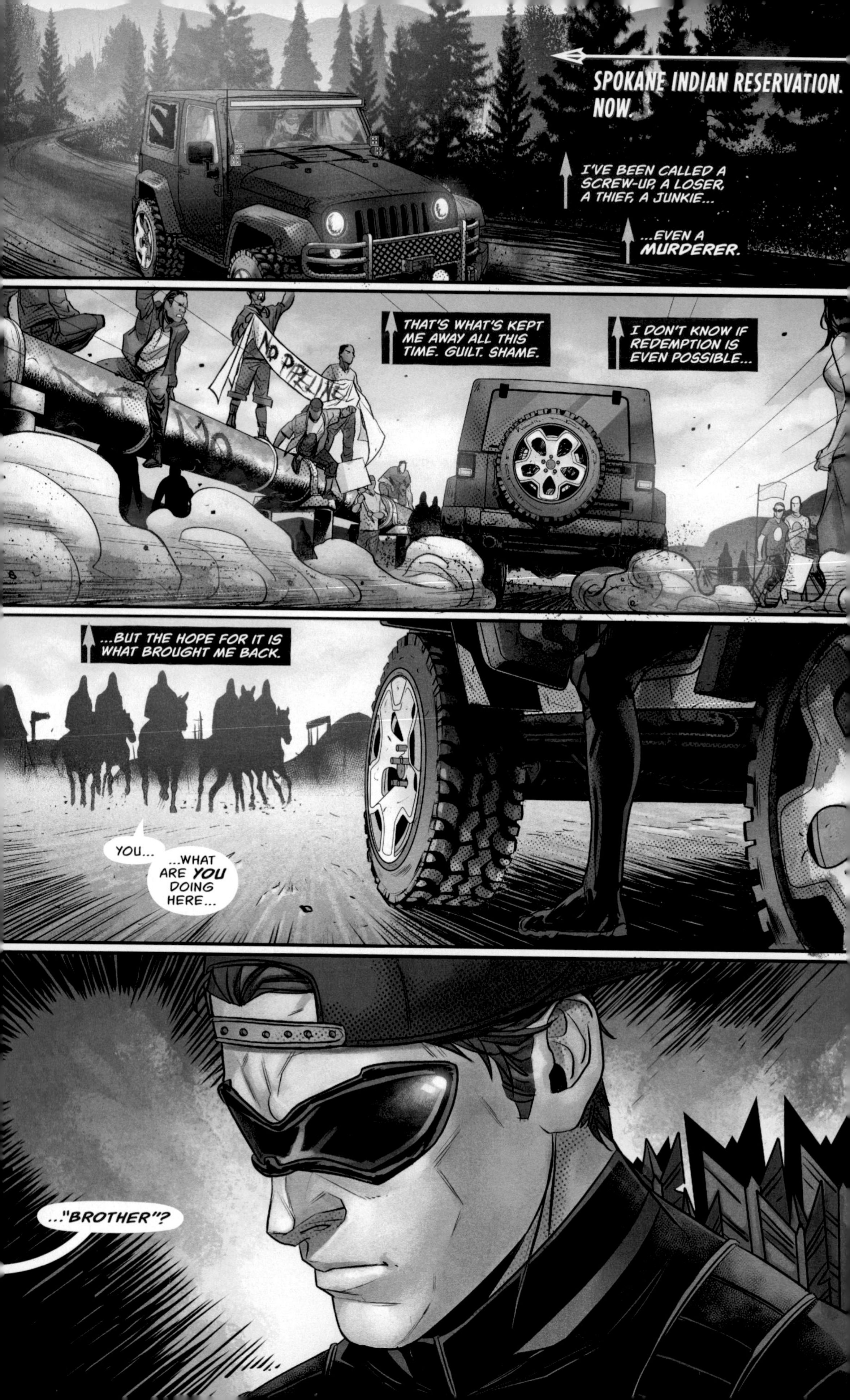
SPOKANE INDIAN RESERVATION. NOW.
I'VE BEEN CALLED A SCREW-UP, A LOSER, A THIEF, A JUNKIE...
...EVEN A MURDERER.
NO PIPELINE
THAT'S WHAT'S KEPT ME AWAY ALL THIS TIME. GUILT. SHAME.
I DON'T KNOW IF REDEMPTION IS EVEN POSSIBLE...
...BUT THE HOPE FOR IT IS WHAT BROUGHT ME BACK.
YOU...
...WHAT ARE YOU DOING HERE...
..."BROTHER"?

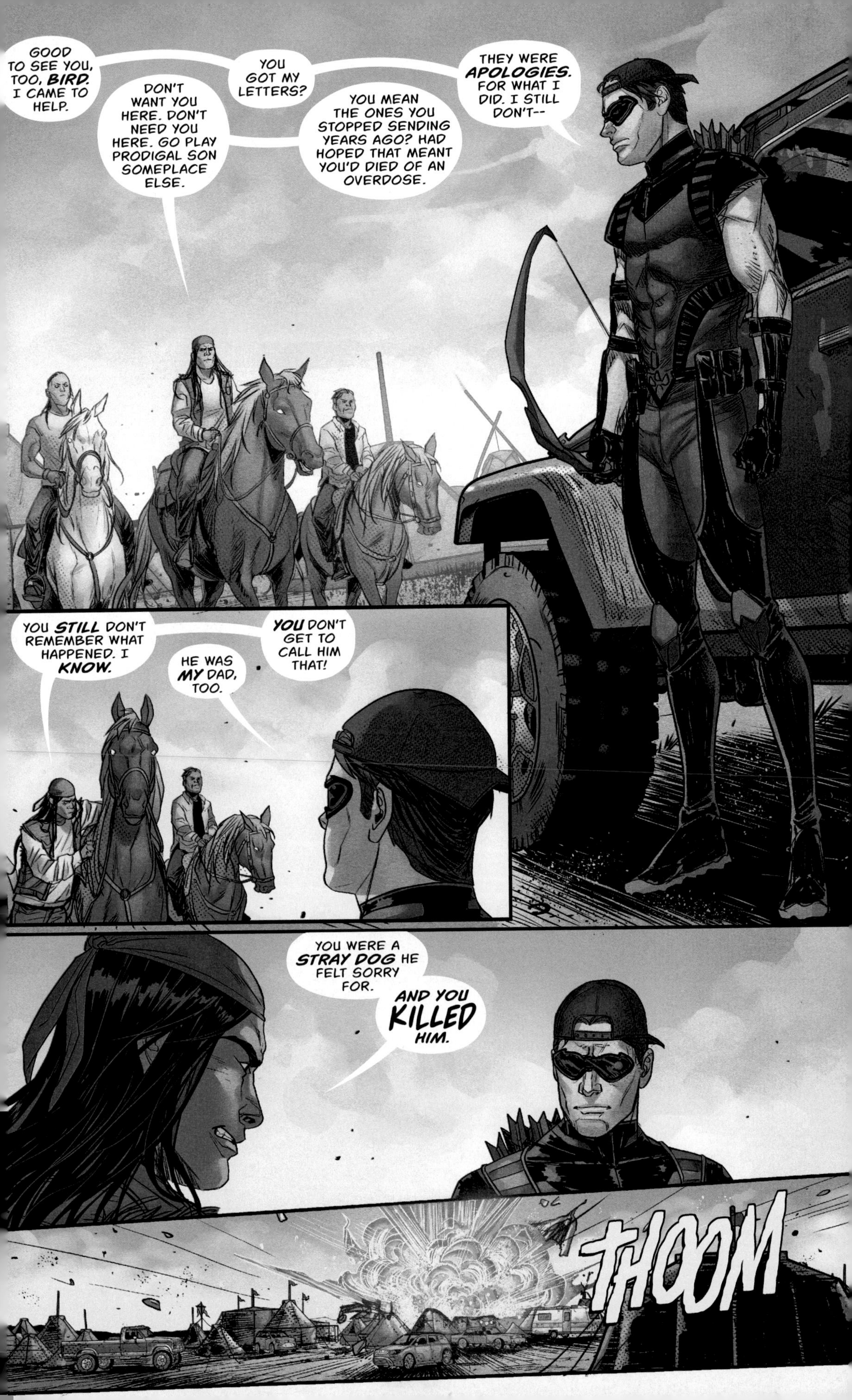
GOOD TO SEE YOU, TOO, **BIRD.** I CAME TO HELP.
DON'T WANT YOU HERE. DON'T NEED YOU HERE. GO PLAY PRODIGAL SON SOMEPLACE ELSE.
YOU GOT MY LETTERS?
YOU MEAN THE ONES YOU STOPPED SENDING YEARS AGO? HAD HOPED THAT MEANT YOU'D DIED OF AN OVERDOSE.
THEY WERE **APOLOGIES.** FOR WHAT I DID. I STILL DON'T--
YOU **STILL** DON'T REMEMBER WHAT HAPPENED. I **KNOW.**
HE WAS **MY** DAD, TOO.
YOU DON'T GET TO CALL HIM THAT!
YOU WERE A **STRAY DOG** HE FELT SORRY FOR.
AND YOU KILLED HIM.
THOOM

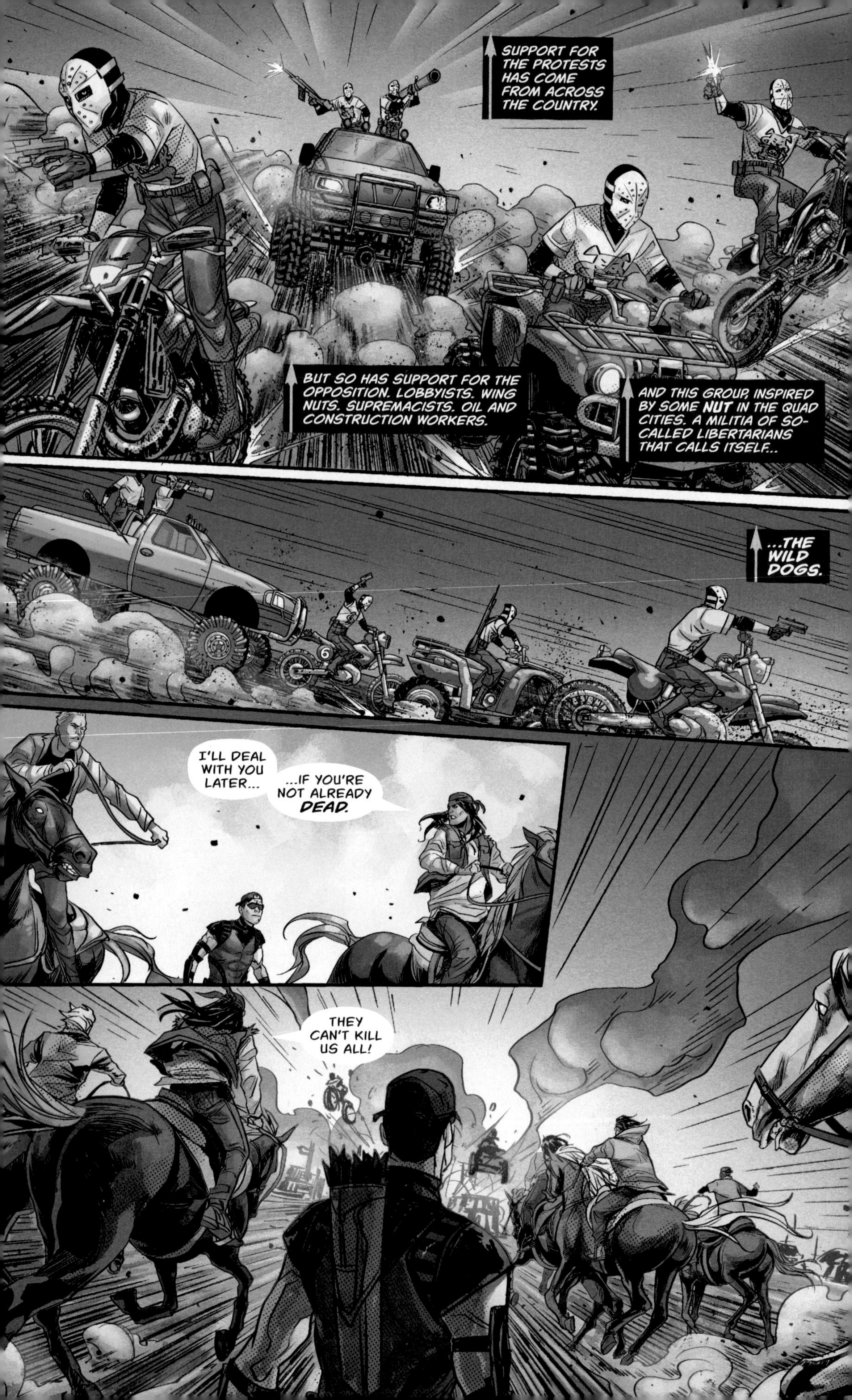
SUPPORT FOR THE PROTESTS HAS COME FROM ACROSS THE COUNTRY.
BUT SO HAS SUPPORT FOR THE OPPOSITION. LOBBYISTS. WING NUTS. SUPREMACISTS. OIL AND CONSTRUCTION WORKERS.
AND THIS GROUP, INSPIRED BY SOME NUT IN THE QUAD CITIES. A MILITIA OF SO-CALLED LIBERTARIANS THAT CALLS ITSELF...
...THE WILD DOGS.
I'LL DEAL WITH YOU LATER...
...IF YOU'RE NOT ALREADY DEAD.
THEY CAN'T KILL US ALL!

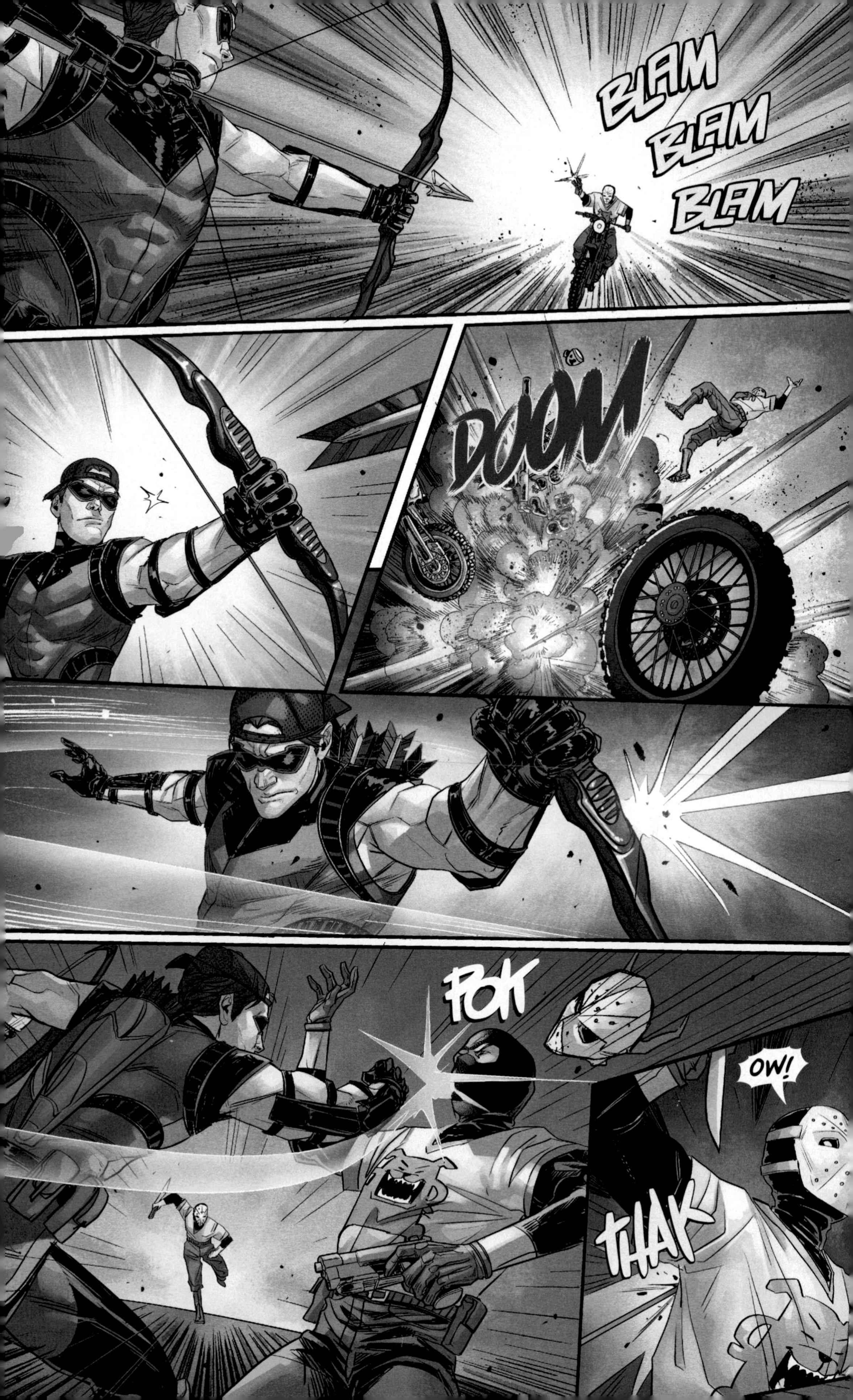
BLAM
BLAM
BLAM
DOOM
POK
OW!
THAK

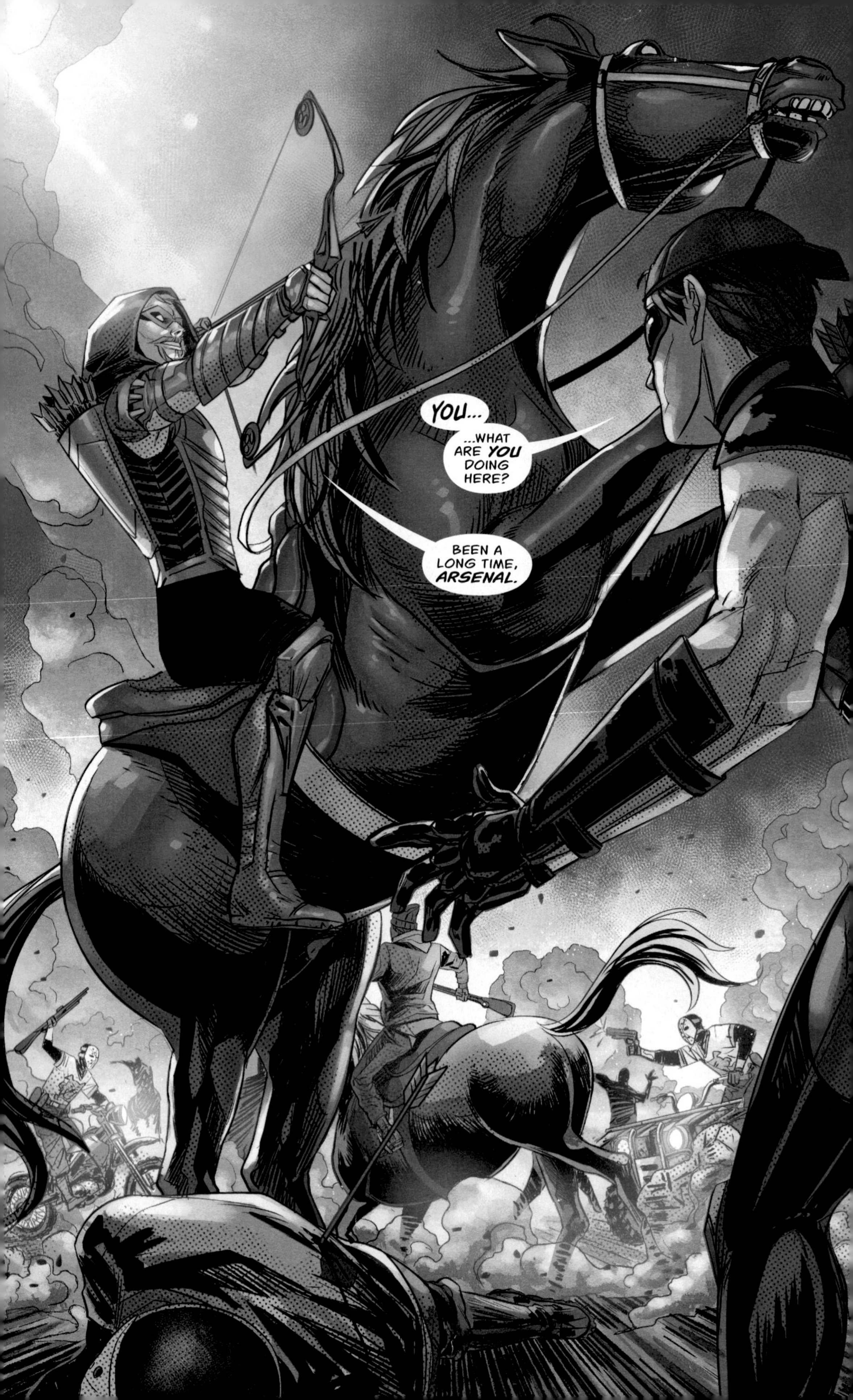
YOU...
...WHAT ARE YOU DOING HERE?
BEEN A LONG TIME, ARSENAL.

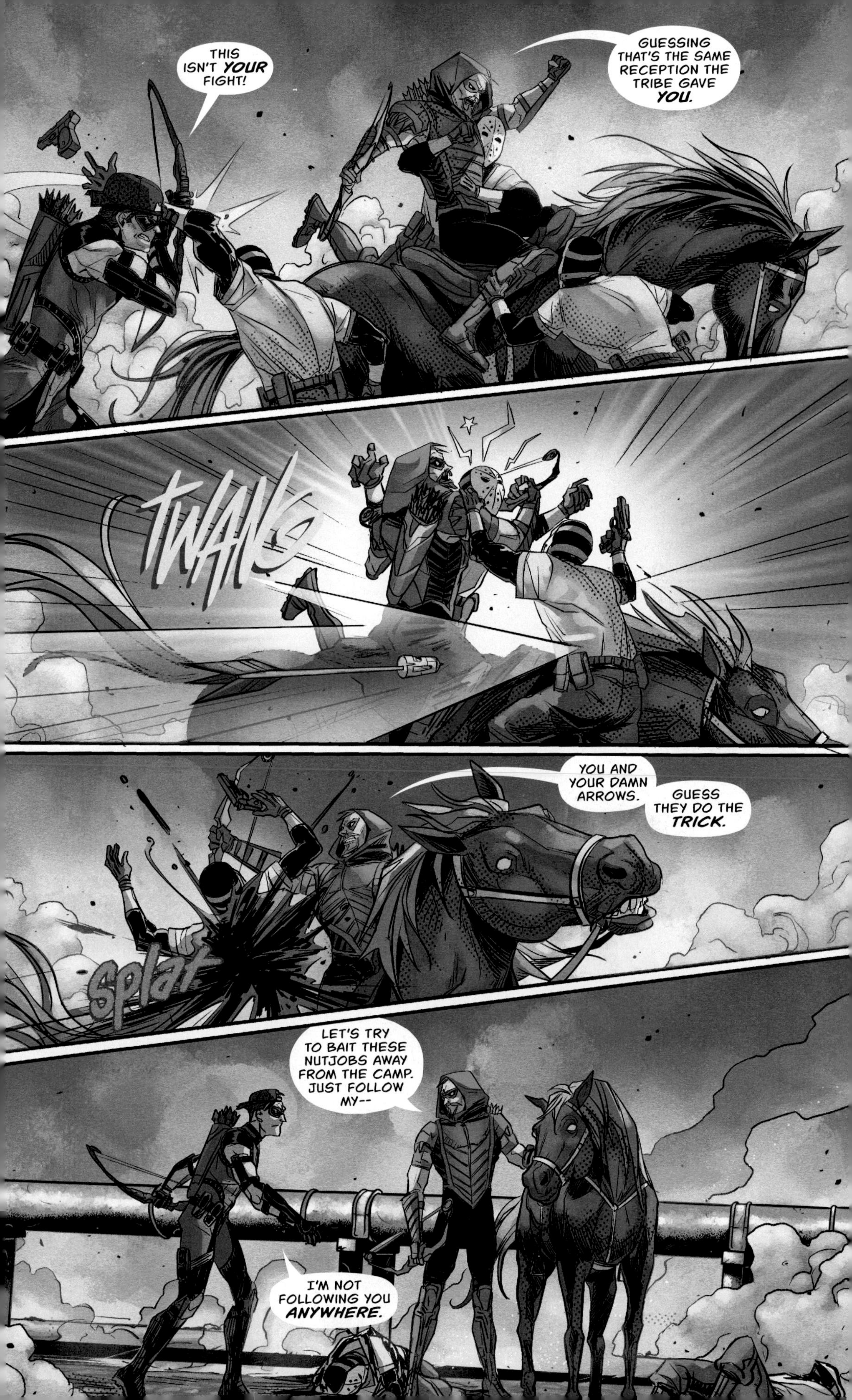
THIS ISN'T YOUR FIGHT!
GUESSING THAT'S THE SAME RECEPTION THE TRIBE GAVE YOU.
TWANG
YOU AND YOUR DAMN ARROWS.
GUESS THEY DO THE TRICK.
splat
LET'S TRY TO BAIT THESE NUTJOBS AWAY FROM THE CAMP. JUST FOLLOW MY--
I'M NOT FOLLOWING YOU ANYWHERE.

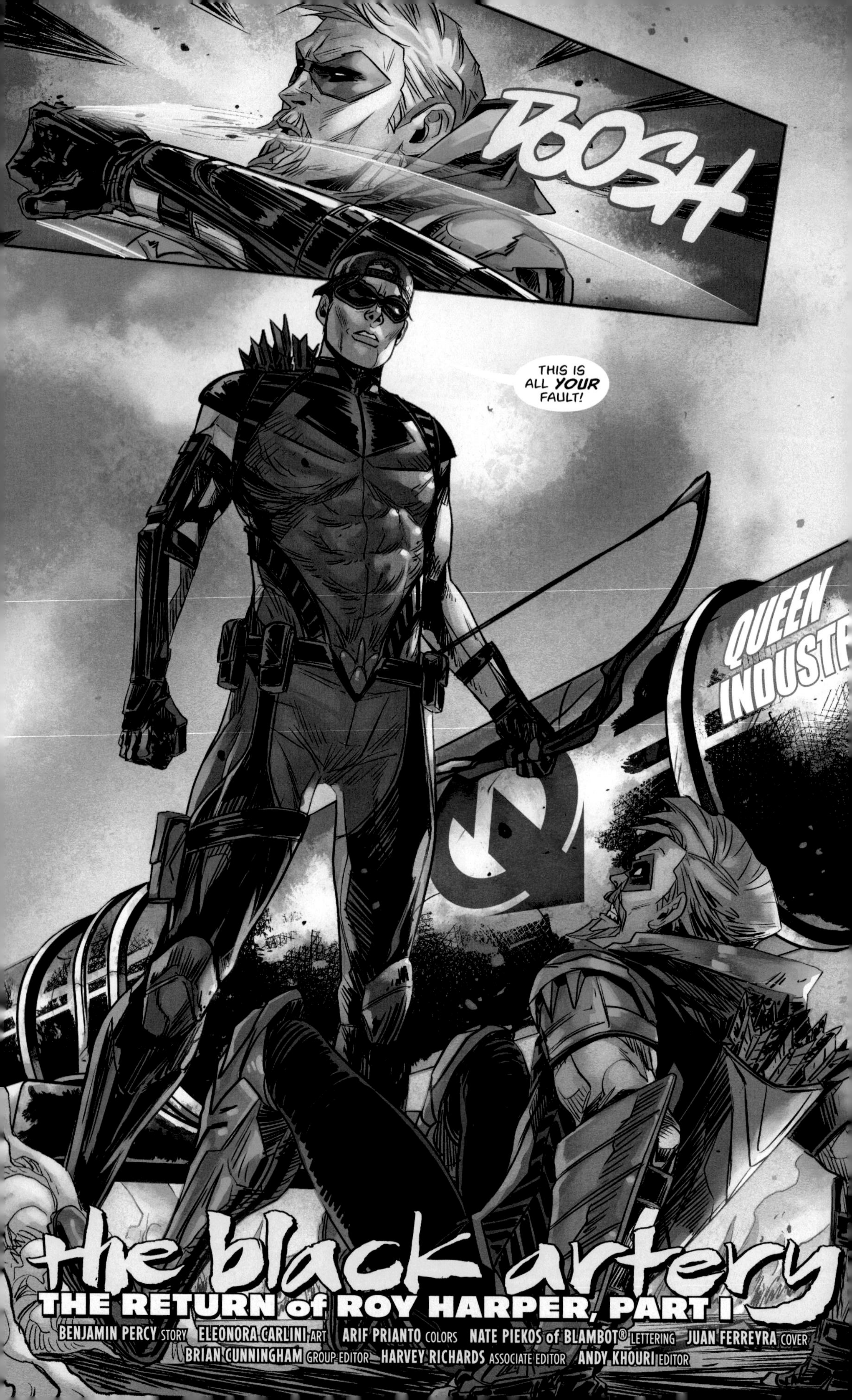
TOOSH
THIS IS ALL YOUR FAULT!
QUEEN INDUST
the black artery
THE RETURN of ROY HARPER, PART I
BENJAMIN PERCY STORY ELEONORA CARLINI ART ARIF PRIANTO COLORS NATE PIEKOS of BLAMBOT® LETTERING JUAN FERREYRA COVER
BRIAN CUNNINGHAM GROUP EDITOR HARVEY RICHARDS ASSOCIATE EDITOR ANDY KHOURI EDITOR

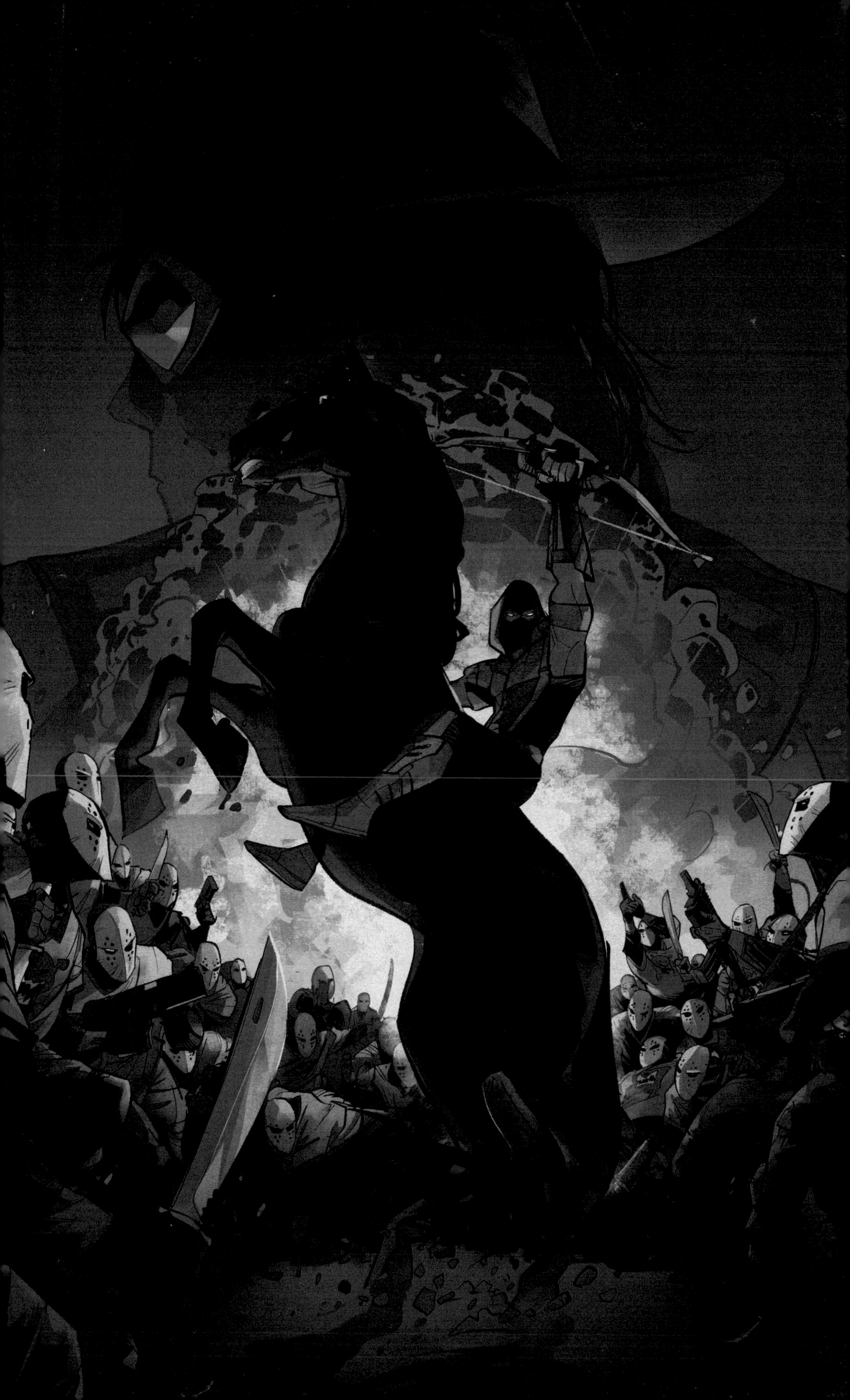

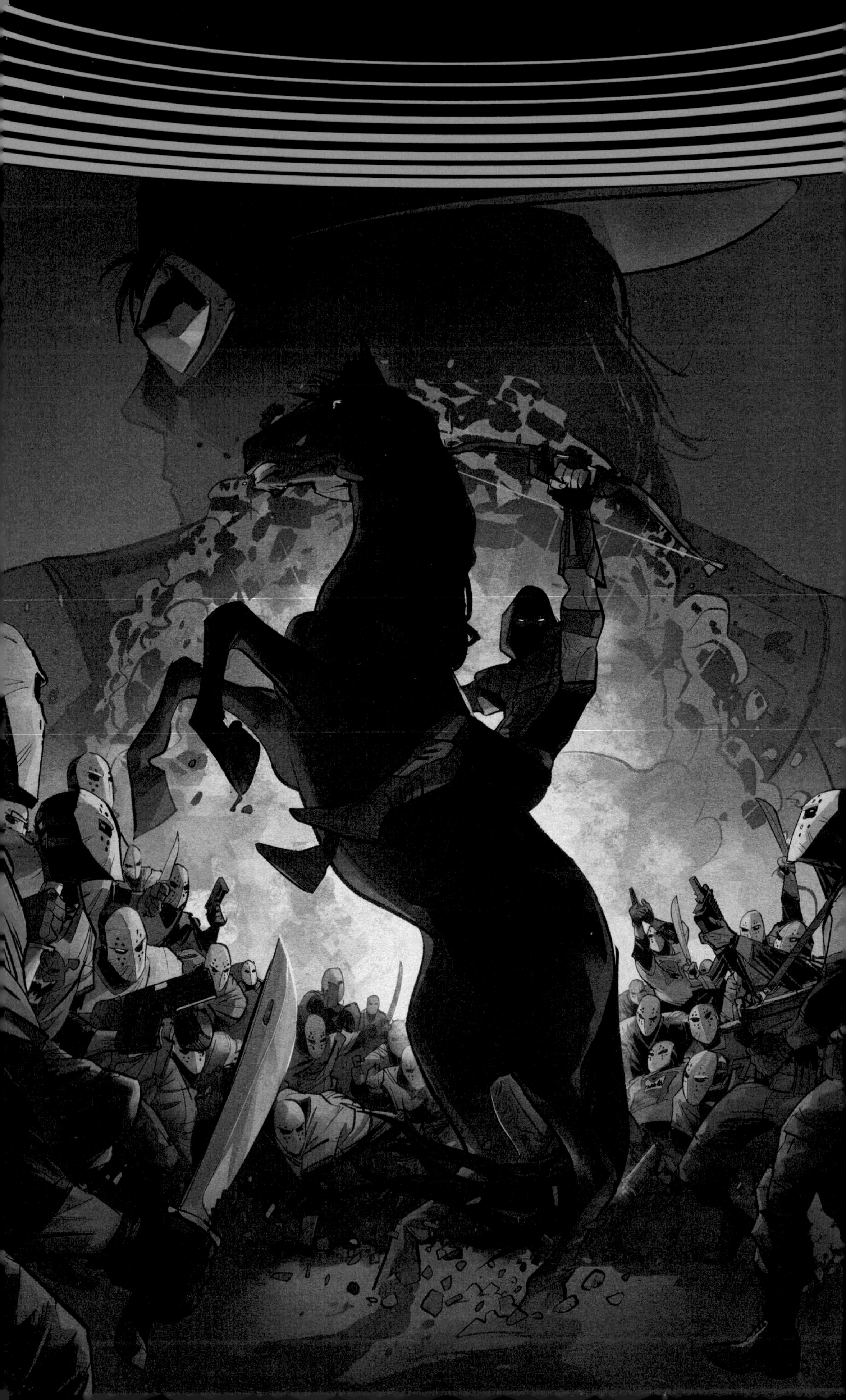

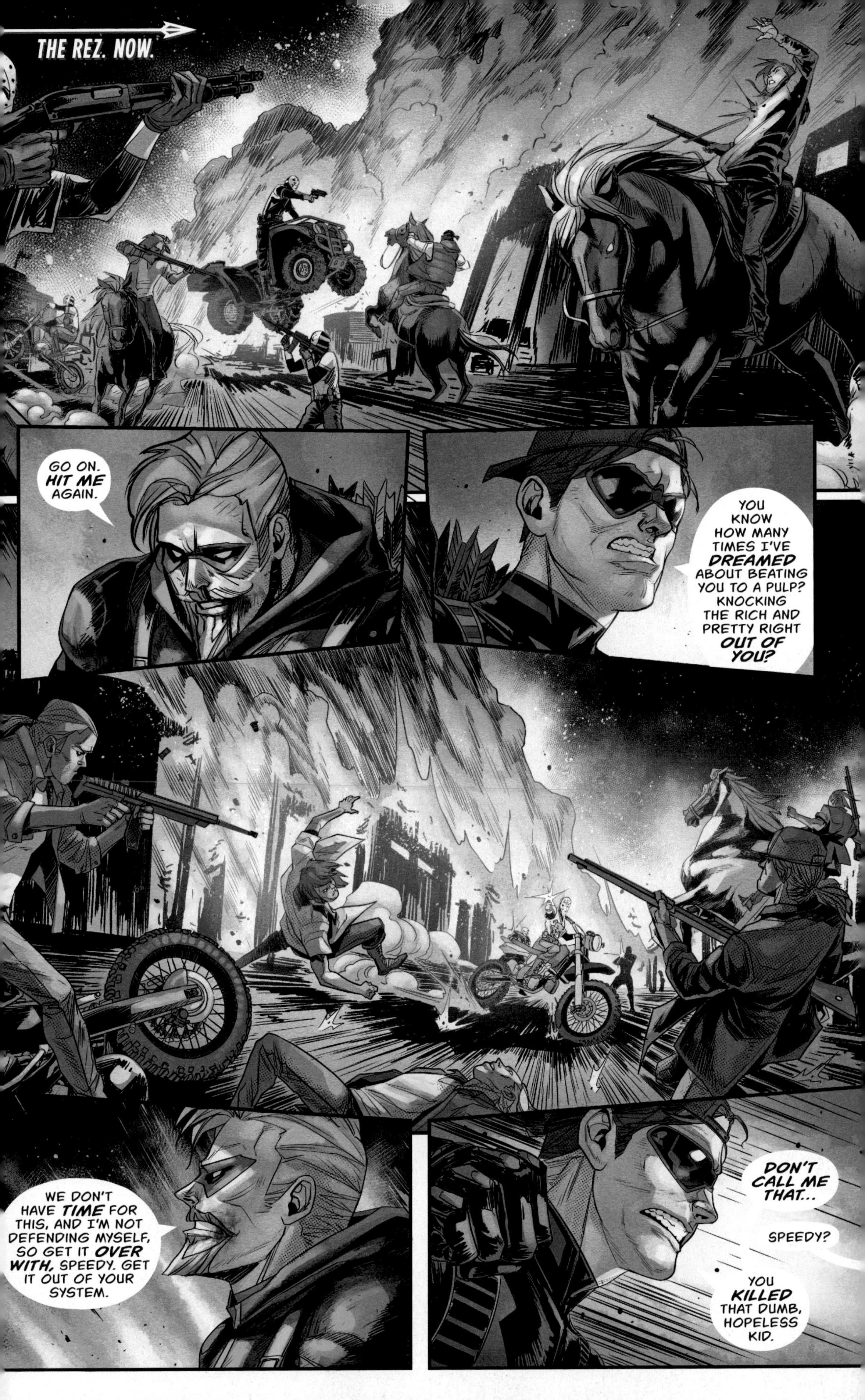
THE REZ. NOW.
GO ON. HIT ME AGAIN.
YOU KNOW HOW MANY TIMES I'VE DREAMED ABOUT BEATING YOU TO A PULP? KNOCKING THE RICH AND PRETTY RIGHT OUT OF YOU?
WE DON'T HAVE TIME FOR THIS, AND I'M NOT DEFENDING MYSELF, SO GET IT OVER WITH, SPEEDY. GET IT OUT OF YOUR SYSTEM.
DON'T CALL ME THAT...
SPEEDY?
YOU KILLED THAT DUMB, HOPELESS KID.

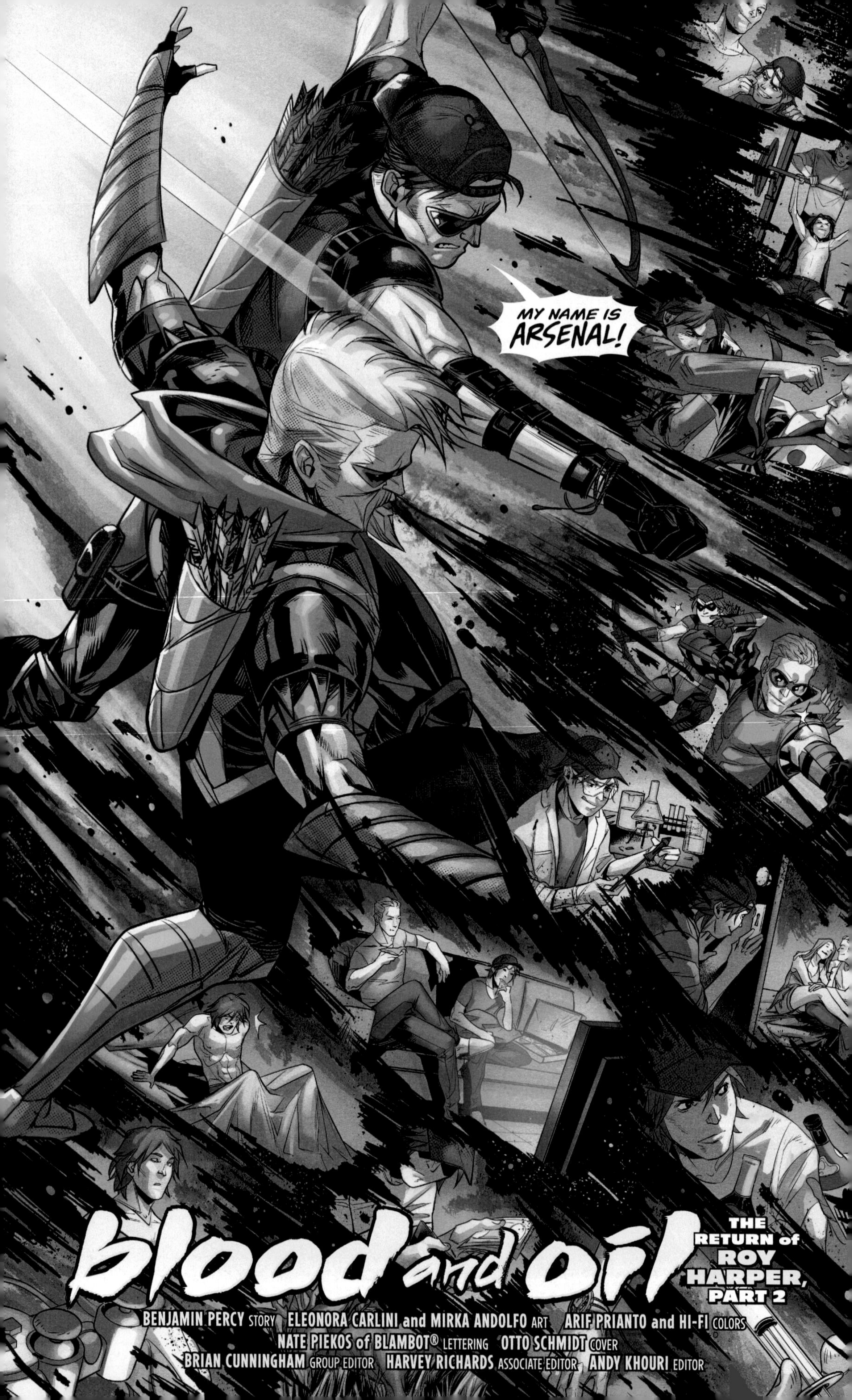
MY NAME IS ARSENAL!
blood and oil
THE RETURN of ROY HARPER, PART 2
BENJAMIN PERCY STORY ELEONORA CARLINI and MIRKA ANDOLFO ART ARIF PRIANTO and HI-FI COLORS
NATE PIEKOS of BLAMBOT® LETTERING OTTO SCHMIDT COVER
BRIAN CUNNINGHAM GROUP EDITOR HARVEY RICHARDS ASSOCIATE EDITOR ANDY KHOURI EDITOR

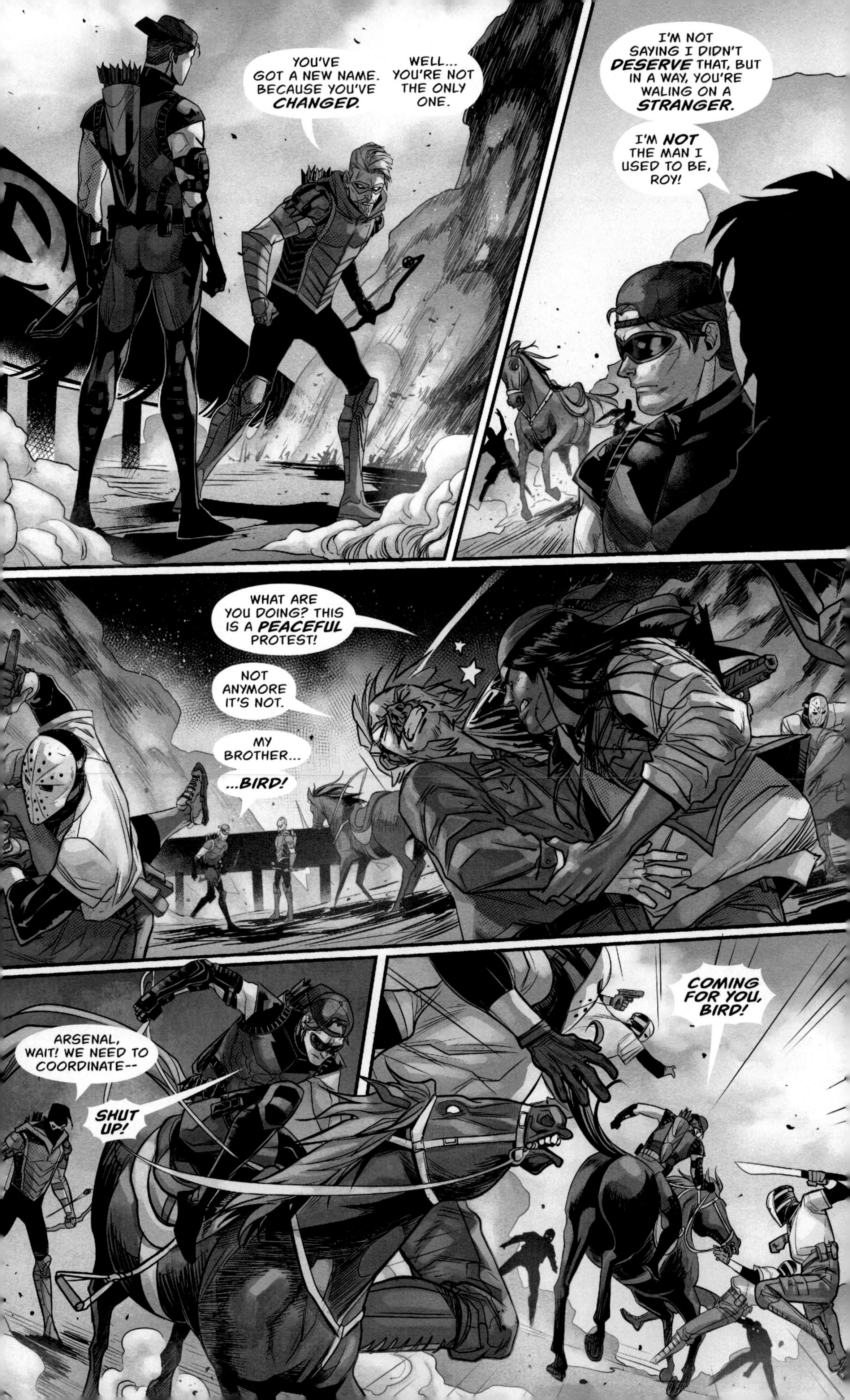
YOU'VE GOT A NEW NAME. BECAUSE YOU'VE CHANGED.
WELL... YOU'RE NOT THE ONLY ONE.
I'M NOT SAYING I DIDN'T DESERVE THAT, BUT IN A WAY, YOU'RE WALING ON A STRANGER.
I'M NOT THE MAN I USED TO BE, ROY!
WHAT ARE YOU DOING? THIS IS A PEACEFUL PROTEST!
NOT ANYMORE IT'S NOT.
MY BROTHER...
...BIRD!
ARSENAL, WAIT! WE NEED TO COORDINATE--
SHUT UP!
COMING FOR YOU, BIRD!

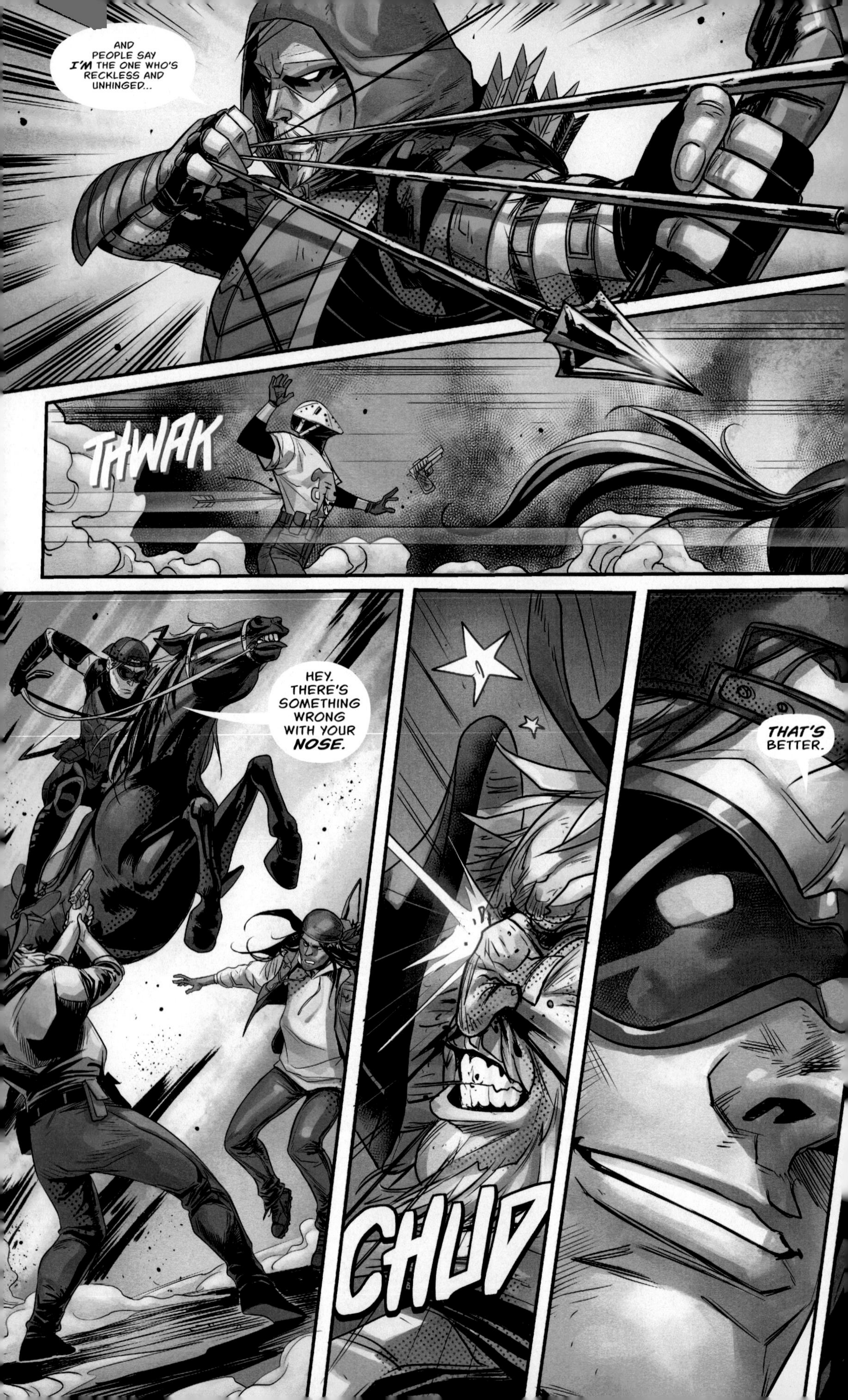
AND PEOPLE SAY I'M THE ONE WHO'S RECKLESS AND UNHINGED...
THWAK
HEY. THERE'S SOMETHING WRONG WITH YOUR NOSE.
CHUD
THAT'S BETTER.

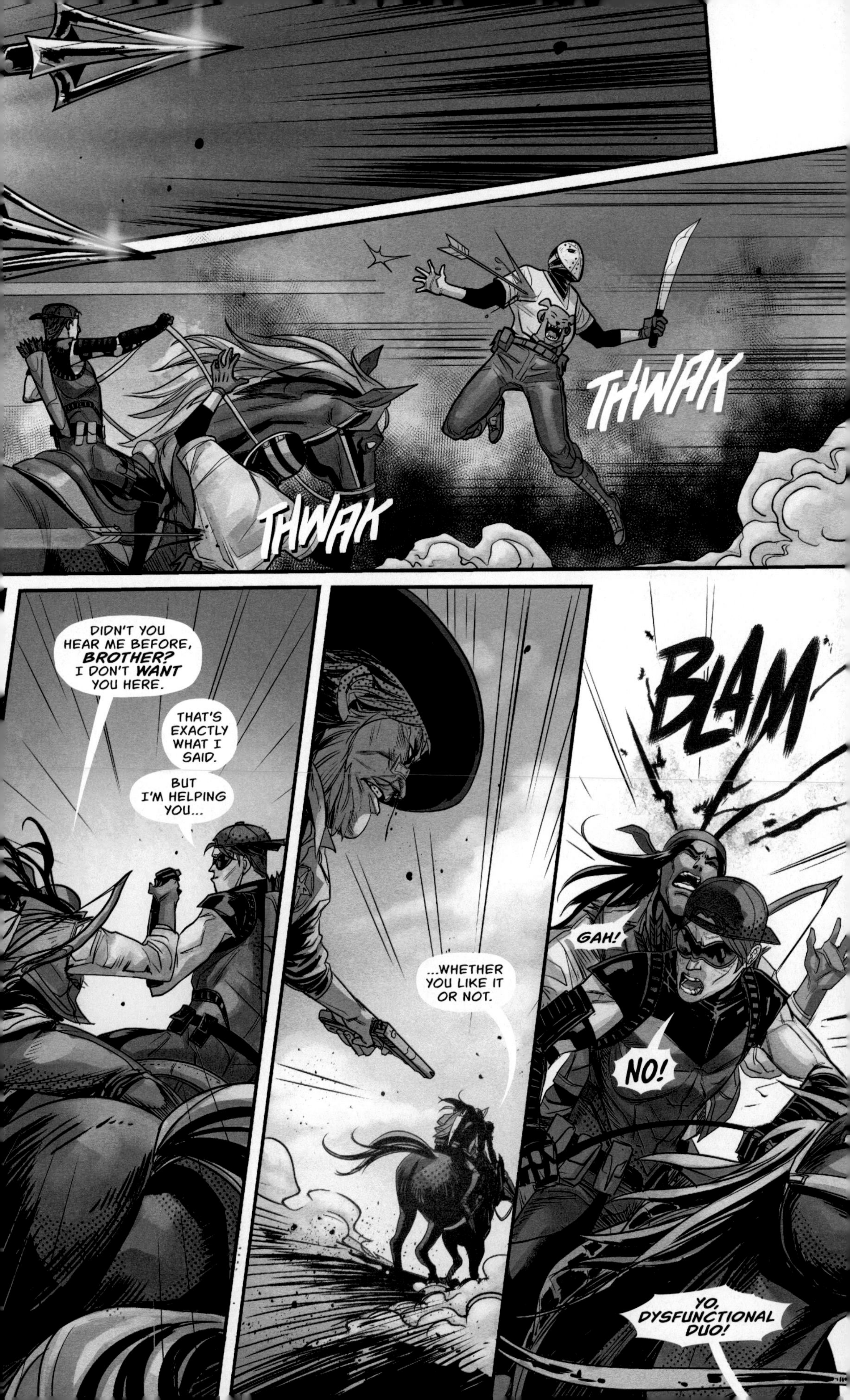
THWAK
THWAK
DIDN'T YOU HEAR ME BEFORE, BROTHER? I DON'T WANT YOU HERE.
THAT'S EXACTLY WHAT I SAID.
BUT I'M HELPING YOU...
...WHETHER YOU LIKE IT OR NOT.
BLAM
GAH!
NO!
YO, DYSFUNCTIONAL DUO!

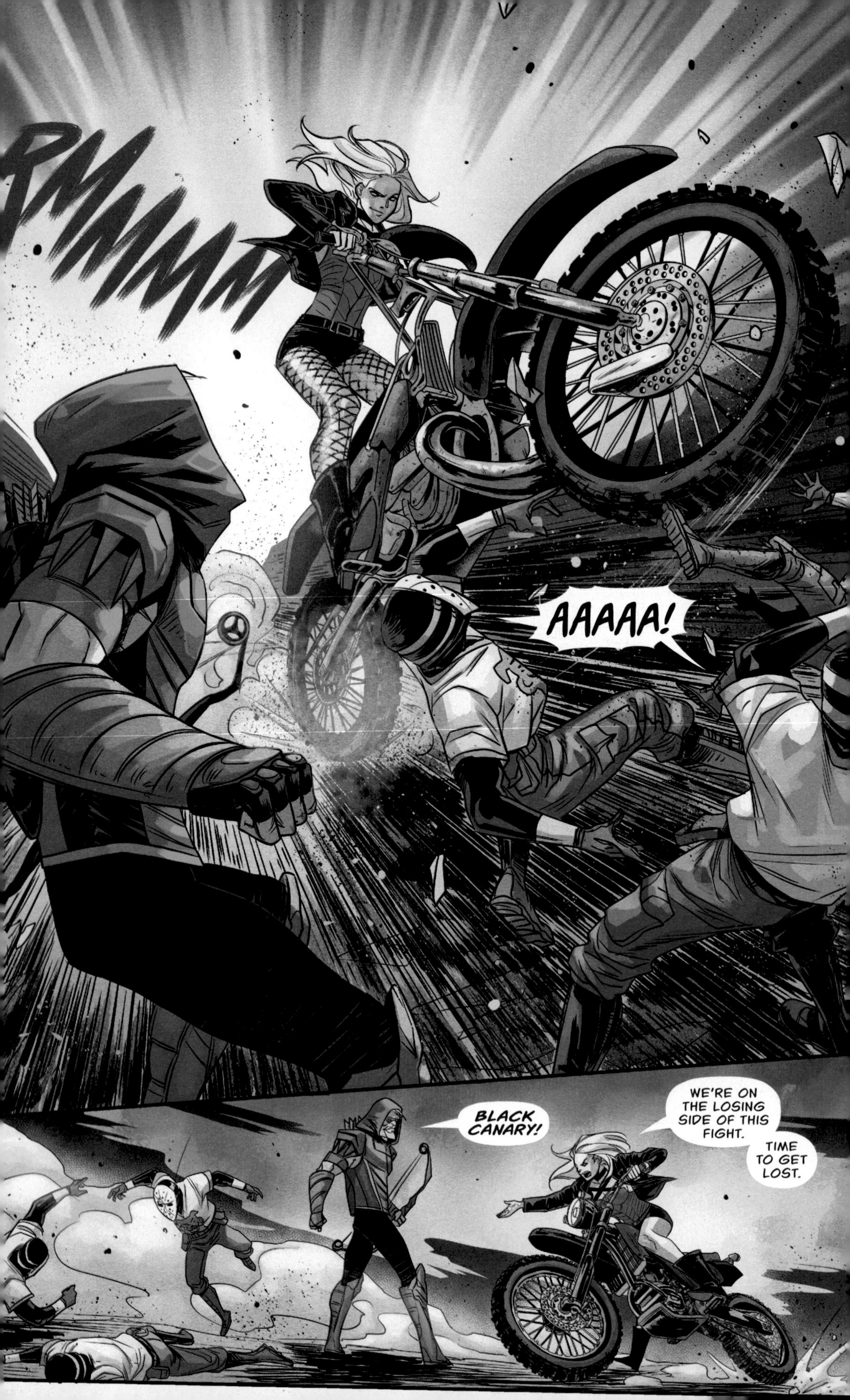
AAAAA!
BLACK CANARY!
WE'RE ON THE LOSING SIDE OF THIS FIGHT.
TIME TO GET LOST.

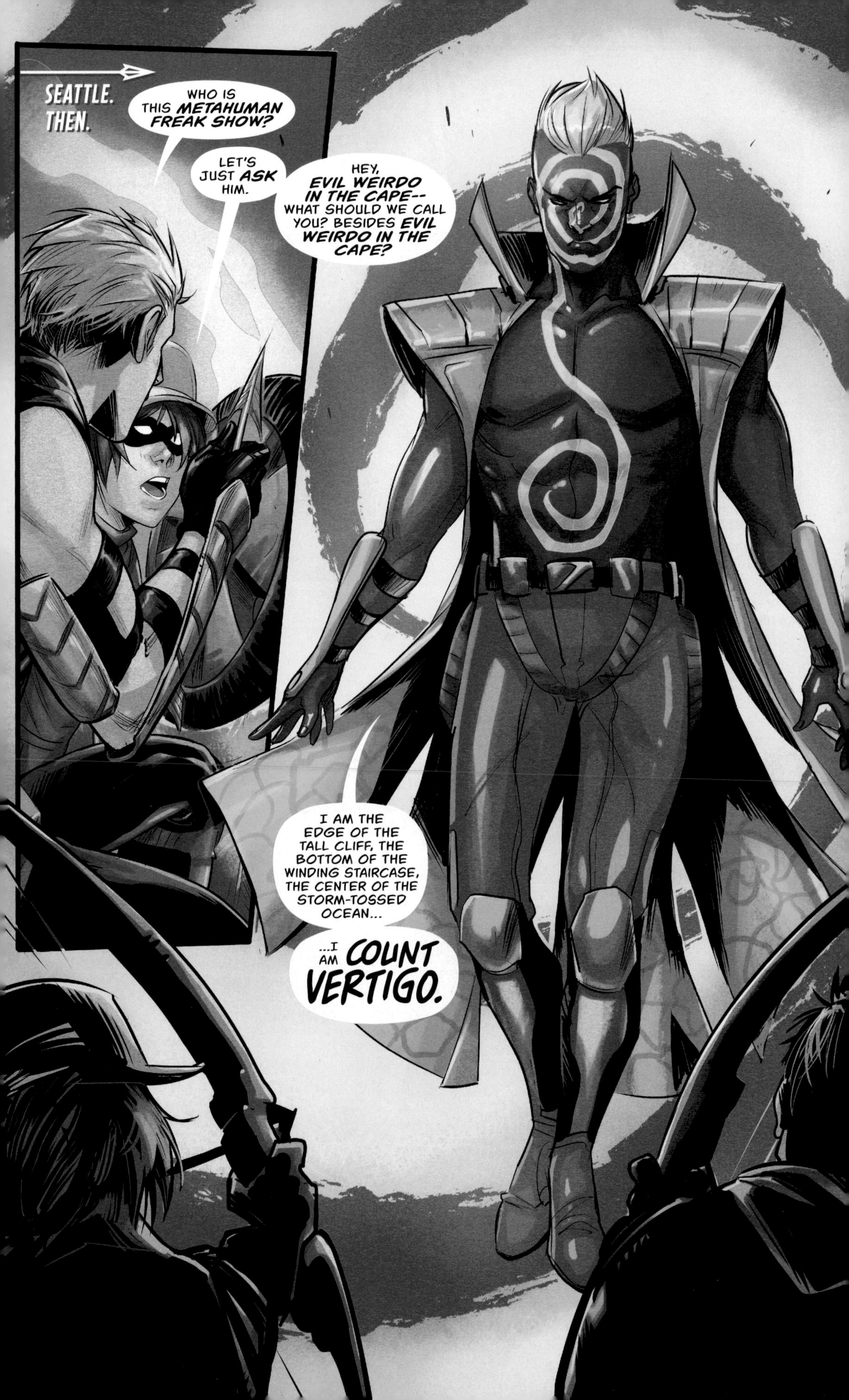
SEATTLE. THEN.
WHO IS THIS METAHUMAN FREAK SHOW?
LET'S JUST ASK HIM.
HEY, EVIL WEIRDO IN THE CAPE-- WHAT SHOULD WE CALL YOU? BESIDES EVIL WEIRDO IN THE CAPE?
I AM THE EDGE OF THE TALL CLIFF, THE BOTTOM OF THE WINDING STAIRCASE, THE CENTER OF THE STORM-TOSSED OCEAN...
...I AM COUNT VERTIGO.

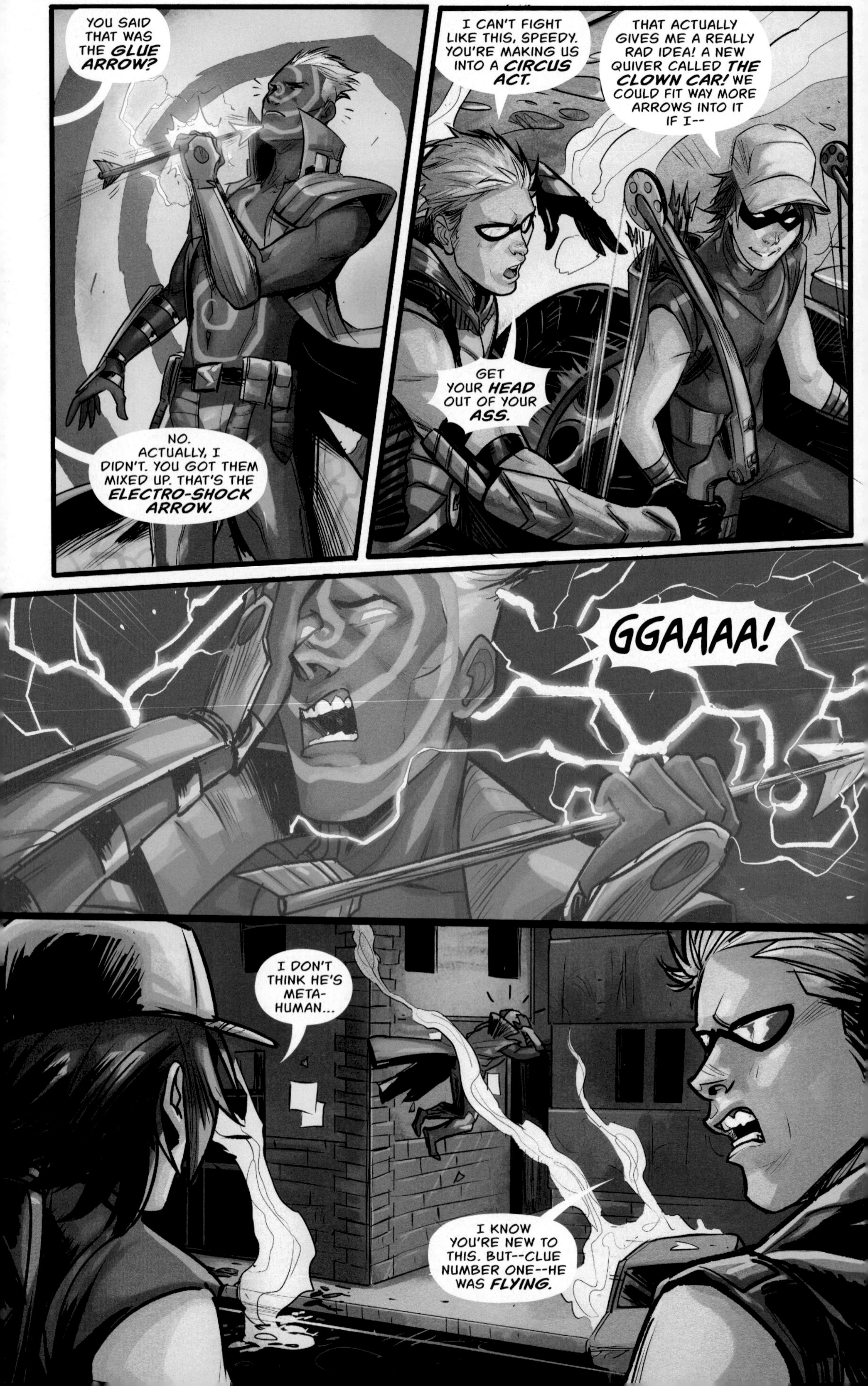
YOU SAID THAT WAS THE GLUE ARROW?
NO. ACTUALLY, I DIDN'T. YOU GOT THEM MIXED UP. THAT'S THE ELECTRO-SHOCK ARROW.
I CAN'T FIGHT LIKE THIS, SPEEDY. YOU'RE MAKING US INTO A CIRCUS ACT.
THAT ACTUALLY GIVES ME A REALLY RAD IDEA! A NEW QUIVER CALLED THE CLOWN CAR! WE COULD FIT WAY MORE ARROWS INTO IT IF I--
GET YOUR HEAD OUT OF YOUR ASS.
GGAAAA!
I DON'T THINK HE'S META-HUMAN...
I KNOW YOU'RE NEW TO THIS. BUT--CLUE NUMBER ONE--HE WAS FLYING.

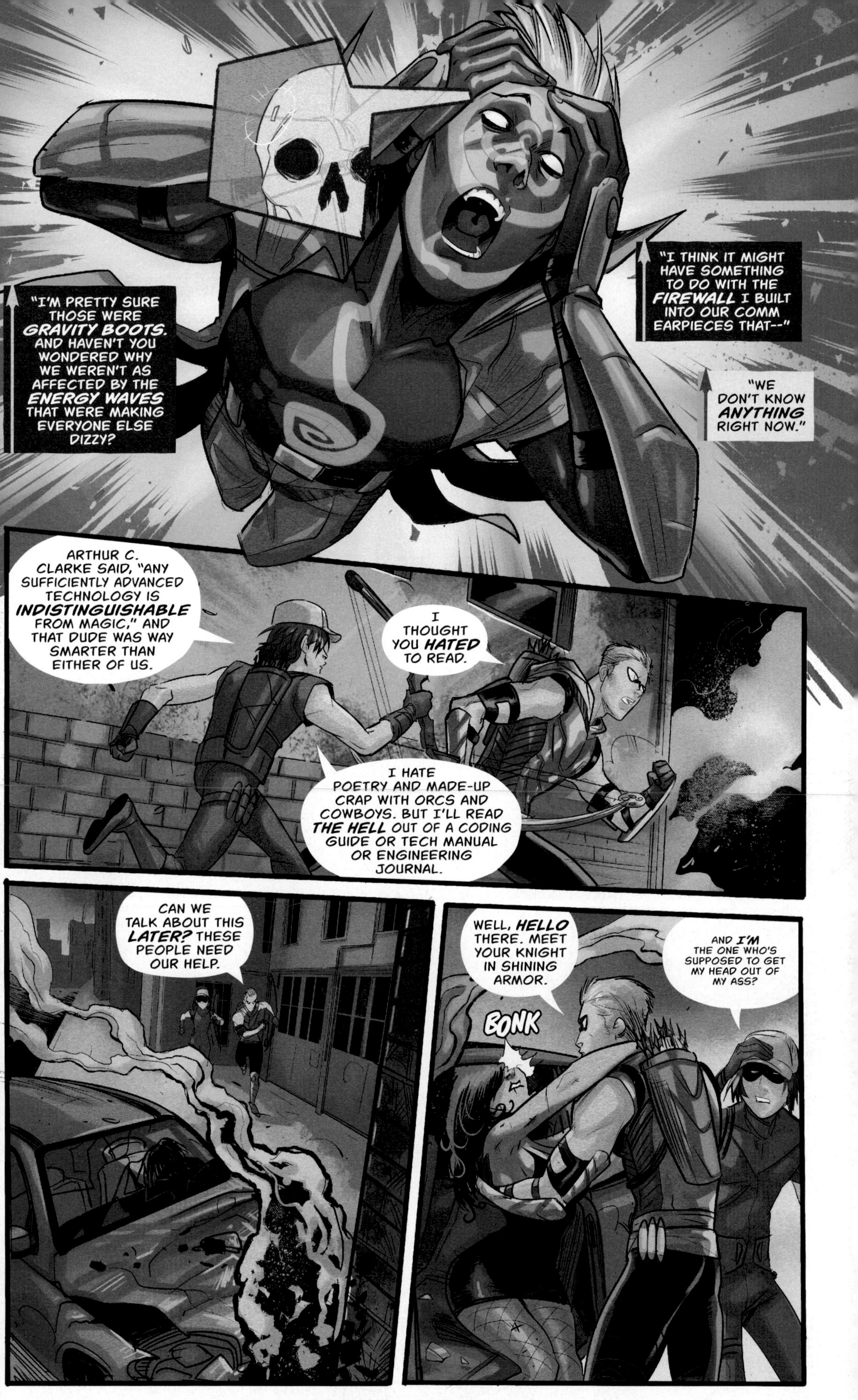
"I'M PRETTY SURE THOSE WERE GRAVITY BOOTS. AND HAVEN'T YOU WONDERED WHY WE WEREN'T AS AFFECTED BY THE ENERGY WAVES THAT WERE MAKING EVERYONE ELSE DIZZY?
"I THINK IT MIGHT HAVE SOMETHING TO DO WITH THE FIREWALL I BUILT INTO OUR COMM EARPIECES THAT--"
"WE DON'T KNOW ANYTHING RIGHT NOW."
ARTHUR C. CLARKE SAID, "ANY SUFFICIENTLY ADVANCED TECHNOLOGY IS INDISTINGUISHABLE FROM MAGIC," AND THAT DUDE WAS WAY SMARTER THAN EITHER OF US.
I THOUGHT YOU HATED TO READ.
I HATE POETRY AND MADE-UP CRAP WITH ORCS AND COWBOYS. BUT I'LL READ THE HELL OUT OF A CODING GUIDE OR TECH MANUAL OR ENGINEERING JOURNAL.
CAN WE TALK ABOUT THIS LATER? THESE PEOPLE NEED OUR HELP.
WELL, HELLO THERE. MEET YOUR KNIGHT IN SHINING ARMOR.
BONK
AND I'M THE ONE WHO'S SUPPOSED TO GET MY HEAD OUT OF MY ASS?

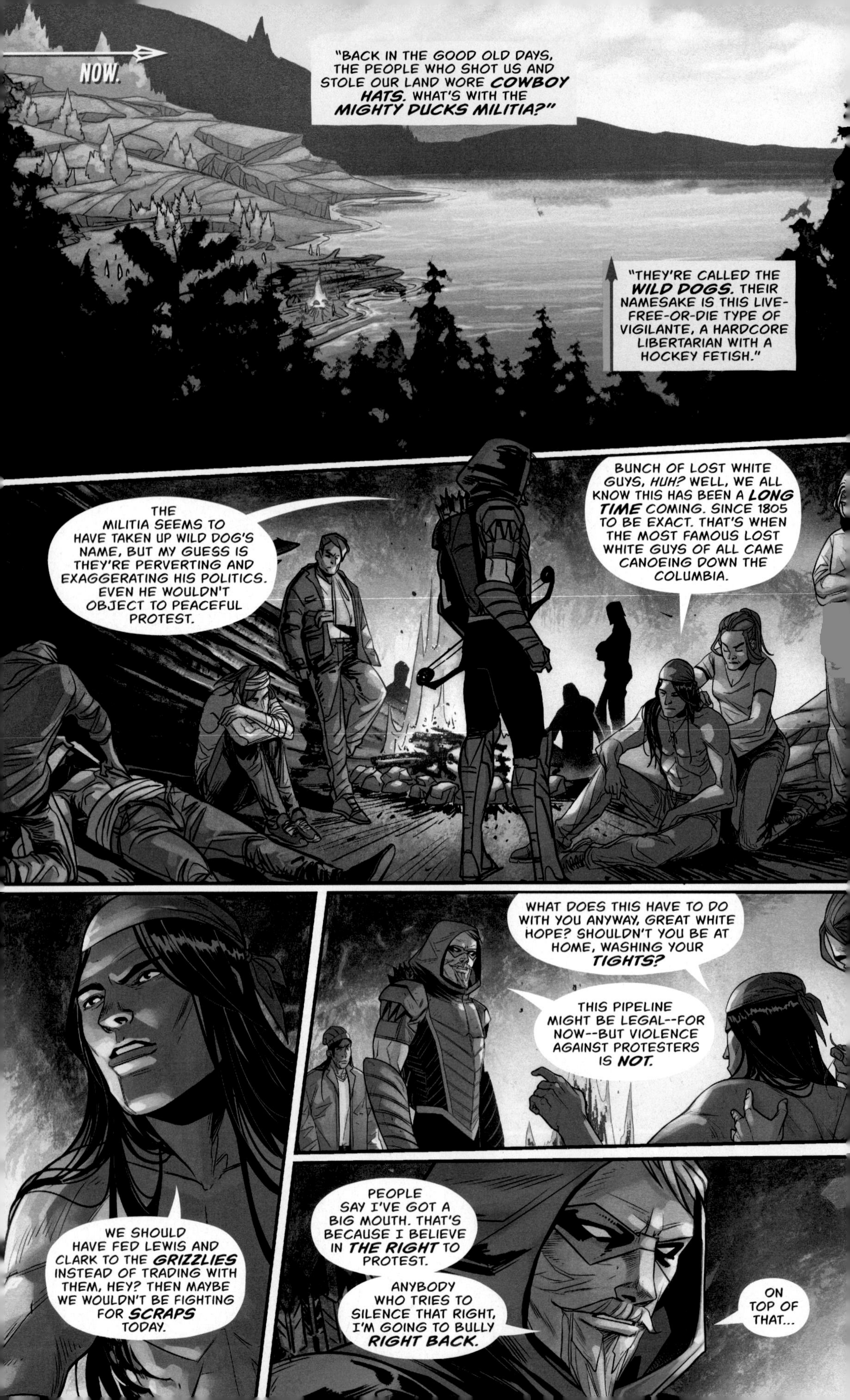

NOW.
"BACK IN THE GOOD OLD DAYS, THE PEOPLE WHO SHOT US AND STOLE OUR LAND WORE COWBOY HATS. WHAT'S WITH THE MIGHTY DUCKS MILITIA?"
"THEY'RE CALLED THE WILD DOGS. THEIR NAMESAKE IS THIS LIVE-FREE-OR-DIE TYPE OF VIGILANTE, A HARDCORE LIBERTARIAN WITH A HOCKEY FETISH."
THE MILITIA SEEMS TO HAVE TAKEN UP WILD DOG'S NAME, BUT MY GUESS IS THEY'RE PERVERTING AND EXAGGERATING HIS POLITICS. EVEN HE WOULDN'T OBJECT TO PEACEFUL PROTEST.
BUNCH OF LOST WHITE GUYS, HUH? WELL, WE ALL KNOW THIS HAS BEEN A LONG TIME COMING. SINCE 1805 TO BE EXACT. THAT'S WHEN THE MOST FAMOUS LOST WHITE GUYS OF ALL CAME CANOEING DOWN THE COLUMBIA.
WE SHOULD HAVE FED LEWIS AND CLARK TO THE GRIZZLIES INSTEAD OF TRADING WITH THEM, HEY? THEN MAYBE WE WOULDN'T BE FIGHTING FOR SCRAPS TODAY.
WHAT DOES THIS HAVE TO DO WITH YOU ANYWAY, GREAT WHITE HOPE? SHOULDN'T YOU BE AT HOME, WASHING YOUR TIGHTS?
THIS PIPELINE MIGHT BE LEGAL--FOR NOW--BUT VIOLENCE AGAINST PROTESTERS IS NOT.
PEOPLE SAY I'VE GOT A BIG MOUTH. THAT'S BECAUSE I BELIEVE IN THE RIGHT TO PROTEST.
ANYBODY WHO TRIES TO SILENCE THAT RIGHT, I'M GOING TO BULLY RIGHT BACK.
ON TOP OF THAT...

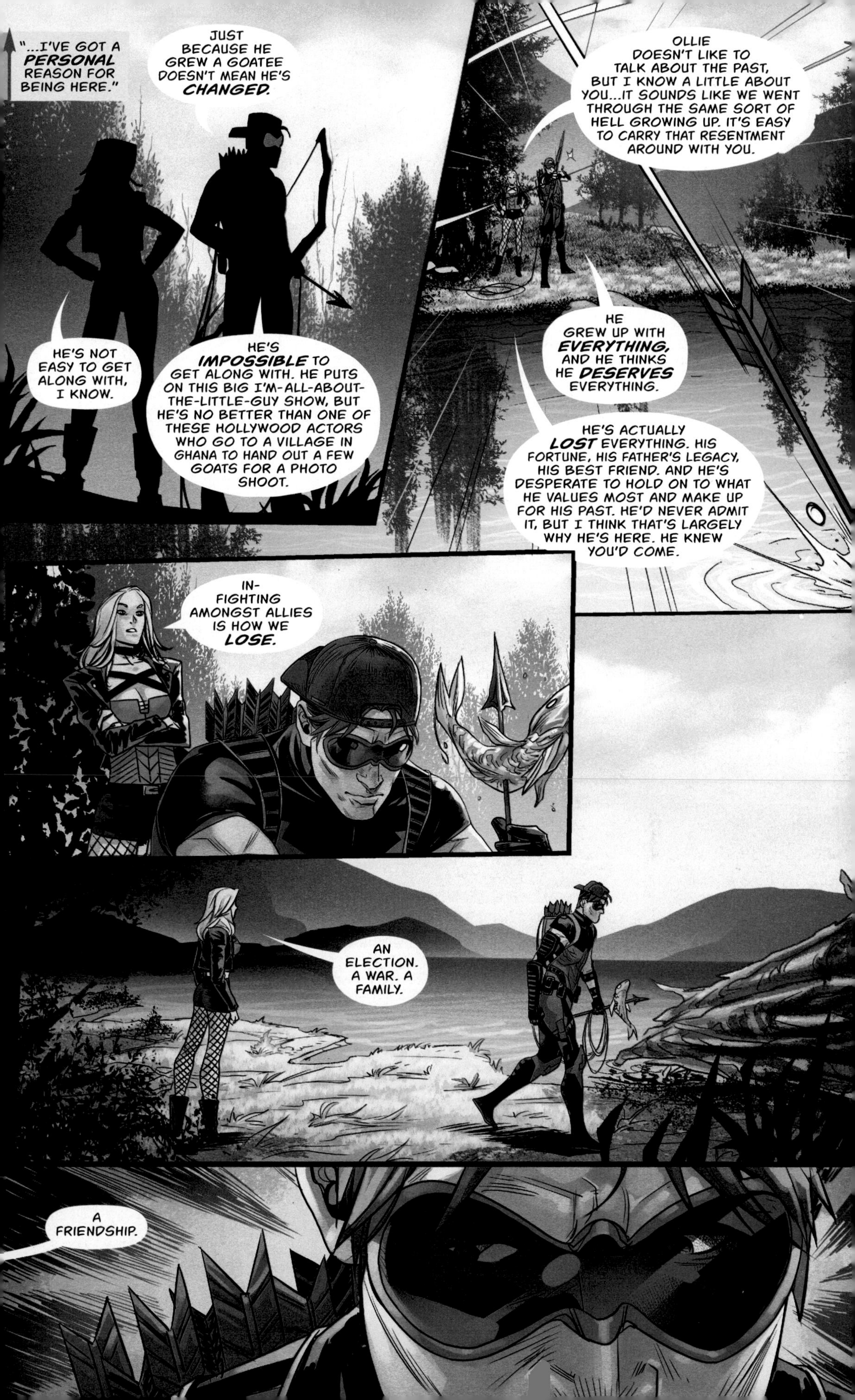
"...I'VE GOT A PERSONAL REASON FOR BEING HERE."
JUST BECAUSE HE GREW A GOATEE DOESN'T MEAN HE'S CHANGED.
HE'S NOT EASY TO GET ALONG WITH, I KNOW.
HE'S IMPOSSIBLE TO GET ALONG WITH. HE PUTS ON THIS BIG I'M-ALL-ABOUT-THE-LITTLE-GUY SHOW, BUT HE'S NO BETTER THAN ONE OF THESE HOLLYWOOD ACTORS WHO GO TO A VILLAGE IN GHANA TO HAND OUT A FEW GOATS FOR A PHOTO SHOOT.
OLLIE DOESN'T LIKE TO TALK ABOUT THE PAST, BUT I KNOW A LITTLE ABOUT YOU...IT SOUNDS LIKE WE WENT THROUGH THE SAME SORT OF HELL GROWING UP. IT'S EASY TO CARRY THAT RESENTMENT AROUND WITH YOU.
HE GREW UP WITH EVERYTHING, AND HE THINKS HE DESERVES EVERYTHING.
HE'S ACTUALLY LOST EVERYTHING. HIS FORTUNE, HIS FATHER'S LEGACY, HIS BEST FRIEND. AND HE'S DESPERATE TO HOLD ON TO WHAT HE VALUES MOST AND MAKE UP FOR HIS PAST. HE'D NEVER ADMIT IT, BUT I THINK THAT'S LARGELY WHY HE'S HERE. HE KNEW YOU'D COME.
IN-FIGHTING AMONGST ALLIES IS HOW WE LOSE.
AN ELECTION. A WAR. A FAMILY.
A FRIENDSHIP.

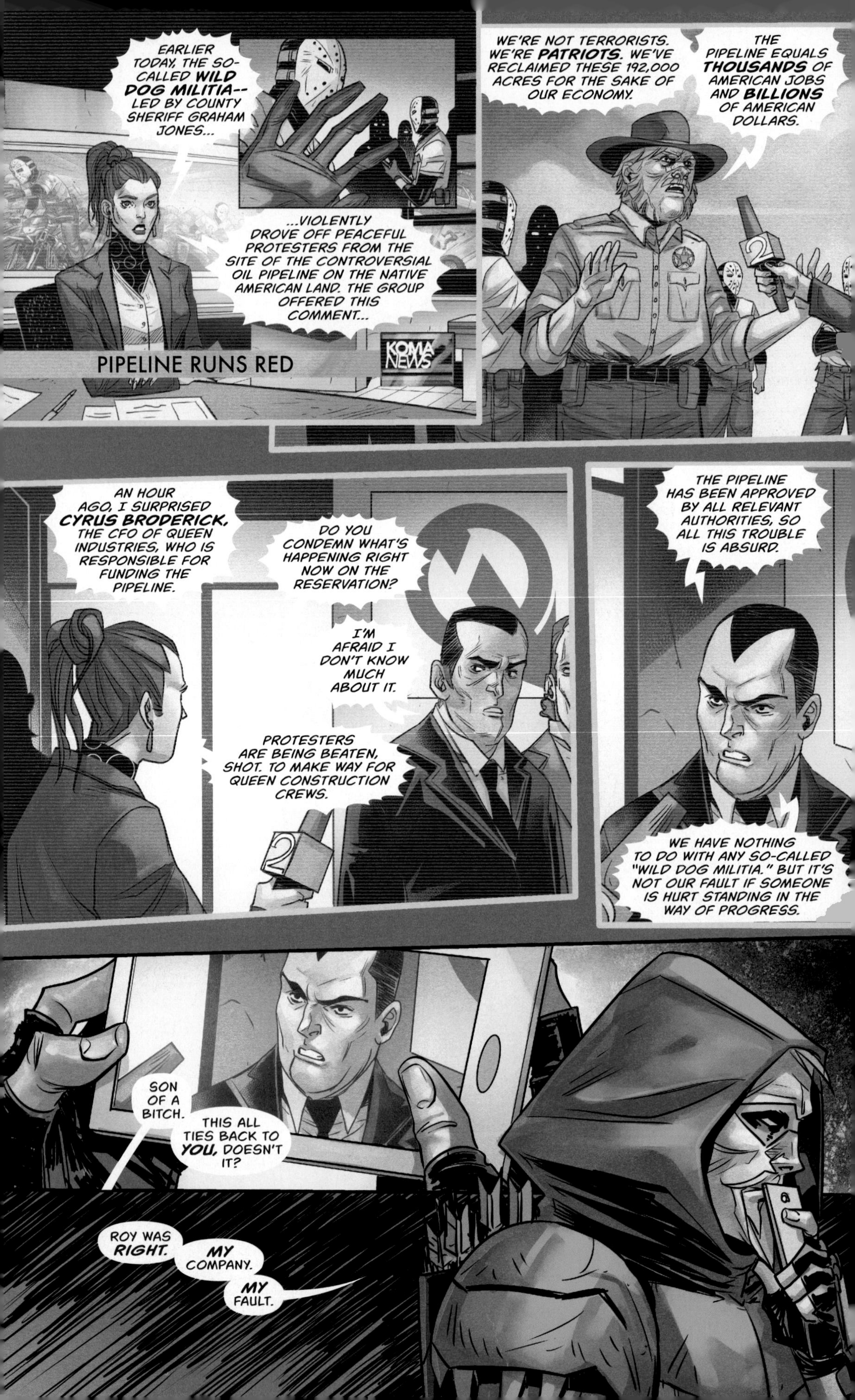

EARLIER TODAY, THE SO-CALLED WILD DOG MILITIA-- LED BY COUNTY SHERIFF GRAHAM JONES...
...VIOLENTLY DROVE OFF PEACEFUL PROTESTERS FROM THE SITE OF THE CONTROVERSIAL OIL PIPELINE ON THE NATIVE AMERICAN LAND. THE GROUP OFFERED THIS COMMENT...
PIPELINE RUNS RED
KOMA NEWS
WE'RE NOT TERRORISTS. WE'RE PATRIOTS. WE'VE RECLAIMED THESE 192,000 ACRES FOR THE SAKE OF OUR ECONOMY.
THE PIPELINE EQUALS THOUSANDS OF AMERICAN JOBS AND BILLIONS OF AMERICAN DOLLARS.
AN HOUR AGO, I SURPRISED CYRUS BRODERICK, THE CFO OF QUEEN INDUSTRIES, WHO IS RESPONSIBLE FOR FUNDING THE PIPELINE.
DO YOU CONDEMN WHAT'S HAPPENING RIGHT NOW ON THE RESERVATION?
I'M AFRAID I DON'T KNOW MUCH ABOUT IT.
PROTESTERS ARE BEING BEATEN, SHOT. TO MAKE WAY FOR QUEEN CONSTRUCTION CREWS.
THE PIPELINE HAS BEEN APPROVED BY ALL RELEVANT AUTHORITIES, SO ALL THIS TROUBLE IS ABSURD.
WE HAVE NOTHING TO DO WITH ANY SO-CALLED "WILD DOG MILITIA." BUT IT'S NOT OUR FAULT IF SOMEONE IS HURT STANDING IN THE WAY OF PROGRESS.
SON OF A BITCH.
THIS ALL TIES BACK TO YOU, DOESN'T IT?
ROY WAS RIGHT.
MY COMPANY.
MY FAULT.

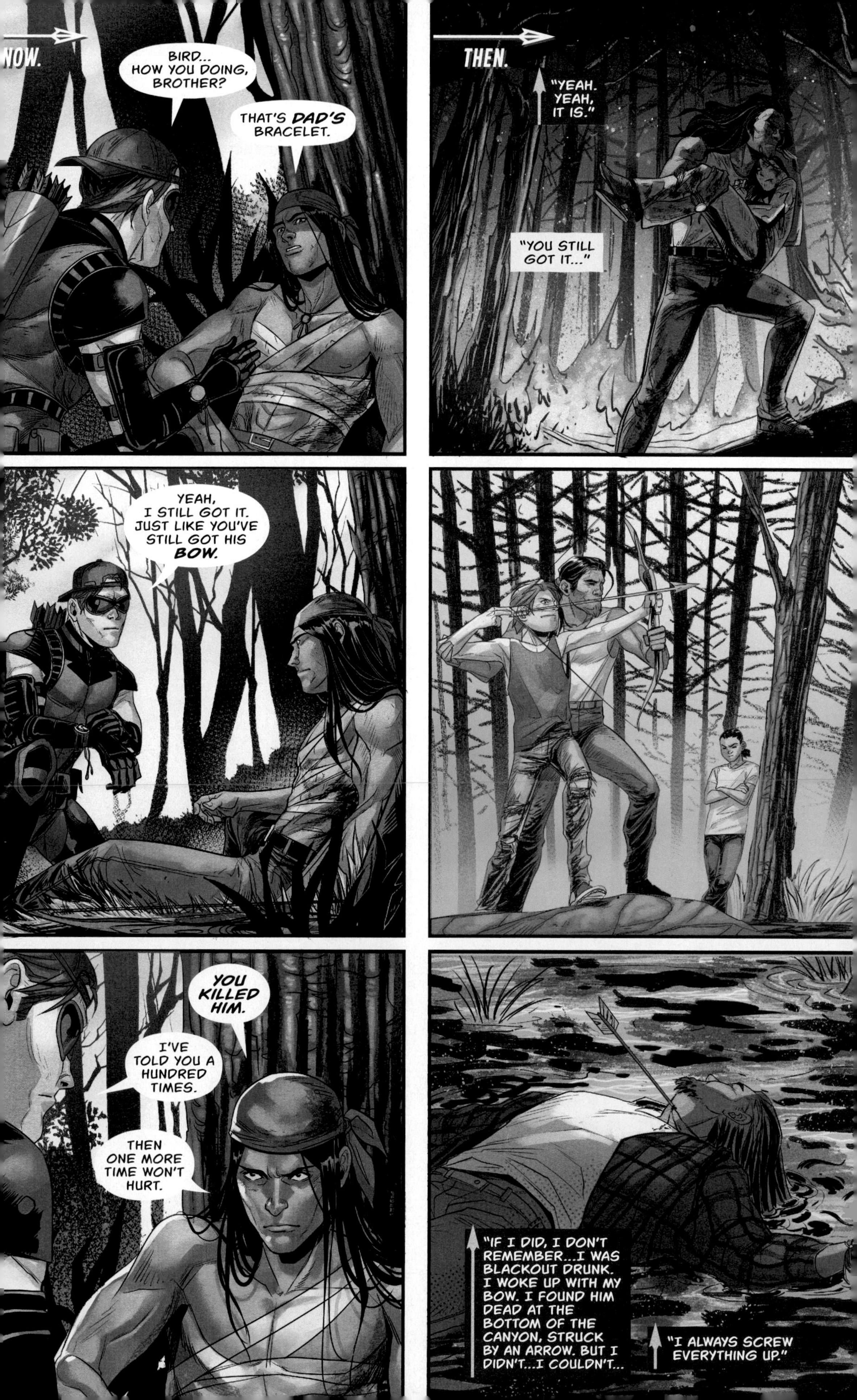

NOW.
BIRD... HOW YOU DOING, BROTHER?
THAT'S DAD'S BRACELET.
THEN.
"YEAH. YEAH, IT IS."
"YOU STILL GOT IT..."
YEAH, I STILL GOT IT. JUST LIKE YOU'VE STILL GOT HIS BOW.
YOU KILLED HIM.
I'VE TOLD YOU A HUNDRED TIMES.
THEN ONE MORE TIME WON'T HURT.
"IF I DID, I DON'T REMEMBER...I WAS BLACKOUT DRUNK. I WOKE UP WITH MY BOW. I FOUND HIM DEAD AT THE BOTTOM OF THE CANYON, STRUCK BY AN ARROW. BUT I DIDN'T...I COULDN'T...
"I ALWAYS SCREW EVERYTHING UP."

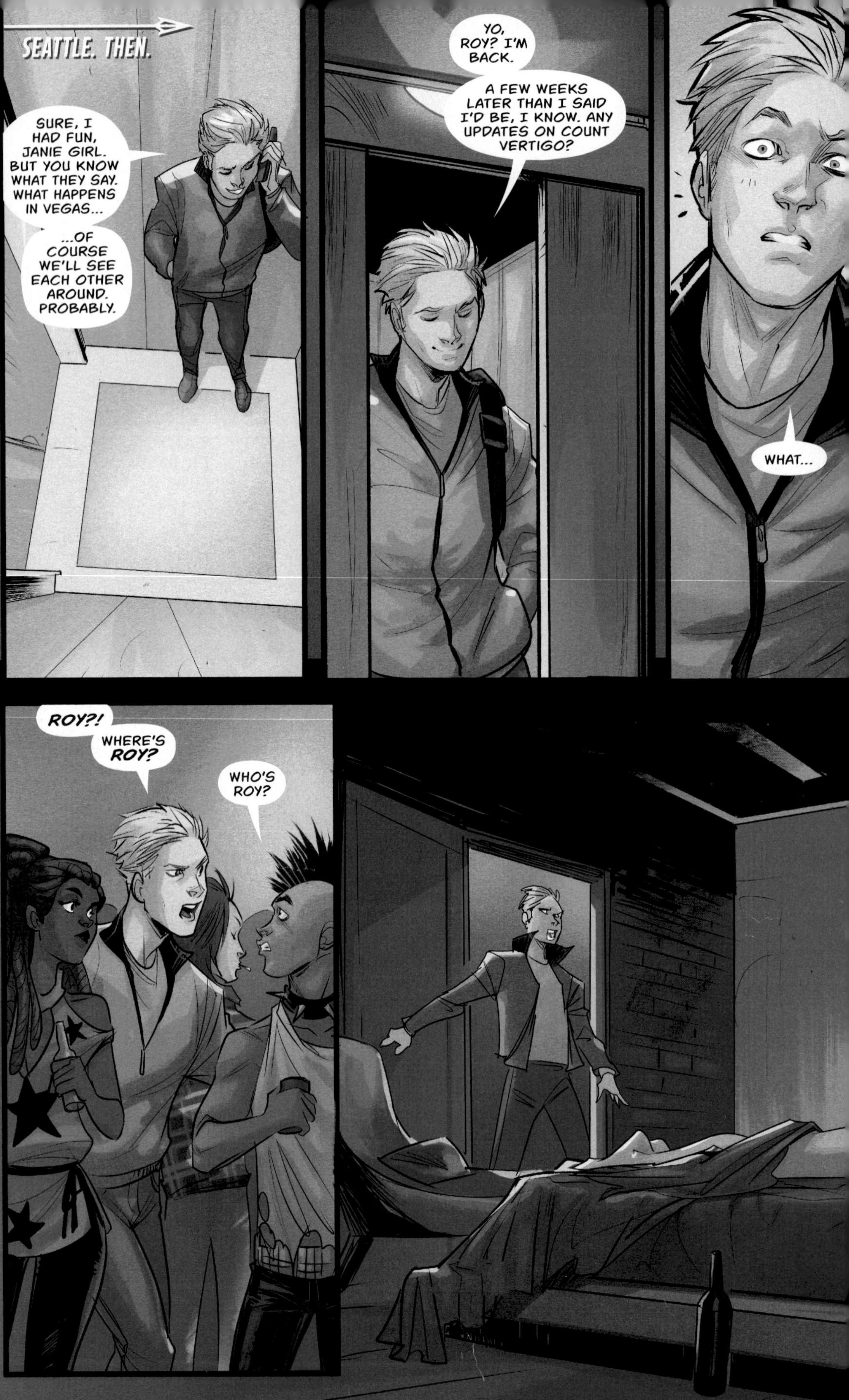
SEATTLE. THEN.
SURE, I HAD FUN, JANIE GIRL. BUT YOU KNOW WHAT THEY SAY. WHAT HAPPENS IN VEGAS...
...OF COURSE WE'LL SEE EACH OTHER AROUND. PROBABLY.
YO, ROY? I'M BACK.
A FEW WEEKS LATER THAN I SAID I'D BE, I KNOW. ANY UPDATES ON COUNT VERTIGO?
WHAT...
ROY?!
WHERE'S ROY?
WHO'S ROY?

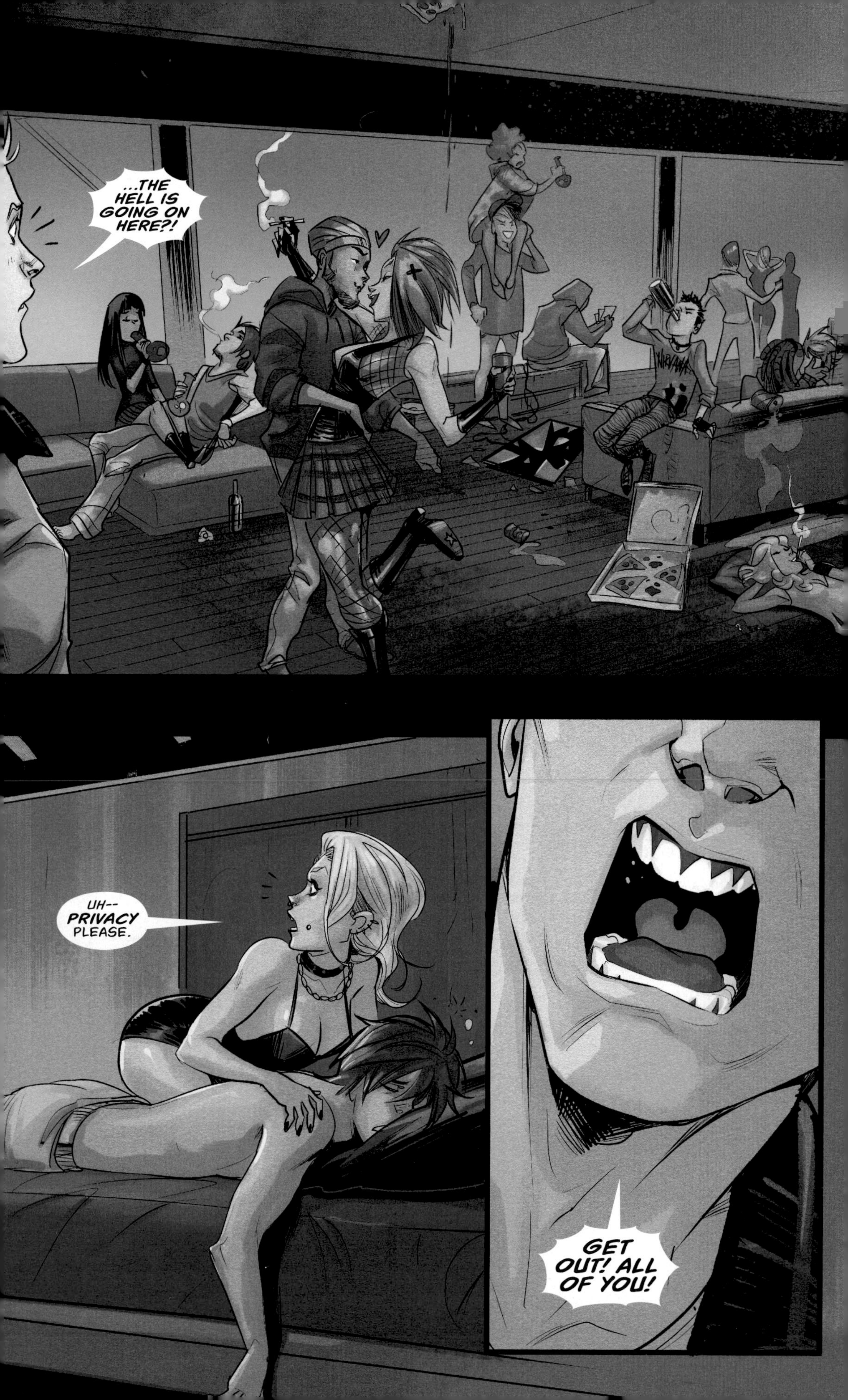
...THE HELL IS GOING ON HERE?!
UH-- PRIVACY PLEASE.
GET OUT! ALL OF YOU!

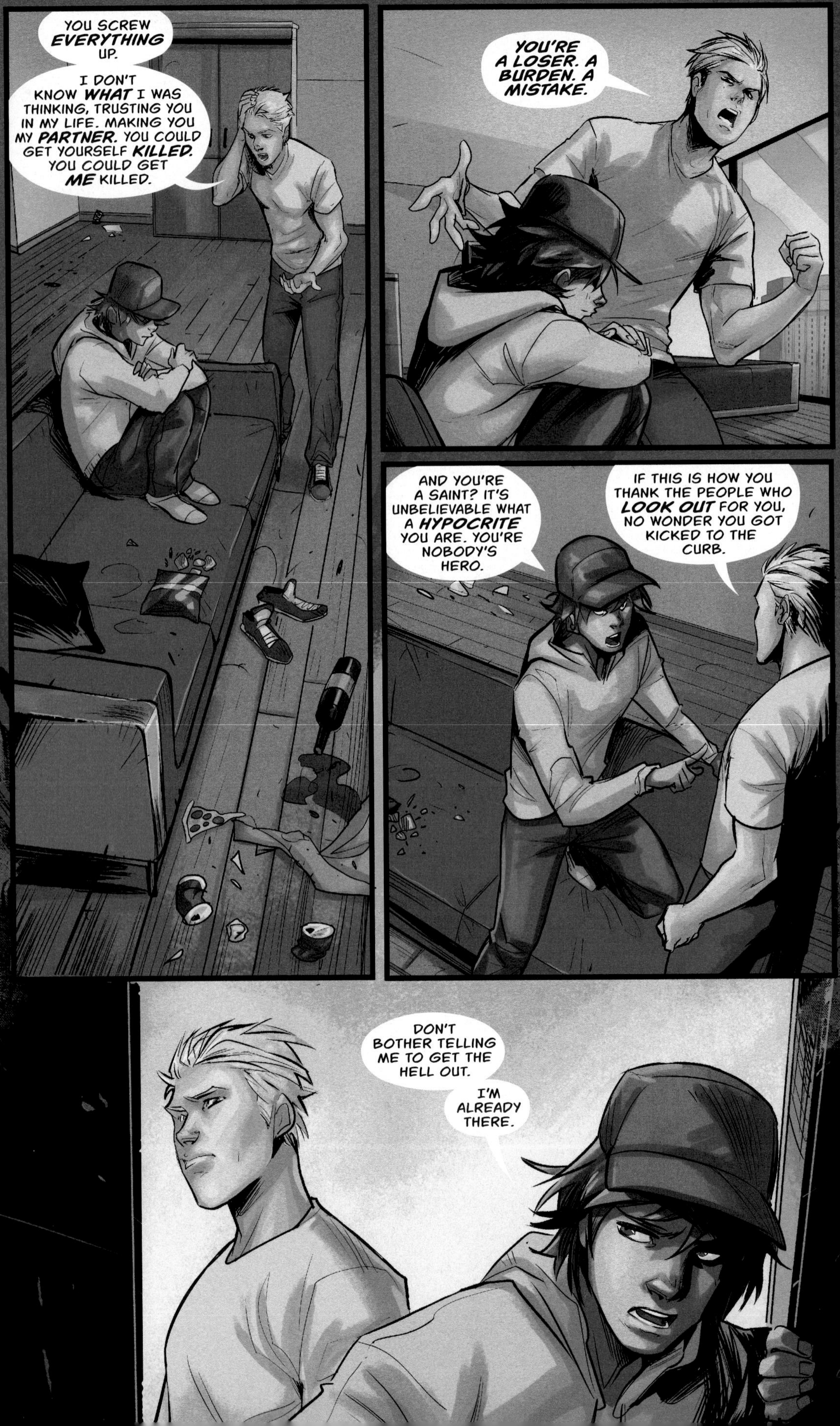

YOU SCREW EVERYTHING UP.
I DON'T KNOW WHAT I WAS THINKING, TRUSTING YOU IN MY LIFE. MAKING YOU MY PARTNER. YOU COULD GET YOURSELF KILLED. YOU COULD GET ME KILLED.
YOU'RE A LOSER. A BURDEN. A MISTAKE.
AND YOU'RE A SAINT? IT'S UNBELIEVABLE WHAT A HYPOCRITE YOU ARE. YOU'RE NOBODY'S HERO.
IF THIS IS HOW YOU THANK THE PEOPLE WHO LOOK OUT FOR YOU, NO WONDER YOU GOT KICKED TO THE CURB.
DON'T BOTHER TELLING ME TO GET THE HELL OUT.
I'M ALREADY THERE.

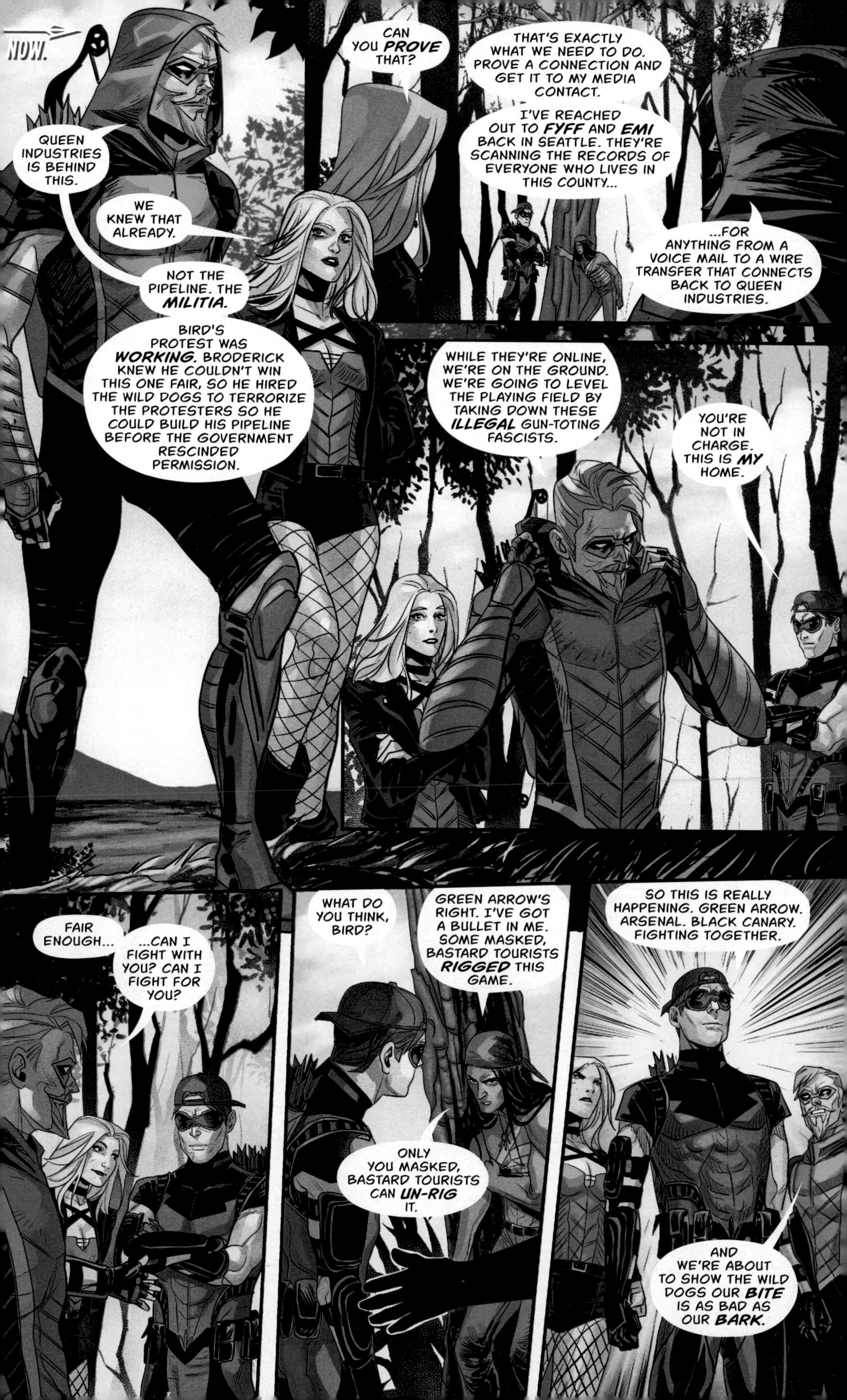
NOW.
QUEEN INDUSTRIES IS BEHIND THIS.
WE KNEW THAT ALREADY.
NOT THE PIPELINE. THE MILITIA.
BIRD'S PROTEST WAS WORKING. BRODERICK KNEW HE COULDN'T WIN THIS ONE FAIR, SO HE HIRED THE WILD DOGS TO TERRORIZE THE PROTESTERS SO HE COULD BUILD HIS PIPELINE BEFORE THE GOVERNMENT RESCINDED PERMISSION.
CAN YOU PROVE THAT?
THAT'S EXACTLY WHAT WE NEED TO DO. PROVE A CONNECTION AND GET IT TO MY MEDIA CONTACT.
I'VE REACHED OUT TO FYFF AND EMI BACK IN SEATTLE. THEY'RE SCANNING THE RECORDS OF EVERYONE WHO LIVES IN THIS COUNTY...
...FOR ANYTHING FROM A VOICE MAIL TO A WIRE TRANSFER THAT CONNECTS BACK TO QUEEN INDUSTRIES.
WHILE THEY'RE ONLINE, WE'RE ON THE GROUND. WE'RE GOING TO LEVEL THE PLAYING FIELD BY TAKING DOWN THESE ILLEGAL GUN-TOTING FASCISTS.
YOU'RE NOT IN CHARGE. THIS IS MY HOME.
FAIR ENOUGH...
...CAN I FIGHT WITH YOU? CAN I FIGHT FOR YOU?
WHAT DO YOU THINK, BIRD?
GREEN ARROW'S RIGHT. I'VE GOT A BULLET IN ME. SOME MASKED, BASTARD TOURISTS RIGGED THIS GAME.
ONLY YOU MASKED, BASTARD TOURISTS CAN UN-RIG IT.
SO THIS IS REALLY HAPPENING. GREEN ARROW. ARSENAL. BLACK CANARY. FIGHTING TOGETHER.
AND WE'RE ABOUT TO SHOW THE WILD DOGS OUR BITE IS AS BAD AS OUR BARK.

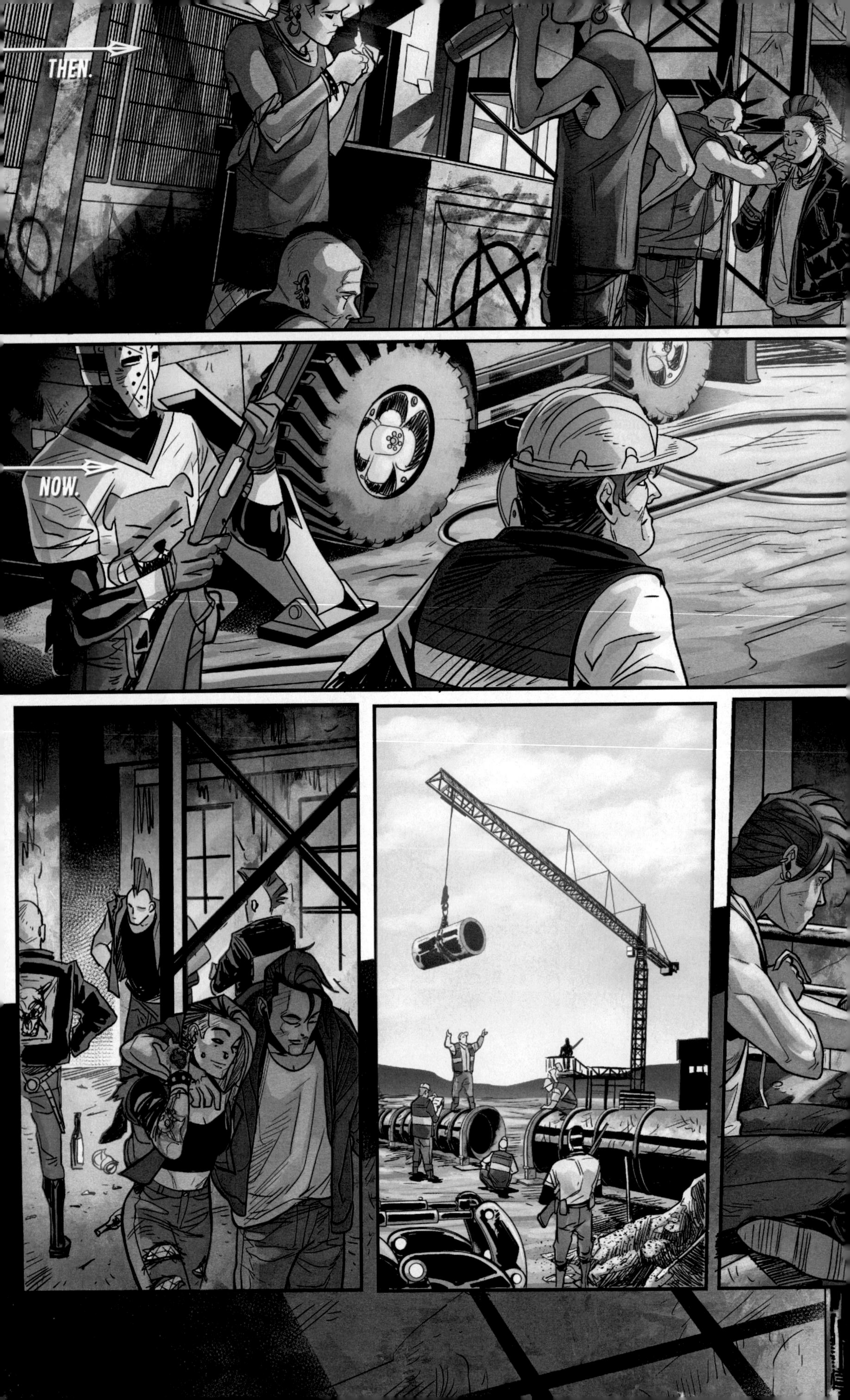
THEN.
NOW.

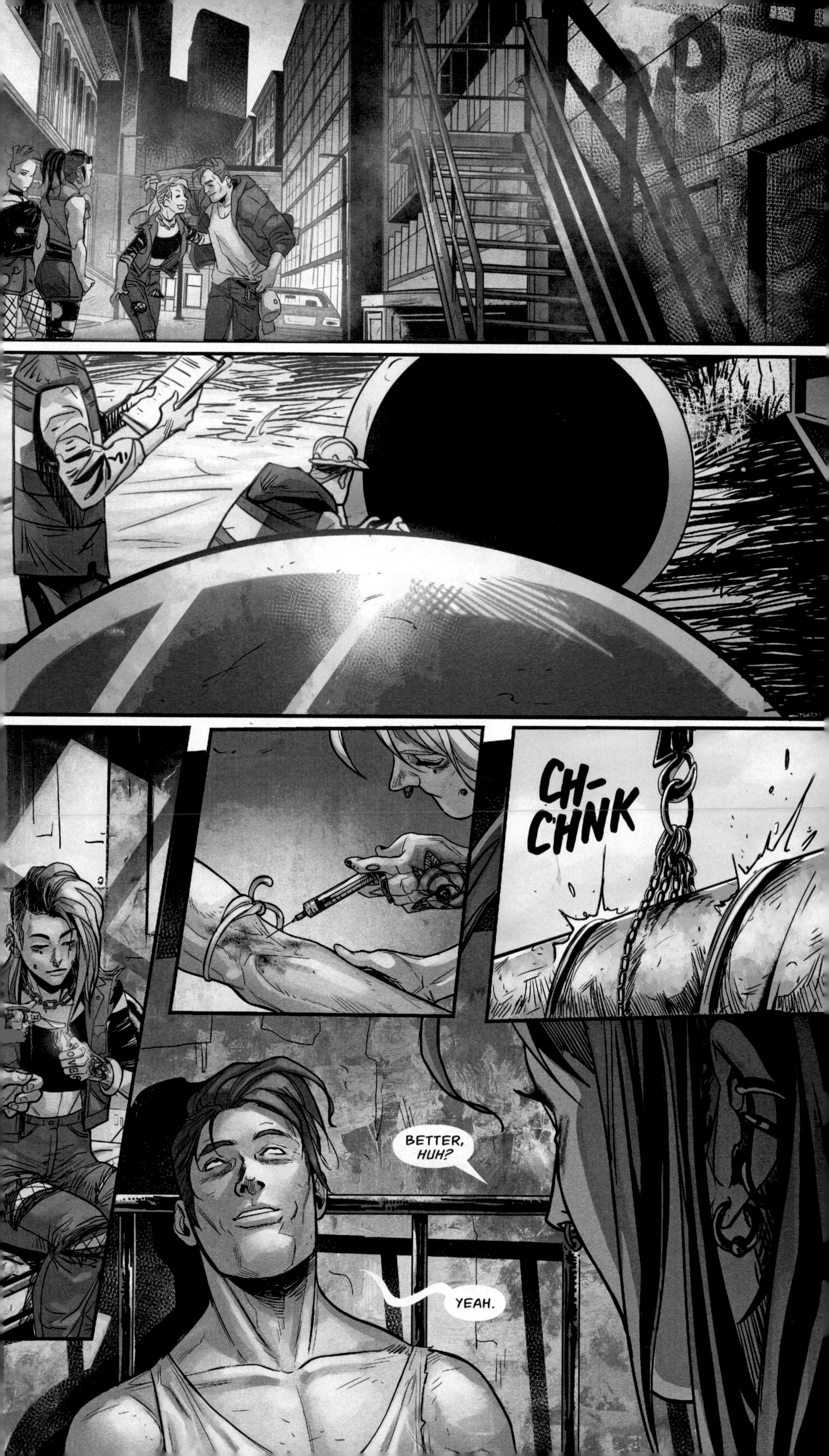
CH-
CHNK
BETTER, HUH?
YEAH.

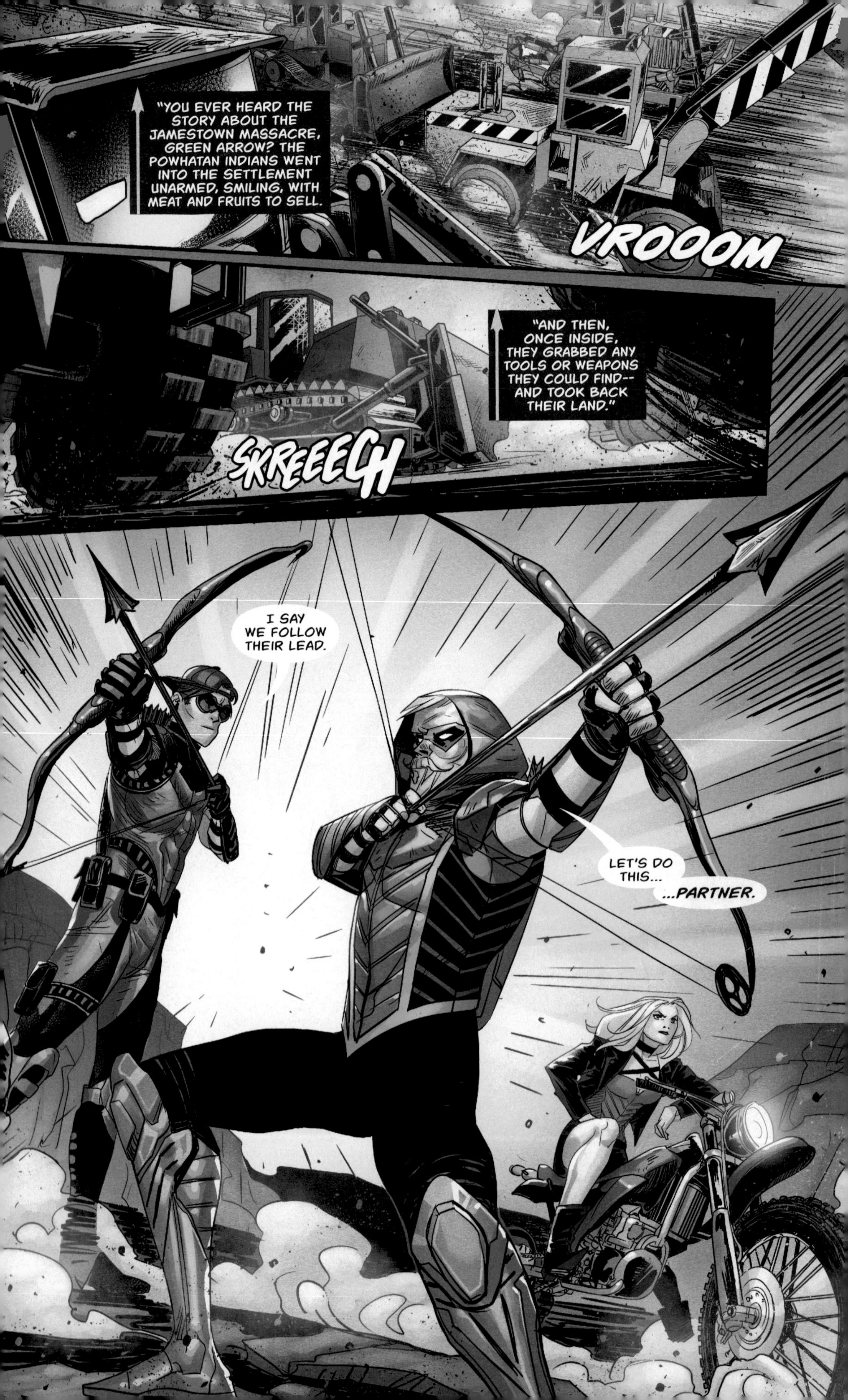
"YOU EVER HEARD THE STORY ABOUT THE JAMESTOWN MASSACRE, GREEN ARROW? THE POWHATAN INDIANS WENT INTO THE SETTLEMENT UNARMED, SMILING, WITH MEAT AND FRUITS TO SELL.
VROOOM
"AND THEN, ONCE INSIDE, THEY GRABBED ANY TOOLS OR WEAPONS THEY COULD FIND-- AND TOOK BACK THEIR LAND."
SKREEEECH
I SAY WE FOLLOW THEIR LEAD.
LET'S DO THIS... ...PARTNER.

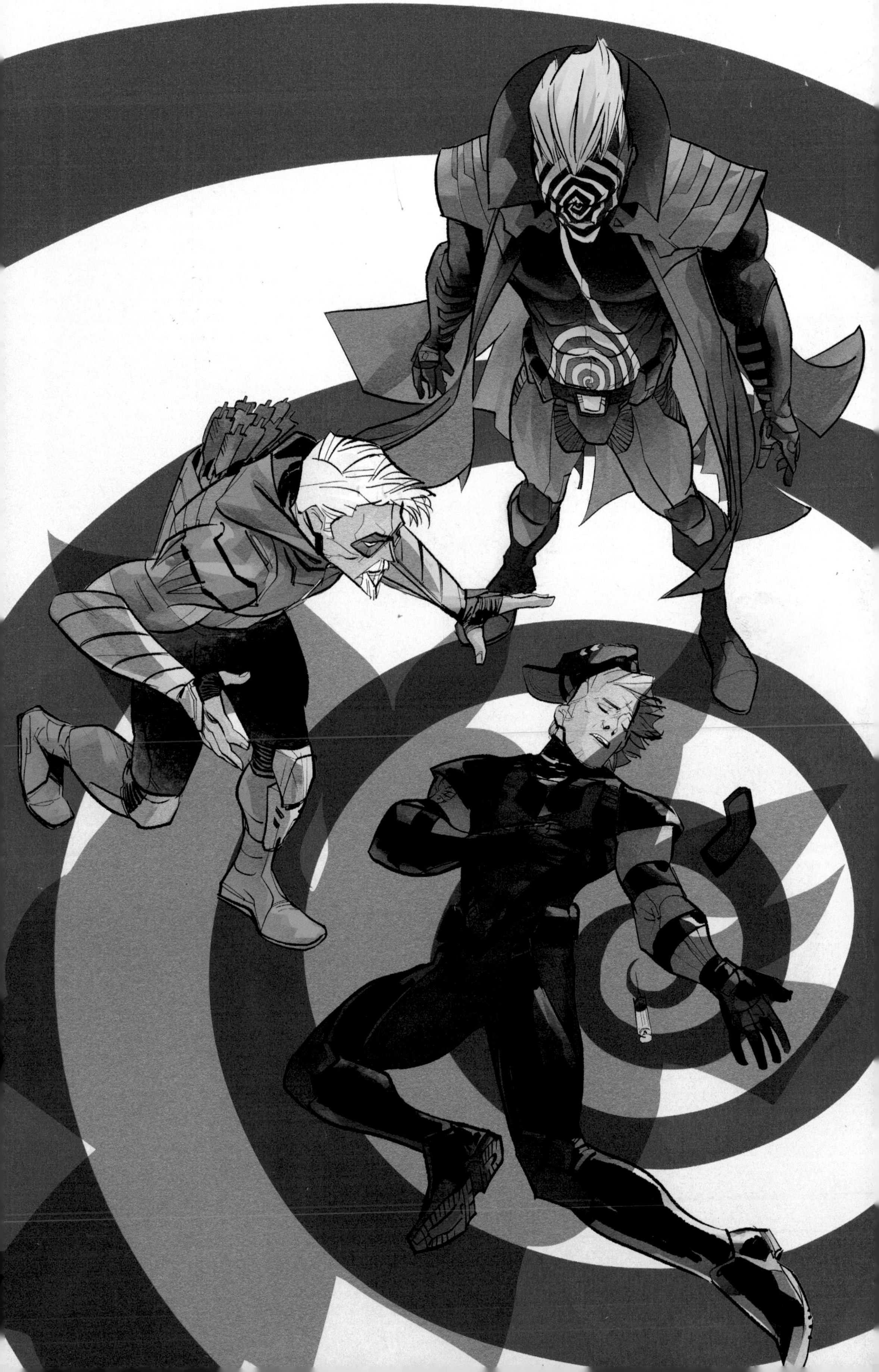

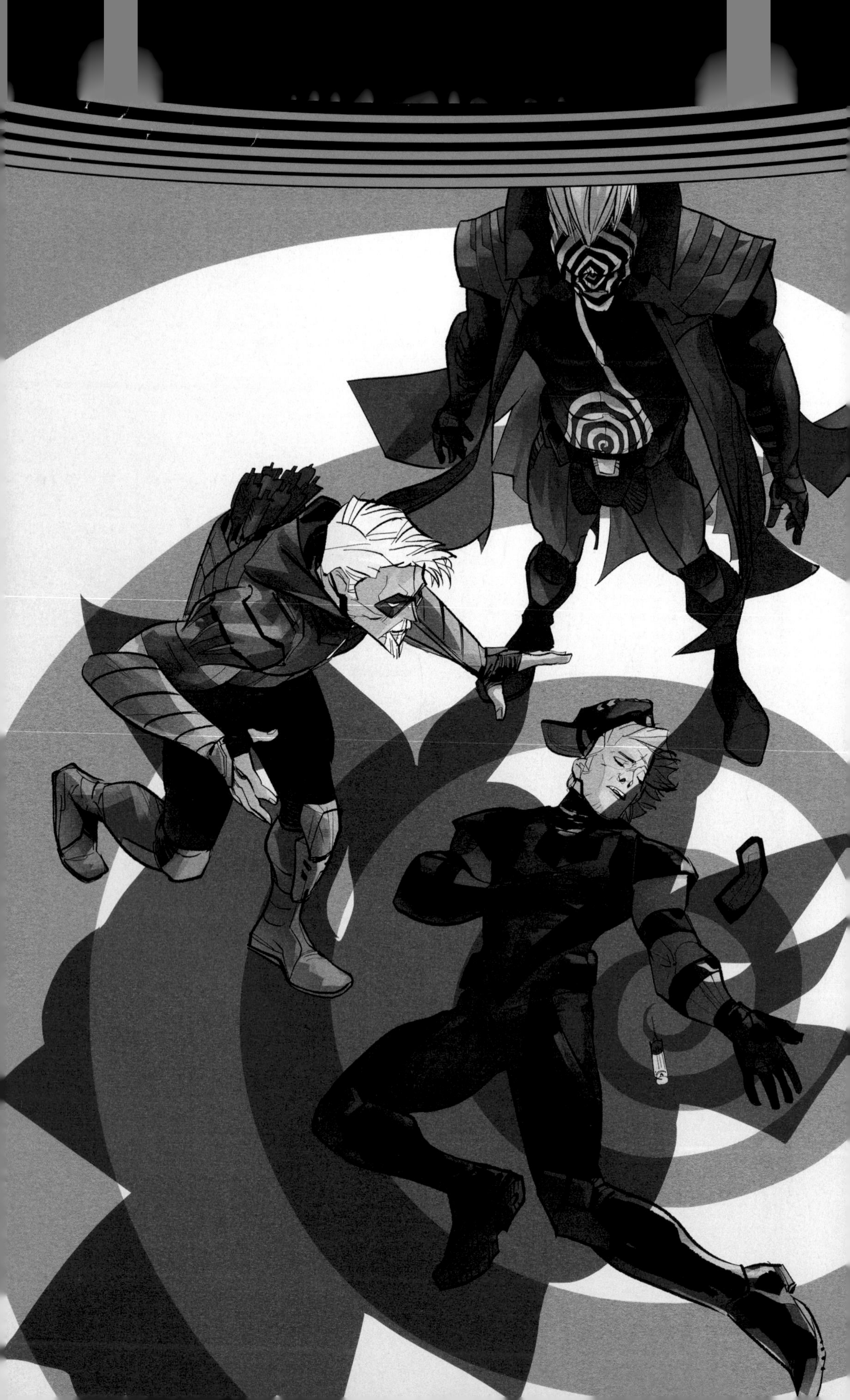

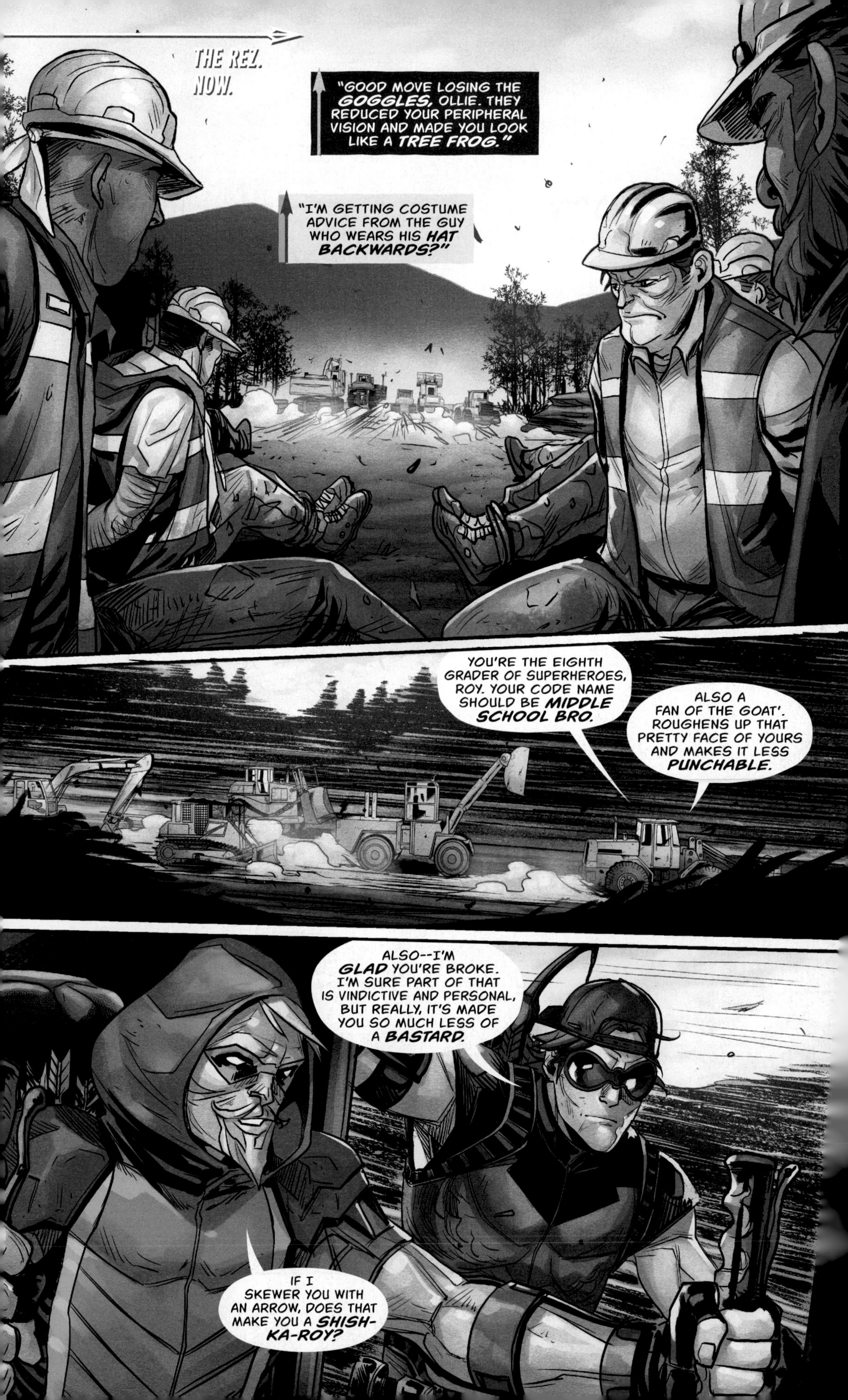
THE REZ. NOW.
"GOOD MOVE LOSING THE GOGGLES, OLLIE. THEY REDUCED YOUR PERIPHERAL VISION AND MADE YOU LOOK LIKE A TREE FROG."
"I'M GETTING COSTUME ADVICE FROM THE GUY WHO WEARS HIS HAT BACKWARDS?"
YOU'RE THE EIGHTH GRADER OF SUPERHEROES, ROY. YOUR CODE NAME SHOULD BE MIDDLE SCHOOL BRO.
ALSO A FAN OF THE GOAT'. ROUGHENS UP THAT PRETTY FACE OF YOURS AND MAKES IT LESS PUNCHABLE.
ALSO--I'M GLAD YOU'RE BROKE. I'M SURE PART OF THAT IS VINDICTIVE AND PERSONAL, BUT REALLY, IT'S MADE YOU SO MUCH LESS OF A BASTARD.
IF I SKEWER YOU WITH AN ARROW, DOES THAT MAKE YOU A SHISH-KA-ROY?

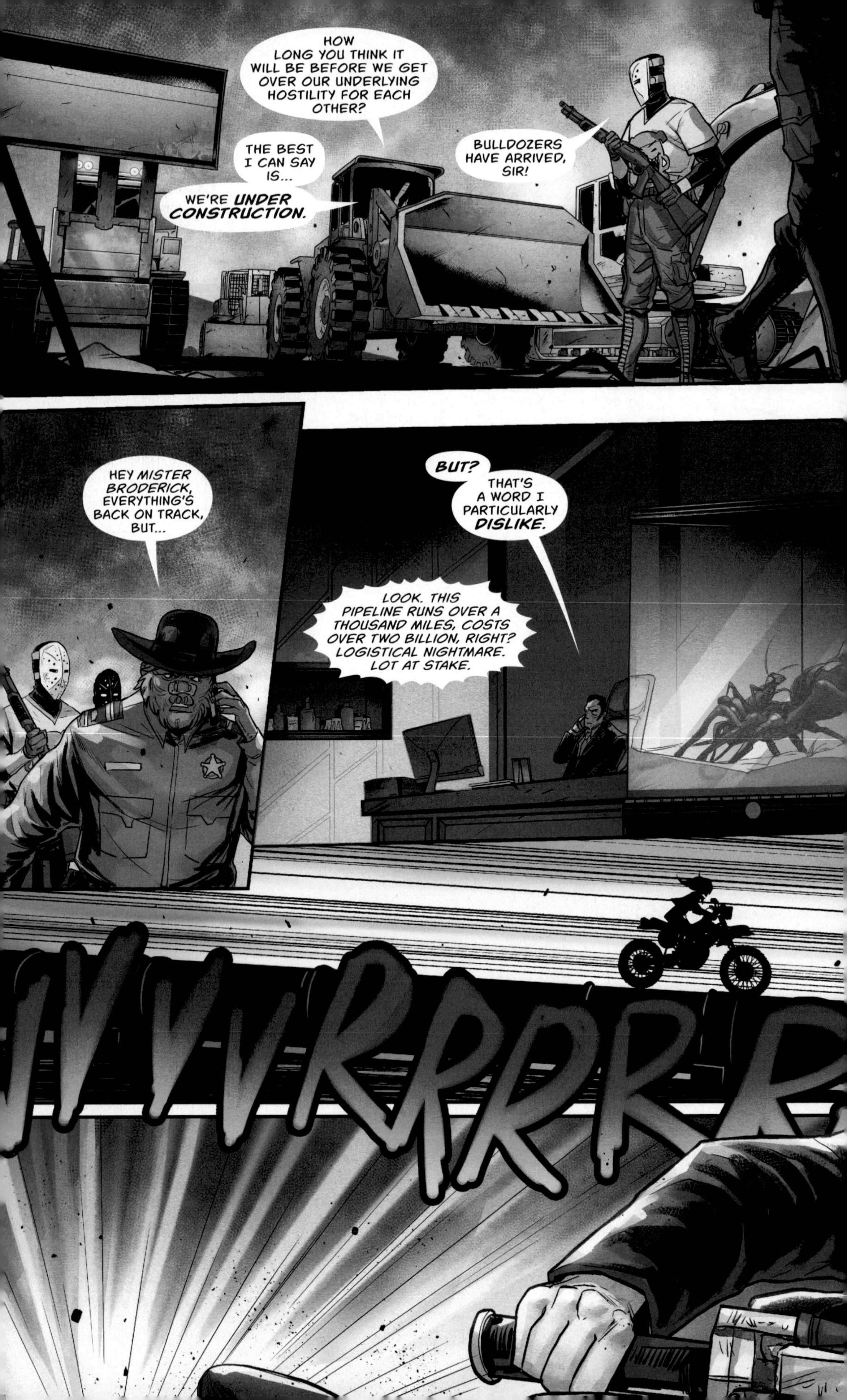

HOW LONG YOU THINK IT WILL BE BEFORE WE GET OVER OUR UNDERLYING HOSTILITY FOR EACH OTHER?
THE BEST I CAN SAY IS...
WE'RE UNDER CONSTRUCTION.
BULLDOZERS HAVE ARRIVED, SIR!
HEY MISTER BRODERICK, EVERYTHING'S BACK ON TRACK, BUT...
BUT? THAT'S A WORD I PARTICULARLY DISLIKE.
LOOK. THIS PIPELINE RUNS OVER A THOUSAND MILES, COSTS OVER TWO BILLION, RIGHT? LOGISTICAL NIGHTMARE. LOT AT STAKE.
VVVRRRRR

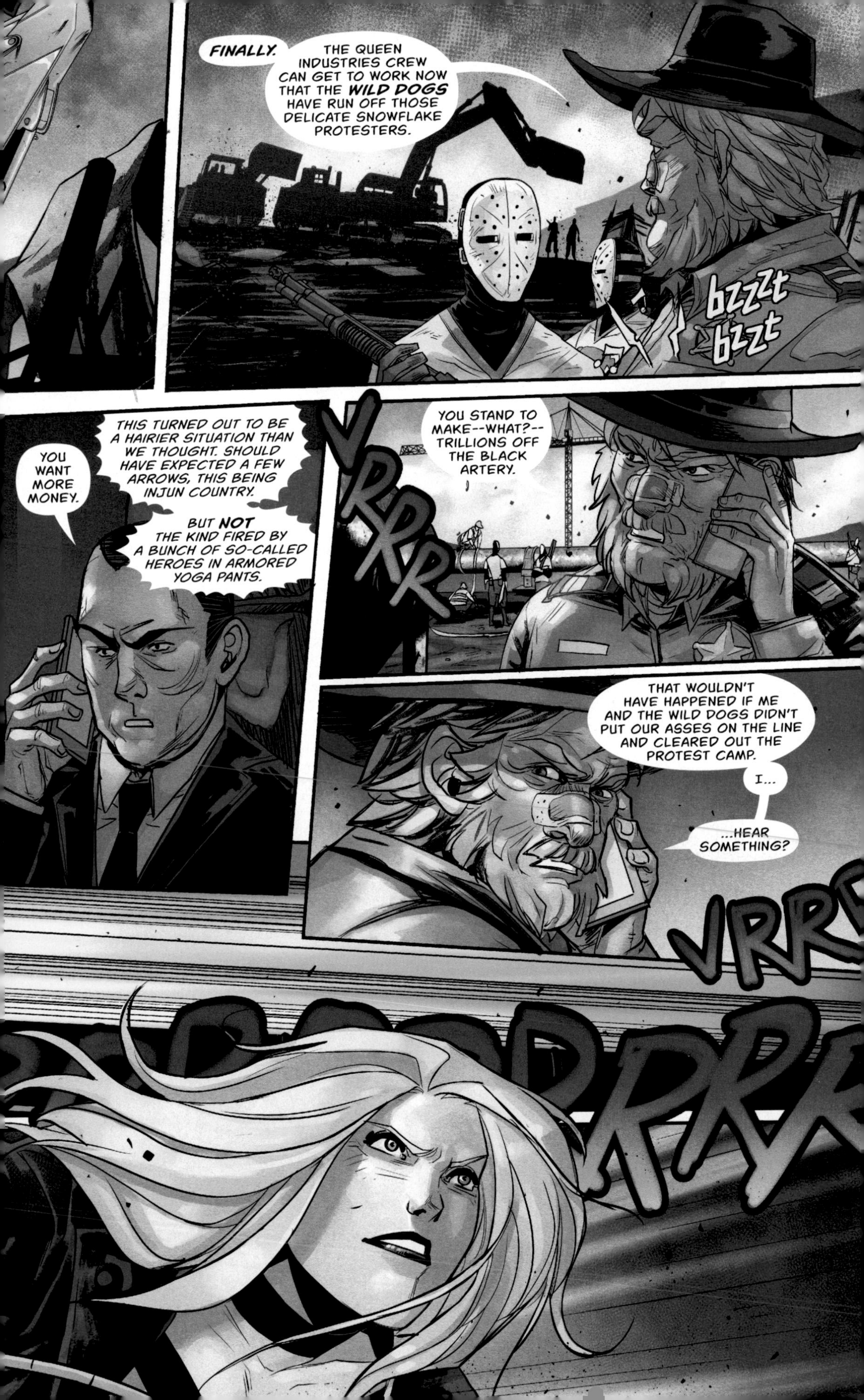

FINALLY.
THE QUEEN INDUSTRIES CREW CAN GET TO WORK NOW THAT THE WILD DOGS HAVE RUN OFF THOSE DELICATE SNOWFLAKE PROTESTERS.
bzzzt bzzt
YOU WANT MORE MONEY.
THIS TURNED OUT TO BE A HAIRIER SITUATION THAN WE THOUGHT. SHOULD HAVE EXPECTED A FEW ARROWS, THIS BEING INJUN COUNTRY.
BUT NOT THE KIND FIRED BY A BUNCH OF SO-CALLED HEROES IN ARMORED YOGA PANTS.
VRRRR
YOU STAND TO MAKE--WHAT?--TRILLIONS OFF THE BLACK ARTERY.
THAT WOULDN'T HAVE HAPPENED IF ME AND THE WILD DOGS DIDN'T PUT OUR ASSES ON THE LINE AND CLEARED OUT THE PROTEST CAMP.
I...
...HEAR SOMETHING?

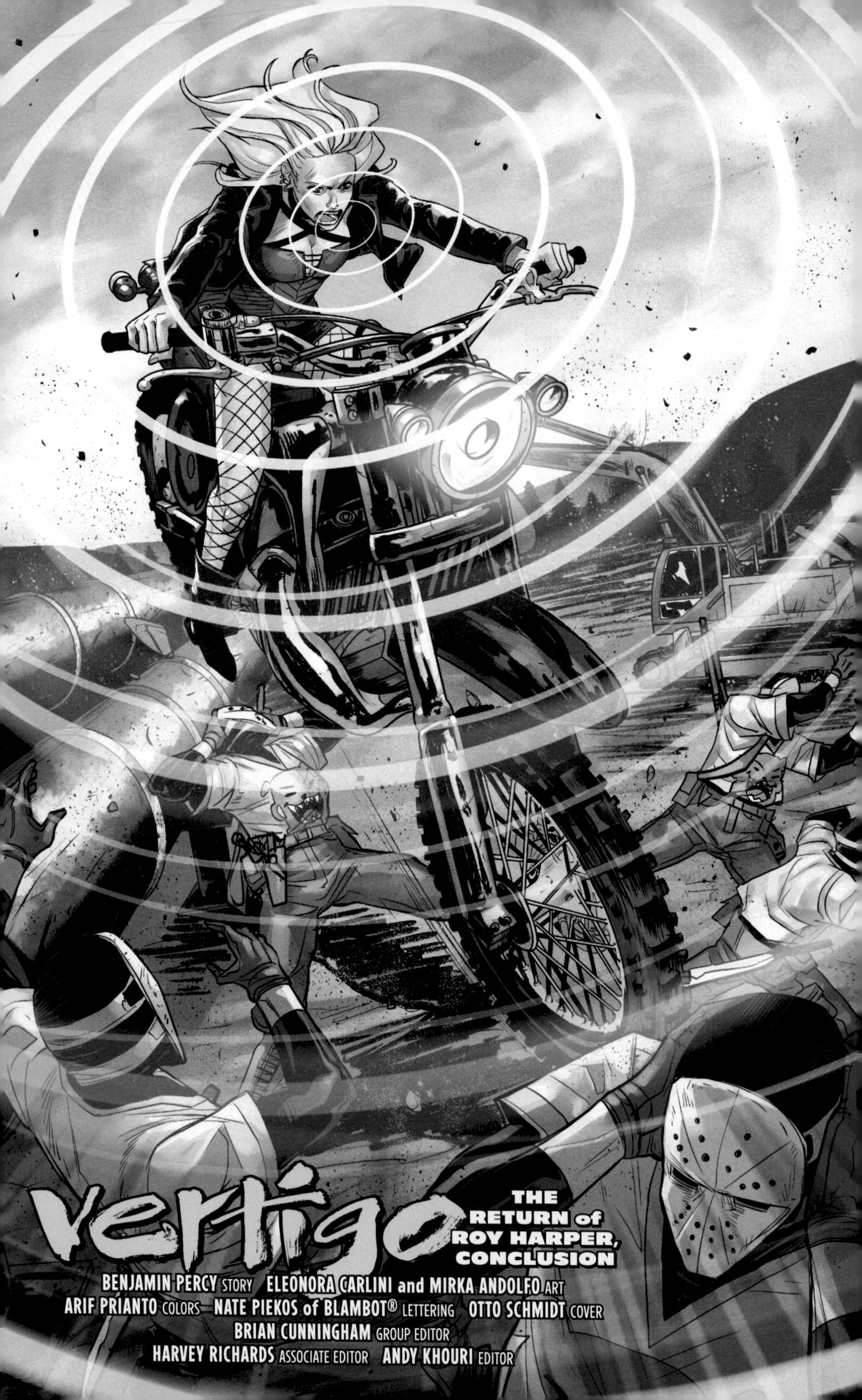
vertigo
THE RETURN of ROY HARPER, CONCLUSION
BENJAMIN PERCY STORY ELEONORA CARLINI and MIRKA ANDOLFO ART
ARIF PRIANTO COLORS NATE PIEKOS of BLAMBOT® LETTERING OTTO SCHMIDT COVER
BRIAN CUNNINGHAM GROUP EDITOR
HARVEY RICHARDS ASSOCIATE EDITOR ANDY KHOURI EDITOR

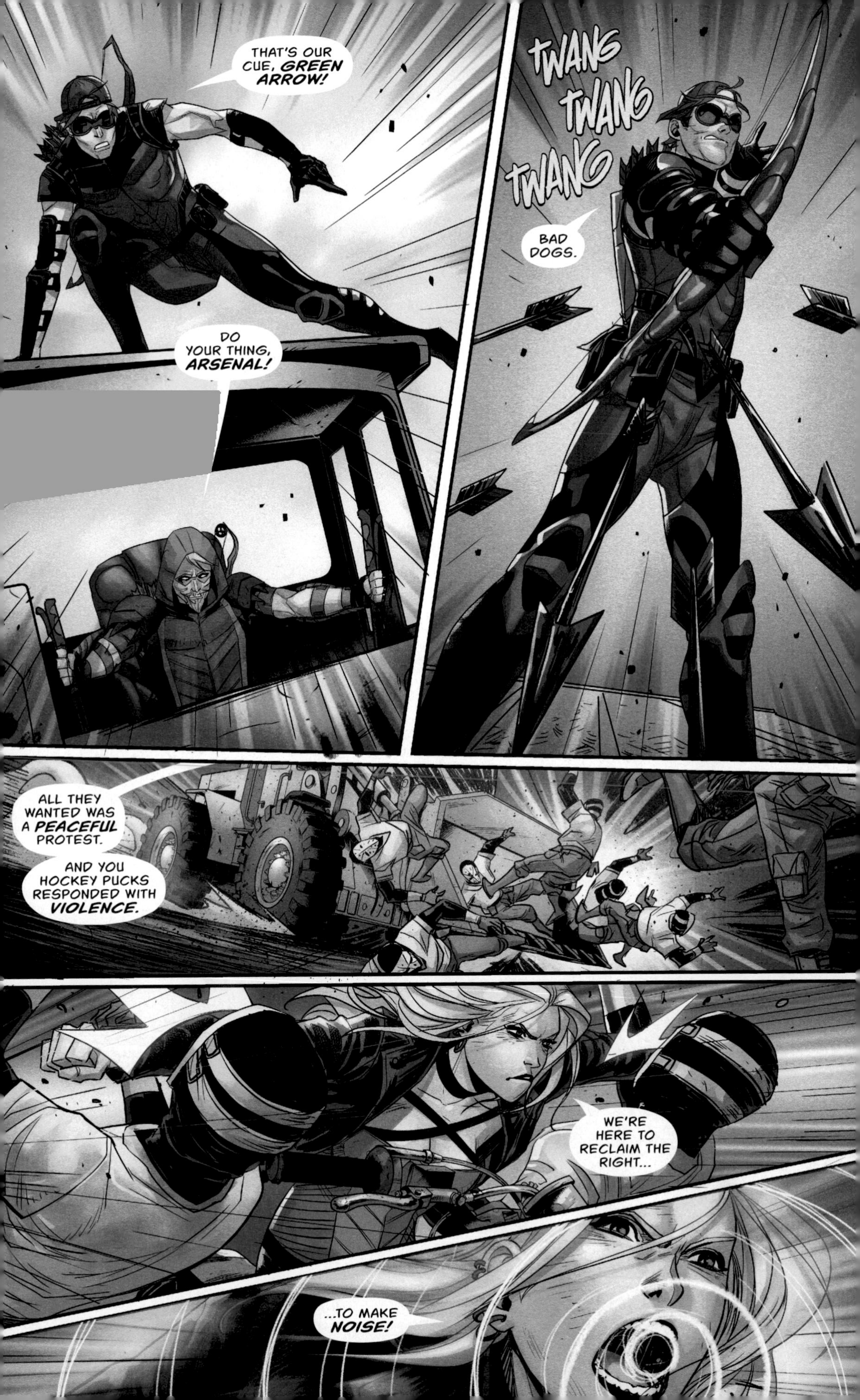
THAT'S OUR CUE, GREEN ARROW!
DO YOUR THING, ARSENAL!
TWANG
TWANG
TWANG
BAD DOGS.
ALL THEY WANTED WAS A PEACEFUL PROTEST.
AND YOU HOCKEY PUCKS RESPONDED WITH VIOLENCE.
WE'RE HERE TO RECLAIM THE RIGHT...
...TO MAKE NOISE!

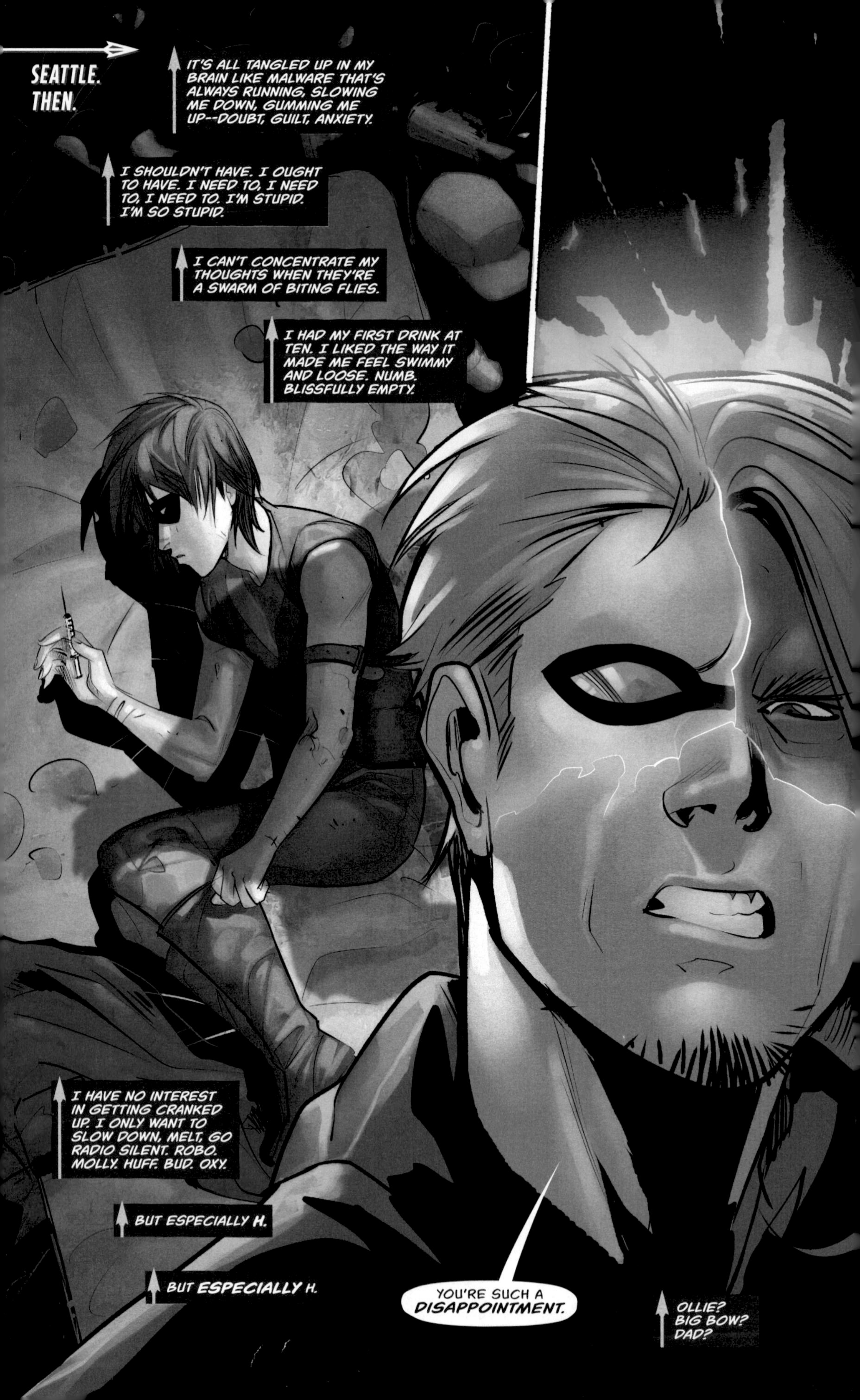

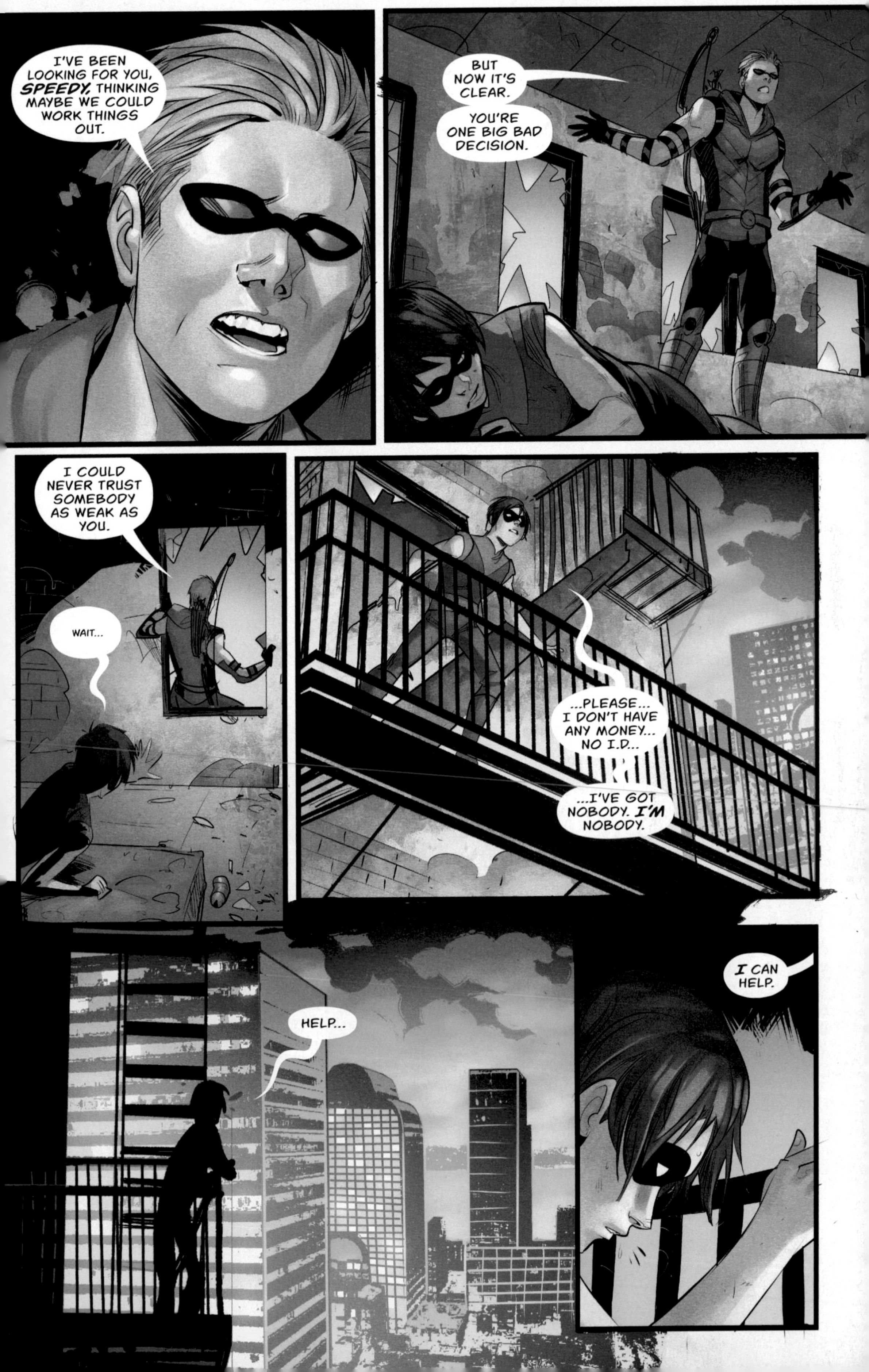
I'VE BEEN LOOKING FOR YOU, SPEEDY, THINKING MAYBE WE COULD WORK THINGS OUT.
BUT NOW IT'S CLEAR.
YOU'RE ONE BIG BAD DECISION.
I COULD NEVER TRUST SOMEBODY AS WEAK AS YOU.
WAIT...
...PLEASE... I DON'T HAVE ANY MONEY... NO I.D...
...I'VE GOT NOBODY. I'M NOBODY.
HELP...
I CAN HELP.

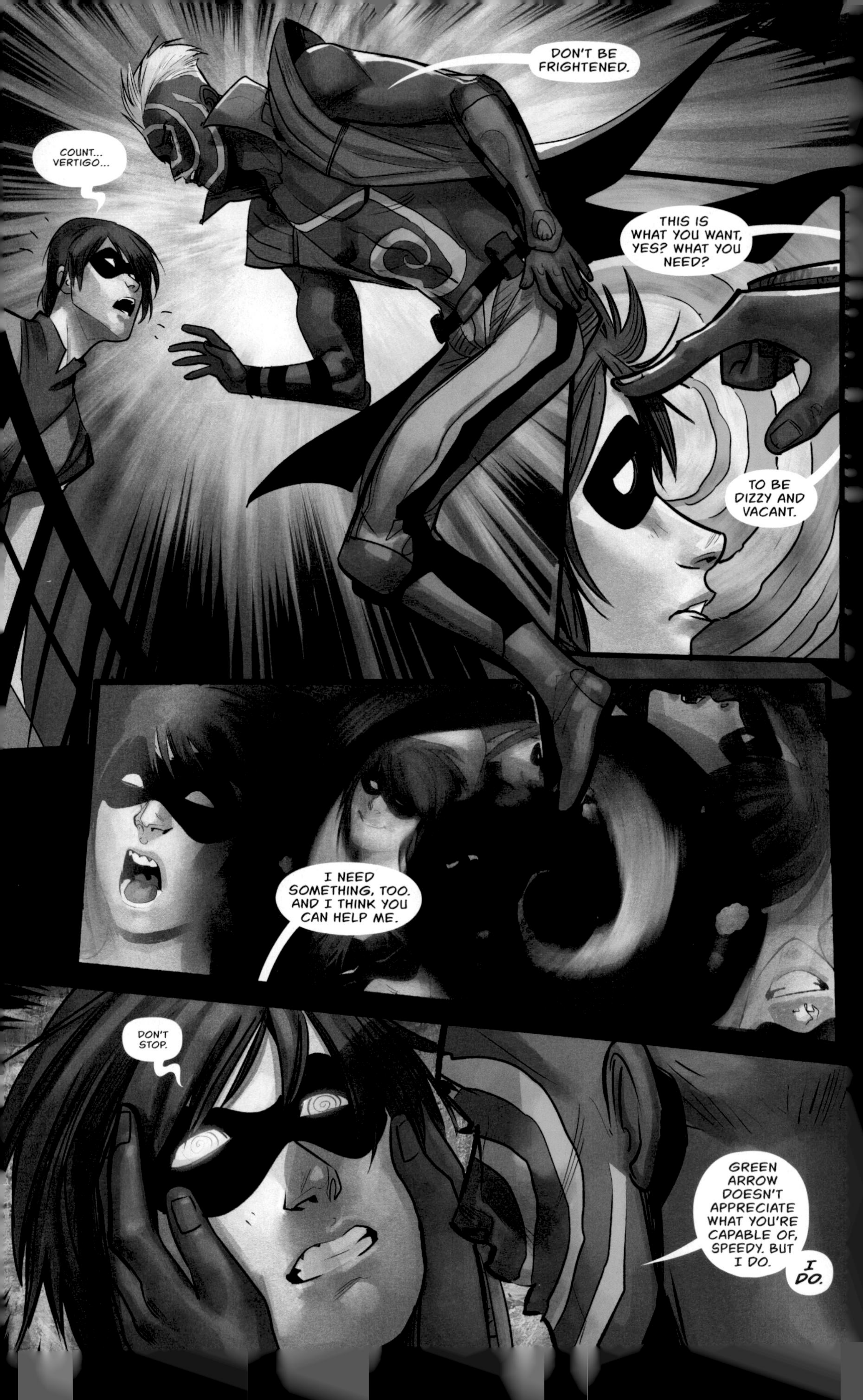
DON'T BE FRIGHTENED.
COUNT... VERTIGO...
THIS IS WHAT YOU WANT, YES? WHAT YOU NEED?
TO BE DIZZY AND VACANT.
I NEED SOMETHING, TOO. AND I THINK YOU CAN HELP ME.
DON'T STOP.
GREEN ARROW DOESN'T APPRECIATE WHAT YOU'RE CAPABLE OF, SPEEDY. BUT I DO.
I DO.

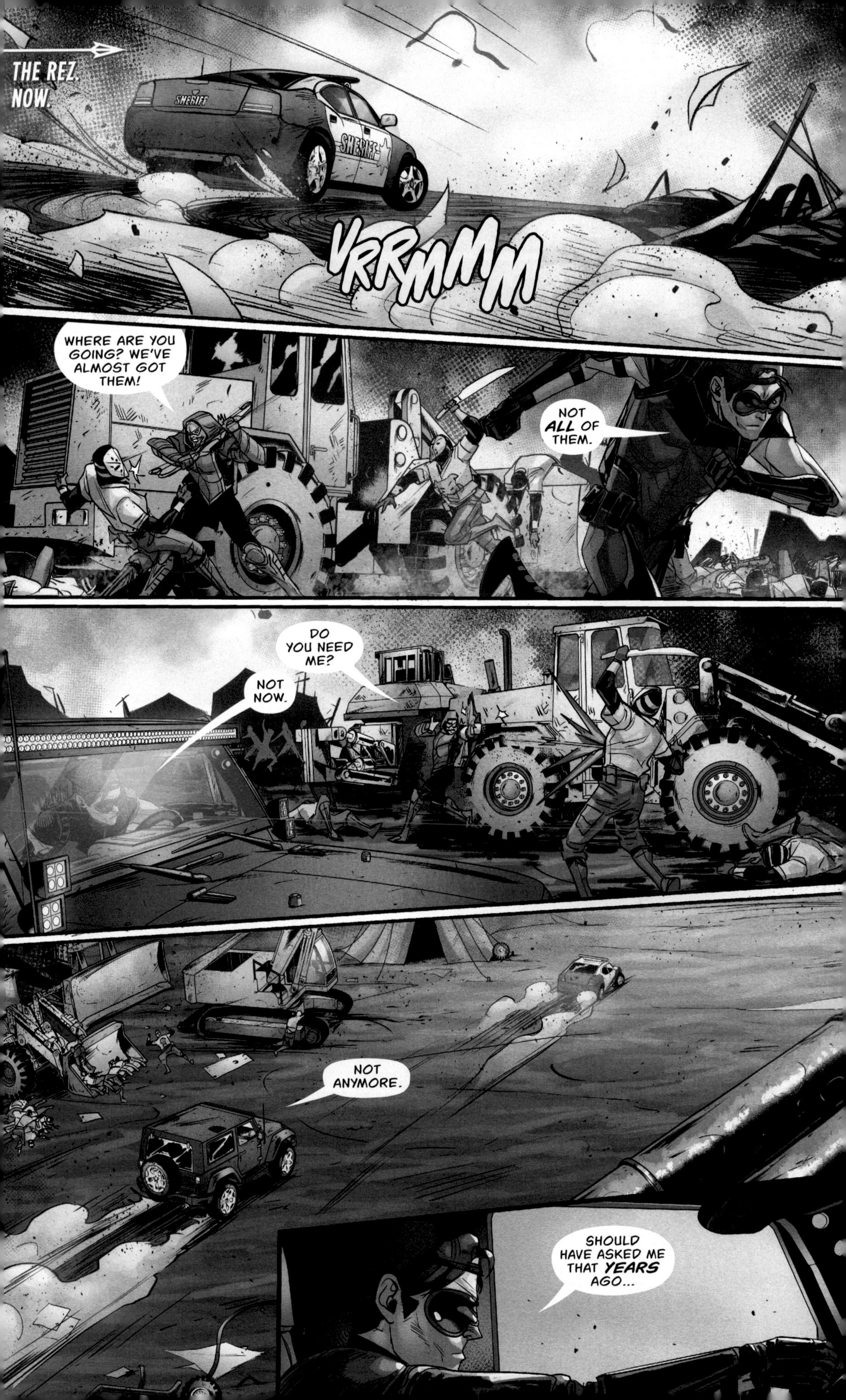
THE REZ.
NOW.
SHERIFF
SHERIFF
VRRMMM
WHERE ARE YOU GOING? WE'VE ALMOST GOT THEM!
NOT ALL OF THEM.
DO YOU NEED ME?
NOT NOW.
NOT ANYMORE.
SHOULD HAVE ASKED ME THAT YEARS AGO...

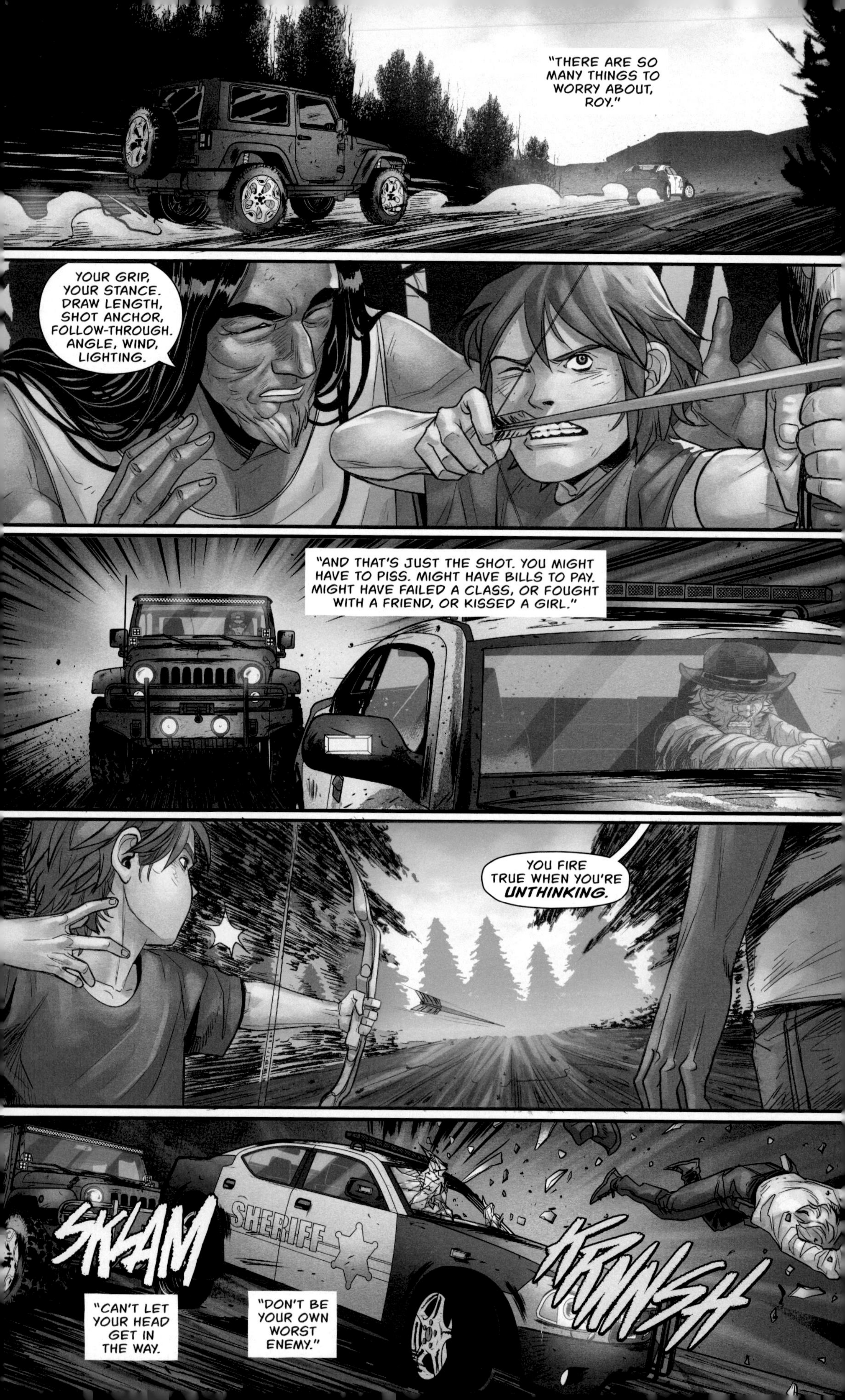
"THERE ARE SO MANY THINGS TO WORRY ABOUT, ROY."
YOUR GRIP, YOUR STANCE. DRAW LENGTH, SHOT ANCHOR, FOLLOW-THROUGH. ANGLE, WIND, LIGHTING.
"AND THAT'S JUST THE SHOT. YOU MIGHT HAVE TO PISS. MIGHT HAVE BILLS TO PAY. MIGHT HAVE FAILED A CLASS, OR FOUGHT WITH A FRIEND, OR KISSED A GIRL."
YOU FIRE TRUE WHEN YOU'RE *UNTHINKING.*
SHERIFF
SKLAM
KRUNSH
"CAN'T LET YOUR HEAD GET IN THE WAY.
"DON'T BE YOUR OWN WORST ENEMY."

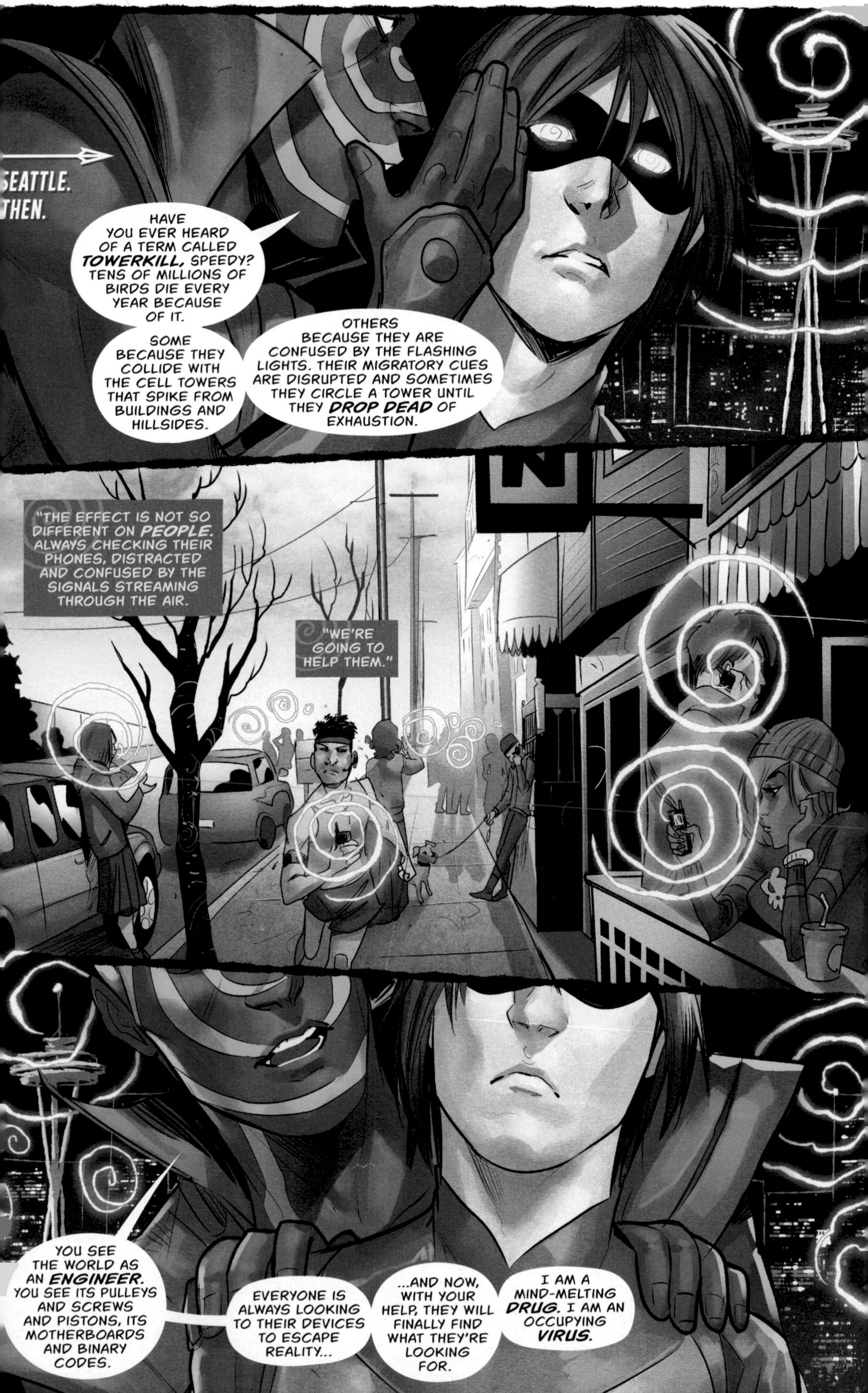

SEATTLE. THEN.
HAVE YOU EVER HEARD OF A TERM CALLED TOWERKILL, SPEEDY? TENS OF MILLIONS OF BIRDS DIE EVERY YEAR BECAUSE OF IT.
SOME BECAUSE THEY COLLIDE WITH THE CELL TOWERS THAT SPIKE FROM BUILDINGS AND HILLSIDES.
OTHERS BECAUSE THEY ARE CONFUSED BY THE FLASHING LIGHTS. THEIR MIGRATORY CUES ARE DISRUPTED AND SOMETIMES THEY CIRCLE A TOWER UNTIL THEY DROP DEAD OF EXHAUSTION.
"THE EFFECT IS NOT SO DIFFERENT ON PEOPLE. ALWAYS CHECKING THEIR PHONES, DISTRACTED AND CONFUSED BY THE SIGNALS STREAMING THROUGH THE AIR.
"WE'RE GOING TO HELP THEM."
YOU SEE THE WORLD AS AN ENGINEER. YOU SEE ITS PULLEYS AND SCREWS AND PISTONS, ITS MOTHERBOARDS AND BINARY CODES.
EVERYONE IS ALWAYS LOOKING TO THEIR DEVICES TO ESCAPE REALITY...
...AND NOW, WITH YOUR HELP, THEY WILL FINALLY FIND WHAT THEY'RE LOOKING FOR.
I AM A MIND-MELTING DRUG. I AM AN OCCUPYING VIRUS.

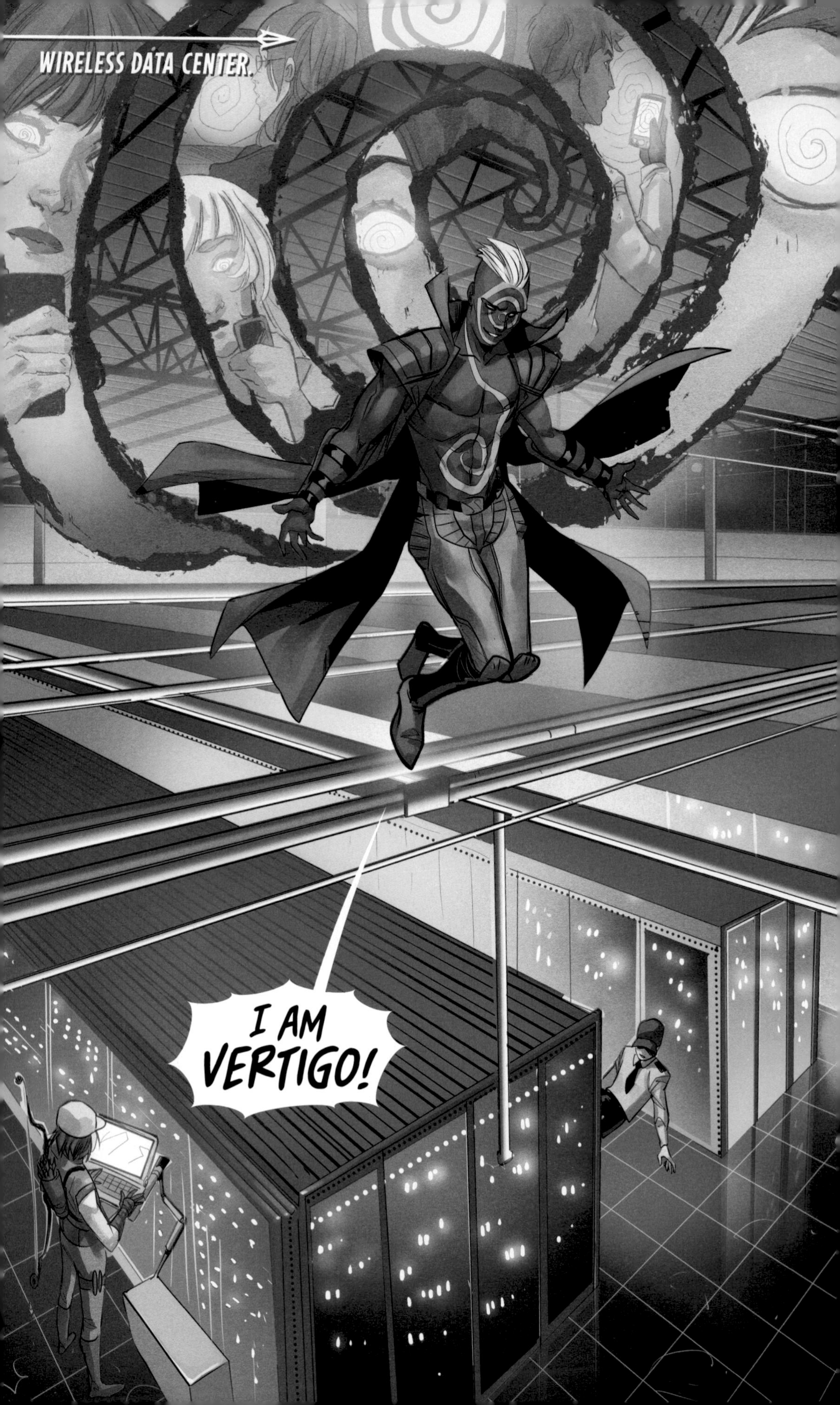
WIRELESS DATA CENTER.
I AM VERTIGO!

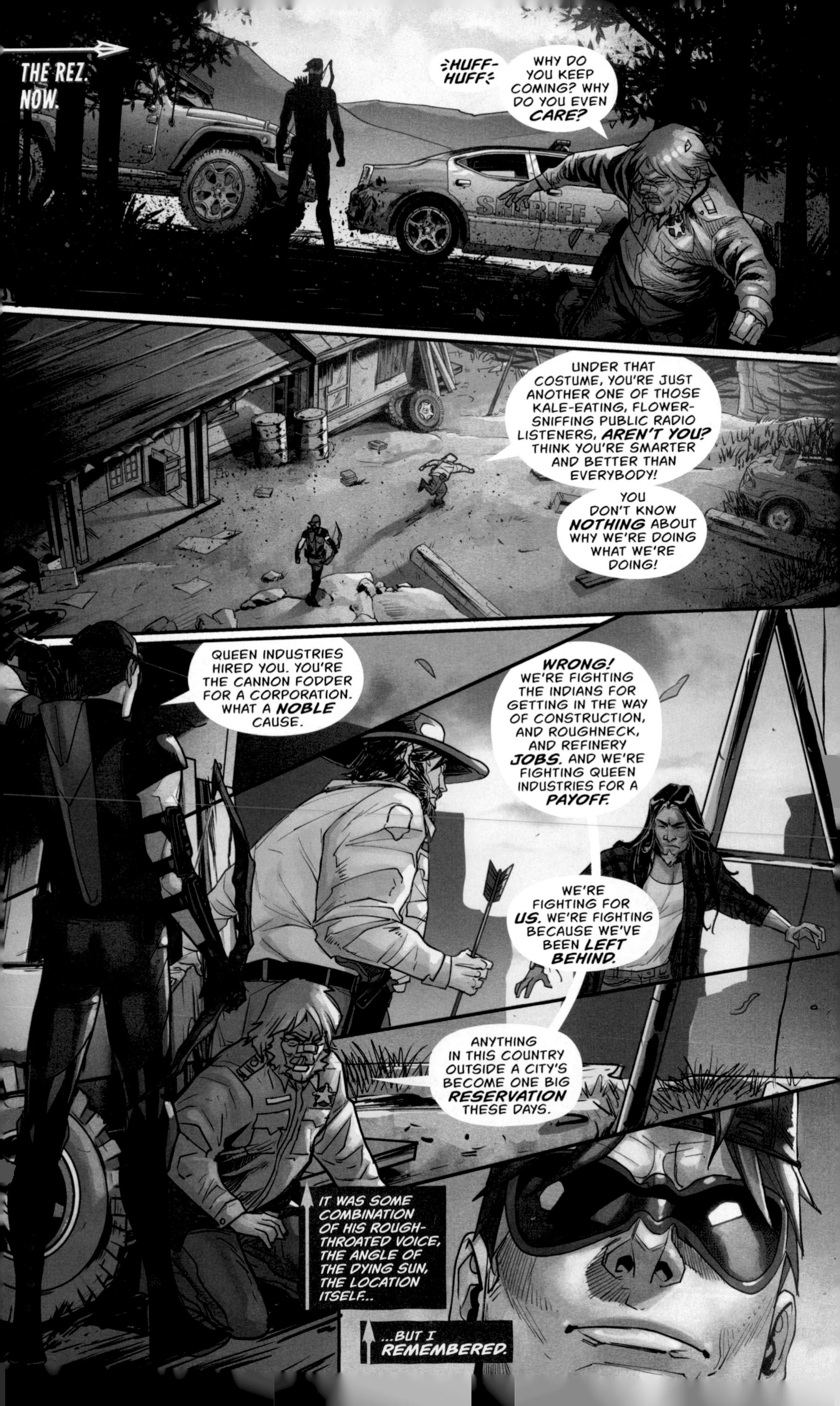
THE REZ. NOW.
HUFF-HUFF
WHY DO YOU KEEP COMING? WHY DO YOU EVEN CARE?
SHERIFF
UNDER THAT COSTUME, YOU'RE JUST ANOTHER ONE OF THOSE KALE-EATING, FLOWER-SNIFFING PUBLIC RADIO LISTENERS, AREN'T YOU? THINK YOU'RE SMARTER AND BETTER THAN EVERYBODY!
YOU DON'T KNOW NOTHING ABOUT WHY WE'RE DOING WHAT WE'RE DOING!
QUEEN INDUSTRIES HIRED YOU. YOU'RE THE CANNON FODDER FOR A CORPORATION. WHAT A NOBLE CAUSE.
WRONG! WE'RE FIGHTING THE INDIANS FOR GETTING IN THE WAY OF CONSTRUCTION, AND ROUGHNECK, AND REFINERY JOBS. AND WE'RE FIGHTING QUEEN INDUSTRIES FOR A PAYOFF.
WE'RE FIGHTING FOR US. WE'RE FIGHTING BECAUSE WE'VE BEEN LEFT BEHIND.
ANYTHING IN THIS COUNTRY OUTSIDE A CITY'S BECOME ONE BIG RESERVATION THESE DAYS.
IT WAS SOME COMBINATION OF HIS ROUGH-THROATED VOICE, THE ANGLE OF THE DYING SUN, THE LOCATION ITSELF...
...BUT I REMEMBERED.

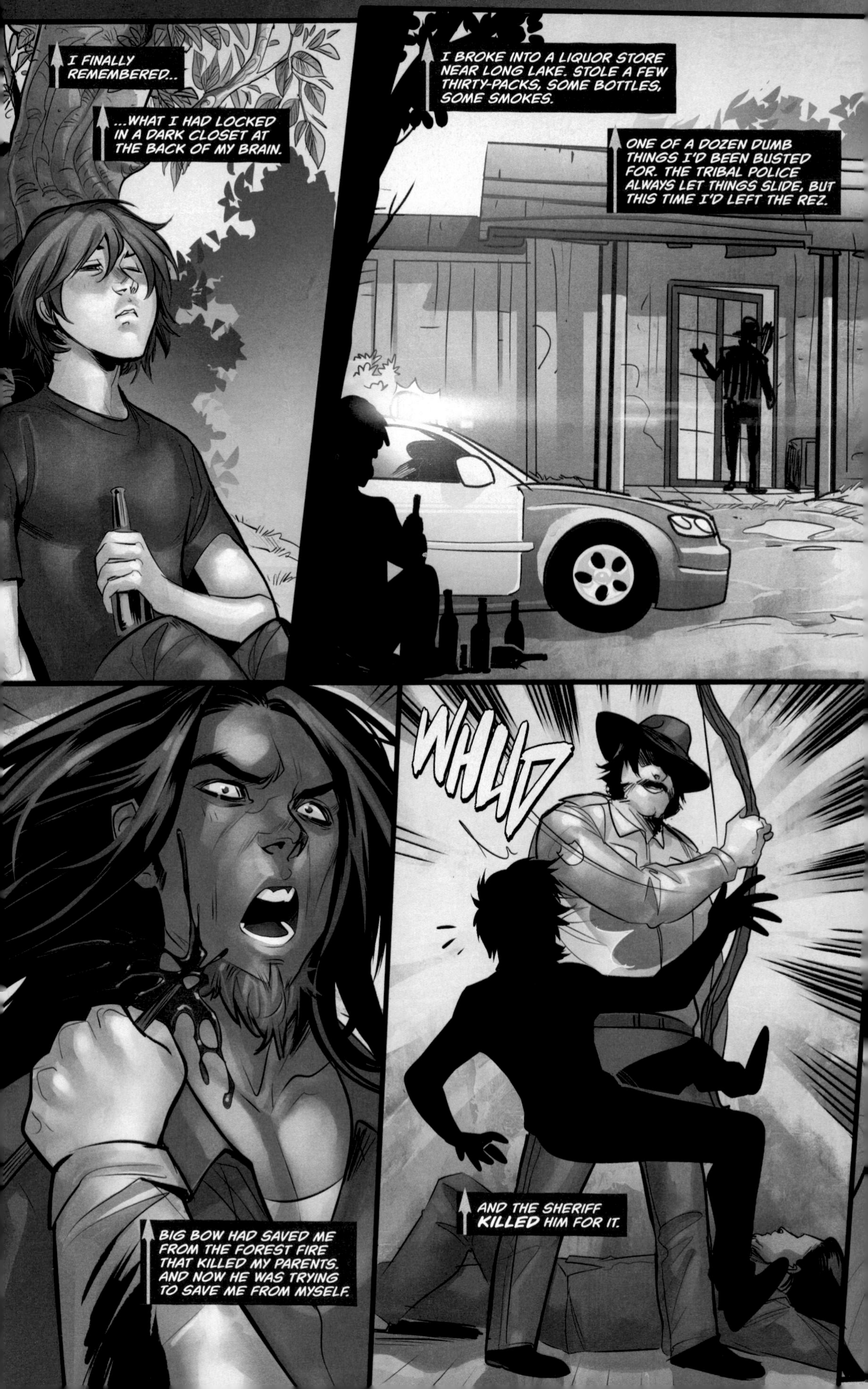
I FINALLY REMEMBERED...
...WHAT I HAD LOCKED IN A DARK CLOSET AT THE BACK OF MY BRAIN.
I BROKE INTO A LIQUOR STORE NEAR LONG LAKE. STOLE A FEW THIRTY-PACKS, SOME BOTTLES, SOME SMOKES.
ONE OF A DOZEN DUMB THINGS I'D BEEN BUSTED FOR. THE TRIBAL POLICE ALWAYS LET THINGS SLIDE, BUT THIS TIME I'D LEFT THE REZ.
BIG BOW HAD SAVED ME FROM THE FOREST FIRE THAT KILLED MY PARENTS. AND NOW HE WAS TRYING TO SAVE ME FROM MYSELF.
WHUD
AND THE SHERIFF **KILLED** HIM FOR IT.

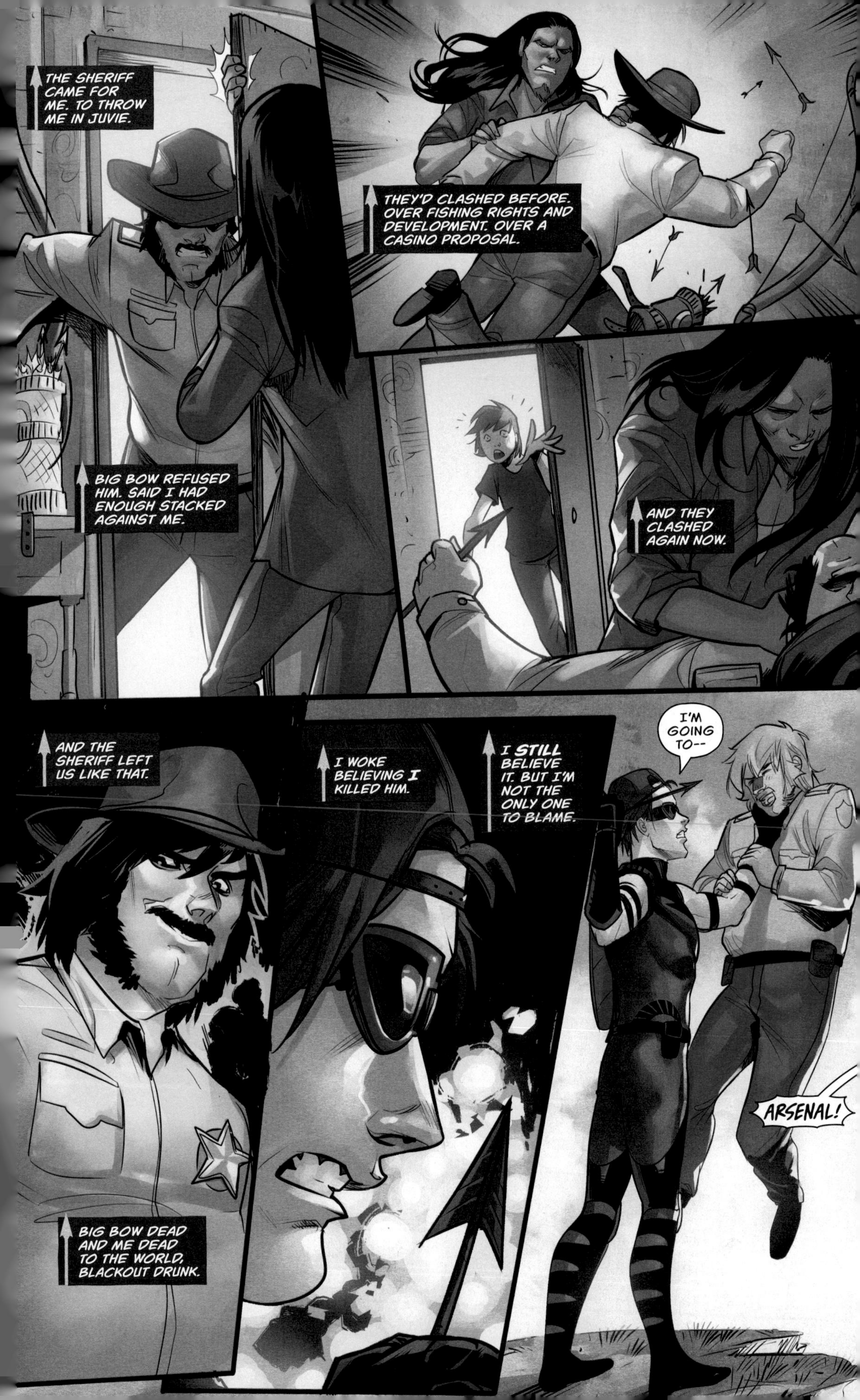
THE SHERIFF CAME FOR ME. TO THROW ME IN JUVIE.
THEY'D CLASHED BEFORE. OVER FISHING RIGHTS AND DEVELOPMENT. OVER A CASINO PROPOSAL.
BIG BOW REFUSED HIM. SAID I HAD ENOUGH STACKED AGAINST ME.
AND THEY CLASHED AGAIN NOW.
AND THE SHERIFF LEFT US LIKE THAT.
BIG BOW DEAD AND ME DEAD TO THE WORLD, BLACKOUT DRUNK.
I WOKE BELIEVING I KILLED HIM.
I STILL BELIEVE IT. BUT I'M NOT THE ONLY ONE TO BLAME.
I'M GOING TO--
ARSENAL!

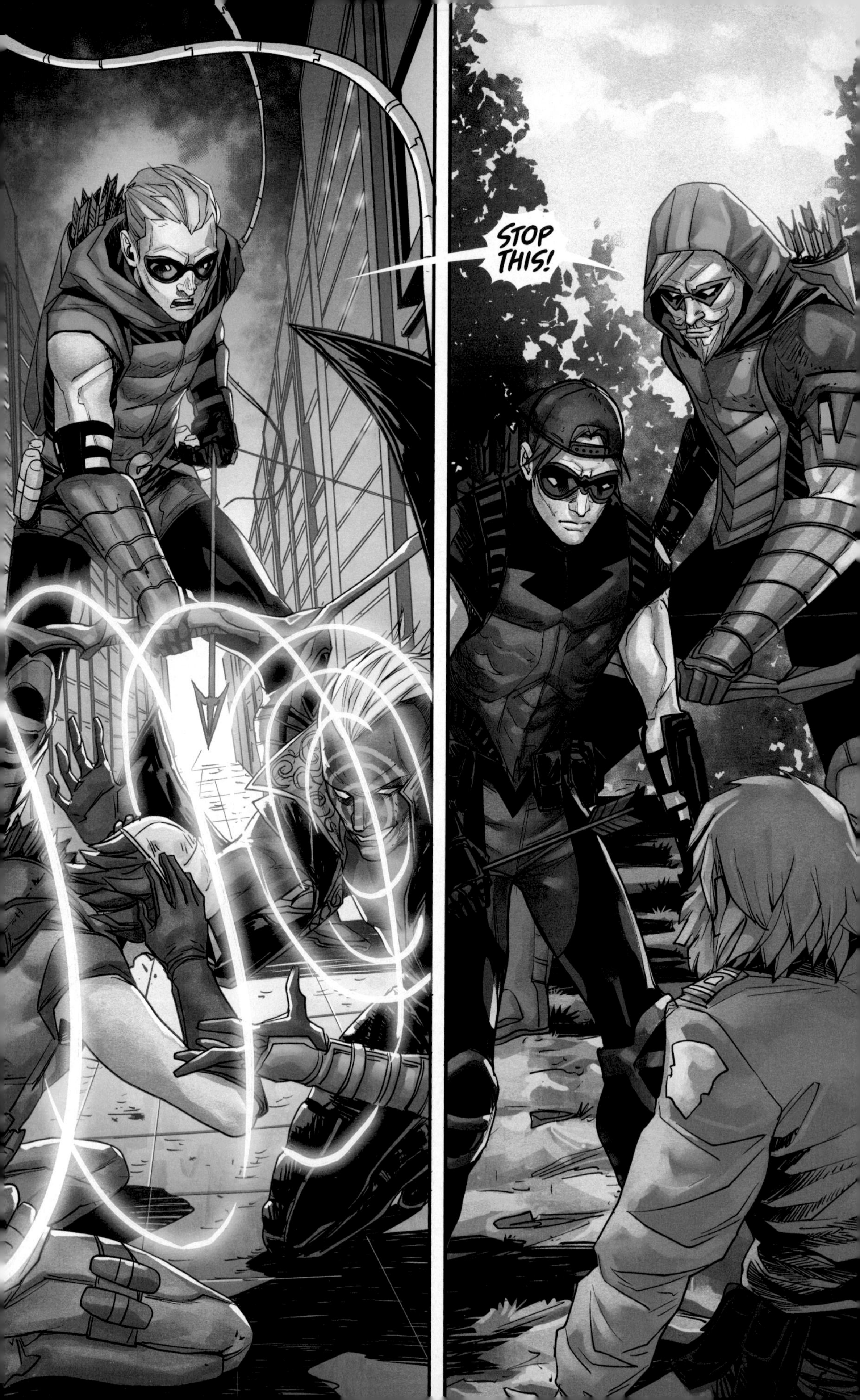
STOP THIS!

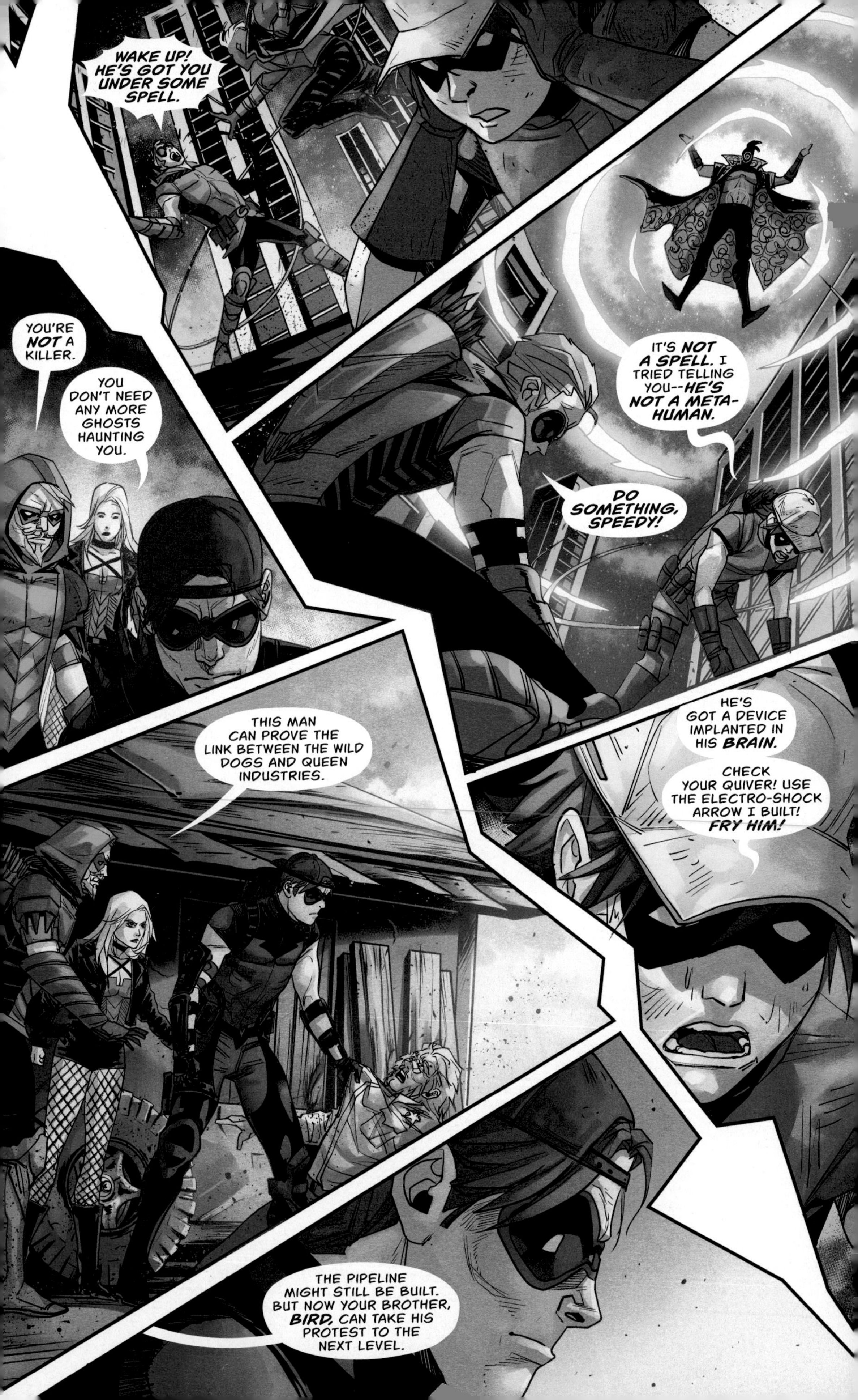
WAKE UP! HE'S GOT YOU UNDER SOME SPELL.
IT'S NOT A SPELL. I TRIED TELLING YOU--HE'S NOT A META-HUMAN.
DO SOMETHING, SPEEDY!
YOU'RE NOT A KILLER.
YOU DON'T NEED ANY MORE GHOSTS HAUNTING YOU.
HE'S GOT A DEVICE IMPLANTED IN HIS BRAIN.
CHECK YOUR QUIVER! USE THE ELECTRO-SHOCK ARROW I BUILT! FRY HIM!
THIS MAN CAN PROVE THE LINK BETWEEN THE WILD DOGS AND QUEEN INDUSTRIES.
THE PIPELINE MIGHT STILL BE BUILT. BUT NOW YOUR BROTHER, BIRD, CAN TAKE HIS PROTEST TO THE NEXT LEVEL.

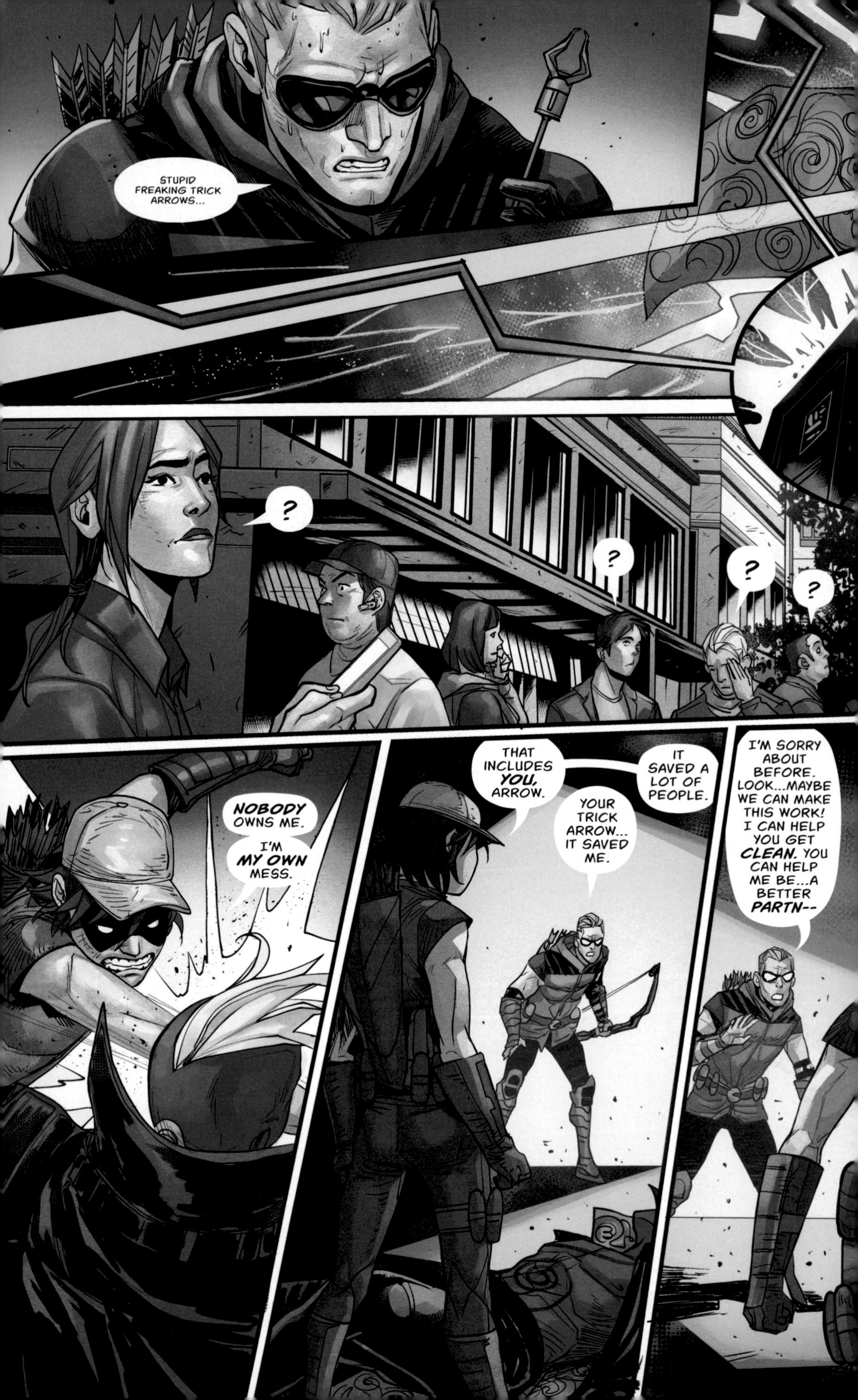
STUPID FREAKING TRICK ARROWS...
?
?
?
?
NOBODY OWNS ME.
I'M MY OWN MESS.
THAT INCLUDES YOU, ARROW.
IT SAVED A LOT OF PEOPLE.
YOUR TRICK ARROW... IT SAVED ME.
I'M SORRY ABOUT BEFORE. LOOK...MAYBE WE CAN MAKE THIS WORK! I CAN HELP YOU GET CLEAN. YOU CAN HELP ME BE...A BETTER PARTN--

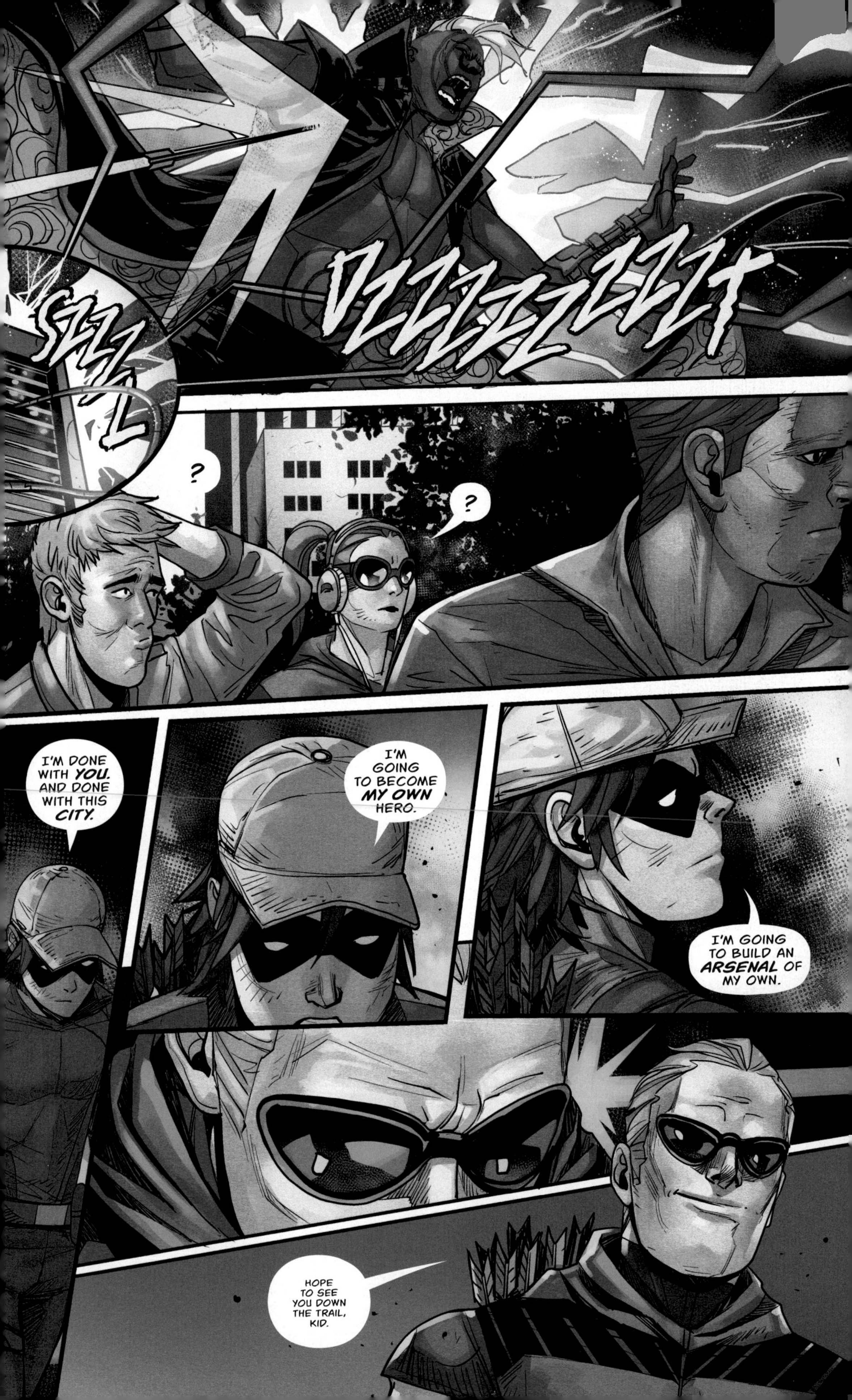
SZZZ
DZZZZZZZZZT
?
?
I'M DONE WITH YOU. AND DONE WITH THIS CITY.
I'M GOING TO BECOME MY OWN HERO.
I'M GOING TO BUILD AN ARSENAL OF MY OWN.
HOPE TO SEE YOU DOWN THE TRAIL, KID.

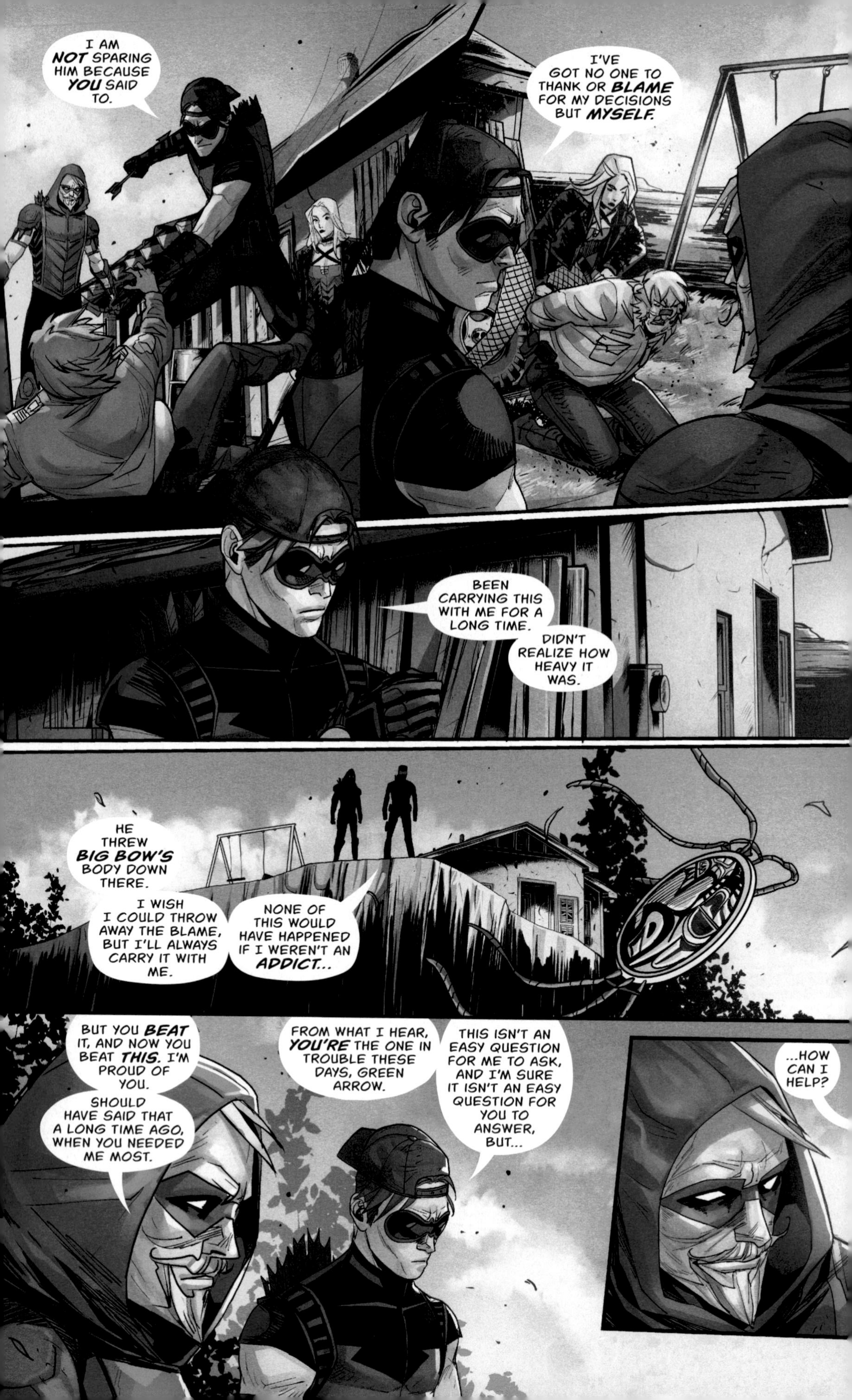

I AM NOT SPARING HIM BECAUSE YOU SAID TO.
I'VE GOT NO ONE TO THANK OR BLAME FOR MY DECISIONS BUT MYSELF.
BEEN CARRYING THIS WITH ME FOR A LONG TIME.
DIDN'T REALIZE HOW HEAVY IT WAS.
HE THREW BIG BOW'S BODY DOWN THERE.
I WISH I COULD THROW AWAY THE BLAME, BUT I'LL ALWAYS CARRY IT WITH ME.
NONE OF THIS WOULD HAVE HAPPENED IF I WEREN'T AN ADDICT...
BUT YOU BEAT IT, AND NOW YOU BEAT THIS. I'M PROUD OF YOU.
SHOULD HAVE SAID THAT A LONG TIME AGO, WHEN YOU NEEDED ME MOST.
FROM WHAT I HEAR, YOU'RE THE ONE IN TROUBLE THESE DAYS, GREEN ARROW.
THIS ISN'T AN EASY QUESTION FOR ME TO ASK, AND I'M SURE IT ISN'T AN EASY QUESTION FOR YOU TO ANSWER, BUT...
...HOW CAN I HELP?

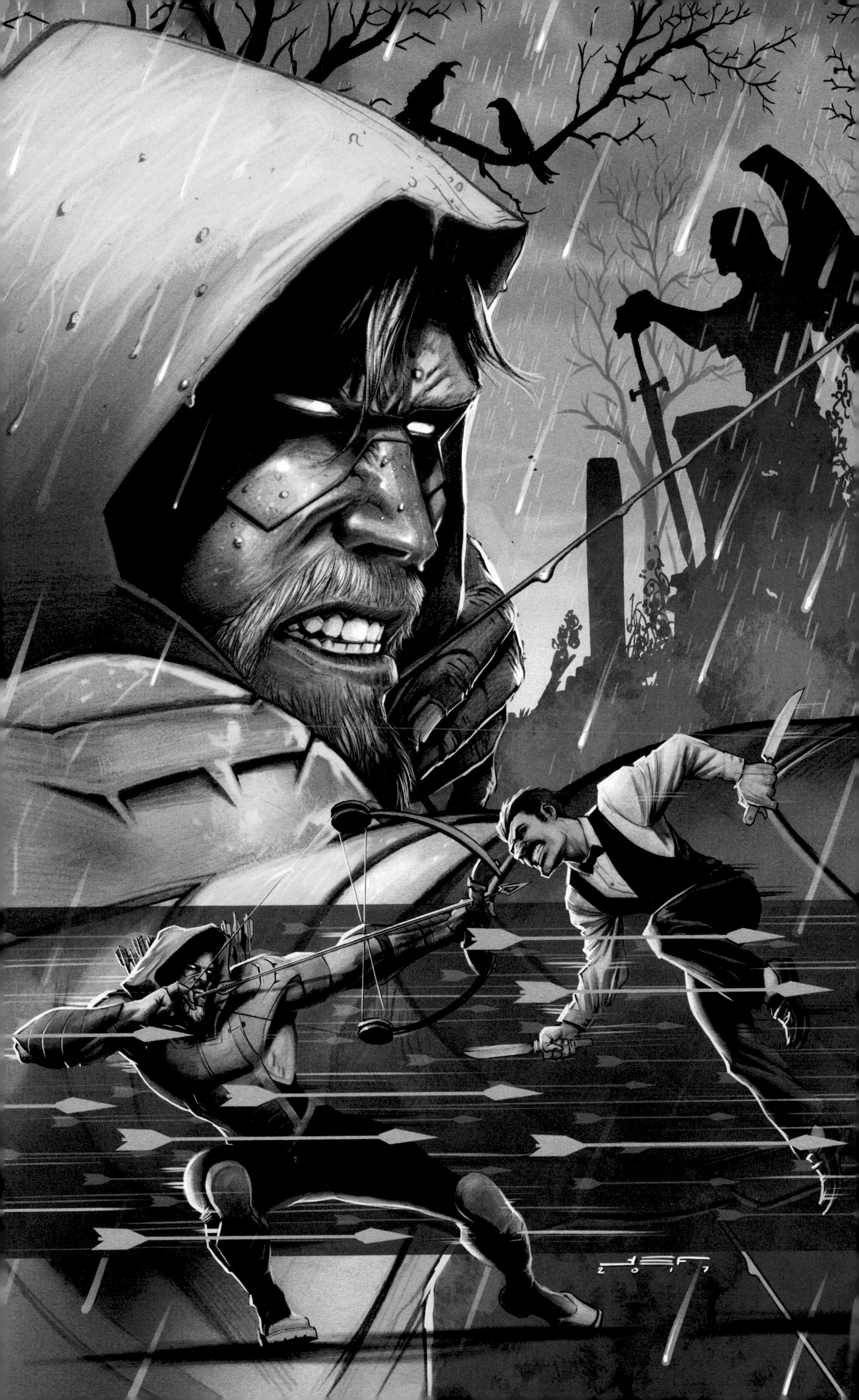

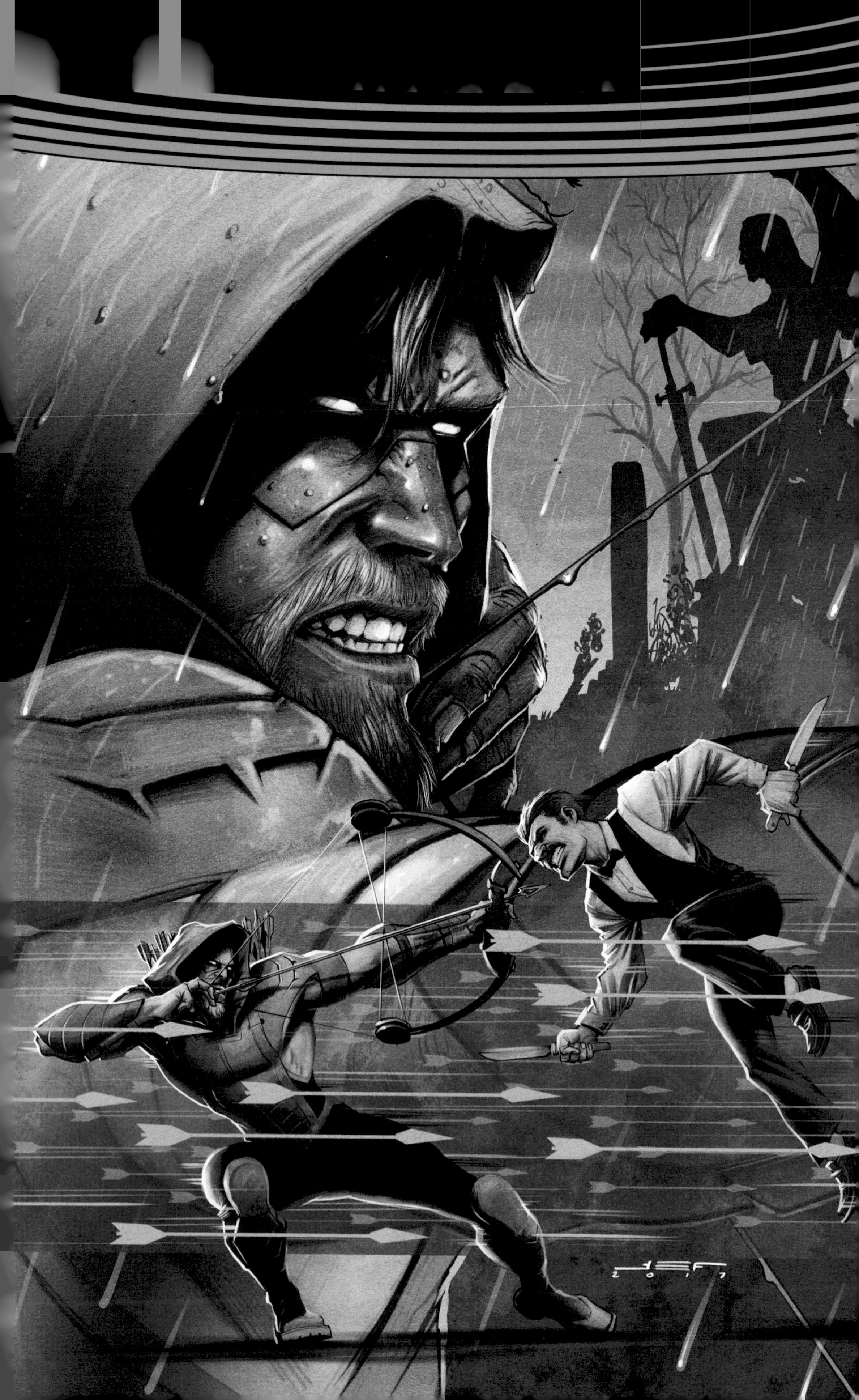

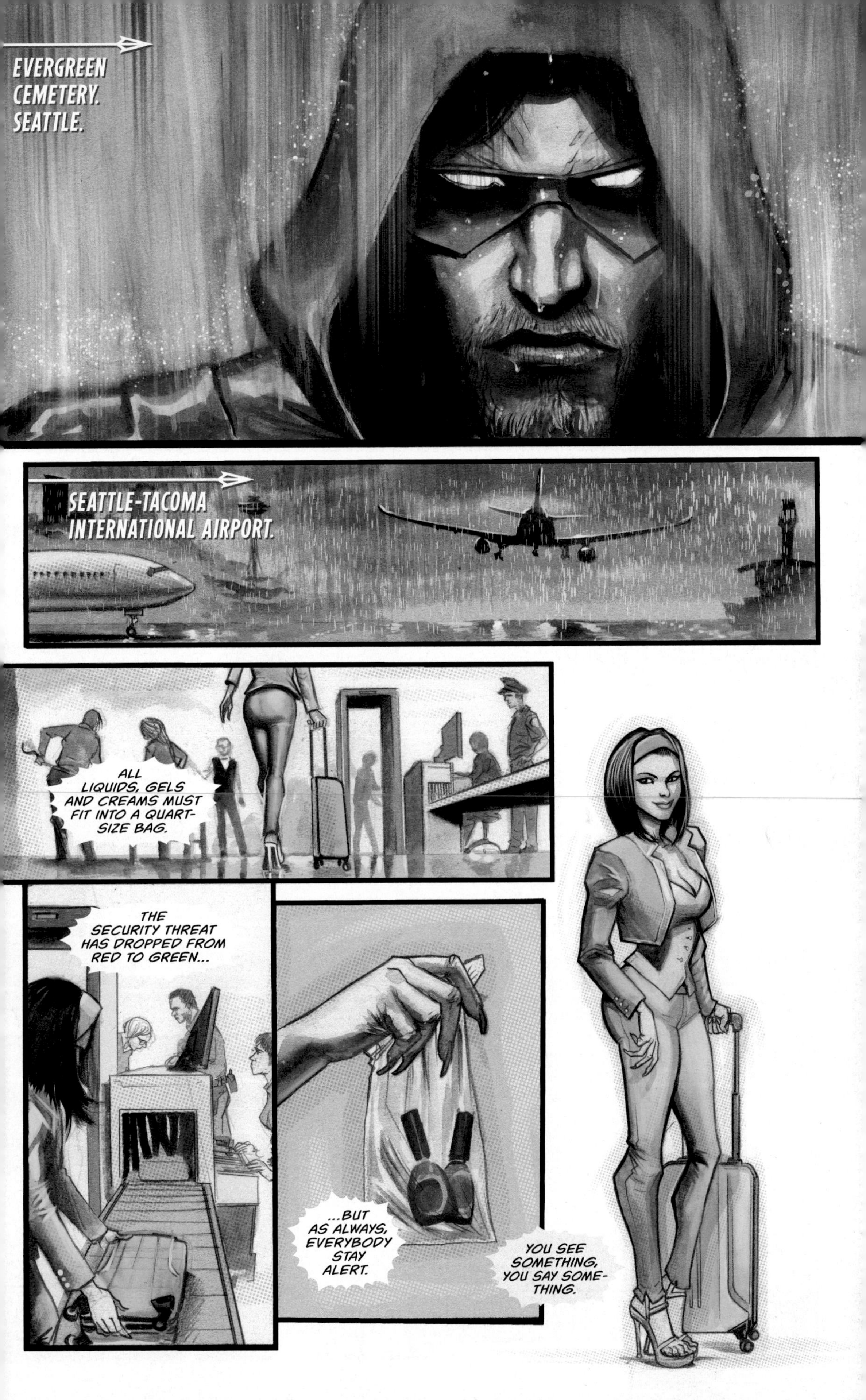
EVERGREEN CEMETERY. SEATTLE.
SEATTLE-TACOMA INTERNATIONAL AIRPORT.
ALL LIQUIDS, GELS AND CREAMS MUST FIT INTO A QUART-SIZE BAG.
THE SECURITY THREAT HAS DROPPED FROM RED TO GREEN...
...BUT AS ALWAYS, EVERYBODY STAY ALERT.
YOU SEE SOMETHING, YOU SAY SOME-THING.

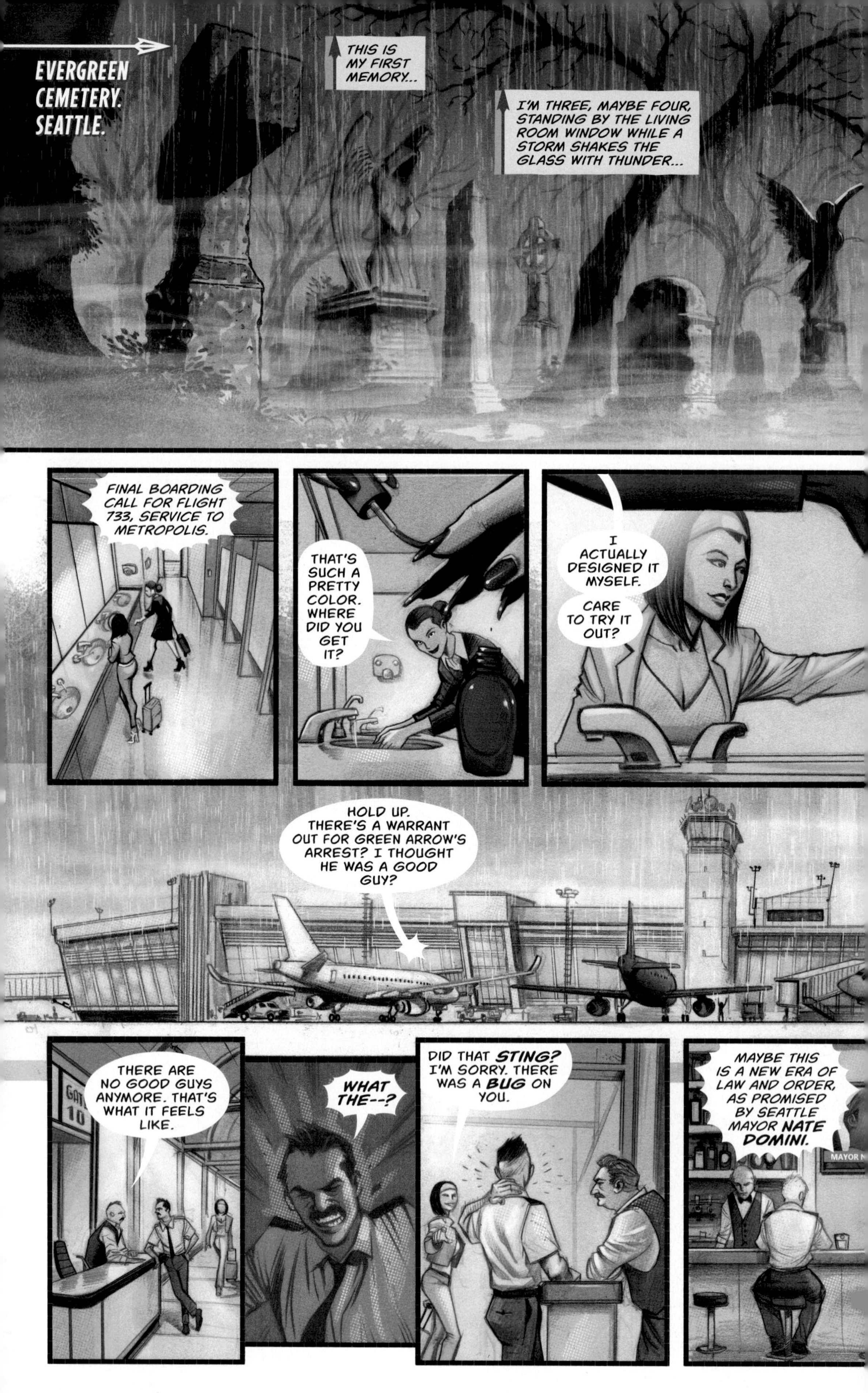
EVERGREEN CEMETERY. SEATTLE.
THIS IS MY FIRST MEMORY...
I'M THREE, MAYBE FOUR, STANDING BY THE LIVING ROOM WINDOW WHILE A STORM SHAKES THE GLASS WITH THUNDER...
FINAL BOARDING CALL FOR FLIGHT 733, SERVICE TO METROPOLIS.
THAT'S SUCH A PRETTY COLOR. WHERE DID YOU GET IT?
I ACTUALLY DESIGNED IT MYSELF.
CARE TO TRY IT OUT?
HOLD UP. THERE'S A WARRANT OUT FOR GREEN ARROW'S ARREST? I THOUGHT HE WAS A GOOD GUY?
GATE 10
THERE ARE NO GOOD GUYS ANYMORE. THAT'S WHAT IT FEELS LIKE.
WHAT THE--?
DID THAT STING? I'M SORRY. THERE WAS A BUG ON YOU.
MAYBE THIS IS A NEW ERA OF LAW AND ORDER, AS PROMISED BY SEATTLE MAYOR NATE DOMINI.

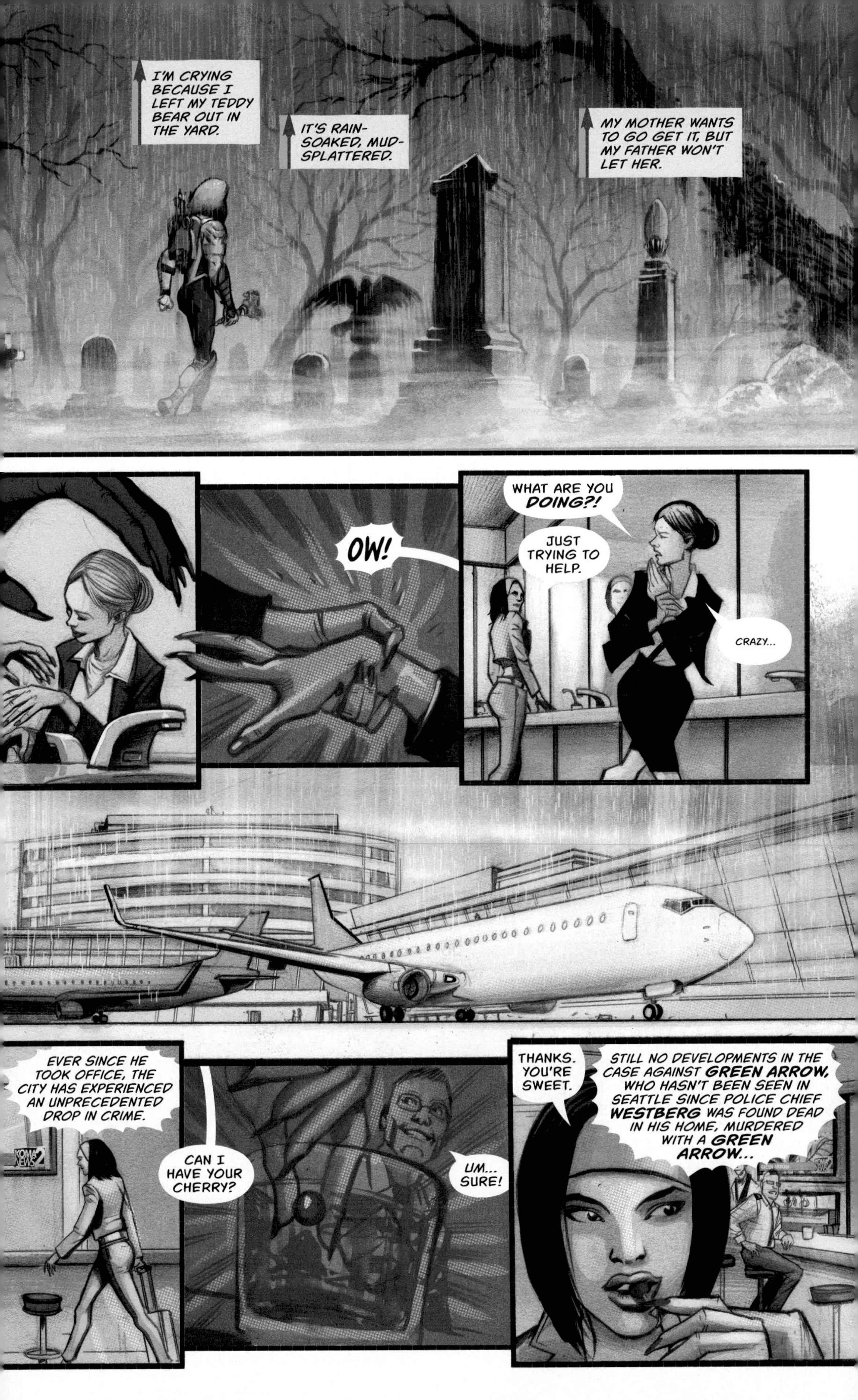

I'M CRYING BECAUSE I LEFT MY TEDDY BEAR OUT IN THE YARD.
IT'S RAIN-SOAKED, MUD-SPLATTERED.
MY MOTHER WANTS TO GO GET IT, BUT MY FATHER WON'T LET HER.
OW!
WHAT ARE YOU DOING?!
JUST TRYING TO HELP.
CRAZY...
EVER SINCE HE TOOK OFFICE, THE CITY HAS EXPERIENCED AN UNPRECEDENTED DROP IN CRIME.
KOMA NEWS 2
CAN I HAVE YOUR CHERRY?
UM... SURE!
THANKS. YOU'RE SWEET.
STILL NO DEVELOPMENTS IN THE CASE AGAINST GREEN ARROW, WHO HASN'T BEEN SEEN IN SEATTLE SINCE POLICE CHIEF WESTBERG WAS FOUND DEAD IN HIS HOME, MURDERED WITH A GREEN ARROW...

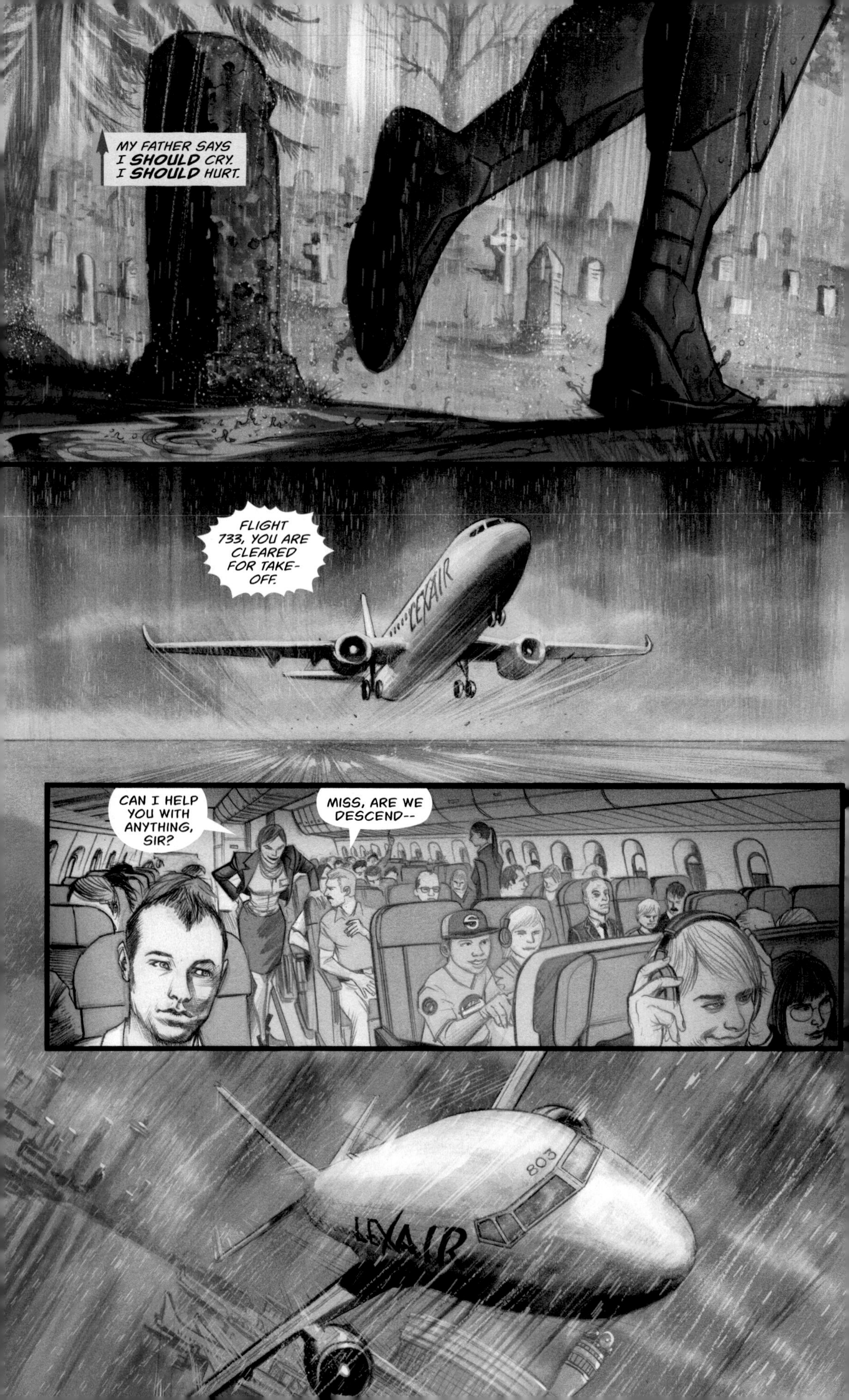
MY FATHER SAYS I SHOULD CRY. I SHOULD HURT.
FLIGHT 733, YOU ARE CLEARED FOR TAKE-OFF.
CAN I HELP YOU WITH ANYTHING, SIR?
MISS, ARE WE DESCEND--

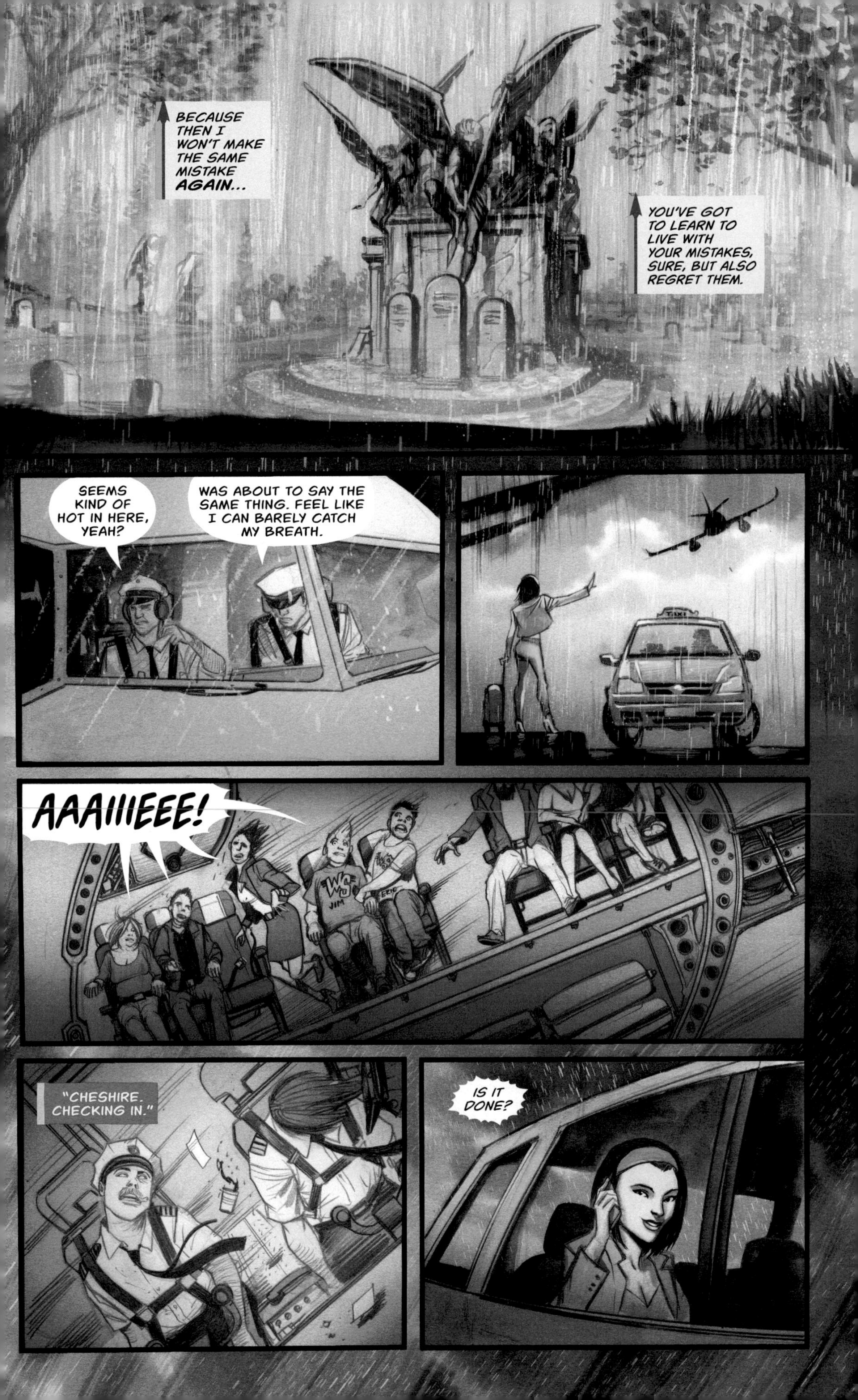
BECAUSE THEN I WON'T MAKE THE SAME MISTAKE AGAIN...
YOU'VE GOT TO LEARN TO LIVE WITH YOUR MISTAKES, SURE, BUT ALSO REGRET THEM.
SEEMS KIND OF HOT IN HERE, YEAH?
WAS ABOUT TO SAY THE SAME THING. FEEL LIKE I CAN BARELY CATCH MY BREATH.
AAAIIIEEE!
"CHESHIRE. CHECKING IN."
IS IT DONE?

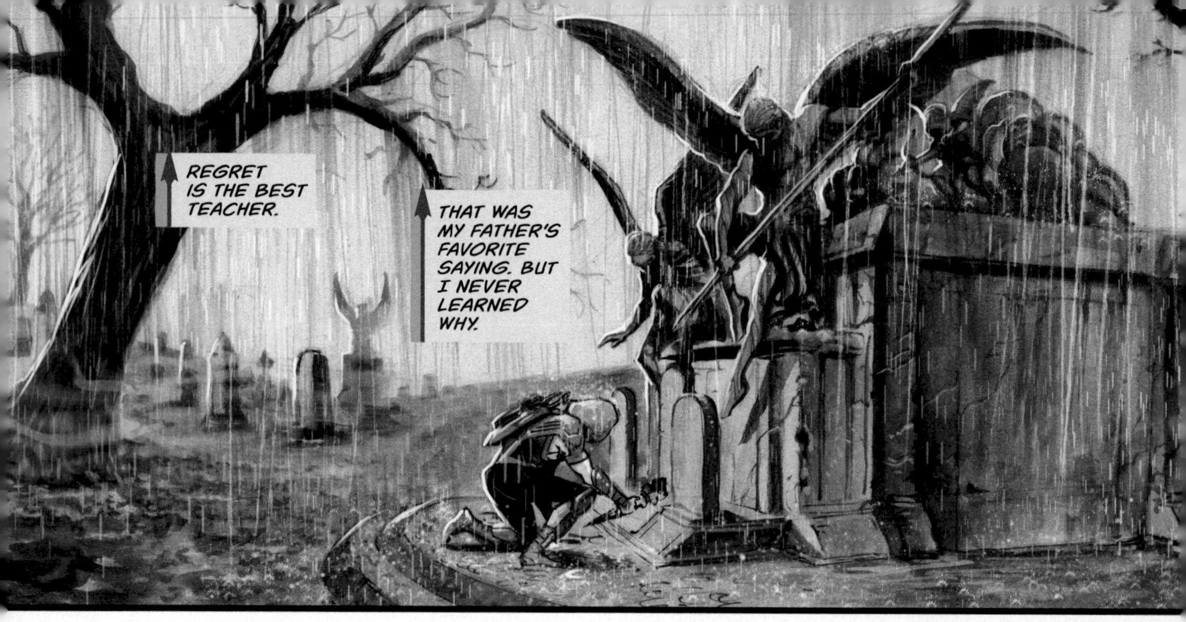
REGRET IS THE BEST TEACHER.
THAT WAS MY FATHER'S FAVORITE SAYING. BUT I NEVER LEARNED WHY.

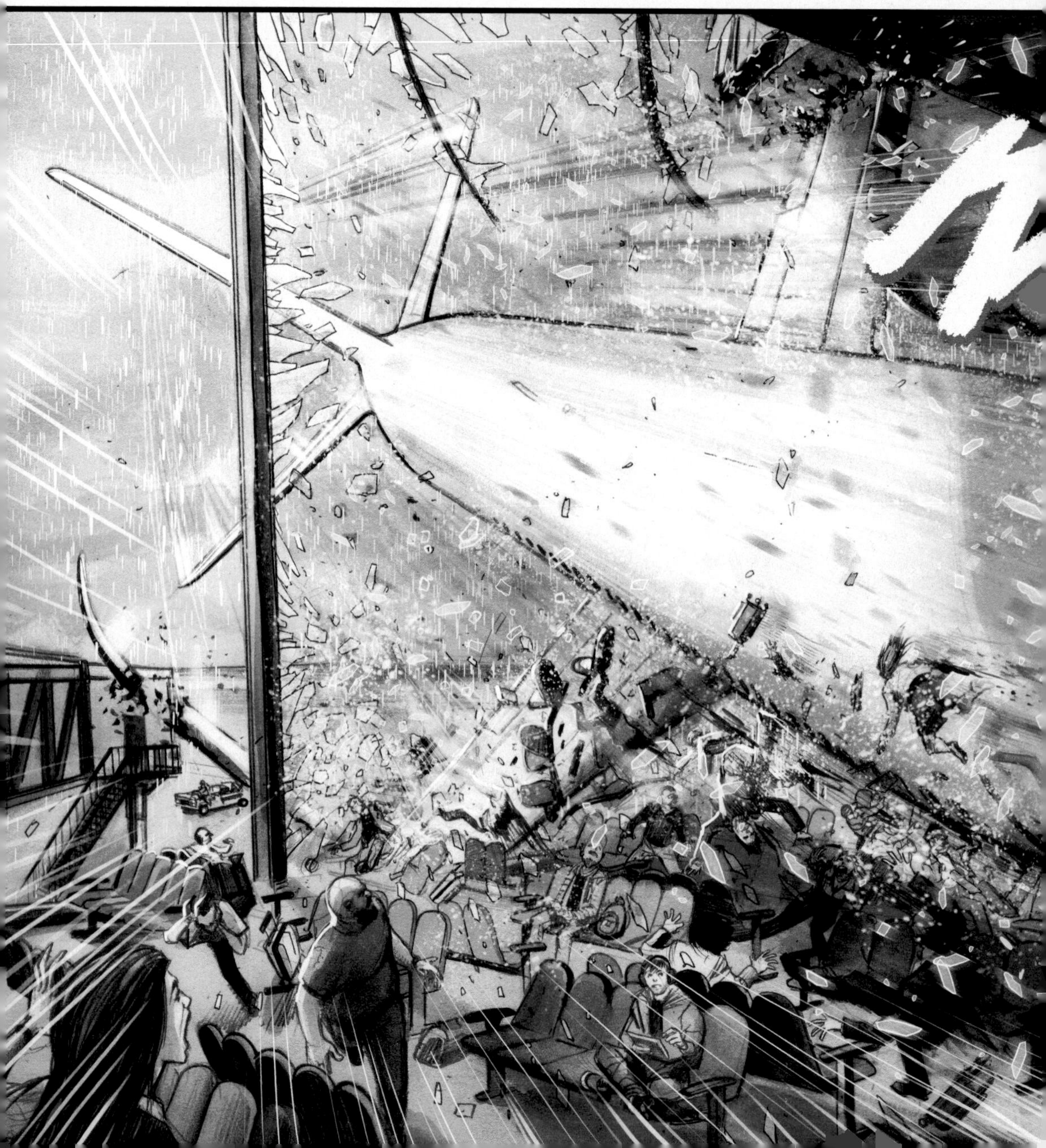

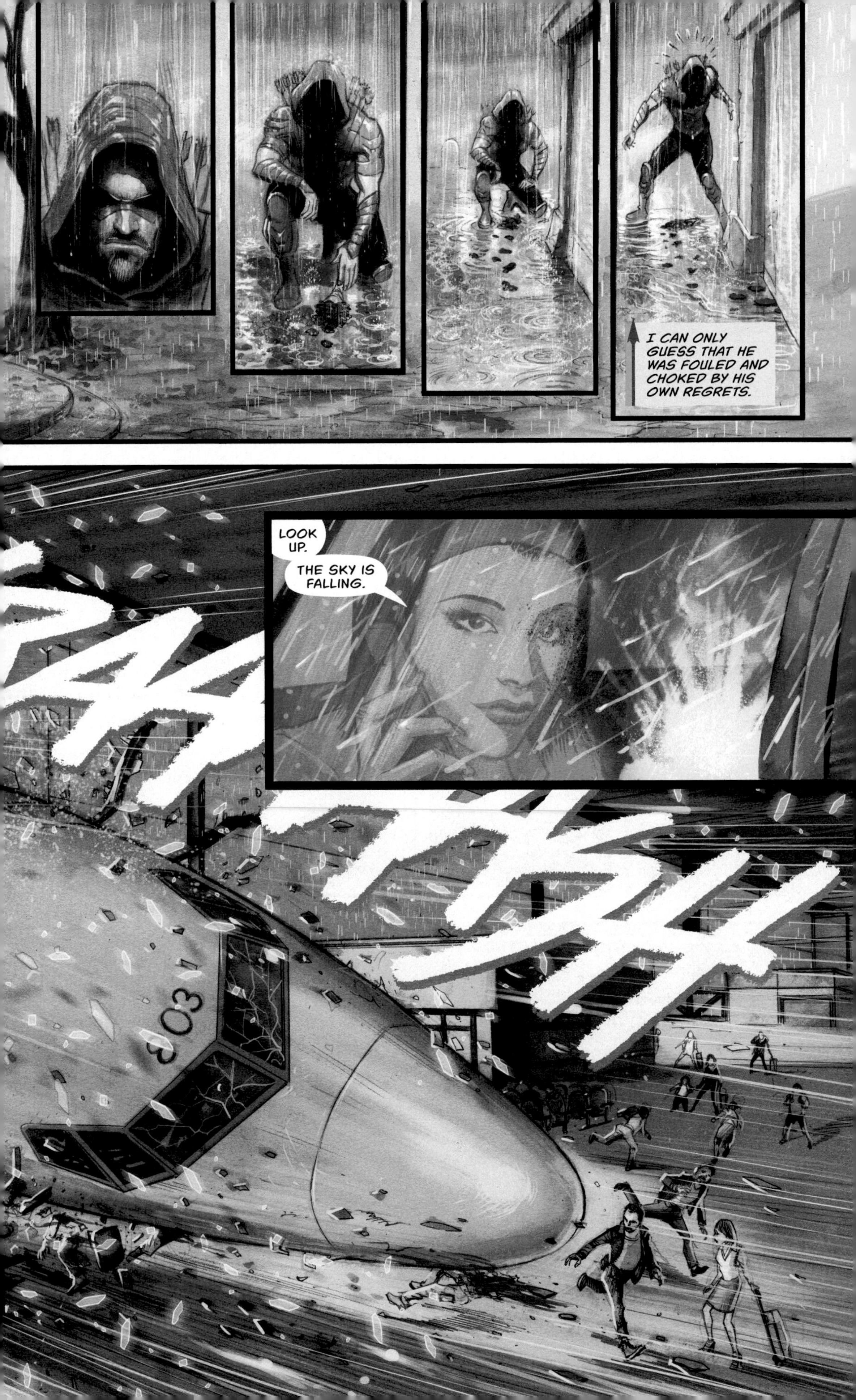
I CAN ONLY GUESS THAT HE WAS FOULED AND CHOKED BY HIS OWN REGRETS.
LOOK UP.
THE SKY IS FALLING.
303

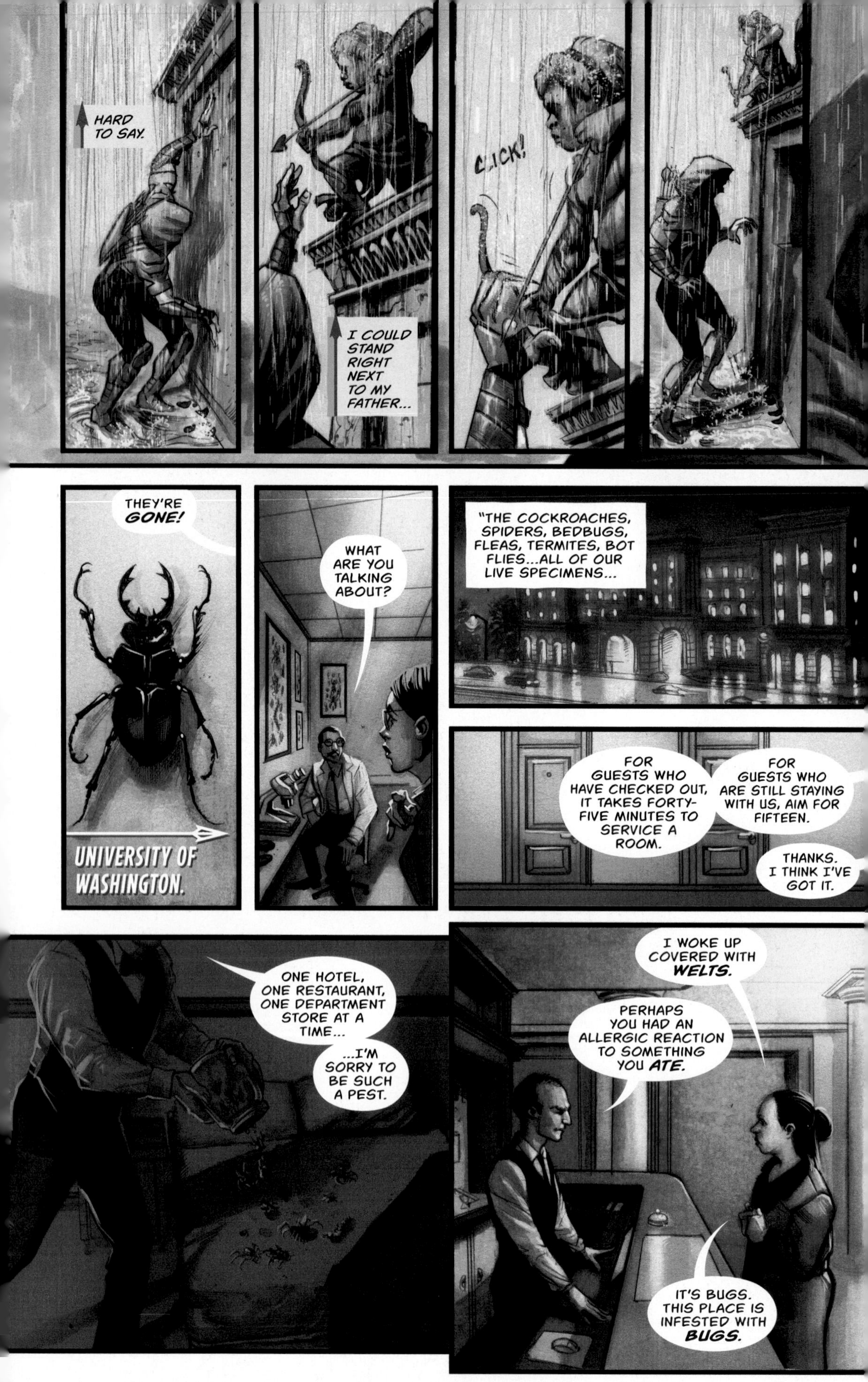
HARD TO SAY.
I COULD STAND RIGHT NEXT TO MY FATHER...
CLICK!
THEY'RE GONE!
UNIVERSITY OF WASHINGTON.
WHAT ARE YOU TALKING ABOUT?
"THE COCKROACHES, SPIDERS, BEDBUGS, FLEAS, TERMITES, BOT FLIES...ALL OF OUR LIVE SPECIMENS...
FOR GUESTS WHO HAVE CHECKED OUT, IT TAKES FORTY-FIVE MINUTES TO SERVICE A ROOM.
FOR GUESTS WHO ARE STILL STAYING WITH US, AIM FOR FIFTEEN.
THANKS. I THINK I'VE GOT IT.
ONE HOTEL, ONE RESTAURANT, ONE DEPARTMENT STORE AT A TIME...
...I'M SORRY TO BE SUCH A PEST.
I WOKE UP COVERED WITH WELTS.
PERHAPS YOU HAD AN ALLERGIC REACTION TO SOMETHING YOU ATE.
IT'S BUGS. THIS PLACE IS INFESTED WITH BUGS.

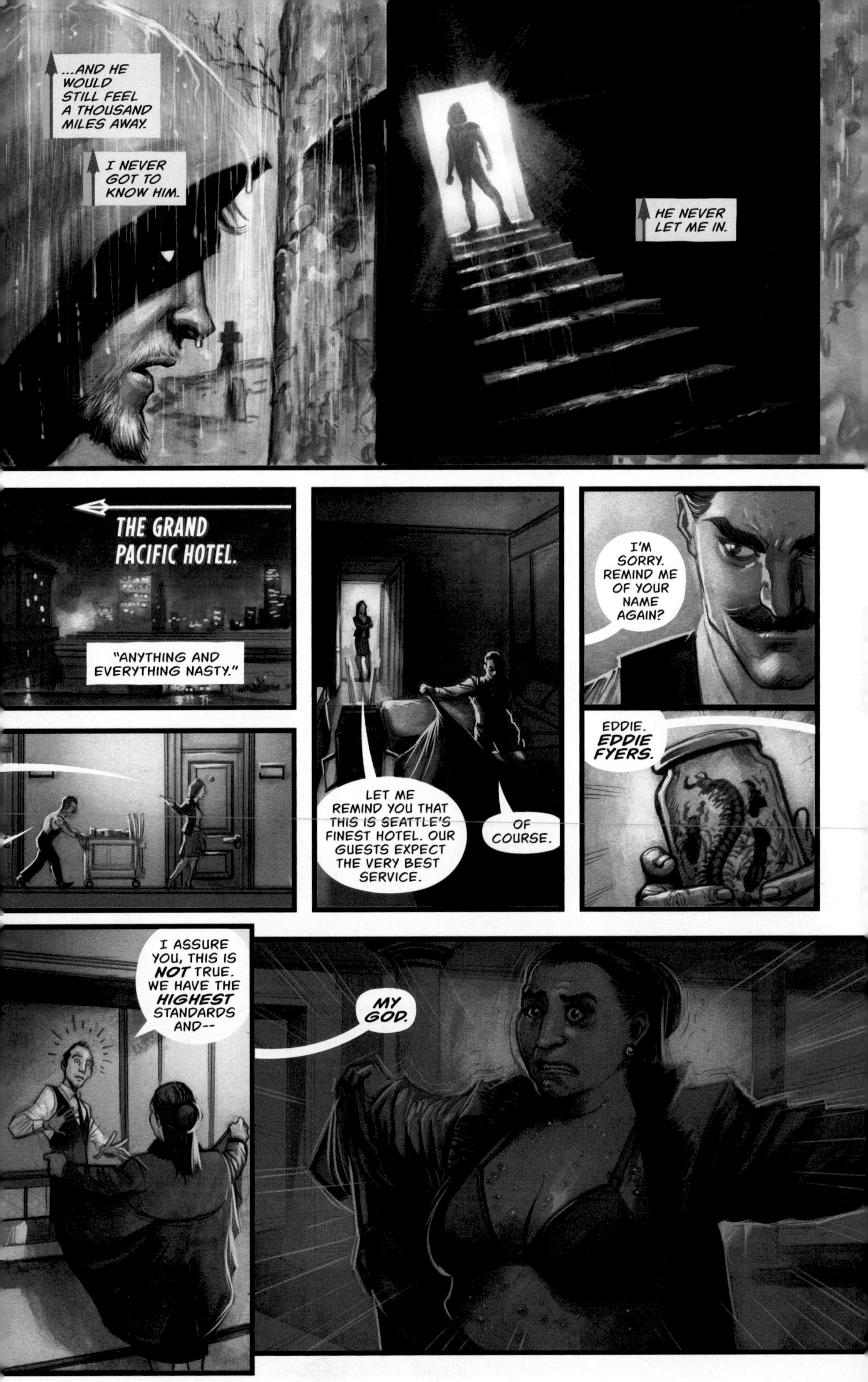
...AND HE WOULD STILL FEEL A THOUSAND MILES AWAY.
I NEVER GOT TO KNOW HIM.
HE NEVER LET ME IN.
THE GRAND PACIFIC HOTEL.
"ANYTHING AND EVERYTHING NASTY."
LET ME REMIND YOU THAT THIS IS SEATTLE'S FINEST HOTEL. OUR GUESTS EXPECT THE VERY BEST SERVICE.
OF COURSE.
I'M SORRY. REMIND ME OF YOUR NAME AGAIN?
EDDIE. EDDIE FYERS.
I ASSURE YOU, THIS IS NOT TRUE. WE HAVE THE HIGHEST STANDARDS AND--
MY GOD.

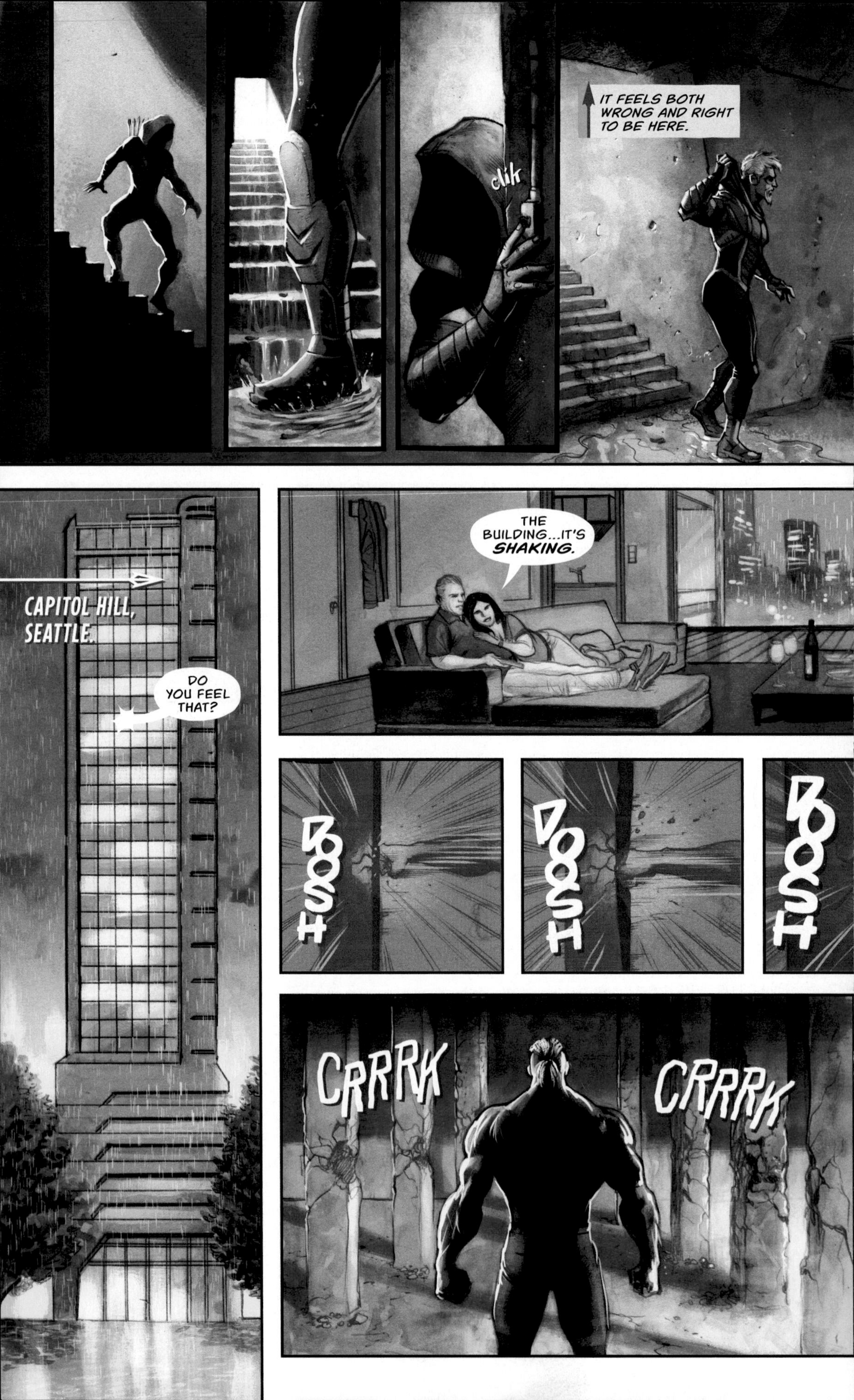
clik
IT FEELS BOTH WRONG AND RIGHT TO BE HERE.
CAPITOL HILL, SEATTLE.
DO YOU FEEL THAT?
THE BUILDING...IT'S *SHAKING.*
DOOSH
DOOSH
DOOSH
CRRRK
CRRRK

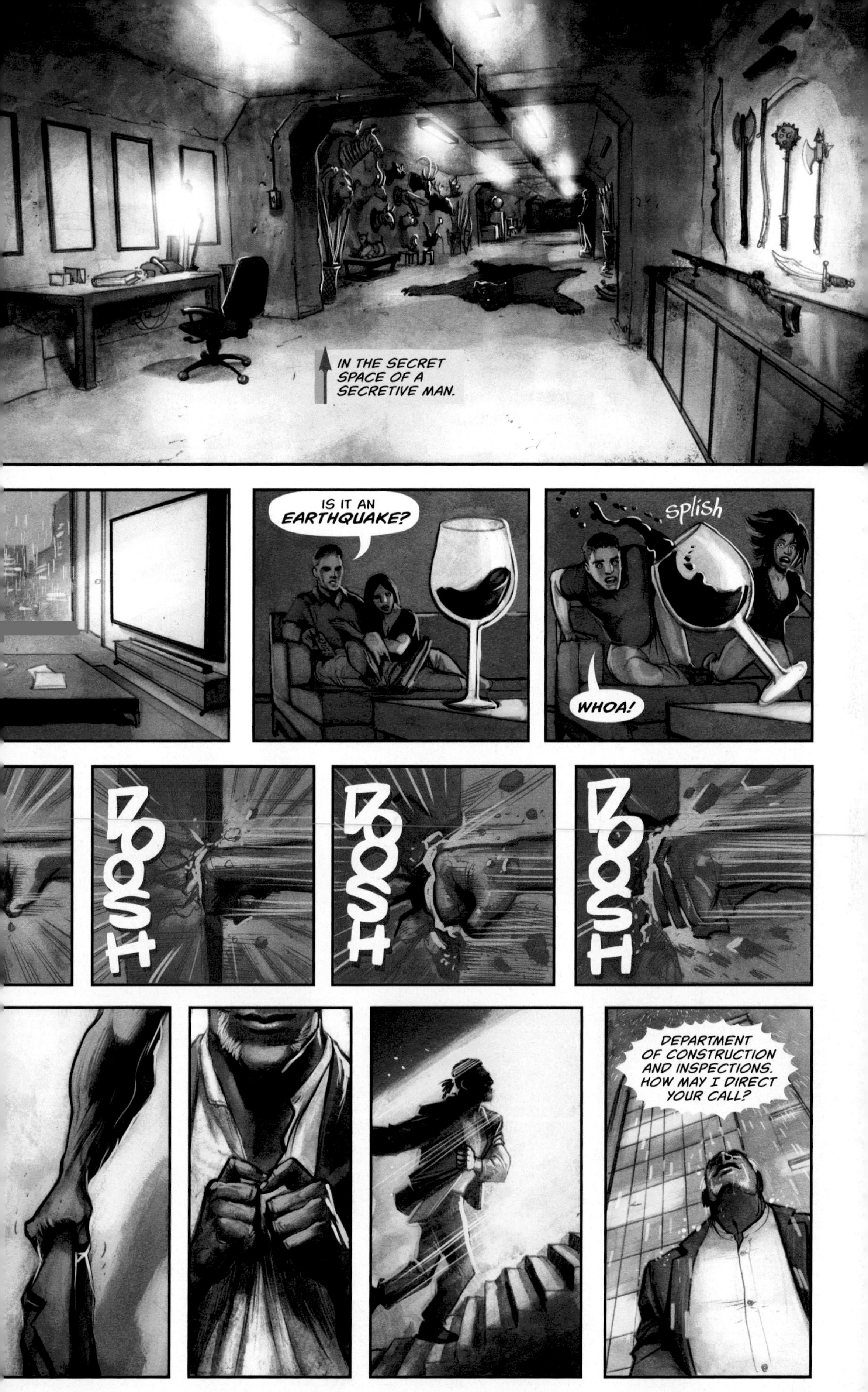
IN THE SECRET SPACE OF A SECRETIVE MAN.
IS IT AN EARTHQUAKE?
splish
WHOA!
BOOSH
BOOSH
BOOSH
DEPARTMENT OF CONSTRUCTION AND INSPECTIONS. HOW MAY I DIRECT YOUR CALL?

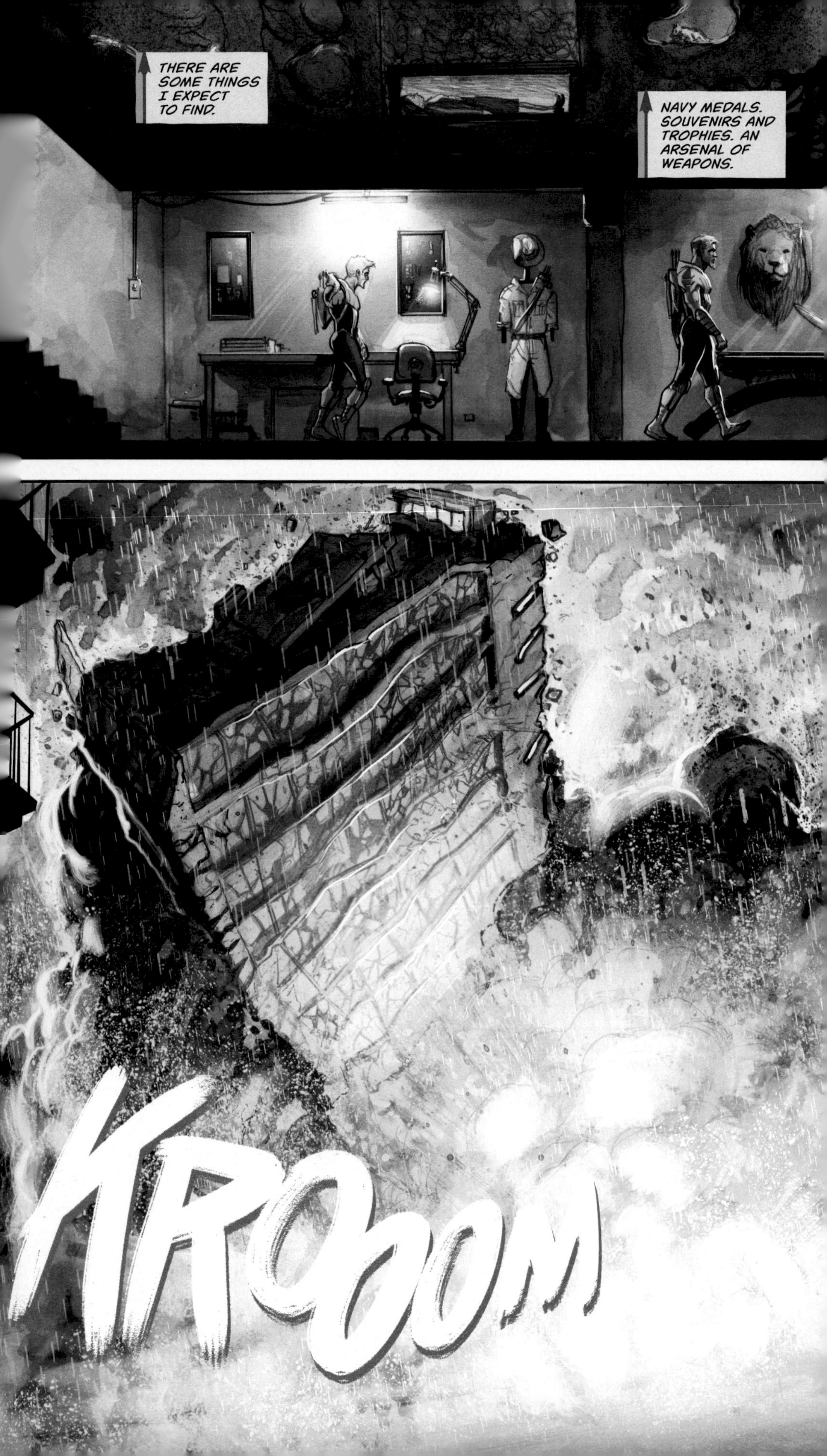
THERE ARE SOME THINGS I EXPECT TO FIND.
NAVY MEDALS. SOUVENIRS AND TROPHIES. AN ARSENAL OF WEAPONS.
KROOOM

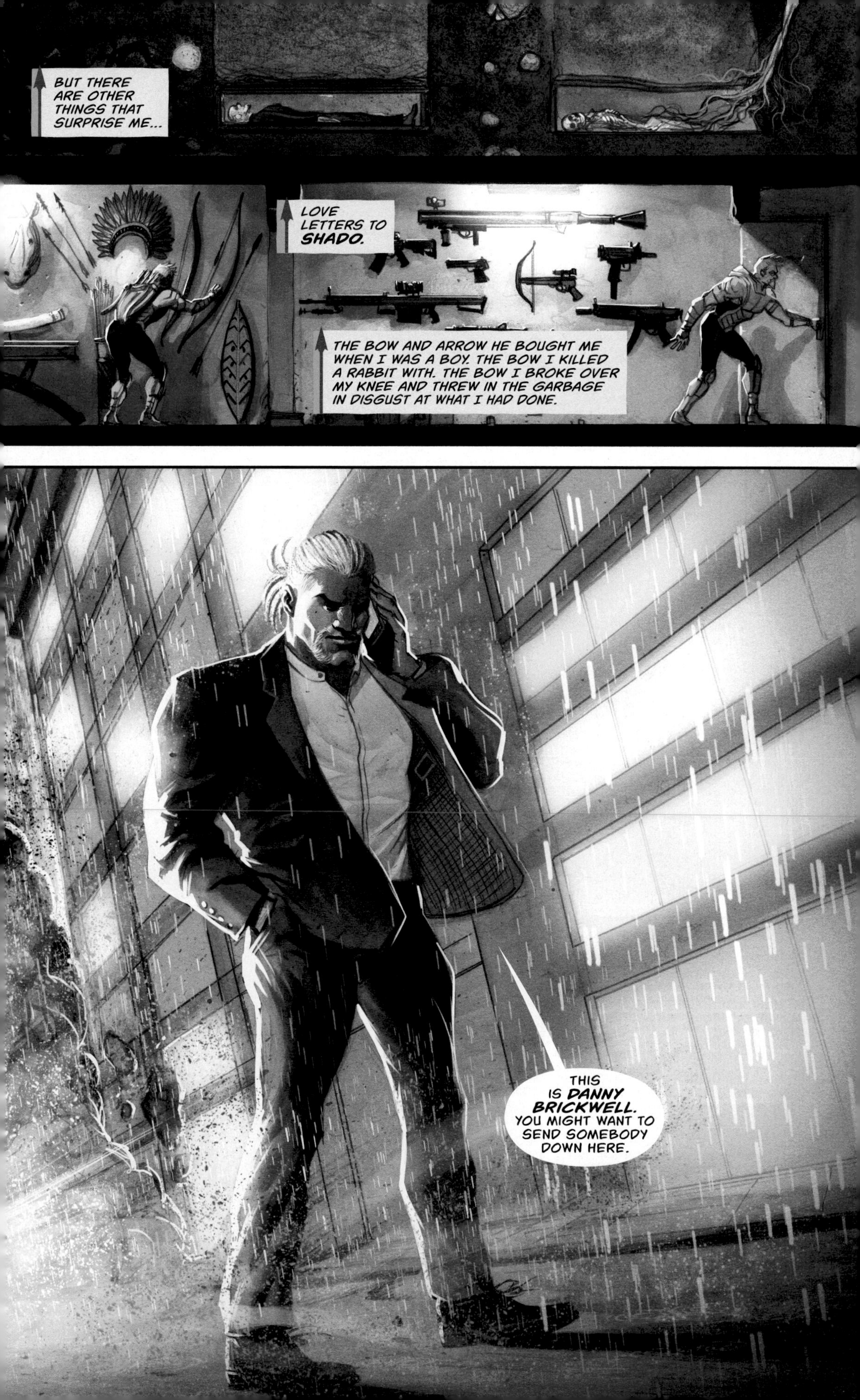
BUT THERE ARE OTHER THINGS THAT SURPRISE ME...
LOVE LETTERS TO SHADO.
THE BOW AND ARROW HE BOUGHT ME WHEN I WAS A BOY. THE BOW I KILLED A RABBIT WITH. THE BOW I BROKE OVER MY KNEE AND THREW IN THE GARBAGE IN DISGUST AT WHAT I HAD DONE.
THIS IS DANNY BRICKWELL. YOU MIGHT WANT TO SEND SOMEBODY DOWN HERE.

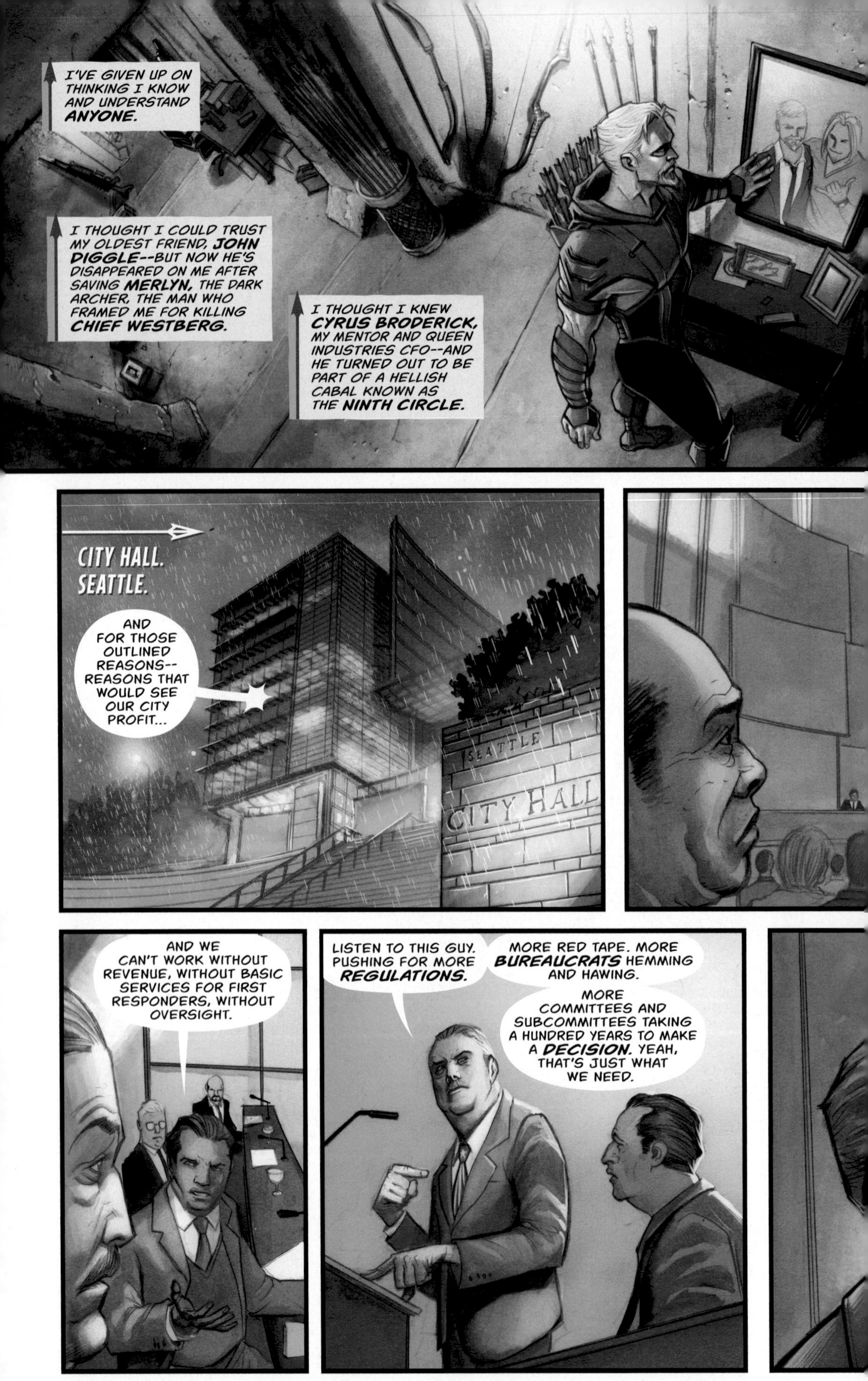
I'VE GIVEN UP ON THINKING I KNOW AND UNDERSTAND **ANYONE.**
I THOUGHT I COULD TRUST MY OLDEST FRIEND, **JOHN DIGGLE**--BUT NOW HE'S DISAPPEARED ON ME AFTER SAVING **MERLYN,** THE DARK ARCHER, THE MAN WHO FRAMED ME FOR KILLING **CHIEF WESTBERG.**
I THOUGHT I KNEW **CYRUS BRODERICK,** MY MENTOR AND QUEEN INDUSTRIES CFO--AND HE TURNED OUT TO BE PART OF A HELLISH CABAL KNOWN AS THE **NINTH CIRCLE.**
CITY HALL. SEATTLE.
AND FOR THOSE OUTLINED REASONS--REASONS THAT WOULD SEE OUR CITY PROFIT...
SEATTLE
CITY HALL
AND WE CAN'T WORK WITHOUT REVENUE, WITHOUT BASIC SERVICES FOR FIRST RESPONDERS, WITHOUT OVERSIGHT.
LISTEN TO THIS GUY. PUSHING FOR MORE **REGULATIONS.**
MORE RED TAPE. MORE **BUREAUCRATS** HEMMING AND HAWING.
MORE COMMITTEES AND SUBCOMMITTEES TAKING A HUNDRED YEARS TO MAKE A **DECISION.** YEAH, THAT'S JUST WHAT WE NEED.

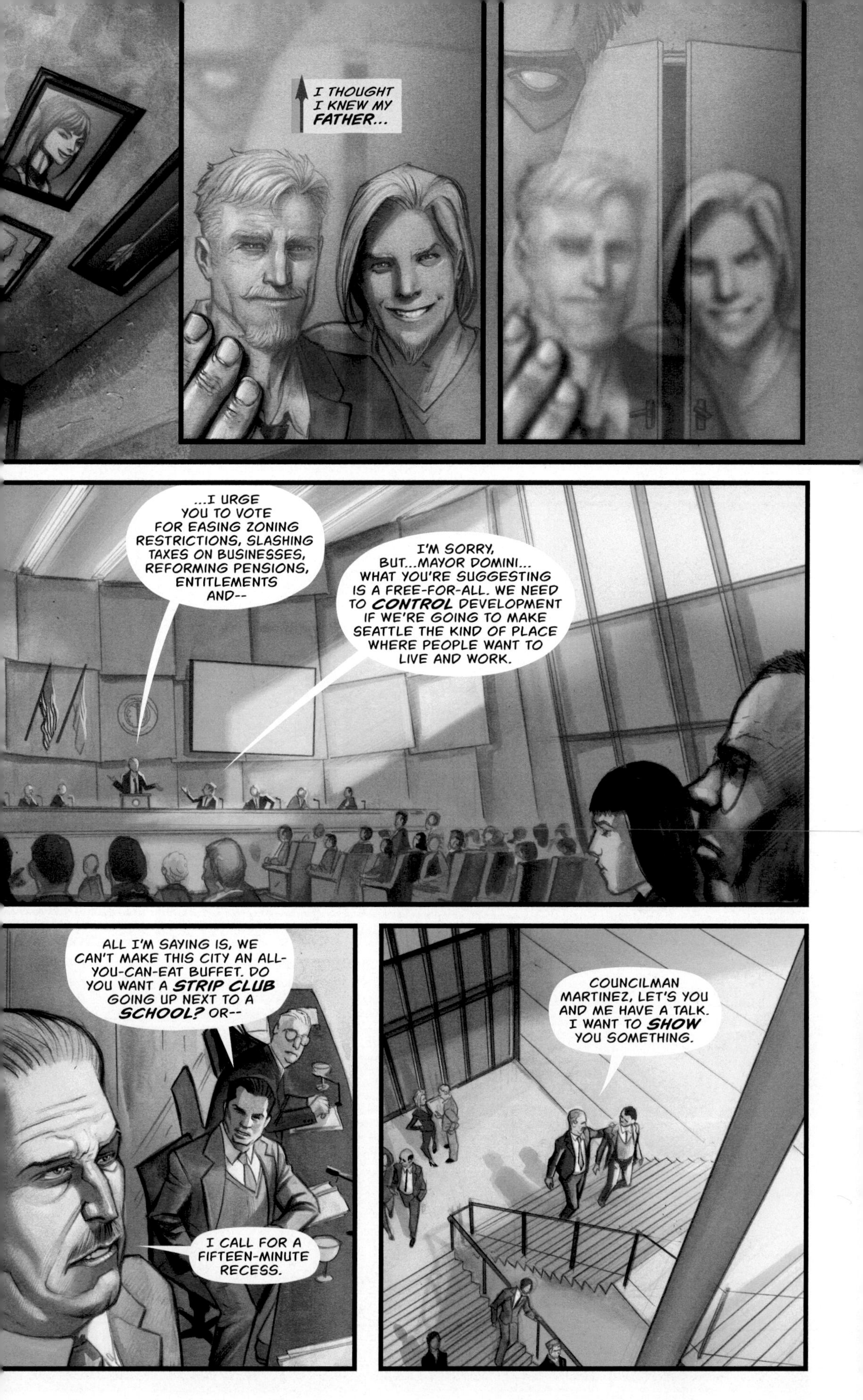
I THOUGHT I KNEW MY FATHER...
...I URGE YOU TO VOTE FOR EASING ZONING RESTRICTIONS, SLASHING TAXES ON BUSINESSES, REFORMING PENSIONS, ENTITLEMENTS AND--
I'M SORRY, BUT...MAYOR DOMINI... WHAT YOU'RE SUGGESTING IS A FREE-FOR-ALL. WE NEED TO CONTROL DEVELOPMENT IF WE'RE GOING TO MAKE SEATTLE THE KIND OF PLACE WHERE PEOPLE WANT TO LIVE AND WORK.
ALL I'M SAYING IS, WE CAN'T MAKE THIS CITY AN ALL-YOU-CAN-EAT BUFFET. DO YOU WANT A STRIP CLUB GOING UP NEXT TO A SCHOOL? OR--
I CALL FOR A FIFTEEN-MINUTE RECESS.
COUNCILMAN MARTINEZ, LET'S YOU AND ME HAVE A TALK. I WANT TO SHOW YOU SOMETHING.

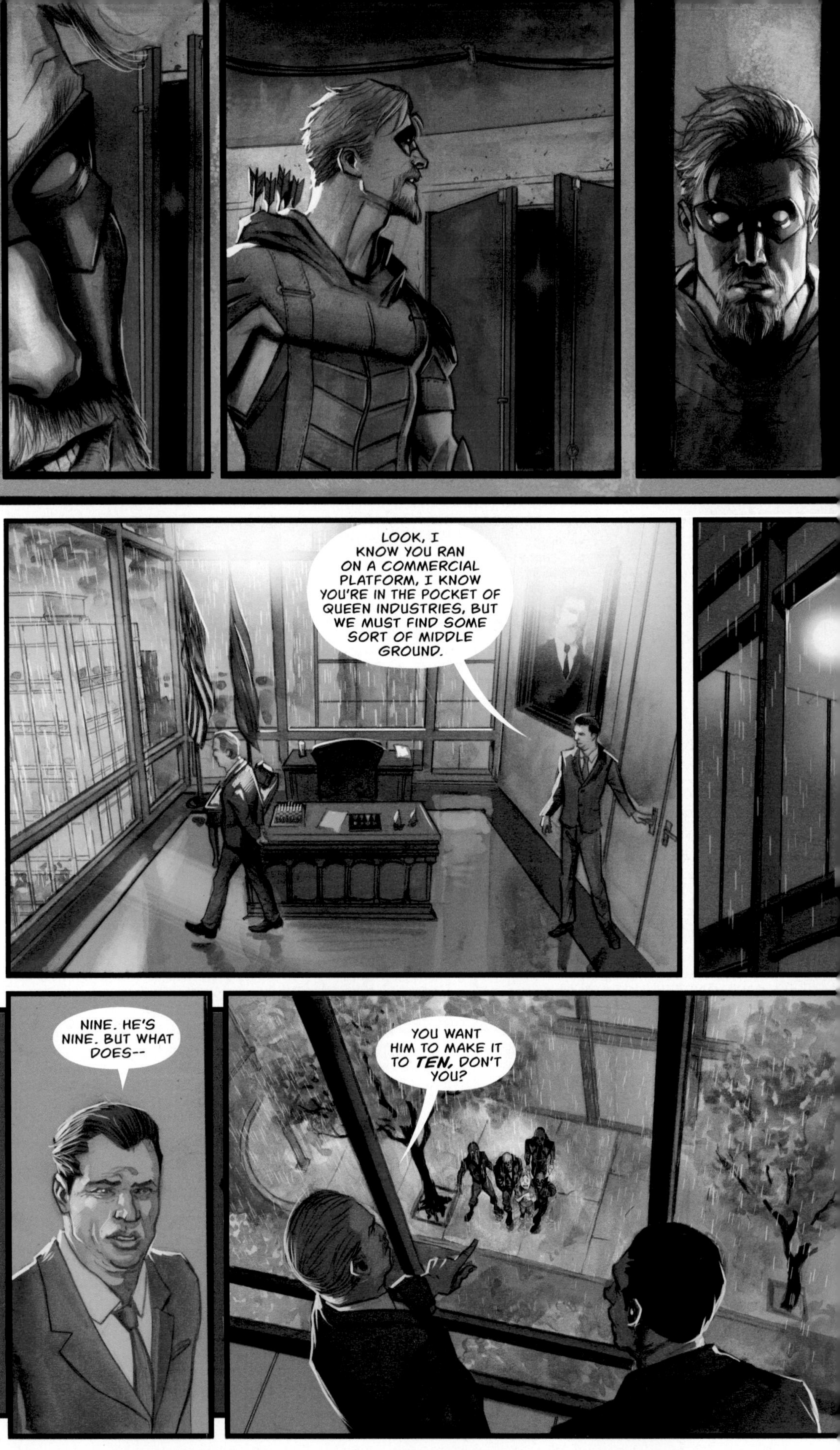
LOOK, I KNOW YOU RAN ON A COMMERCIAL PLATFORM, I KNOW YOU'RE IN THE POCKET OF QUEEN INDUSTRIES, BUT WE MUST FIND SOME SORT OF MIDDLE GROUND.
NINE. HE'S NINE. BUT WHAT DOES--
YOU WANT HIM TO MAKE IT TO TEN, DON'T YOU?

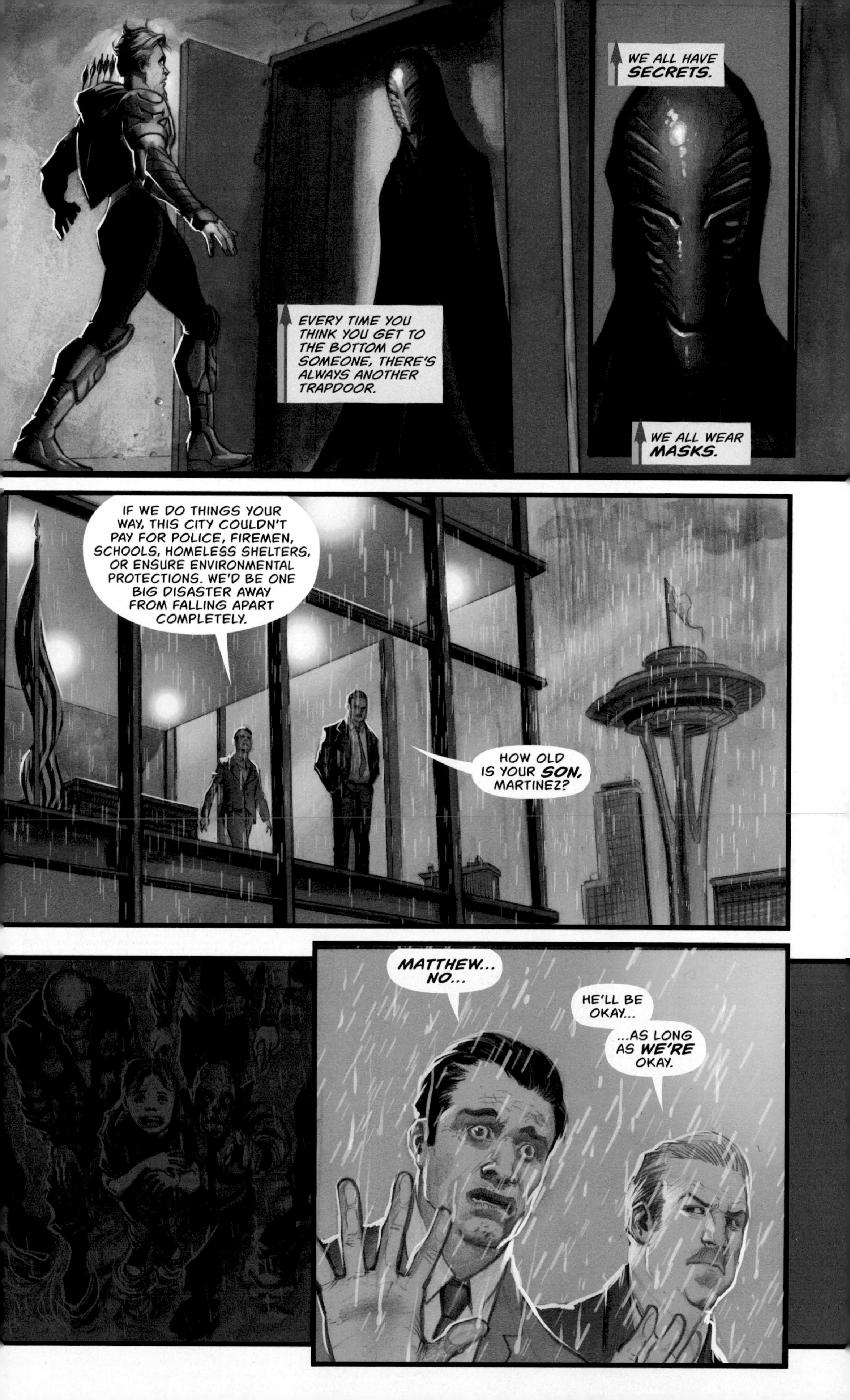
EVERY TIME YOU THINK YOU GET TO THE BOTTOM OF SOMEONE, THERE'S ALWAYS ANOTHER TRAPDOOR.
WE ALL HAVE SECRETS.
WE ALL WEAR MASKS.
IF WE DO THINGS YOUR WAY, THIS CITY COULDN'T PAY FOR POLICE, FIREMEN, SCHOOLS, HOMELESS SHELTERS, OR ENSURE ENVIRONMENTAL PROTECTIONS. WE'D BE ONE BIG DISASTER AWAY FROM FALLING APART COMPLETELY.
HOW OLD IS YOUR SON, MARTINEZ?
MATTHEW... NO...
HE'LL BE OKAY...
...AS LONG AS WE'RE OKAY.

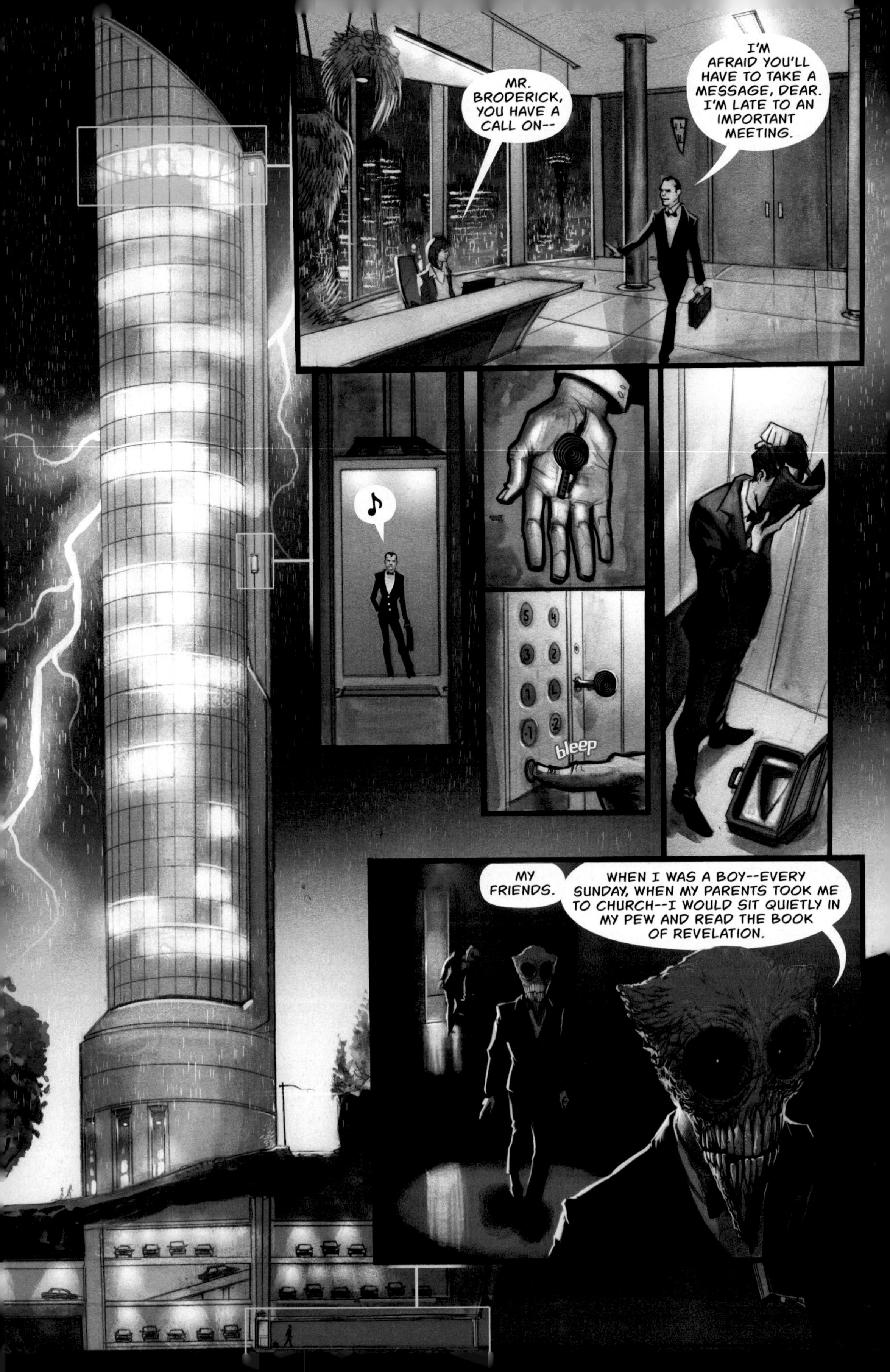
MR. BRODERICK, YOU HAVE A CALL ON--
I'M AFRAID YOU'LL HAVE TO TAKE A MESSAGE, DEAR. I'M LATE TO AN IMPORTANT MEETING.
♪
bleep
MY FRIENDS.
WHEN I WAS A BOY--EVERY SUNDAY, WHEN MY PARENTS TOOK ME TO CHURCH--I WOULD SIT QUIETLY IN MY PEW AND READ THE BOOK OF REVELATION.

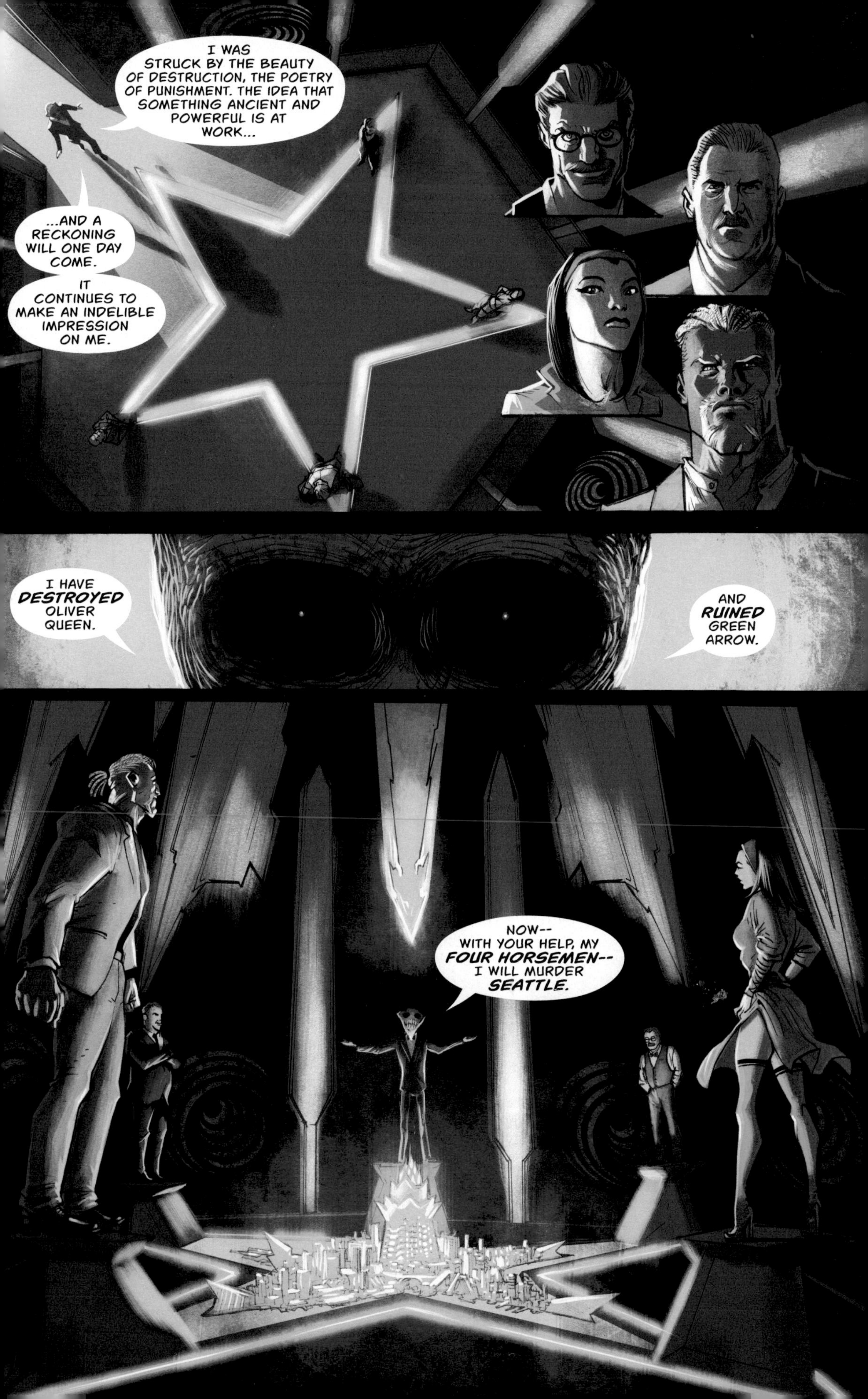

I WAS STRUCK BY THE BEAUTY OF DESTRUCTION, THE POETRY OF PUNISHMENT. THE IDEA THAT SOMETHING ANCIENT AND POWERFUL IS AT WORK...
...AND A RECKONING WILL ONE DAY COME.
IT CONTINUES TO MAKE AN INDELIBLE IMPRESSION ON ME.
I HAVE DESTROYED OLIVER QUEEN.
AND RUINED GREEN ARROW.
NOW-- WITH YOUR HELP, MY FOUR HORSEMEN-- I WILL MURDER SEATTLE.

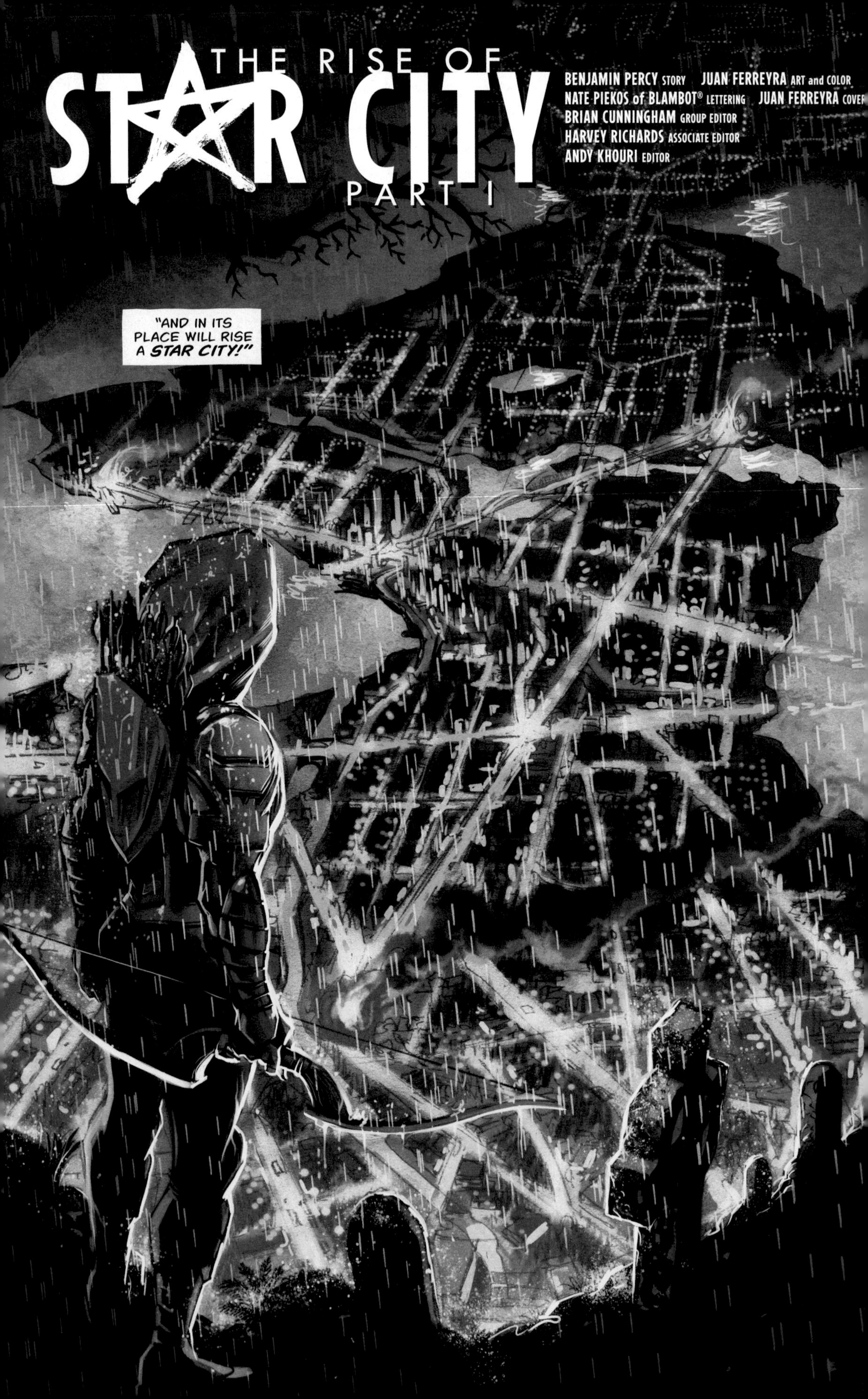
THE RISE OF
STAR CITY
PART I
BENJAMIN PERCY STORY JUAN FERREYRA ART and COLOR
NATE PIEKOS of BLAMBOT® LETTERING JUAN FERREYRA COVER
BRIAN CUNNINGHAM GROUP EDITOR
HARVEY RICHARDS ASSOCIATE EDITOR
ANDY KHOURI EDITOR
"AND IN ITS PLACE WILL RISE A STAR CITY!"

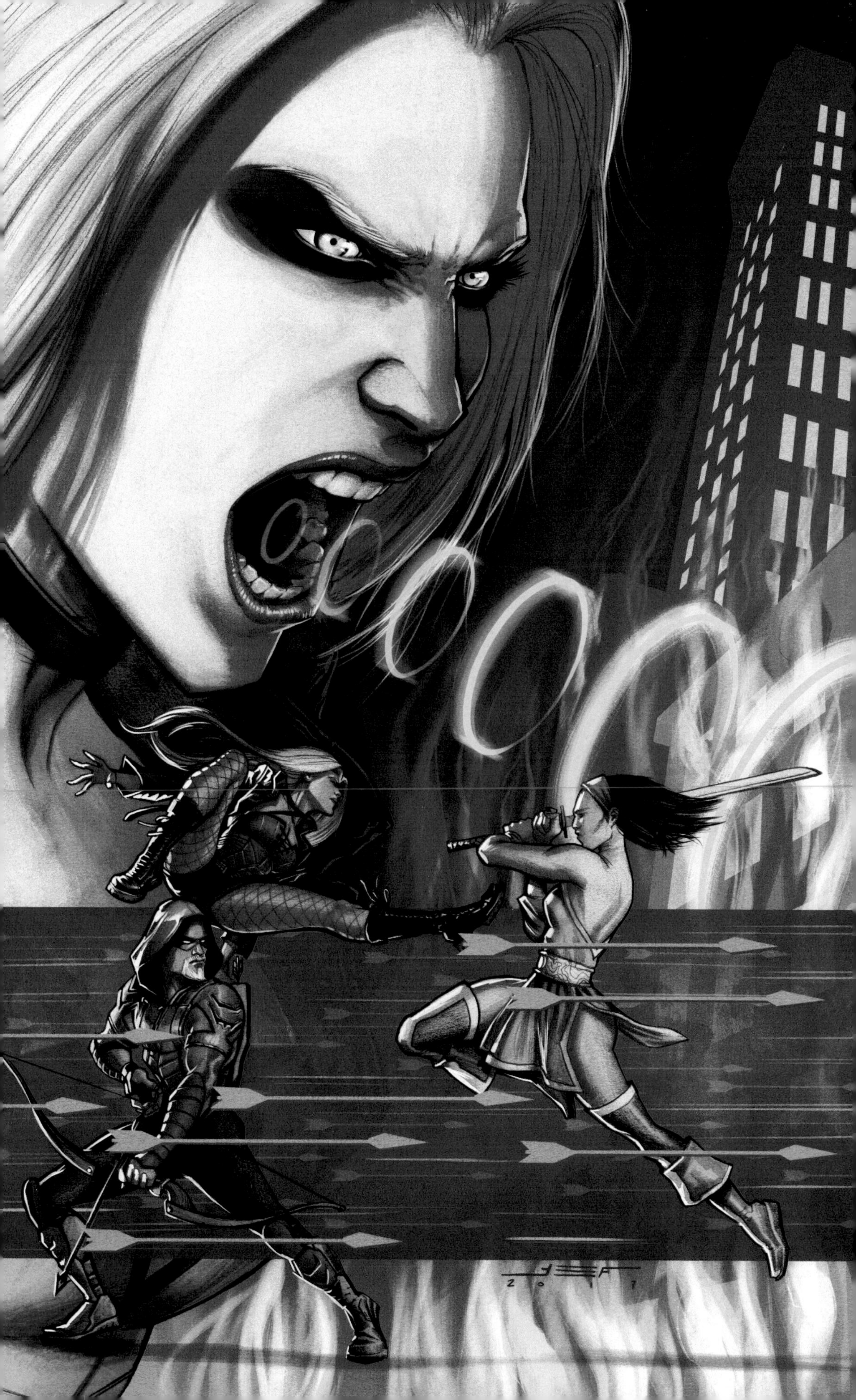

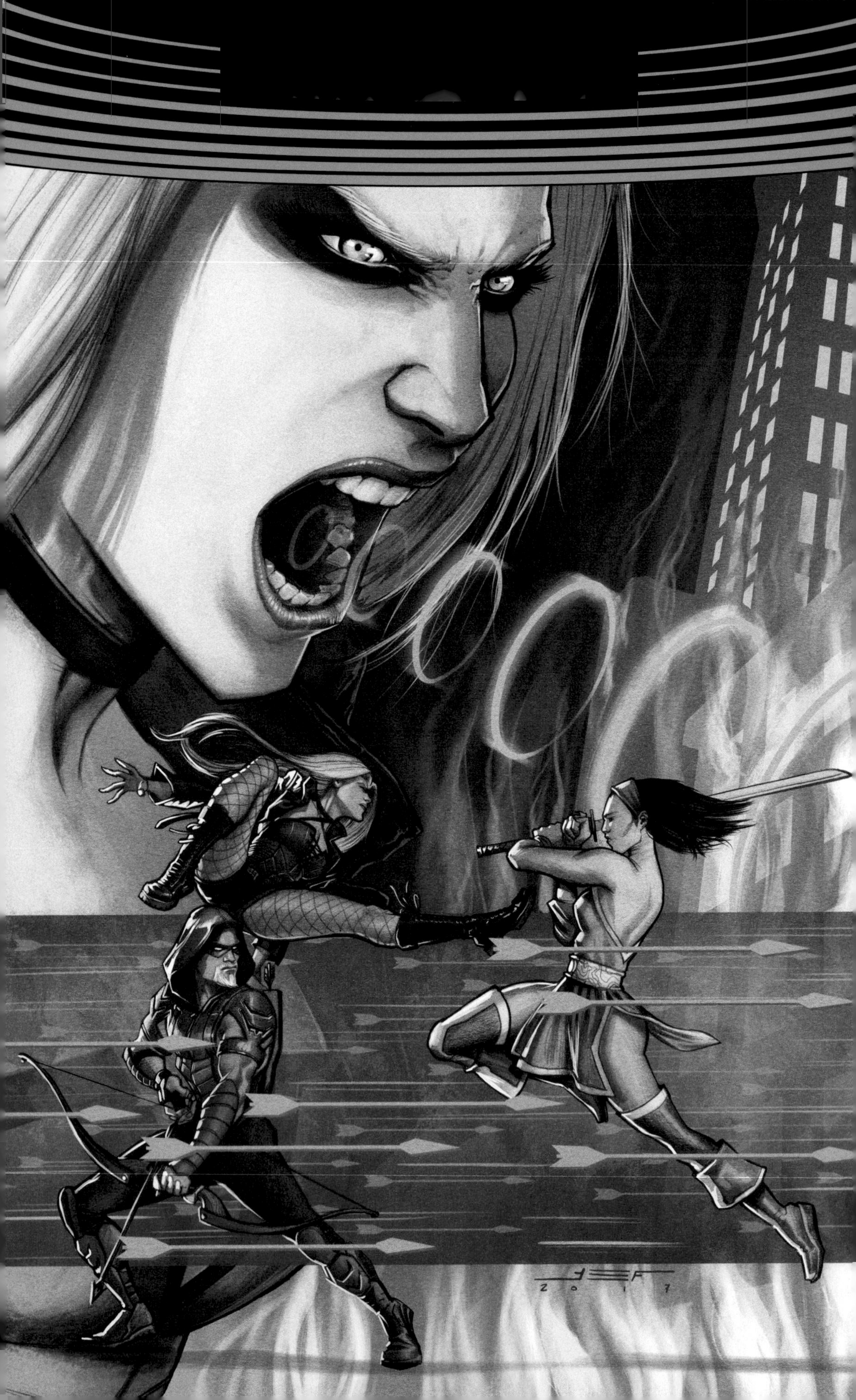

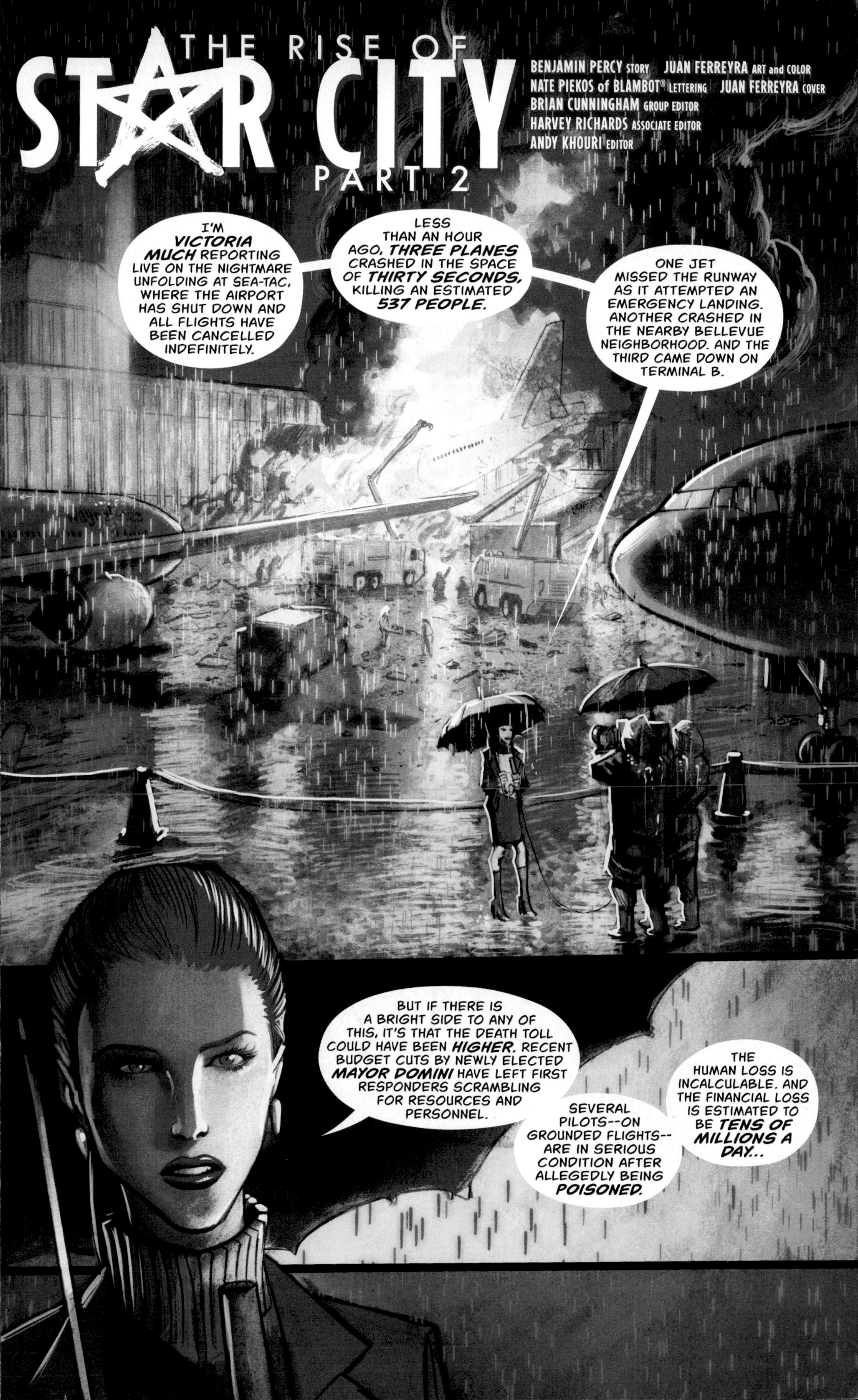
THE RISE OF
STAR CITY
PART 2
BENJAMIN PERCY STORY JUAN FERREYRA ART and COLOR
NATE PIEKOS of BLAMBOT® LETTERING JUAN FERREYRA COVER
BRIAN CUNNINGHAM GROUP EDITOR
HARVEY RICHARDS ASSOCIATE EDITOR
ANDY KHOURI EDITOR
I'M VICTORIA MUCH REPORTING LIVE ON THE NIGHTMARE UNFOLDING AT SEA-TAC, WHERE THE AIRPORT HAS SHUT DOWN AND ALL FLIGHTS HAVE BEEN CANCELLED INDEFINITELY.
LESS THAN AN HOUR AGO, THREE PLANES CRASHED IN THE SPACE OF THIRTY SECONDS, KILLING AN ESTIMATED 537 PEOPLE.
ONE JET MISSED THE RUNWAY AS IT ATTEMPTED AN EMERGENCY LANDING. ANOTHER CRASHED IN THE NEARBY BELLEVUE NEIGHBORHOOD. AND THE THIRD CAME DOWN ON TERMINAL B.
BUT IF THERE IS A BRIGHT SIDE TO ANY OF THIS, IT'S THAT THE DEATH TOLL COULD HAVE BEEN HIGHER. RECENT BUDGET CUTS BY NEWLY ELECTED MAYOR DOMINI HAVE LEFT FIRST RESPONDERS SCRAMBLING FOR RESOURCES AND PERSONNEL.
SEVERAL PILOTS--ON GROUNDED FLIGHTS--ARE IN SERIOUS CONDITION AFTER ALLEGEDLY BEING POISONED.
THE HUMAN LOSS IS INCALCULABLE. AND THE FINANCIAL LOSS IS ESTIMATED TO BE TENS OF MILLIONS A DAY...

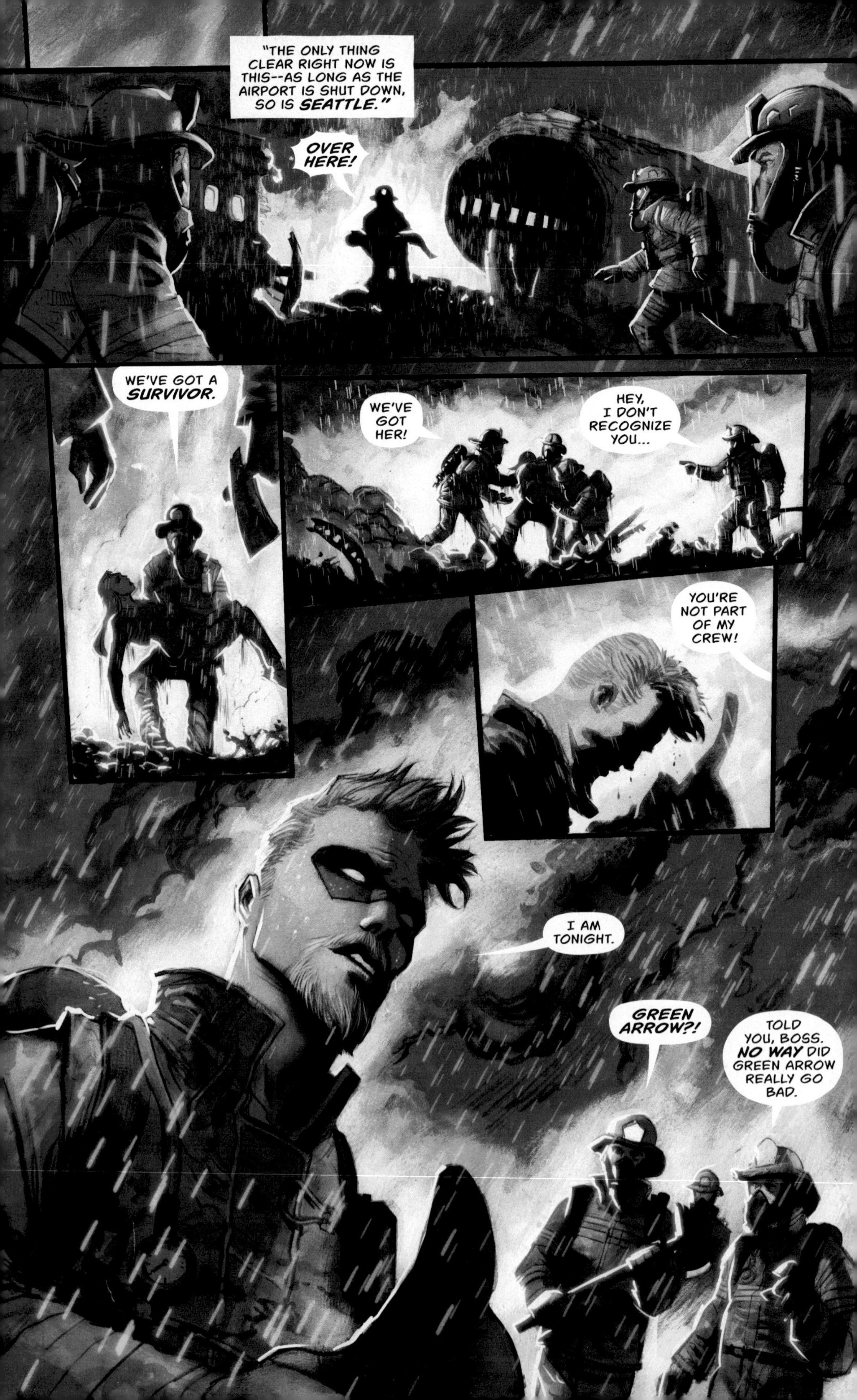
"THE ONLY THING CLEAR RIGHT NOW IS THIS--AS LONG AS THE AIRPORT IS SHUT DOWN, SO IS *SEATTLE.*"
OVER HERE!
WE'VE GOT A *SURVIVOR.*
WE'VE GOT HER!
HEY, I DON'T RECOGNIZE YOU...
YOU'RE NOT PART OF MY CREW!
I AM TONIGHT.
GREEN ARROW?!
TOLD YOU, BOSS. ***NO WAY*** DID GREEN ARROW REALLY GO BAD.

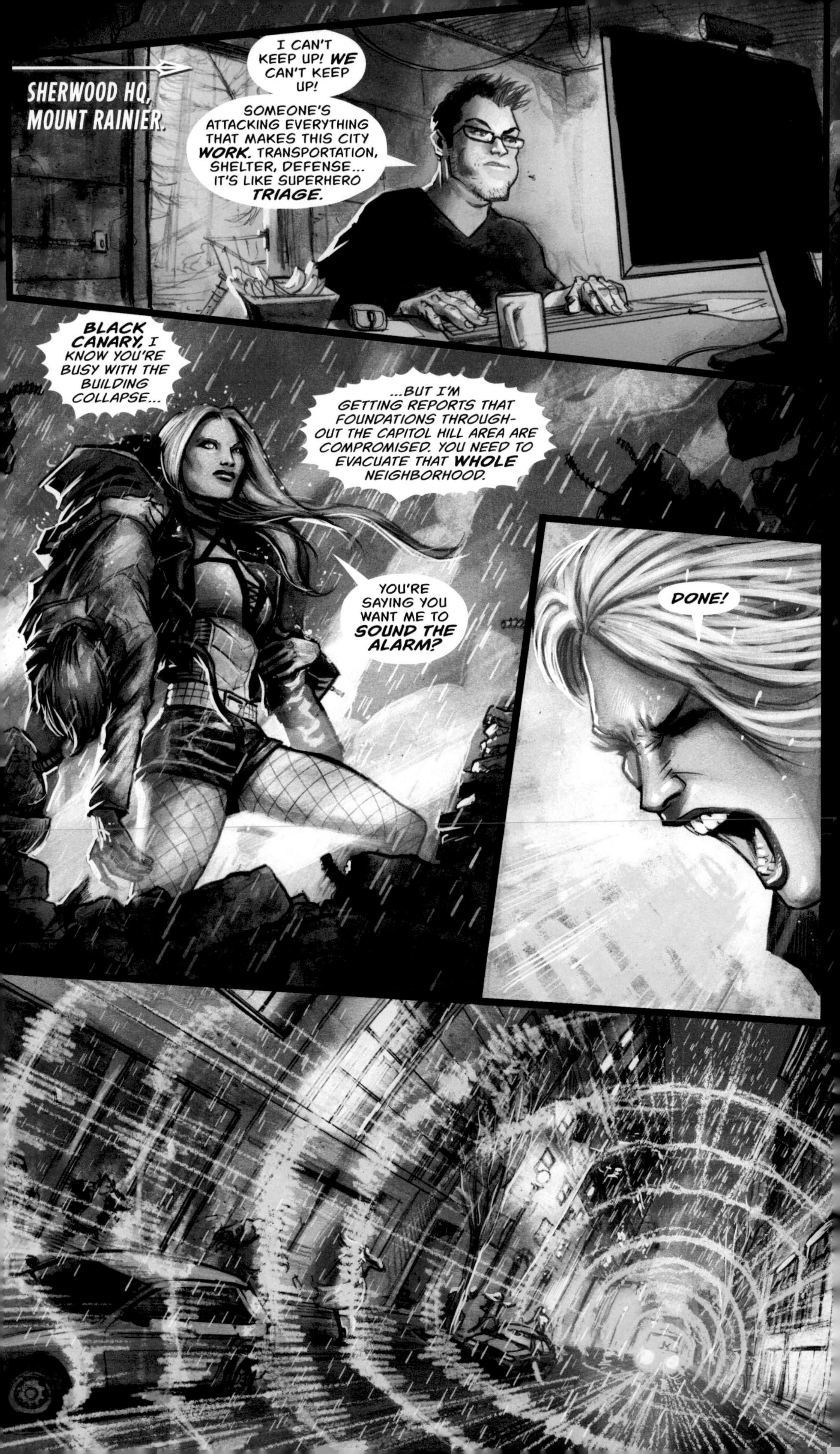
SHERWOOD HQ, MOUNT RAINIER.
I CAN'T KEEP UP! WE CAN'T KEEP UP!
SOMEONE'S ATTACKING EVERYTHING THAT MAKES THIS CITY WORK. TRANSPORTATION, SHELTER, DEFENSE... IT'S LIKE SUPERHERO TRIAGE.
BLACK CANARY, I KNOW YOU'RE BUSY WITH THE BUILDING COLLAPSE...
...BUT I'M GETTING REPORTS THAT FOUNDATIONS THROUGH-OUT THE CAPITOL HILL AREA ARE COMPROMISED. YOU NEED TO EVACUATE THAT WHOLE NEIGHBORHOOD.
YOU'RE SAYING YOU WANT ME TO SOUND THE ALARM?
DONE!

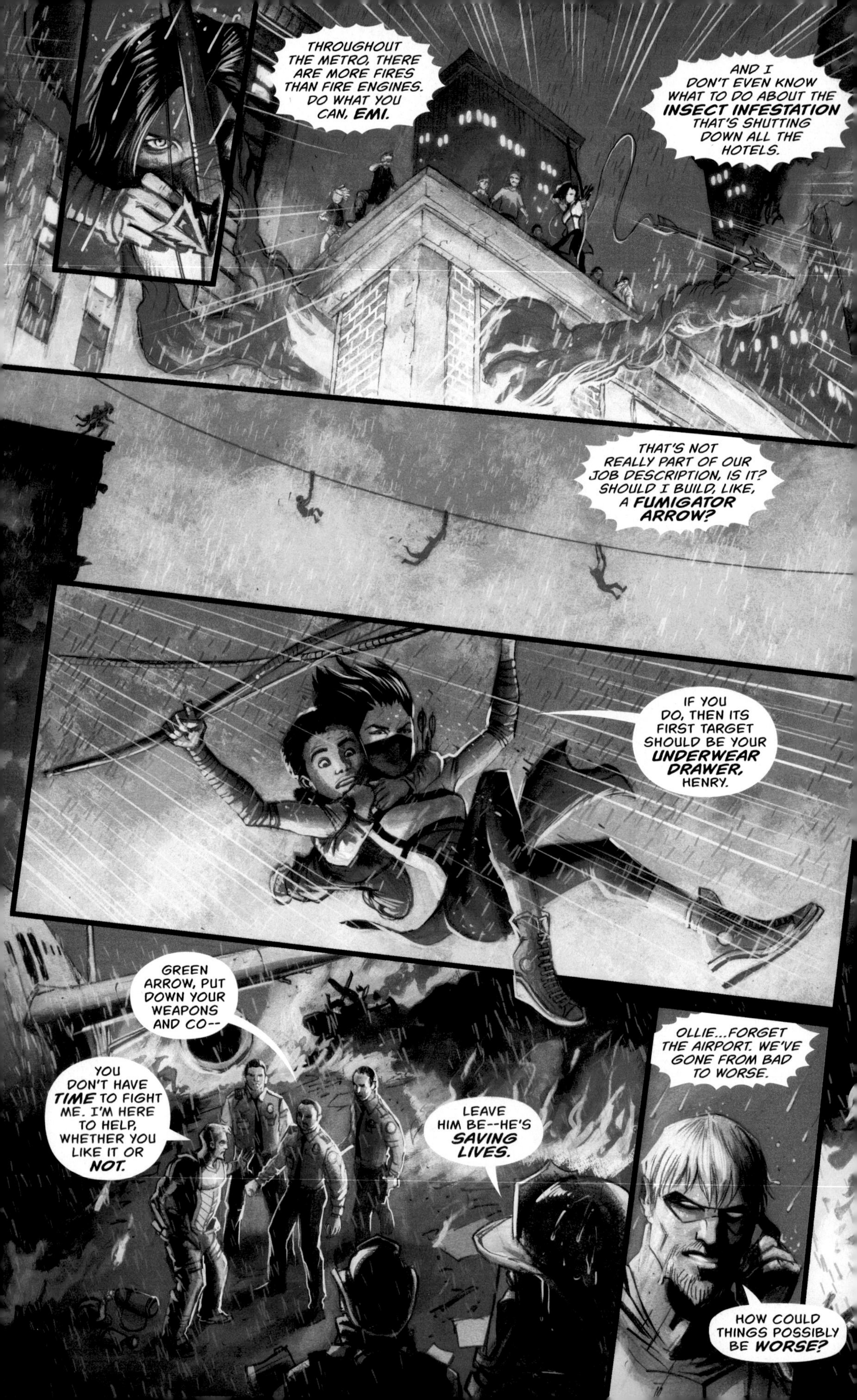
THROUGHOUT THE METRO, THERE ARE MORE FIRES THAN FIRE ENGINES. DO WHAT YOU CAN, EMI.
AND I DON'T EVEN KNOW WHAT TO DO ABOUT THE INSECT INFESTATION THAT'S SHUTTING DOWN ALL THE HOTELS.
THAT'S NOT REALLY PART OF OUR JOB DESCRIPTION, IS IT? SHOULD I BUILD, LIKE, A FUMIGATOR ARROW?
IF YOU DO, THEN ITS FIRST TARGET SHOULD BE YOUR UNDERWEAR DRAWER, HENRY.
GREEN ARROW, PUT DOWN YOUR WEAPONS AND CO--
YOU DON'T HAVE TIME TO FIGHT ME. I'M HERE TO HELP, WHETHER YOU LIKE IT OR NOT.
LEAVE HIM BE--HE'S SAVING LIVES.
OLLIE...FORGET THE AIRPORT. WE'VE GONE FROM BAD TO WORSE.
HOW COULD THINGS POSSIBLY BE WORSE?

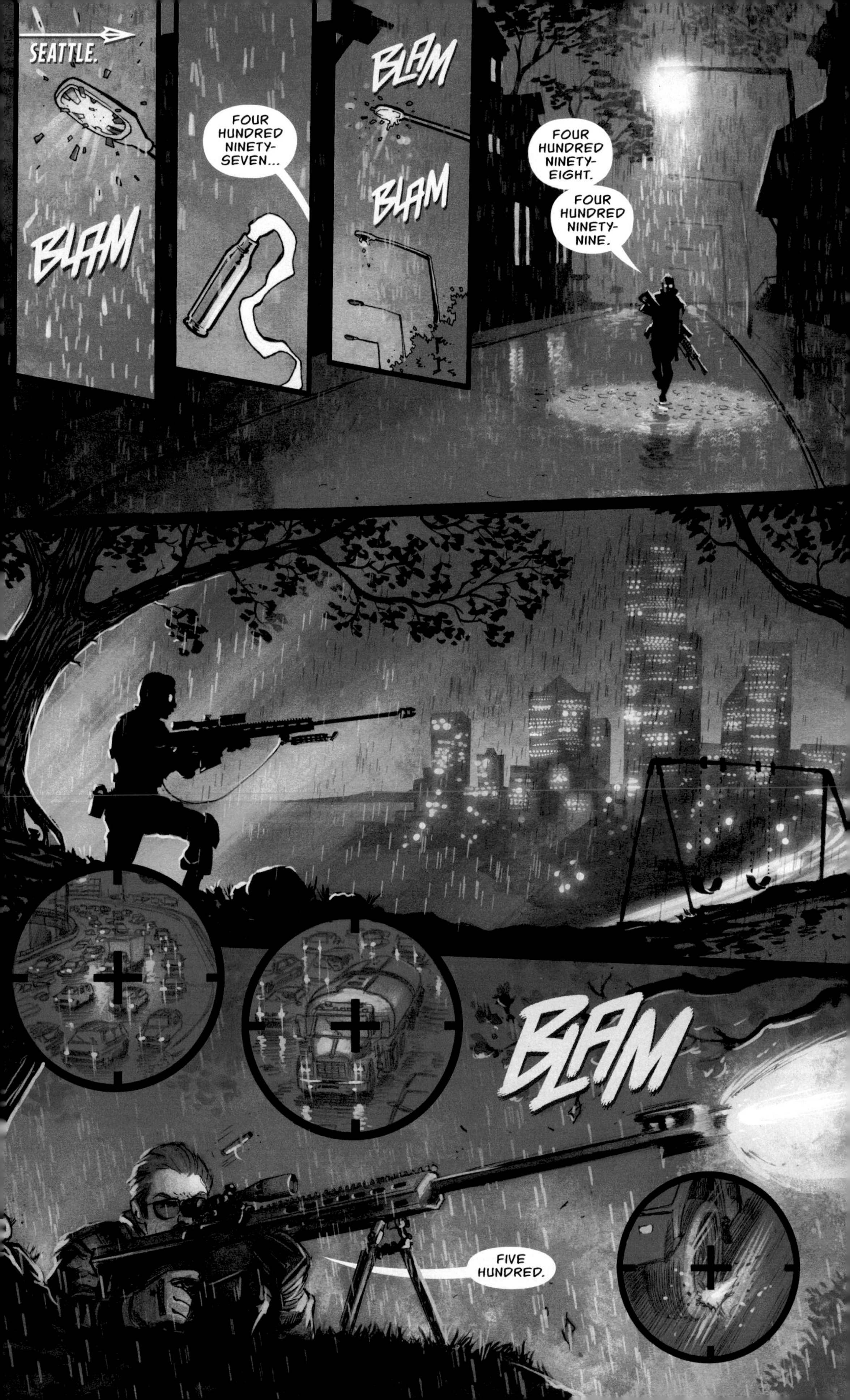
SEATTLE.
BLAM
FOUR HUNDRED NINETY-SEVEN...
BLAM
BLAM
FOUR HUNDRED NINETY-EIGHT.
FOUR HUNDRED NINETY-NINE.
BLAM
FIVE HUNDRED.

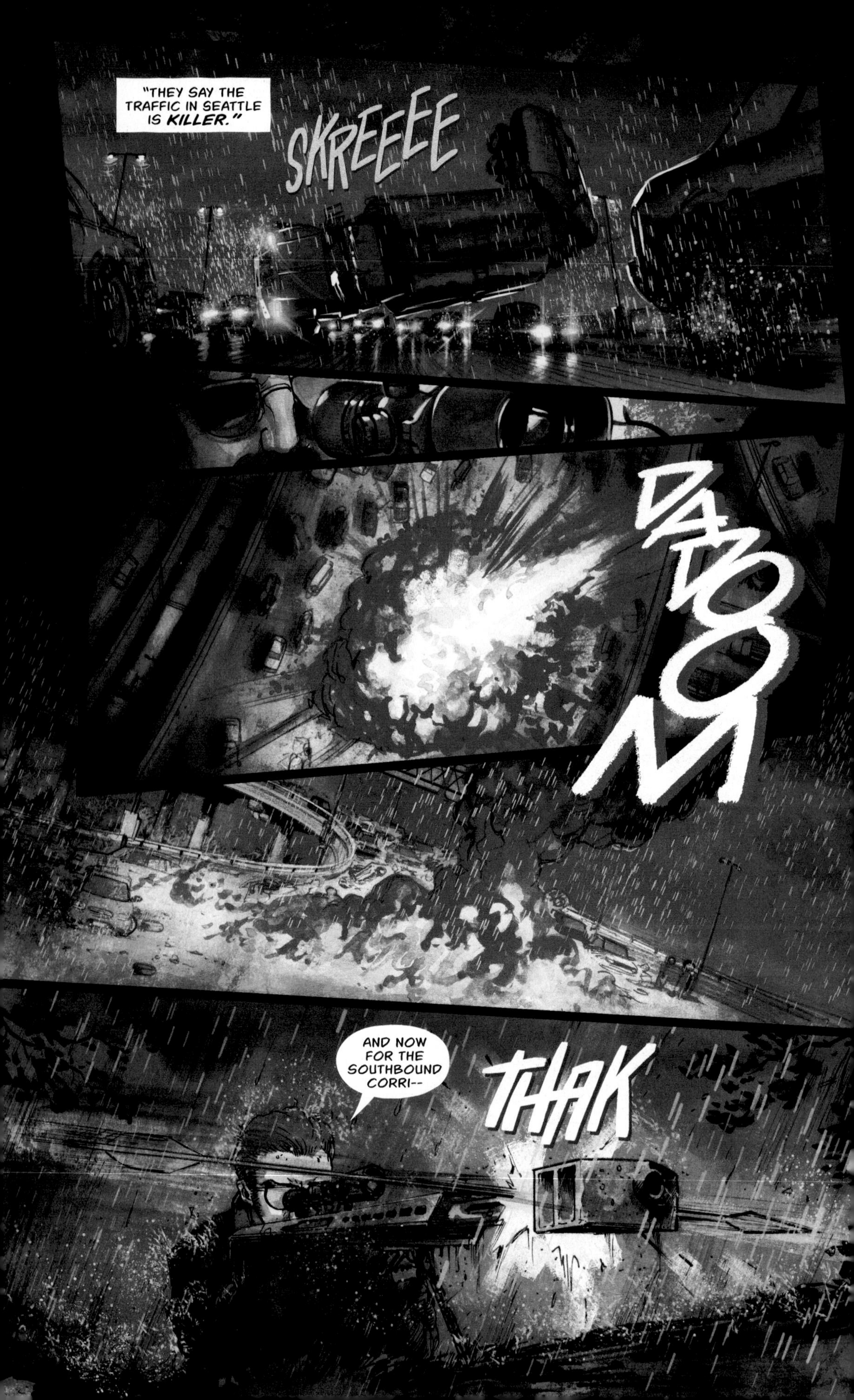
"THEY SAY THE TRAFFIC IN SEATTLE IS KILLER."
SKREEEE
DABOOM
AND NOW FOR THE SOUTHBOUND CORRI--
THAK

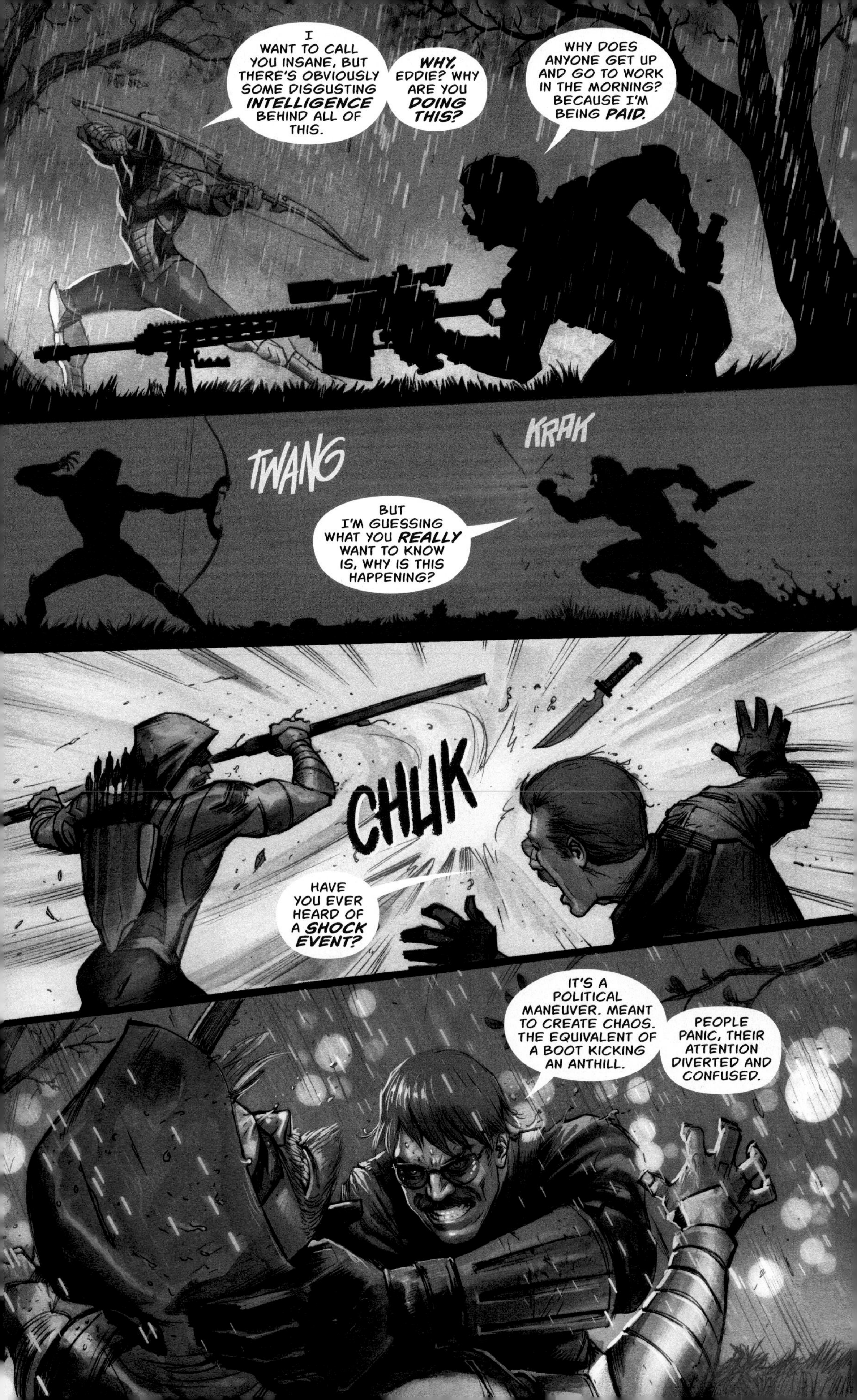
I WANT TO CALL YOU INSANE, BUT THERE'S OBVIOUSLY SOME DISGUSTING INTELLIGENCE BEHIND ALL OF THIS.
WHY, EDDIE? WHY ARE YOU DOING THIS?
WHY DOES ANYONE GET UP AND GO TO WORK IN THE MORNING? BECAUSE I'M BEING PAID.
TWANG
KRAK
BUT I'M GUESSING WHAT YOU REALLY WANT TO KNOW IS, WHY IS THIS HAPPENING?
CHUK
HAVE YOU EVER HEARD OF A SHOCK EVENT?
IT'S A POLITICAL MANEUVER. MEANT TO CREATE CHAOS. THE EQUIVALENT OF A BOOT KICKING AN ANTHILL.
PEOPLE PANIC, THEIR ATTENTION DIVERTED AND CONFUSED.

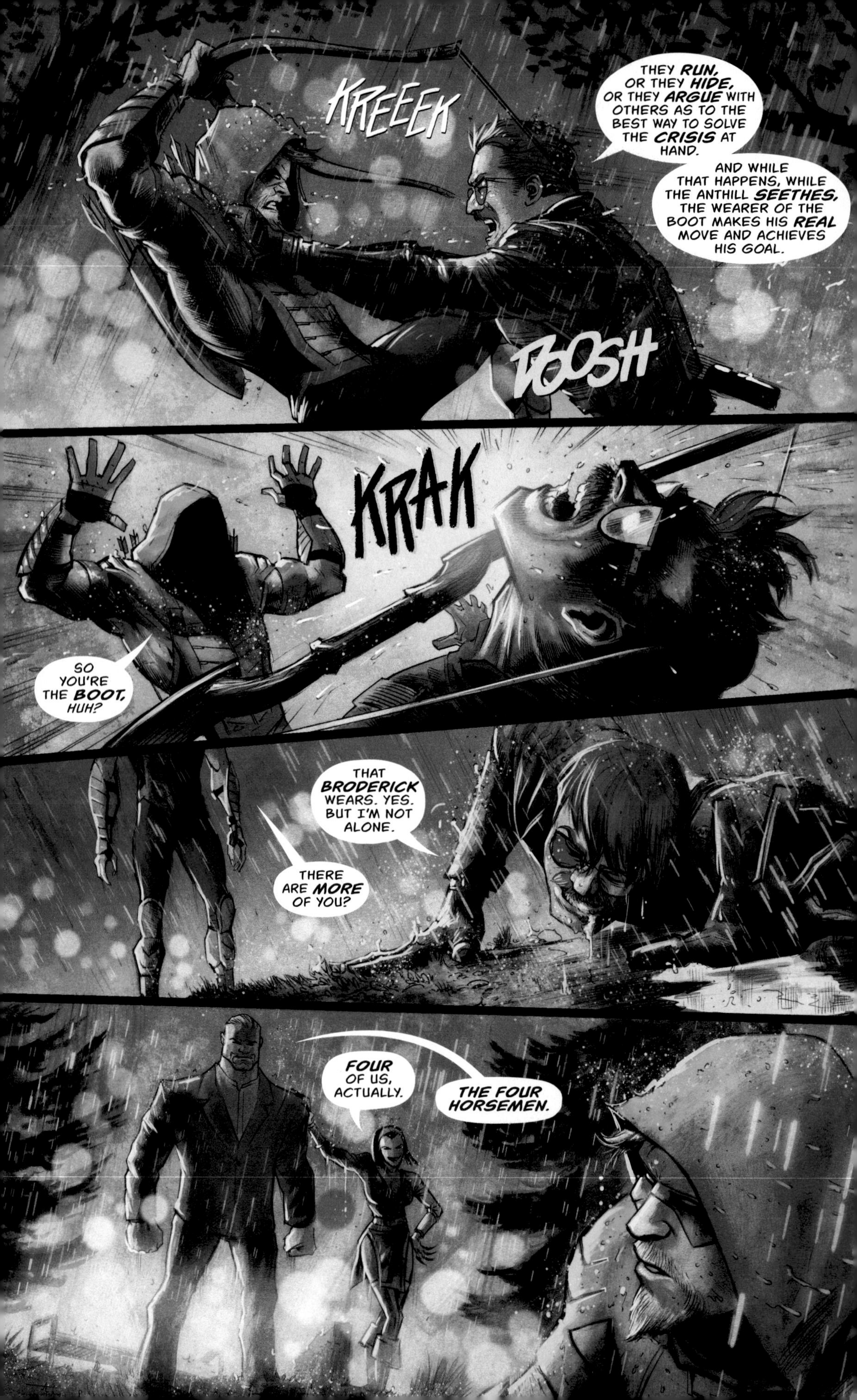
KREEEK
THEY RUN, OR THEY HIDE, OR THEY ARGUE WITH OTHERS AS TO THE BEST WAY TO SOLVE THE CRISIS AT HAND.
AND WHILE THAT HAPPENS, WHILE THE ANTHILL SEETHES, THE WEARER OF THE BOOT MAKES HIS REAL MOVE AND ACHIEVES HIS GOAL.
DOOSH
KRAK
SO YOU'RE THE BOOT, HUH?
THAT BRODERICK WEARS. YES. BUT I'M NOT ALONE.
THERE ARE MORE OF YOU?
FOUR OF US, ACTUALLY.
THE FOUR HORSEMEN.

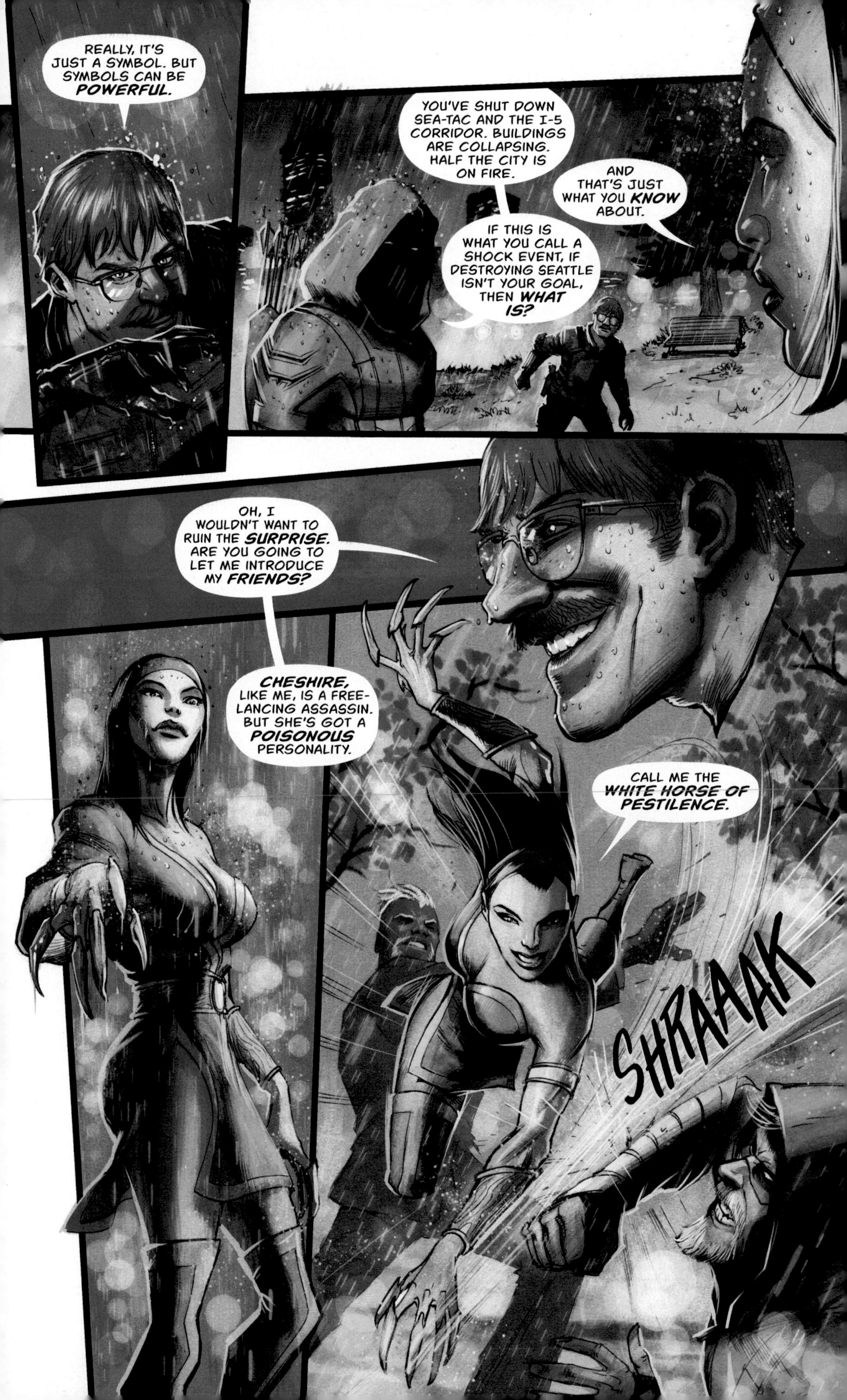
REALLY, IT'S JUST A SYMBOL. BUT SYMBOLS CAN BE POWERFUL.
YOU'VE SHUT DOWN SEA-TAC AND THE I-5 CORRIDOR. BUILDINGS ARE COLLAPSING. HALF THE CITY IS ON FIRE.
IF THIS IS WHAT YOU CALL A SHOCK EVENT, IF DESTROYING SEATTLE ISN'T YOUR GOAL, THEN WHAT IS?
AND THAT'S JUST WHAT YOU KNOW ABOUT.
OH, I WOULDN'T WANT TO RUIN THE SURPRISE. ARE YOU GOING TO LET ME INTRODUCE MY FRIENDS?
CHESHIRE, LIKE ME, IS A FREE-LANCING ASSASSIN. BUT SHE'S GOT A POISONOUS PERSONALITY.
CALL ME THE WHITE HORSE OF PESTILENCE.
SHRAAAK

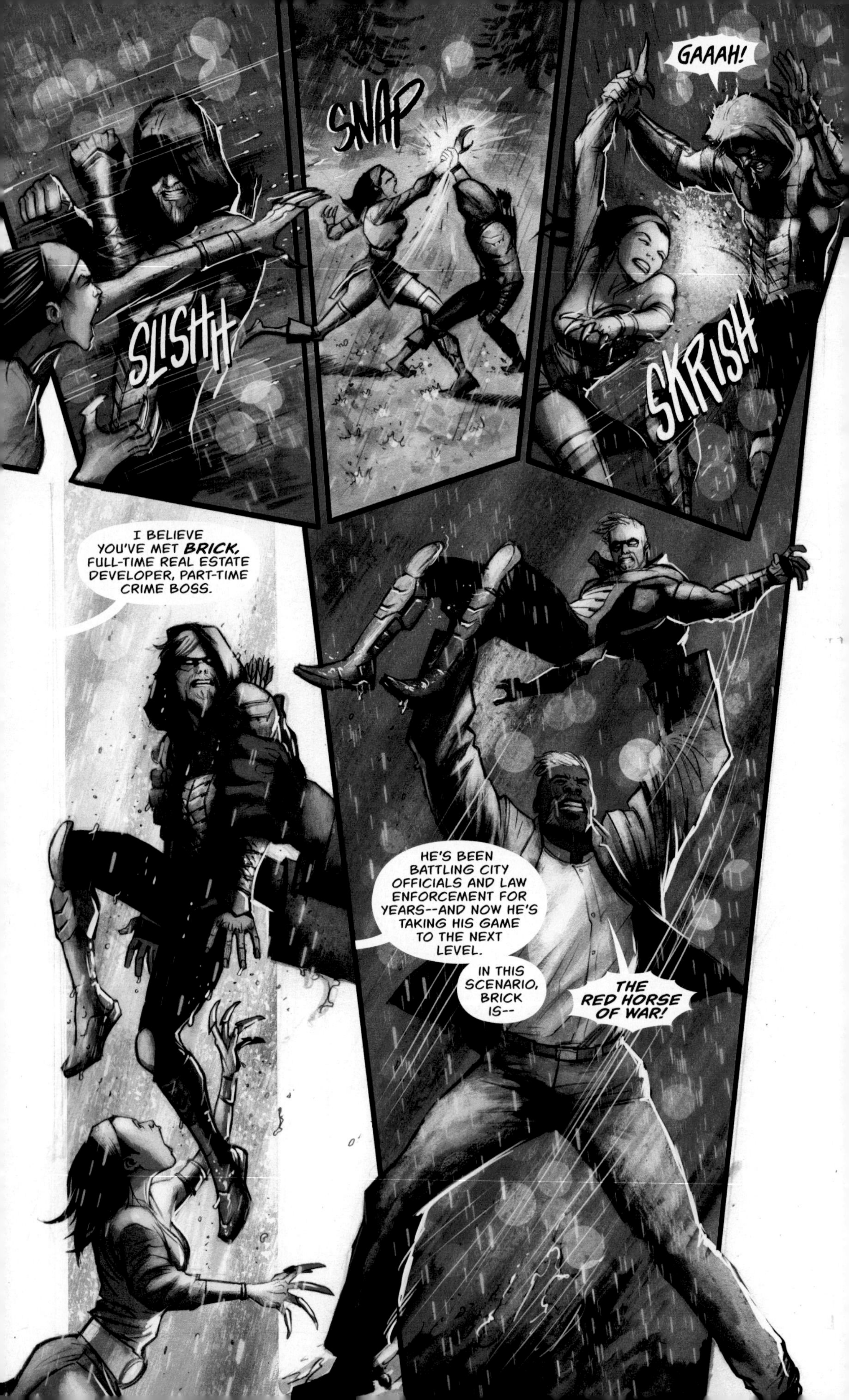
SLISHH
SNAP
GAAAH!
SKRISH
I BELIEVE YOU'VE MET **BRICK,** FULL-TIME REAL ESTATE DEVELOPER, PART-TIME CRIME BOSS.
HE'S BEEN BATTLING CITY OFFICIALS AND LAW ENFORCEMENT FOR YEARS--AND NOW HE'S TAKING HIS GAME TO THE NEXT LEVEL.
IN THIS SCENARIO, BRICK IS--
THE RED HORSE OF WAR!

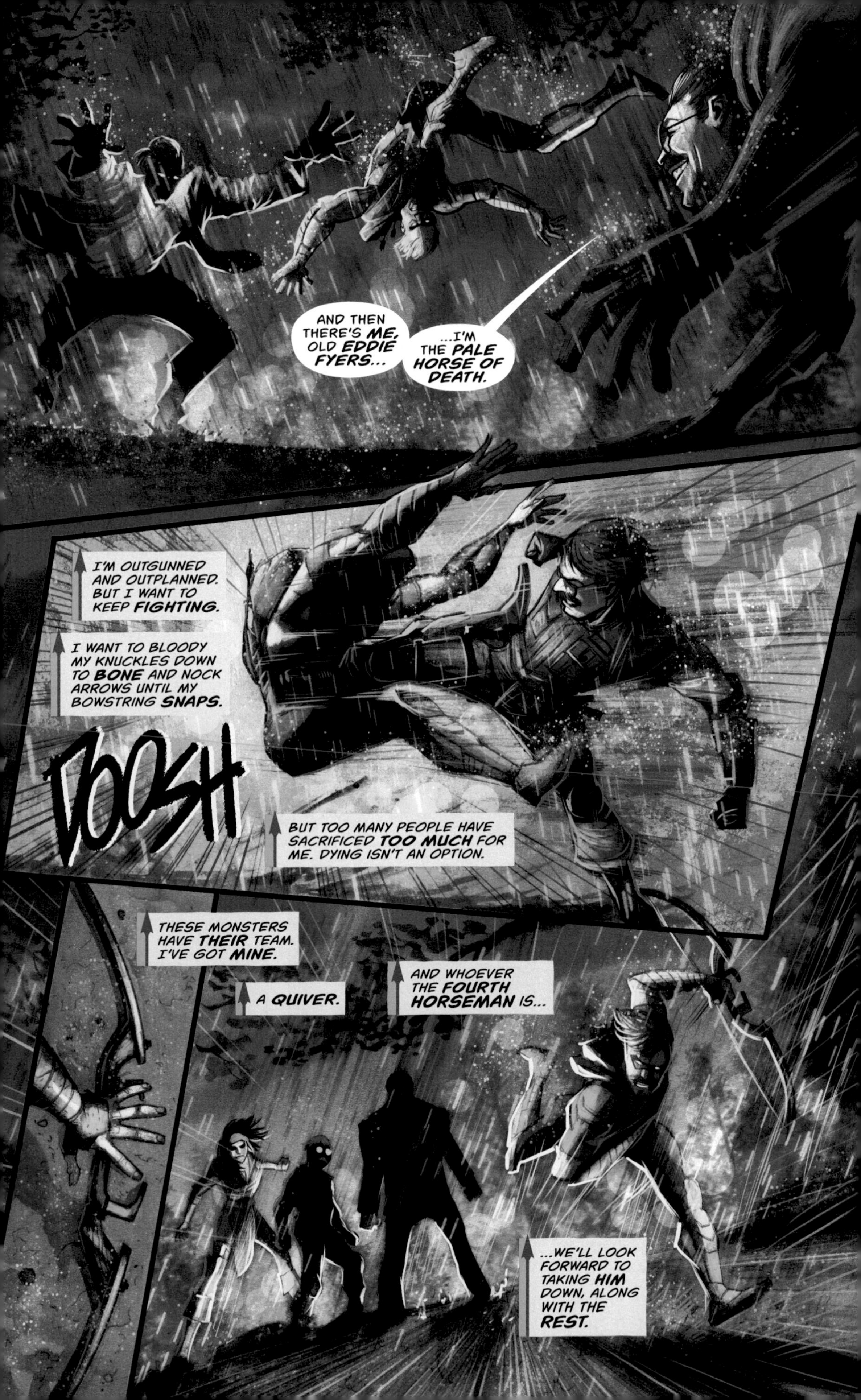

AND THEN THERE'S ME, OLD EDDIE FYERS...
...I'M THE PALE HORSE OF DEATH.
I'M OUTGUNNED AND OUTPLANNED. BUT I WANT TO KEEP FIGHTING.
I WANT TO BLOODY MY KNUCKLES DOWN TO BONE AND NOCK ARROWS UNTIL MY BOWSTRING SNAPS.
DOOSH
BUT TOO MANY PEOPLE HAVE SACRIFICED TOO MUCH FOR ME. DYING ISN'T AN OPTION.
THESE MONSTERS HAVE THEIR TEAM. I'VE GOT MINE.
A QUIVER.
AND WHOEVER THE FOURTH HORSEMAN IS...
...WE'LL LOOK FORWARD TO TAKING HIM DOWN, ALONG WITH THE REST.

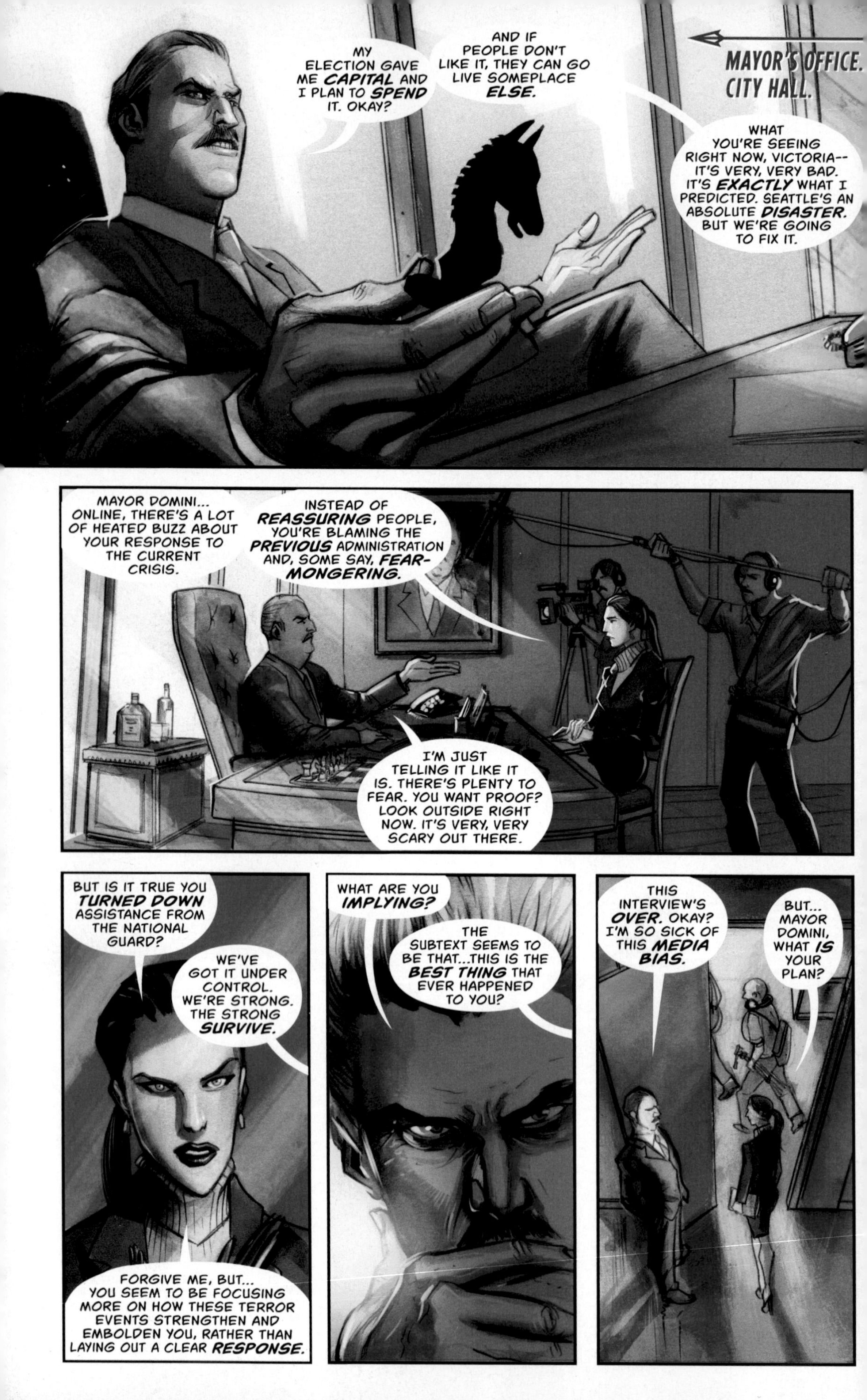
MAYOR'S OFFICE. CITY HALL.
MY ELECTION GAVE ME CAPITAL AND I PLAN TO SPEND IT. OKAY?
AND IF PEOPLE DON'T LIKE IT, THEY CAN GO LIVE SOMEPLACE ELSE.
WHAT YOU'RE SEEING RIGHT NOW, VICTORIA-- IT'S VERY, VERY BAD. IT'S EXACTLY WHAT I PREDICTED. SEATTLE'S AN ABSOLUTE DISASTER. BUT WE'RE GOING TO FIX IT.
MAYOR DOMINI... ONLINE, THERE'S A LOT OF HEATED BUZZ ABOUT YOUR RESPONSE TO THE CURRENT CRISIS.
INSTEAD OF REASSURING PEOPLE, YOU'RE BLAMING THE PREVIOUS ADMINISTRATION AND, SOME SAY, FEAR-MONGERING.
I'M JUST TELLING IT LIKE IT IS. THERE'S PLENTY TO FEAR. YOU WANT PROOF? LOOK OUTSIDE RIGHT NOW. IT'S VERY, VERY SCARY OUT THERE.
BUT IS IT TRUE YOU TURNED DOWN ASSISTANCE FROM THE NATIONAL GUARD?
WE'VE GOT IT UNDER CONTROL. WE'RE STRONG. THE STRONG SURVIVE.
FORGIVE ME, BUT... YOU SEEM TO BE FOCUSING MORE ON HOW THESE TERROR EVENTS STRENGTHEN AND EMBOLDEN YOU, RATHER THAN LAYING OUT A CLEAR RESPONSE.
WHAT ARE YOU IMPLYING?
THE SUBTEXT SEEMS TO BE THAT...THIS IS THE BEST THING THAT EVER HAPPENED TO YOU?
THIS INTERVIEW'S OVER. OKAY? I'M SO SICK OF THIS MEDIA BIAS.
BUT... MAYOR DOMINI, WHAT IS YOUR PLAN?

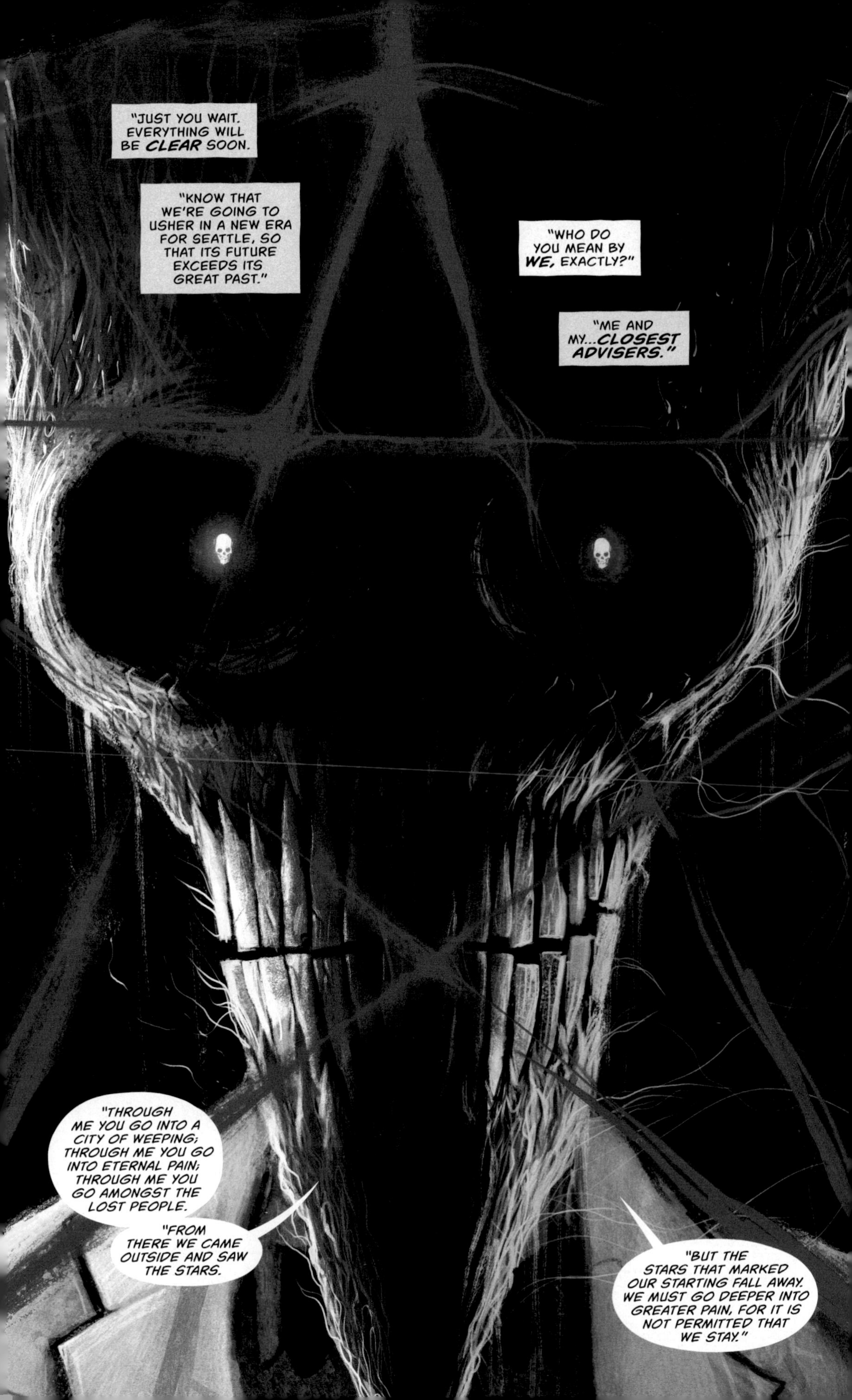
"JUST YOU WAIT. EVERYTHING WILL BE CLEAR SOON.
"KNOW THAT WE'RE GOING TO USHER IN A NEW ERA FOR SEATTLE, SO THAT ITS FUTURE EXCEEDS ITS GREAT PAST."
"WHO DO YOU MEAN BY WE, EXACTLY?"
"ME AND MY...CLOSEST ADVISERS."
"THROUGH ME YOU GO INTO A CITY OF WEEPING; THROUGH ME YOU GO INTO ETERNAL PAIN; THROUGH ME YOU GO AMONGST THE LOST PEOPLE.
"FROM THERE WE CAME OUTSIDE AND SAW THE STARS.
"BUT THE STARS THAT MARKED OUR STARTING FALL AWAY. WE MUST GO DEEPER INTO GREATER PAIN, FOR IT IS NOT PERMITTED THAT WE STAY."

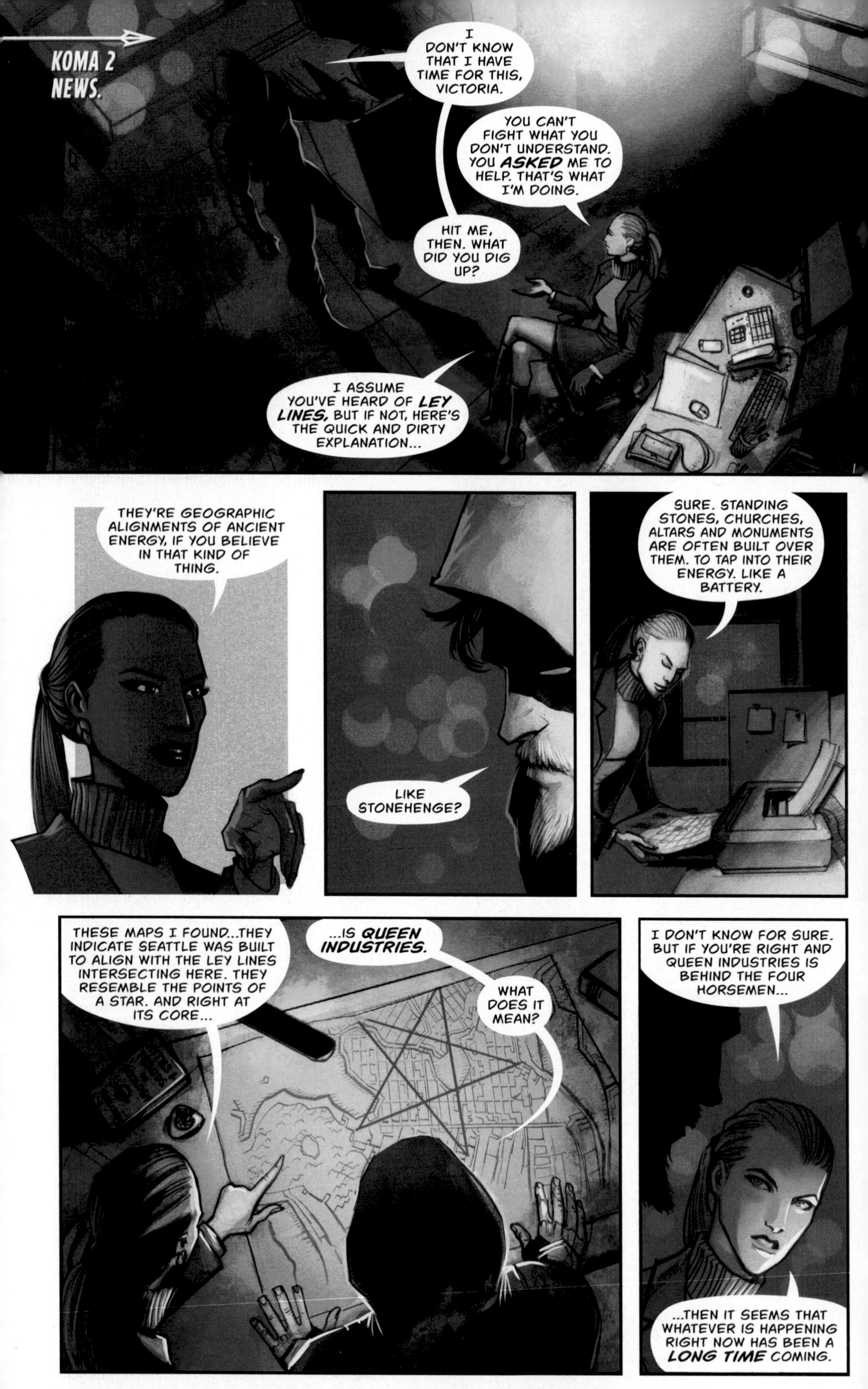
KOMA 2 NEWS.
I DON'T KNOW THAT I HAVE TIME FOR THIS, VICTORIA.
YOU CAN'T FIGHT WHAT YOU DON'T UNDERSTAND. YOU ASKED ME TO HELP. THAT'S WHAT I'M DOING.
HIT ME, THEN. WHAT DID YOU DIG UP?
I ASSUME YOU'VE HEARD OF LEY LINES, BUT IF NOT, HERE'S THE QUICK AND DIRTY EXPLANATION...
THEY'RE GEOGRAPHIC ALIGNMENTS OF ANCIENT ENERGY, IF YOU BELIEVE IN THAT KIND OF THING.
LIKE STONEHENGE?
SURE. STANDING STONES, CHURCHES, ALTARS AND MONUMENTS ARE OFTEN BUILT OVER THEM. TO TAP INTO THEIR ENERGY. LIKE A BATTERY.
THESE MAPS I FOUND...THEY INDICATE SEATTLE WAS BUILT TO ALIGN WITH THE LEY LINES INTERSECTING HERE. THEY RESEMBLE THE POINTS OF A STAR. AND RIGHT AT ITS CORE...
...IS QUEEN INDUSTRIES.
WHAT DOES IT MEAN?
I DON'T KNOW FOR SURE. BUT IF YOU'RE RIGHT AND QUEEN INDUSTRIES IS BEHIND THE FOUR HORSEMEN...
...THEN IT SEEMS THAT WHATEVER IS HAPPENING RIGHT NOW HAS BEEN A LONG TIME COMING.

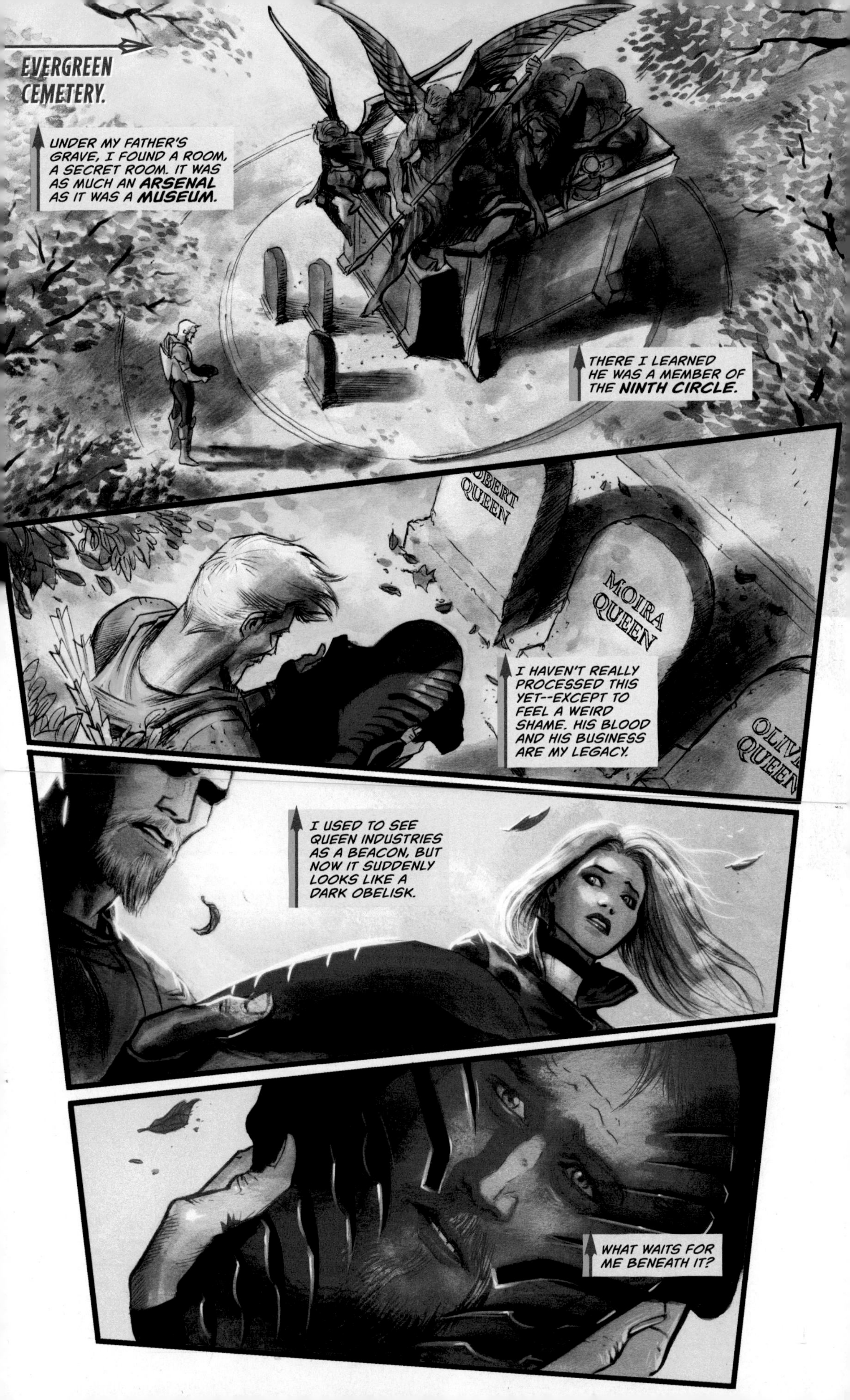
EVERGREEN CEMETERY.
UNDER MY FATHER'S GRAVE, I FOUND A ROOM, A SECRET ROOM. IT WAS AS MUCH AN ARSENAL AS IT WAS A MUSEUM.
THERE I LEARNED HE WAS A MEMBER OF THE NINTH CIRCLE.
MOIRA QUEEN
I HAVEN'T REALLY PROCESSED THIS YET--EXCEPT TO FEEL A WEIRD SHAME. HIS BLOOD AND HIS BUSINESS ARE MY LEGACY.
I USED TO SEE QUEEN INDUSTRIES AS A BEACON, BUT NOW IT SUDDENLY LOOKS LIKE A DARK OBELISK.
WHAT WAITS FOR ME BENEATH IT?

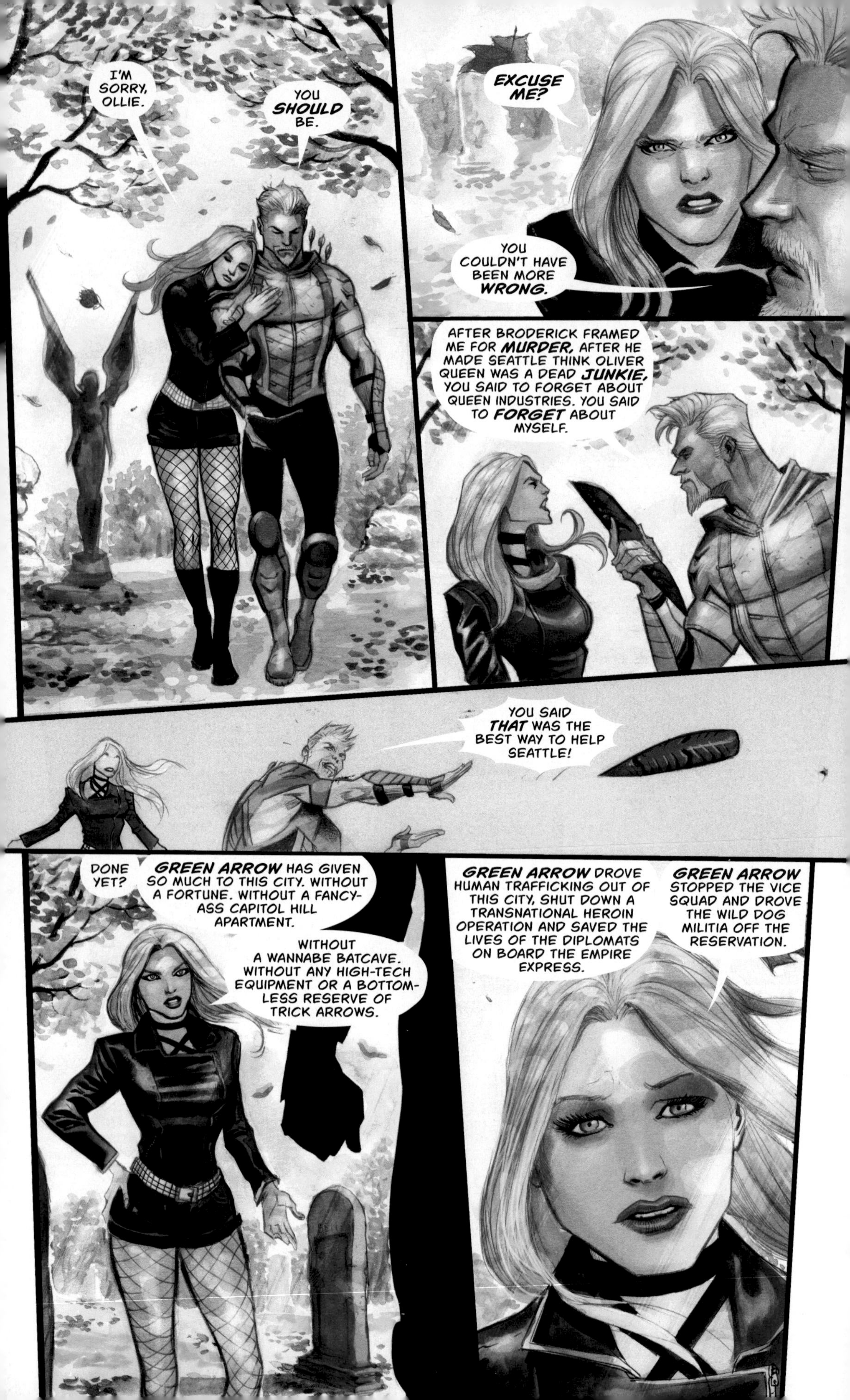
I'M SORRY, OLLIE.
YOU SHOULD BE.
EXCUSE ME?
YOU COULDN'T HAVE BEEN MORE WRONG.
AFTER BRODERICK FRAMED ME FOR MURDER, AFTER HE MADE SEATTLE THINK OLIVER QUEEN WAS A DEAD JUNKIE, YOU SAID TO FORGET ABOUT QUEEN INDUSTRIES. YOU SAID TO FORGET ABOUT MYSELF.
YOU SAID THAT WAS THE BEST WAY TO HELP SEATTLE!
DONE YET?
GREEN ARROW HAS GIVEN SO MUCH TO THIS CITY. WITHOUT A FORTUNE. WITHOUT A FANCY-ASS CAPITOL HILL APARTMENT.
WITHOUT A WANNABE BATCAVE. WITHOUT ANY HIGH-TECH EQUIPMENT OR A BOTTOMLESS RESERVE OF TRICK ARROWS.
GREEN ARROW DROVE HUMAN TRAFFICKING OUT OF THIS CITY, SHUT DOWN A TRANSNATIONAL HEROIN OPERATION AND SAVED THE LIVES OF THE DIPLOMATS ON BOARD THE EMPIRE EXPRESS.
GREEN ARROW STOPPED THE VICE SQUAD AND DROVE THE WILD DOG MILITIA OFF THE RESERVATION.

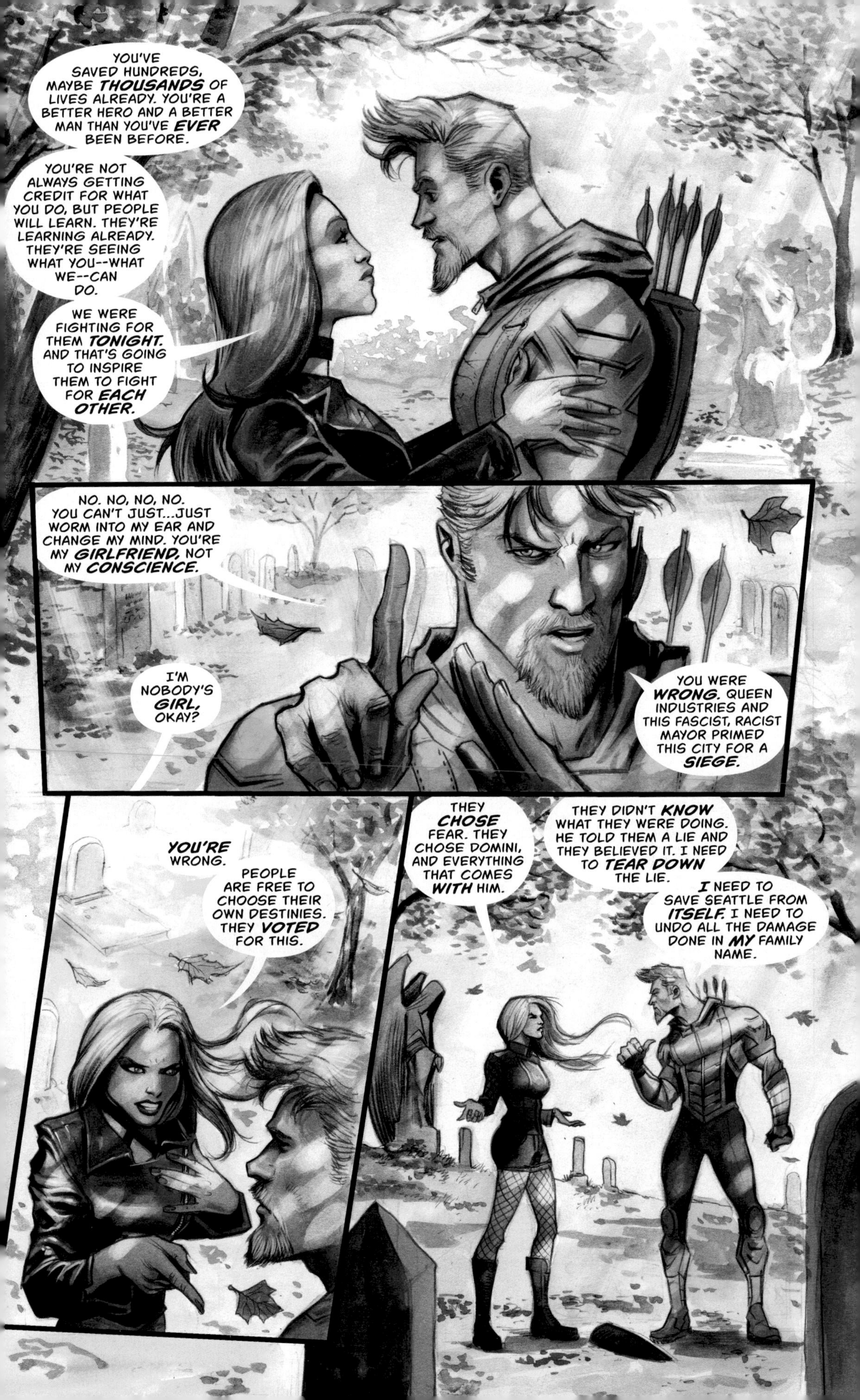
YOU'VE SAVED HUNDREDS, MAYBE THOUSANDS OF LIVES ALREADY. YOU'RE A BETTER HERO AND A BETTER MAN THAN YOU'VE EVER BEEN BEFORE.
YOU'RE NOT ALWAYS GETTING CREDIT FOR WHAT YOU DO, BUT PEOPLE WILL LEARN. THEY'RE LEARNING ALREADY. THEY'RE SEEING WHAT YOU--WHAT WE--CAN DO.
WE WERE FIGHTING FOR THEM TONIGHT. AND THAT'S GOING TO INSPIRE THEM TO FIGHT FOR EACH OTHER.
NO. NO, NO, NO. YOU CAN'T JUST...JUST WORM INTO MY EAR AND CHANGE MY MIND. YOU'RE MY GIRLFRIEND, NOT MY CONSCIENCE.
I'M NOBODY'S GIRL, OKAY?
YOU WERE WRONG. QUEEN INDUSTRIES AND THIS FASCIST, RACIST MAYOR PRIMED THIS CITY FOR A SIEGE.
YOU'RE WRONG.
PEOPLE ARE FREE TO CHOOSE THEIR OWN DESTINIES. THEY VOTED FOR THIS.
THEY CHOSE FEAR. THEY CHOSE DOMINI, AND EVERYTHING THAT COMES WITH HIM.
THEY DIDN'T KNOW WHAT THEY WERE DOING. HE TOLD THEM A LIE AND THEY BELIEVED IT. I NEED TO TEAR DOWN THE LIE.
I NEED TO SAVE SEATTLE FROM ITSELF. I NEED TO UNDO ALL THE DAMAGE DONE IN MY FAMILY NAME.

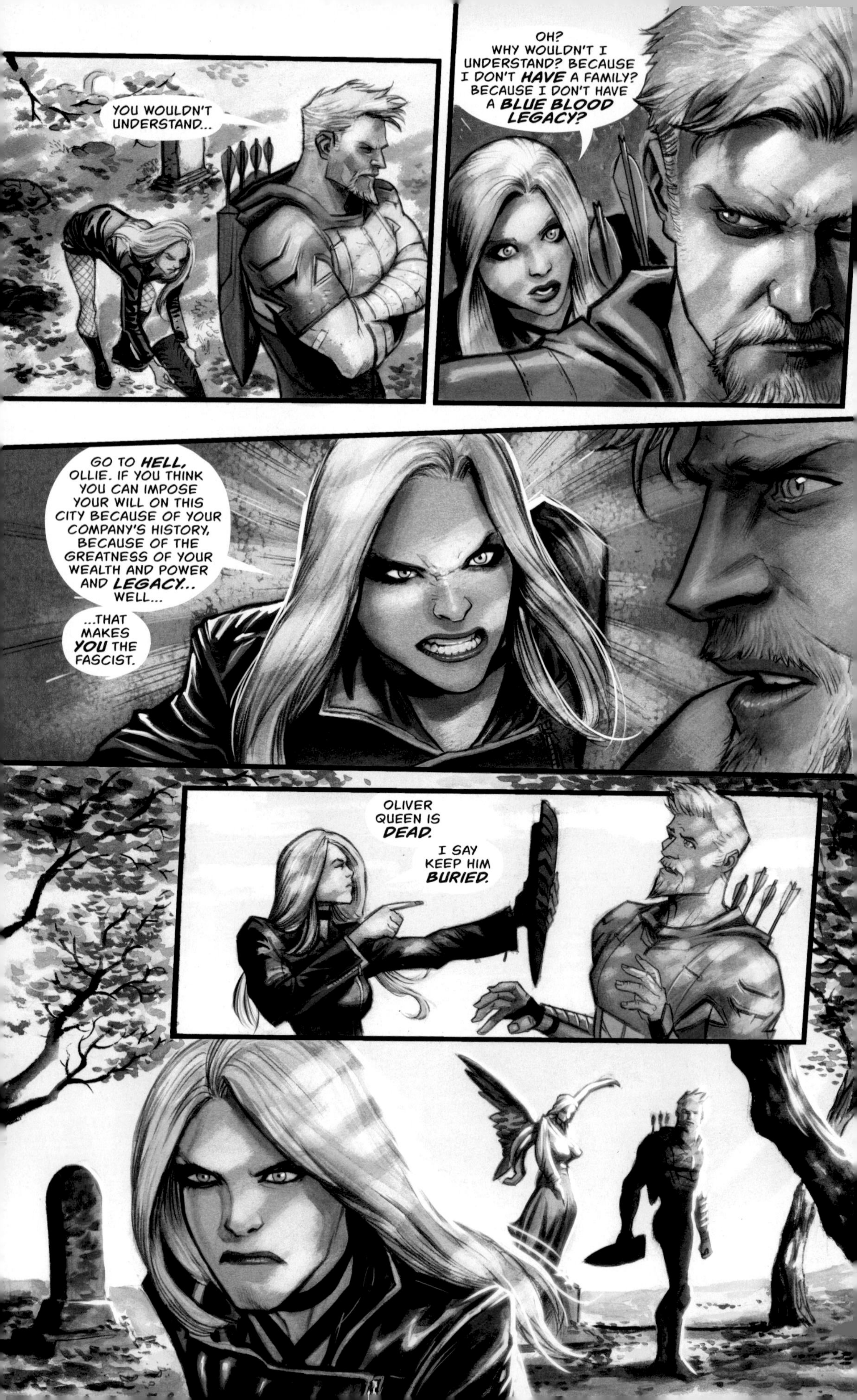
YOU WOULDN'T UNDERSTAND...
OH? WHY WOULDN'T I UNDERSTAND? BECAUSE I DON'T **HAVE** A FAMILY? BECAUSE I DON'T HAVE A **BLUE BLOOD LEGACY?**
GO TO **HELL,** OLLIE. IF YOU THINK YOU CAN IMPOSE YOUR WILL ON THIS CITY BECAUSE OF YOUR COMPANY'S HISTORY, BECAUSE OF THE GREATNESS OF YOUR WEALTH AND POWER AND **LEGACY...** WELL...
...THAT MAKES **YOU** THE FASCIST.
OLIVER QUEEN IS **DEAD.**
I SAY KEEP HIM **BURIED.**

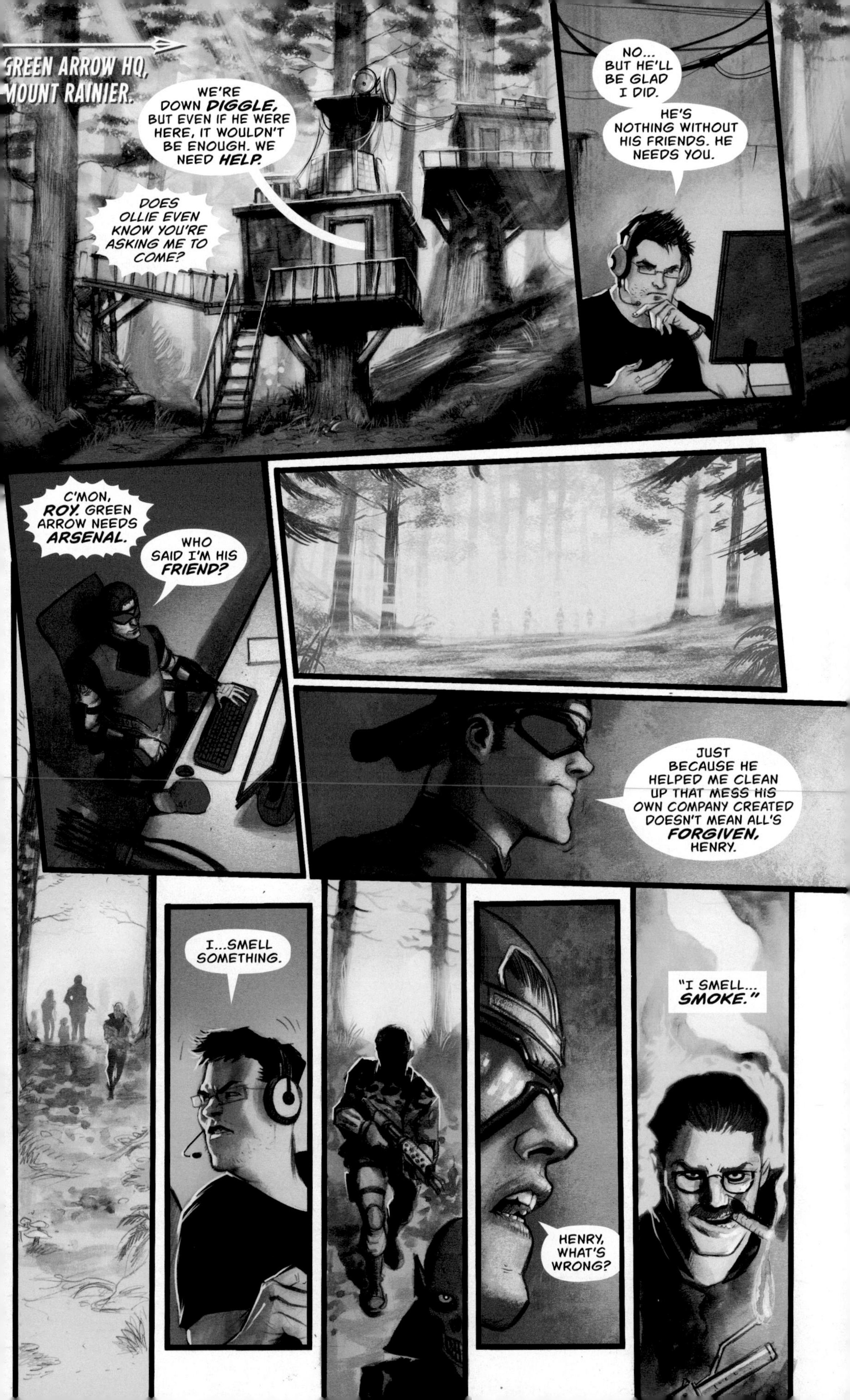
GREEN ARROW HQ, MOUNT RAINIER.
WE'RE DOWN DIGGLE, BUT EVEN IF HE WERE HERE, IT WOULDN'T BE ENOUGH. WE NEED HELP.
DOES OLLIE EVEN KNOW YOU'RE ASKING ME TO COME?
NO... BUT HE'LL BE GLAD I DID.
HE'S NOTHING WITHOUT HIS FRIENDS. HE NEEDS YOU.
C'MON, ROY. GREEN ARROW NEEDS ARSENAL.
WHO SAID I'M HIS FRIEND?
JUST BECAUSE HE HELPED ME CLEAN UP THAT MESS HIS OWN COMPANY CREATED DOESN'T MEAN ALL'S FORGIVEN, HENRY.
I...SMELL SOMETHING.
HENRY, WHAT'S WRONG?
"I SMELL... SMOKE."

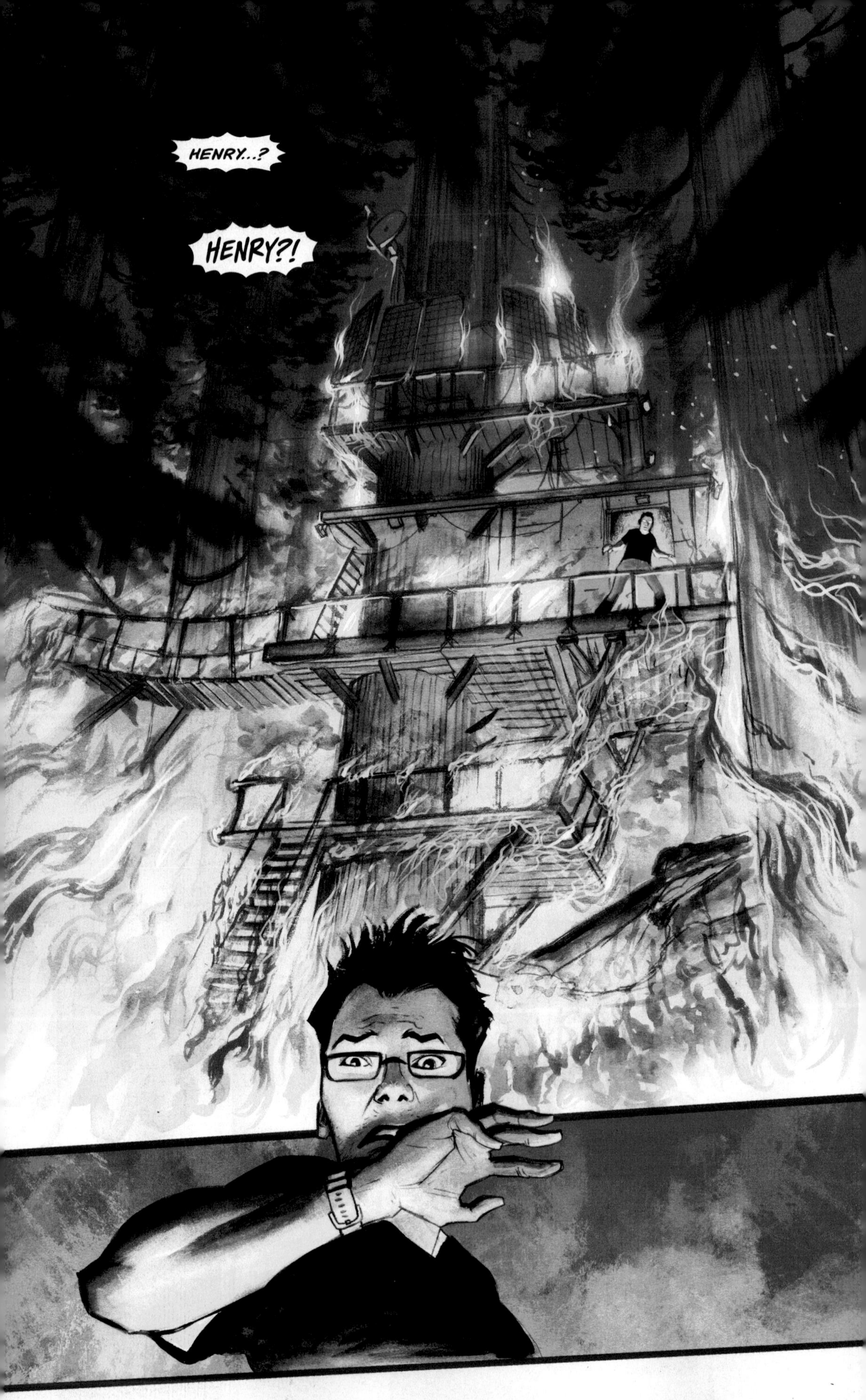
HENRY...?
HENRY?!

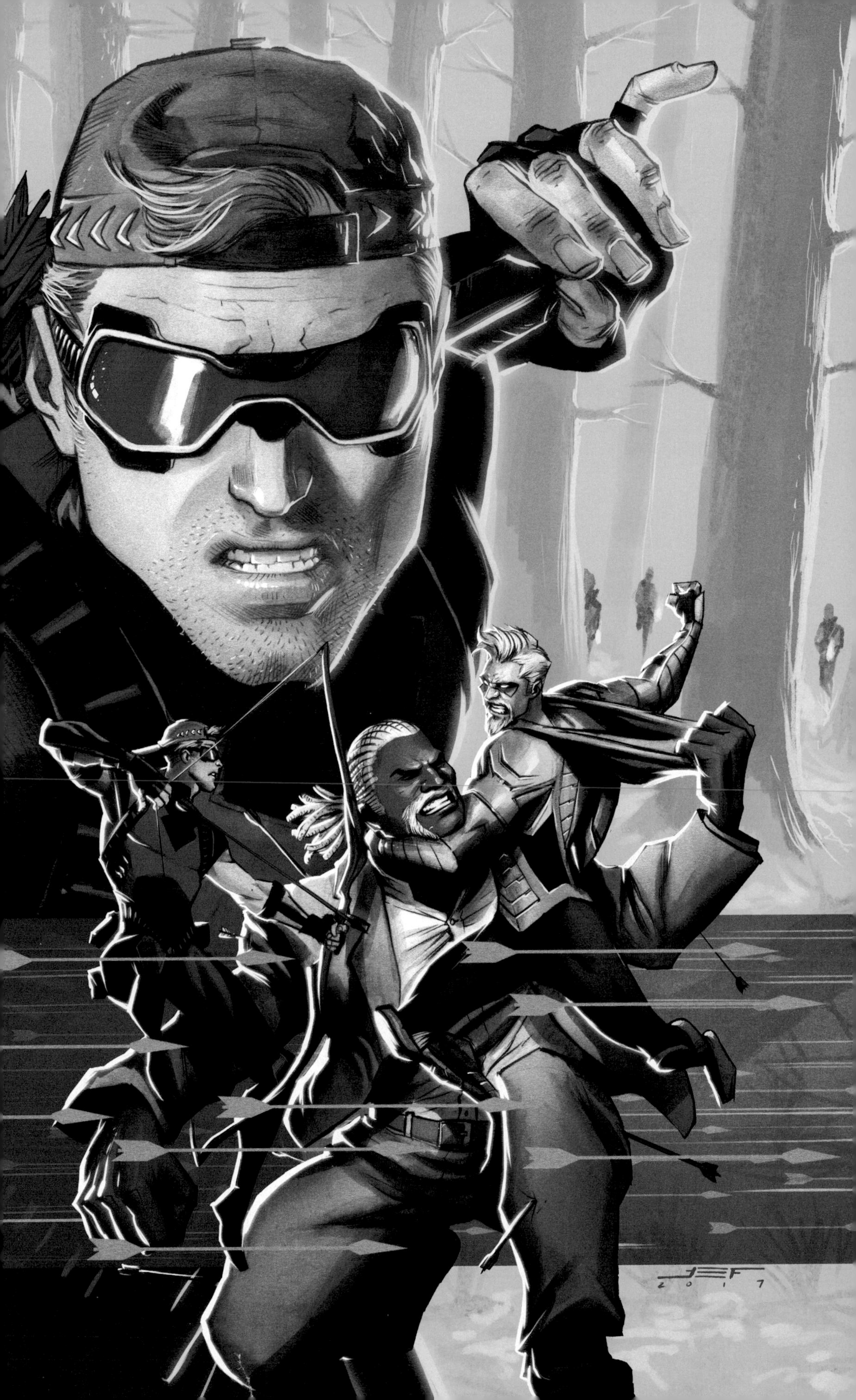
JEF
2017

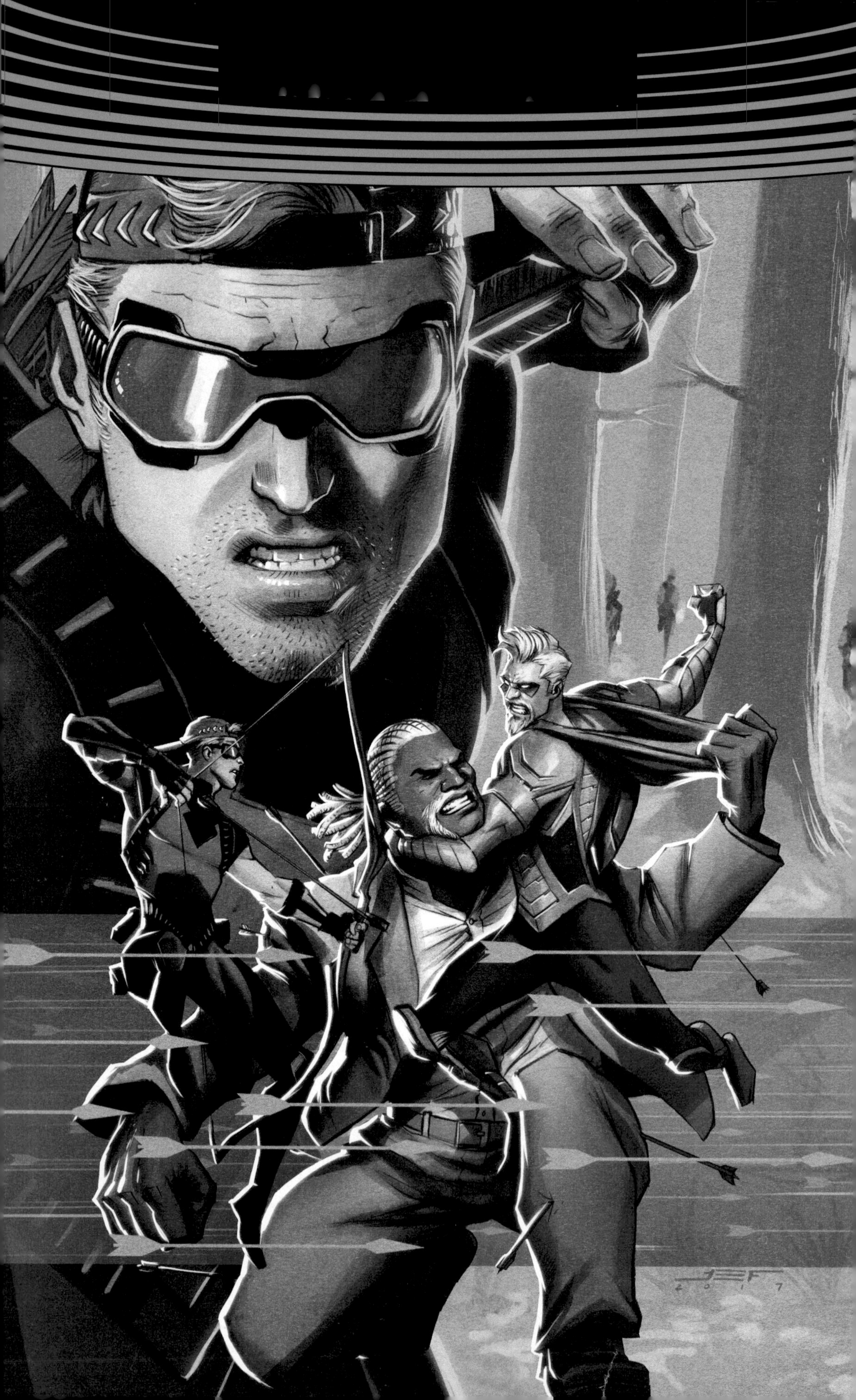

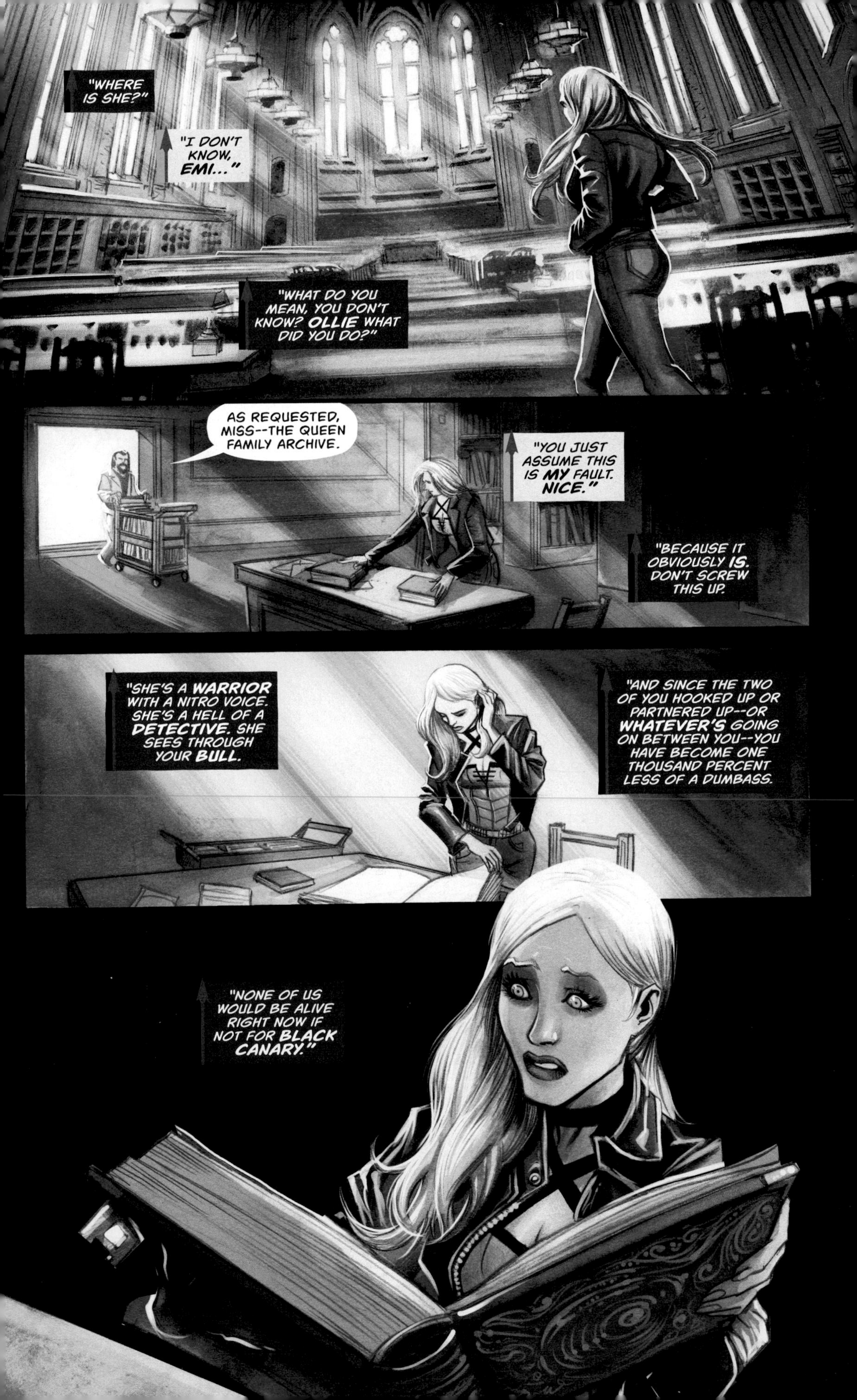
"WHERE IS SHE?"
"I DON'T KNOW, EMI..."
"WHAT DO YOU MEAN, YOU DON'T KNOW? OLLIE WHAT DID YOU DO?"
AS REQUESTED, MISS--THE QUEEN FAMILY ARCHIVE.
"YOU JUST ASSUME THIS IS MY FAULT. NICE."
"BECAUSE IT OBVIOUSLY IS. DON'T SCREW THIS UP.
"SHE'S A WARRIOR WITH A NITRO VOICE. SHE'S A HELL OF A DETECTIVE. SHE SEES THROUGH YOUR BULL.
"AND SINCE THE TWO OF YOU HOOKED UP OR PARTNERED UP--OR WHATEVER'S GOING ON BETWEEN YOU--YOU HAVE BECOME ONE THOUSAND PERCENT LESS OF A DUMBASS.
"NONE OF US WOULD BE ALIVE RIGHT NOW IF NOT FOR BLACK CANARY."

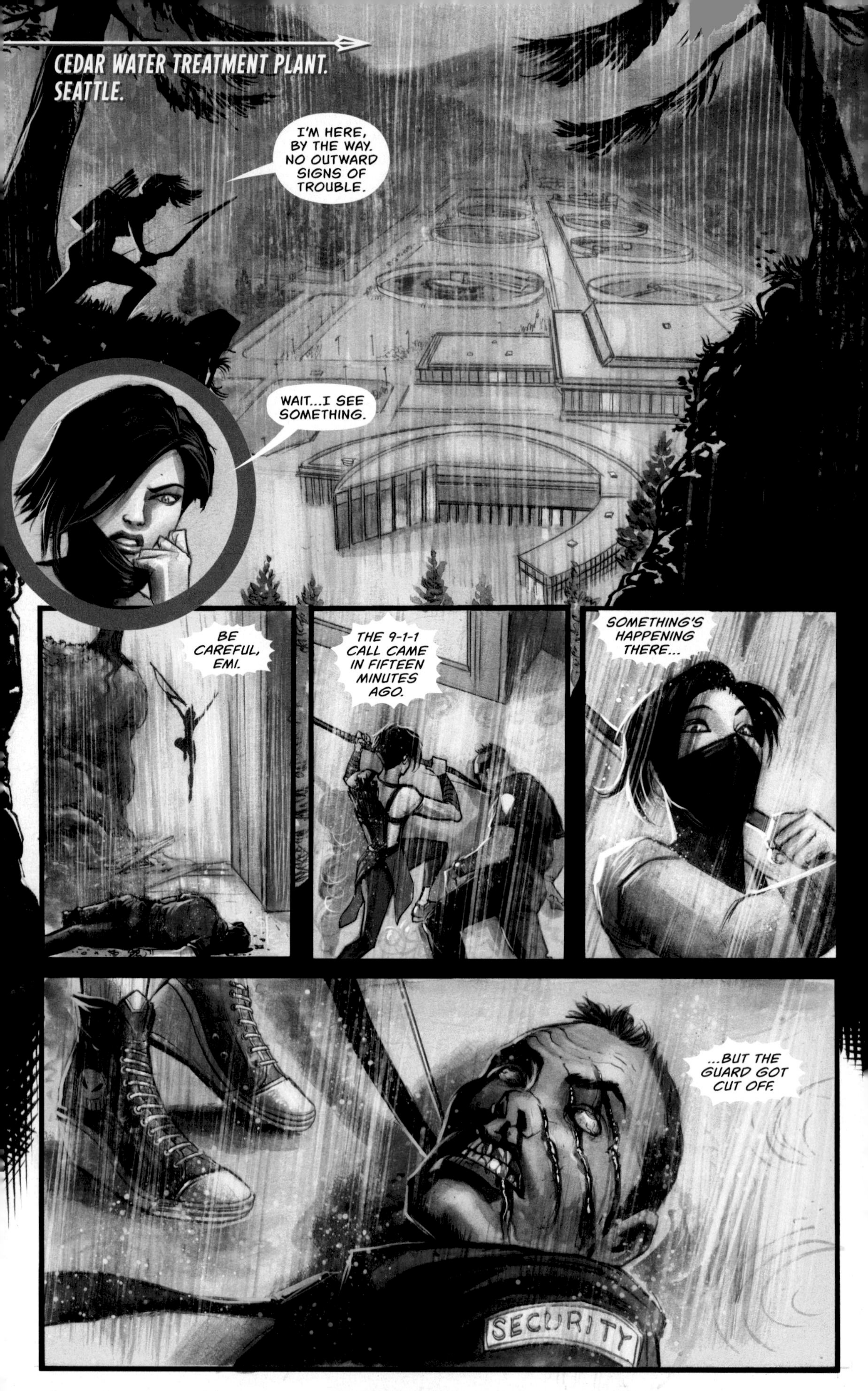
CEDAR WATER TREATMENT PLANT.
SEATTLE.
I'M HERE, BY THE WAY. NO OUTWARD SIGNS OF TROUBLE.
WAIT...I SEE SOMETHING.
BE CAREFUL, EMI.
THE 9-1-1 CALL CAME IN FIFTEEN MINUTES AGO.
SOMETHING'S HAPPENING THERE...
...BUT THE GUARD GOT CUT OFF.
SECURITY

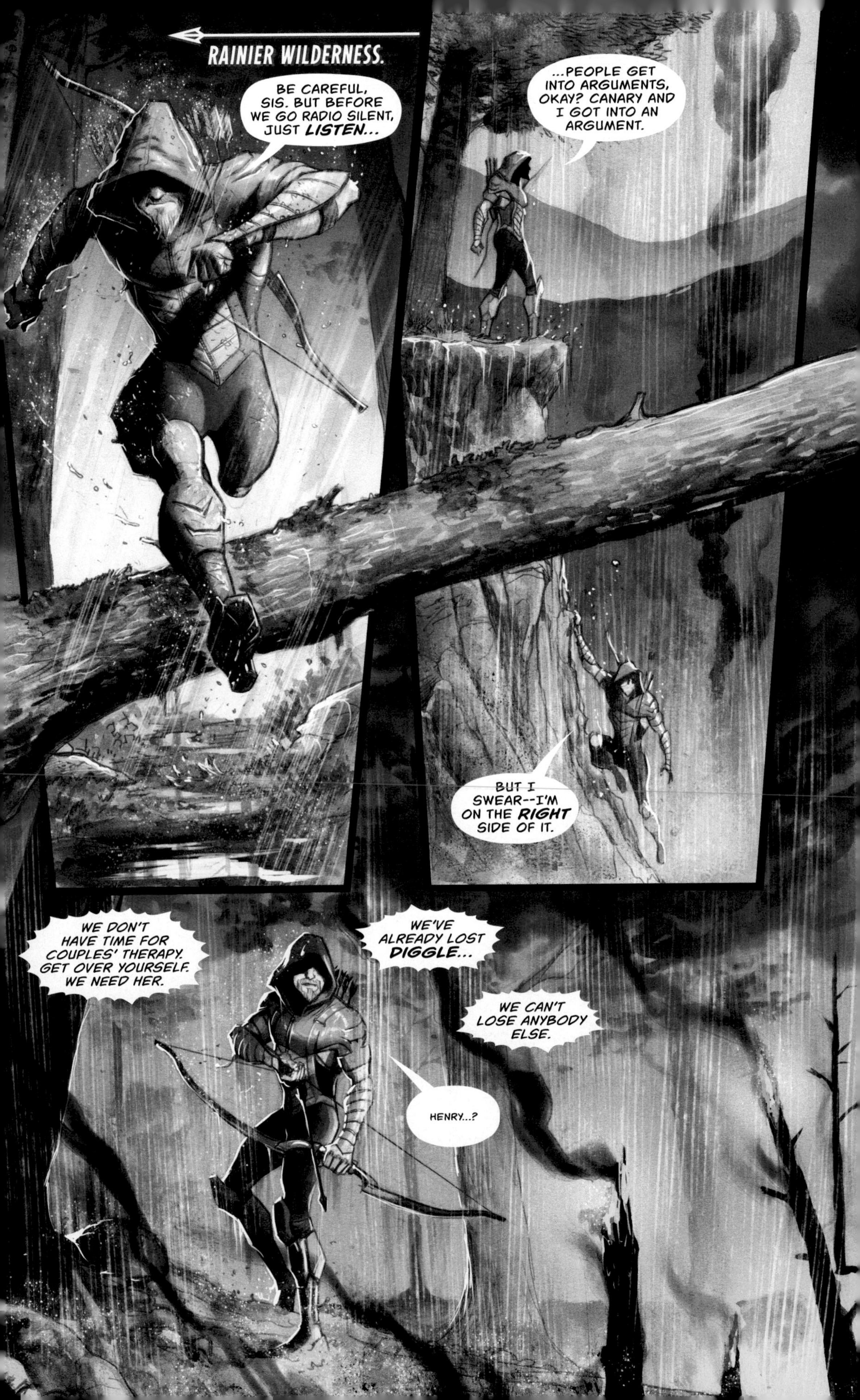
RAINIER WILDERNESS.
BE CAREFUL, SIS. BUT BEFORE WE GO RADIO SILENT, JUST LISTEN...
...PEOPLE GET INTO ARGUMENTS, OKAY? CANARY AND I GOT INTO AN ARGUMENT.
BUT I SWEAR--I'M ON THE RIGHT SIDE OF IT.
WE DON'T HAVE TIME FOR COUPLES' THERAPY. GET OVER YOURSELF. WE NEED HER.
WE'VE ALREADY LOST DIGGLE...
WE CAN'T LOSE ANYBODY ELSE.
HENRY...?

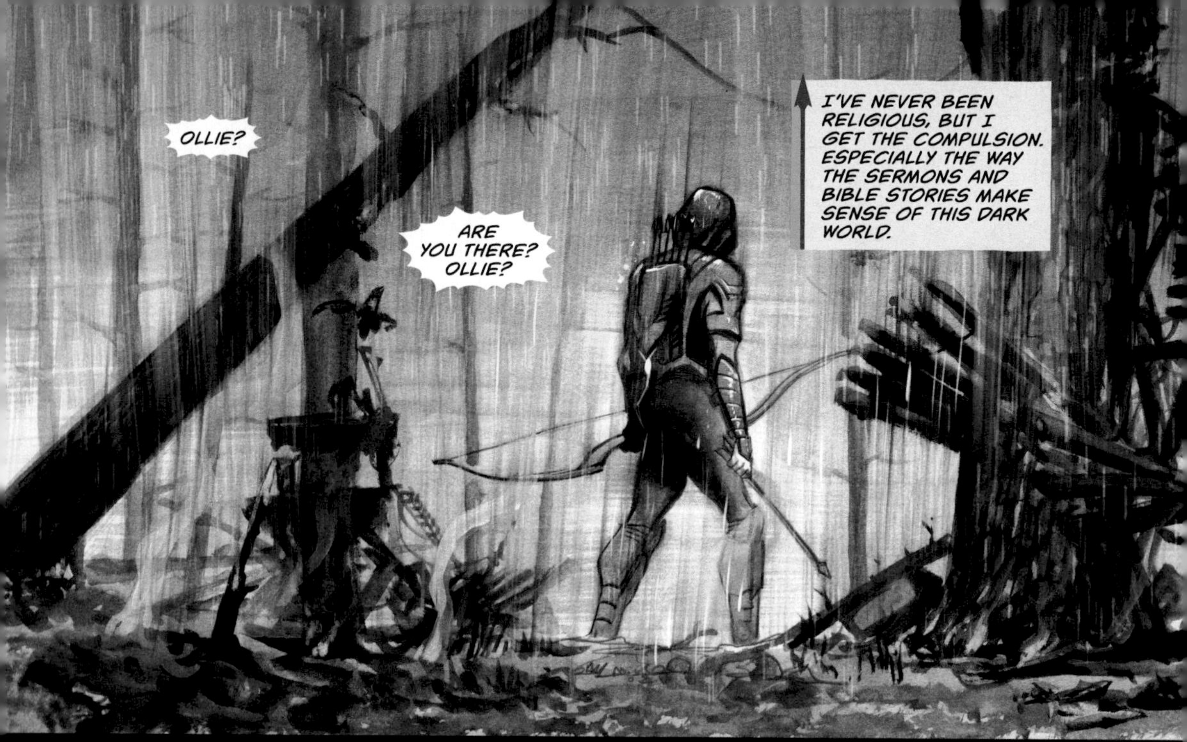
I'VE NEVER BEEN RELIGIOUS, BUT I GET THE COMPULSION. ESPECIALLY THE WAY THE SERMONS AND BIBLE STORIES MAKE SENSE OF THIS DARK WORLD.
OLLIE?
ARE YOU THERE? OLLIE?

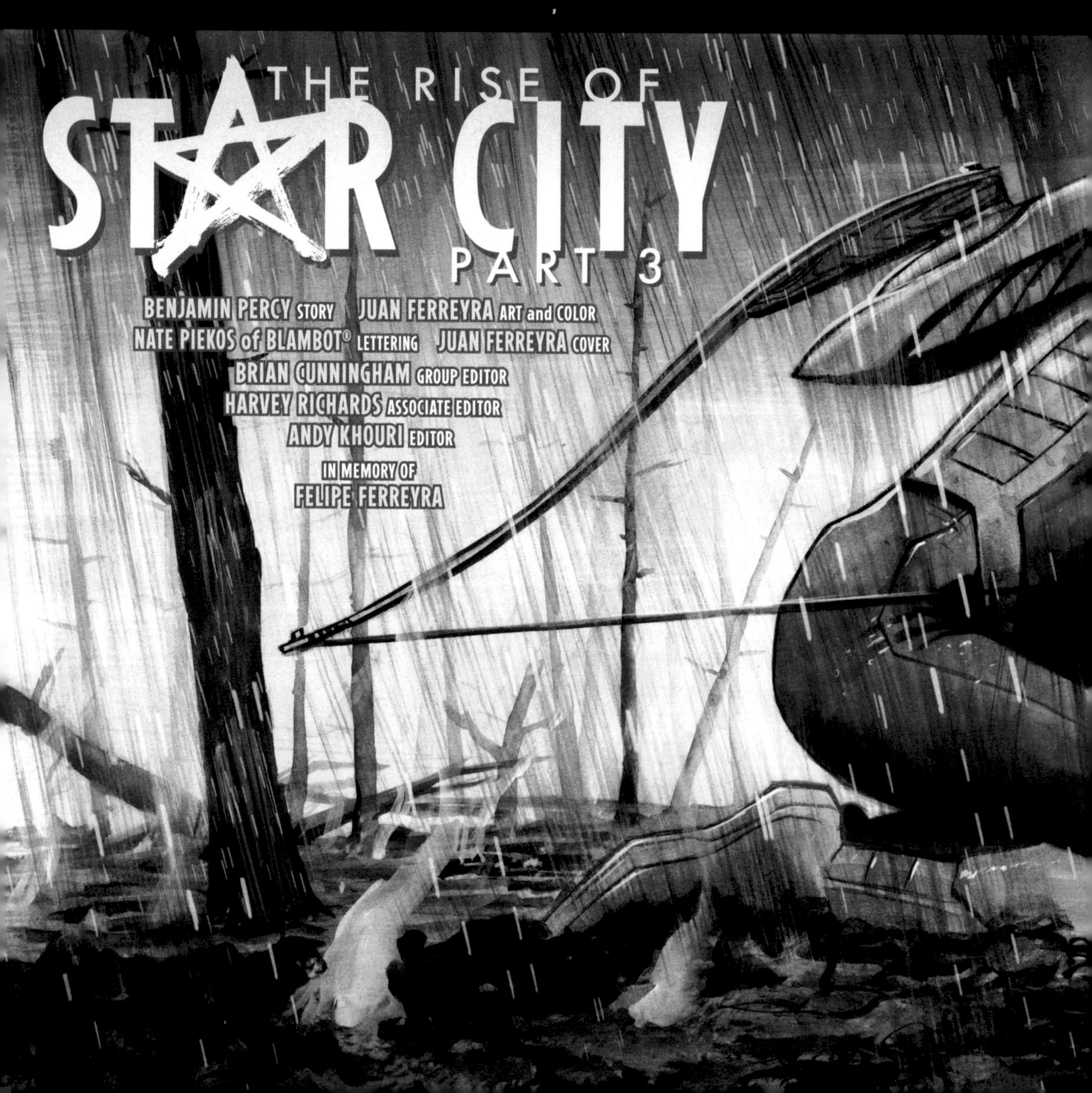
THE RISE OF
STAR CITY
PART 3
BENJAMIN PERCY STORY JUAN FERREYRA ART and COLOR
NATE PIEKOS of BLAMBOT® LETTERING JUAN FERREYRA COVER
BRIAN CUNNINGHAM GROUP EDITOR
HARVEY RICHARDS ASSOCIATE EDITOR
ANDY KHOURI EDITOR
IN MEMORY OF
FELIPE FERREYRA

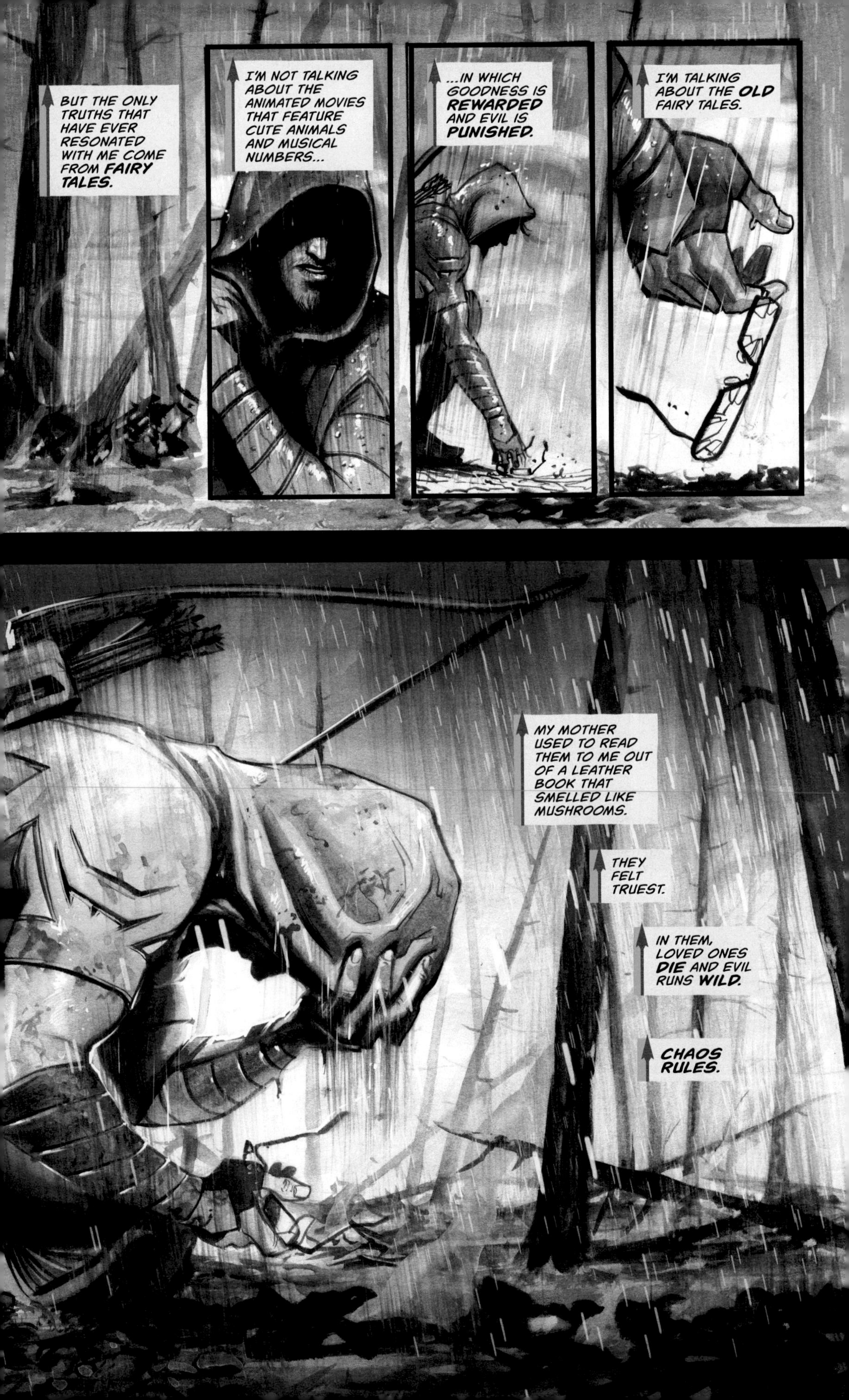
BUT THE ONLY TRUTHS THAT HAVE EVER RESONATED WITH ME COME FROM FAIRY TALES.
I'M NOT TALKING ABOUT THE ANIMATED MOVIES THAT FEATURE CUTE ANIMALS AND MUSICAL NUMBERS...
...IN WHICH GOODNESS IS REWARDED AND EVIL IS PUNISHED.
I'M TALKING ABOUT THE OLD FAIRY TALES.
MY MOTHER USED TO READ THEM TO ME OUT OF A LEATHER BOOK THAT SMELLED LIKE MUSHROOMS.
THEY FELT TRUEST.
IN THEM, LOVED ONES DIE AND EVIL RUNS WILD.
CHAOS RULES.

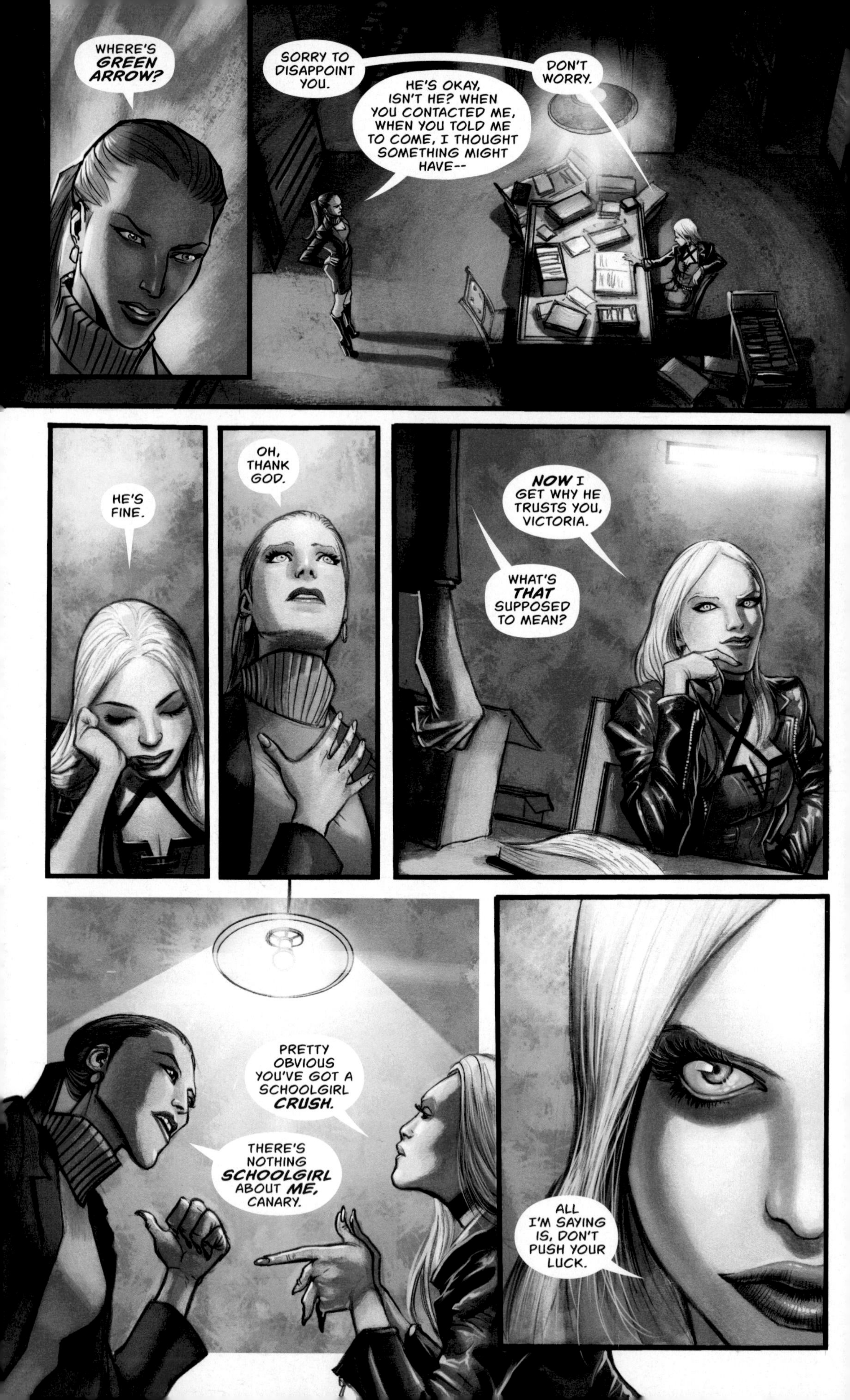
WHERE'S GREEN ARROW?
SORRY TO DISAPPOINT YOU.
DON'T WORRY.
HE'S OKAY, ISN'T HE? WHEN YOU CONTACTED ME, WHEN YOU TOLD ME TO COME, I THOUGHT SOMETHING MIGHT HAVE--
HE'S FINE.
OH, THANK GOD.
NOW I GET WHY HE TRUSTS YOU, VICTORIA.
WHAT'S THAT SUPPOSED TO MEAN?
PRETTY OBVIOUS YOU'VE GOT A SCHOOLGIRL CRUSH.
THERE'S NOTHING SCHOOLGIRL ABOUT ME, CANARY.
ALL I'M SAYING IS, DON'T PUSH YOUR LUCK.

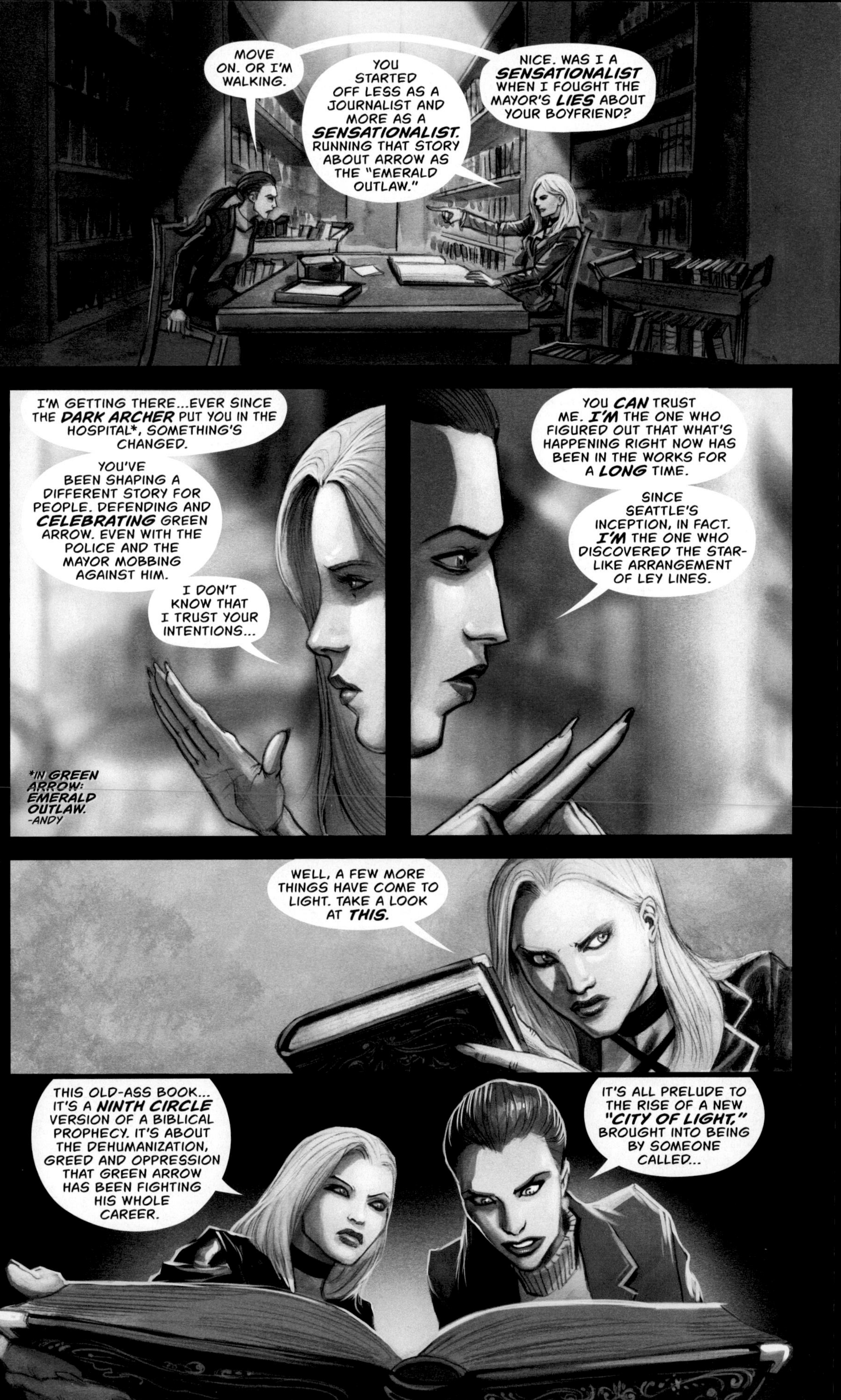
MOVE ON. OR I'M WALKING.
YOU STARTED OFF LESS AS A JOURNALIST AND MORE AS A SENSATIONALIST. RUNNING THAT STORY ABOUT ARROW AS THE "EMERALD OUTLAW."
NICE. WAS I A SENSATIONALIST WHEN I FOUGHT THE MAYOR'S LIES ABOUT YOUR BOYFRIEND?
I'M GETTING THERE...EVER SINCE THE DARK ARCHER PUT YOU IN THE HOSPITAL*, SOMETHING'S CHANGED.
YOU'VE BEEN SHAPING A DIFFERENT STORY FOR PEOPLE. DEFENDING AND CELEBRATING GREEN ARROW. EVEN WITH THE POLICE AND THE MAYOR MOBBING AGAINST HIM.
I DON'T KNOW THAT I TRUST YOUR INTENTIONS...
*IN GREEN ARROW: EMERALD OUTLAW. -ANDY
YOU CAN TRUST ME. I'M THE ONE WHO FIGURED OUT THAT WHAT'S HAPPENING RIGHT NOW HAS BEEN IN THE WORKS FOR A LONG TIME.
SINCE SEATTLE'S INCEPTION, IN FACT. I'M THE ONE WHO DISCOVERED THE STAR-LIKE ARRANGEMENT OF LEY LINES.
WELL, A FEW MORE THINGS HAVE COME TO LIGHT. TAKE A LOOK AT THIS.
THIS OLD-ASS BOOK... IT'S A NINTH CIRCLE VERSION OF A BIBLICAL PROPHECY. IT'S ABOUT THE DEHUMANIZATION, GREED AND OPPRESSION THAT GREEN ARROW HAS BEEN FIGHTING HIS WHOLE CAREER.
IT'S ALL PRELUDE TO THE RISE OF A NEW "CITY OF LIGHT," BROUGHT INTO BEING BY SOMEONE CALLED...

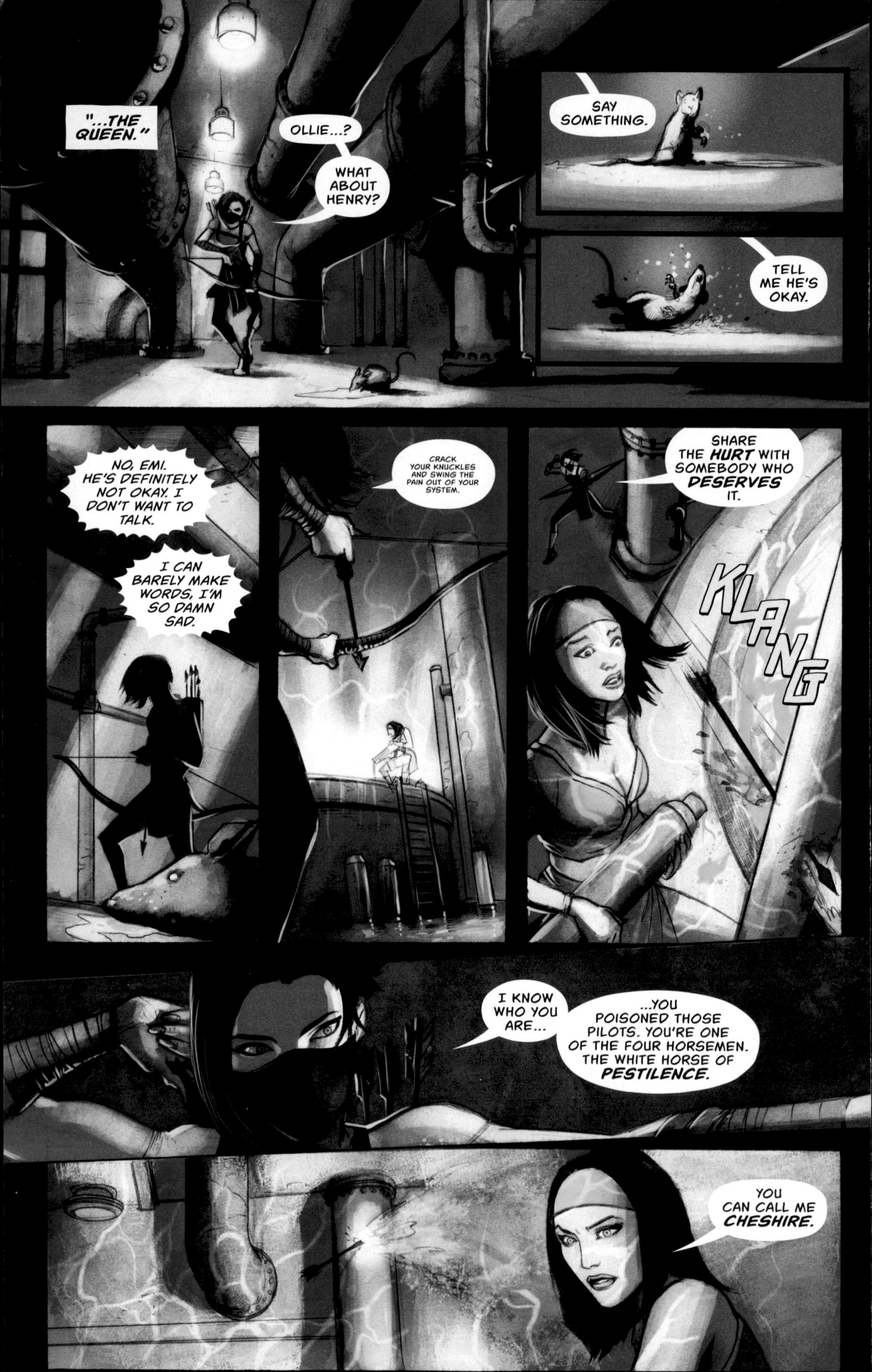
"...THE QUEEN."
OLLIE...?
WHAT ABOUT HENRY?
SAY SOMETHING.
TELL ME HE'S OKAY.
NO, EMI. HE'S DEFINITELY NOT OKAY. I DON'T WANT TO TALK.
I CAN BARELY MAKE WORDS, I'M SO DAMN SAD.
CRACK YOUR KNUCKLES AND SWING THE PAIN OUT OF YOUR SYSTEM.
SHARE THE HURT WITH SOMEBODY WHO DESERVES IT.
KLANG
I KNOW WHO YOU ARE...
...YOU POISONED THOSE PILOTS. YOU'RE ONE OF THE FOUR HORSEMEN. THE WHITE HORSE OF PESTILENCE.
YOU CAN CALL ME CHESHIRE.

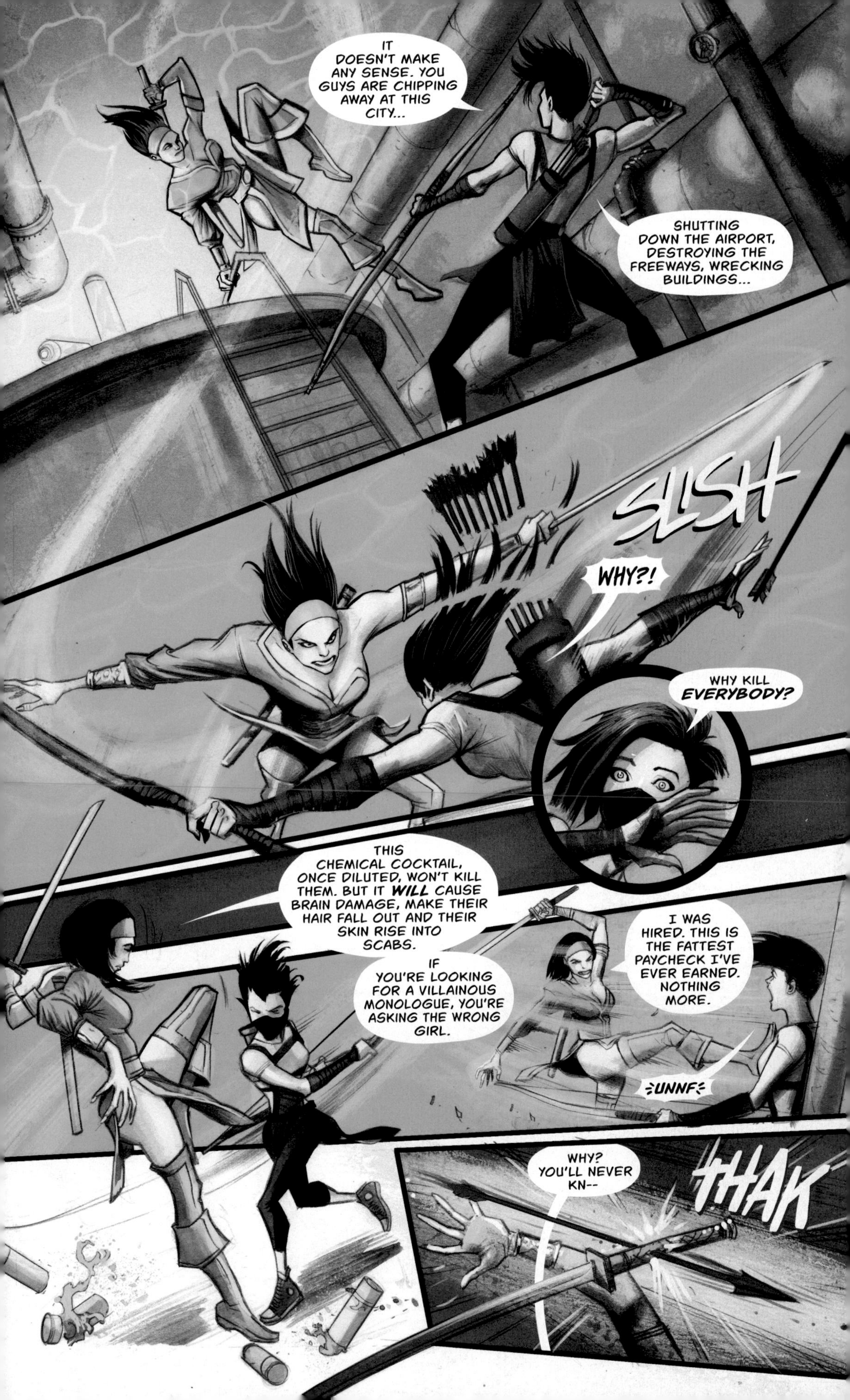
IT DOESN'T MAKE ANY SENSE. YOU GUYS ARE CHIPPING AWAY AT THIS CITY...
SHUTTING DOWN THE AIRPORT, DESTROYING THE FREEWAYS, WRECKING BUILDINGS...
SLISH
WHY?!
WHY KILL EVERYBODY?
THIS CHEMICAL COCKTAIL, ONCE DILUTED, WON'T KILL THEM. BUT IT WILL CAUSE BRAIN DAMAGE, MAKE THEIR HAIR FALL OUT AND THEIR SKIN RISE INTO SCABS.
IF YOU'RE LOOKING FOR A VILLAINOUS MONOLOGUE, YOU'RE ASKING THE WRONG GIRL.
I WAS HIRED. THIS IS THE FATTEST PAYCHECK I'VE EVER EARNED. NOTHING MORE.
UNNF
WHY? YOU'LL NEVER KN--
THAK

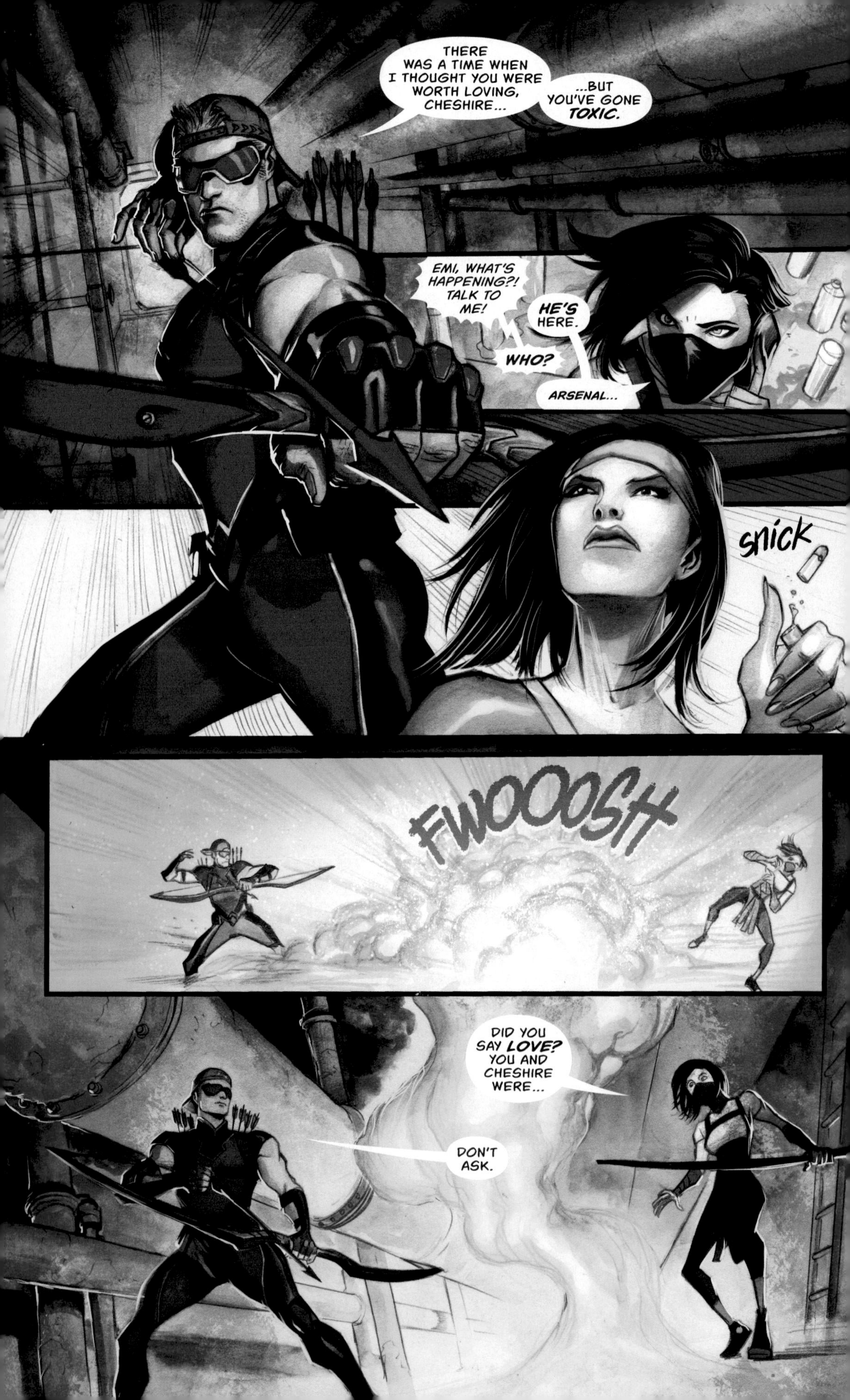
THERE WAS A TIME WHEN I THOUGHT YOU WERE WORTH LOVING, CHESHIRE...
...BUT YOU'VE GONE TOXIC.
EMI, WHAT'S HAPPENING?! TALK TO ME!
HE'S HERE.
WHO?
ARSENAL...
snick
FWOOOSH
DID YOU SAY LOVE? YOU AND CHESHIRE WERE...
DON'T ASK.

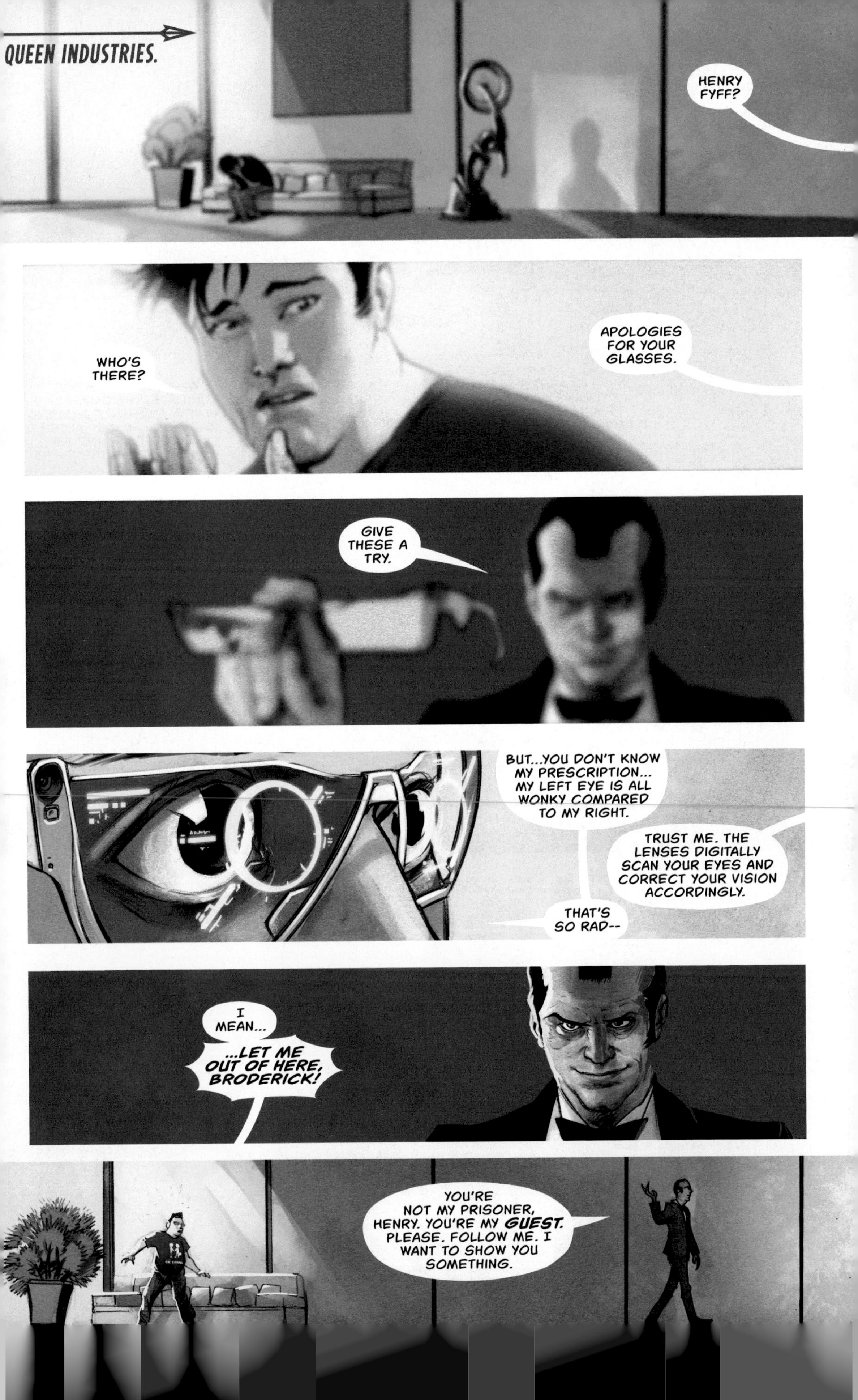
QUEEN INDUSTRIES.
HENRY FYFF?
WHO'S THERE?
APOLOGIES FOR YOUR GLASSES.
GIVE THESE A TRY.
BUT...YOU DON'T KNOW MY PRESCRIPTION... MY LEFT EYE IS ALL WONKY COMPARED TO MY RIGHT.
TRUST ME. THE LENSES DIGITALLY SCAN YOUR EYES AND CORRECT YOUR VISION ACCORDINGLY.
THAT'S SO RAD--
I MEAN...
...LET ME OUT OF HERE, BRODERICK!
YOU'RE NOT MY PRISONER, HENRY. YOU'RE MY GUEST. PLEASE. FOLLOW ME. I WANT TO SHOW YOU SOMETHING.

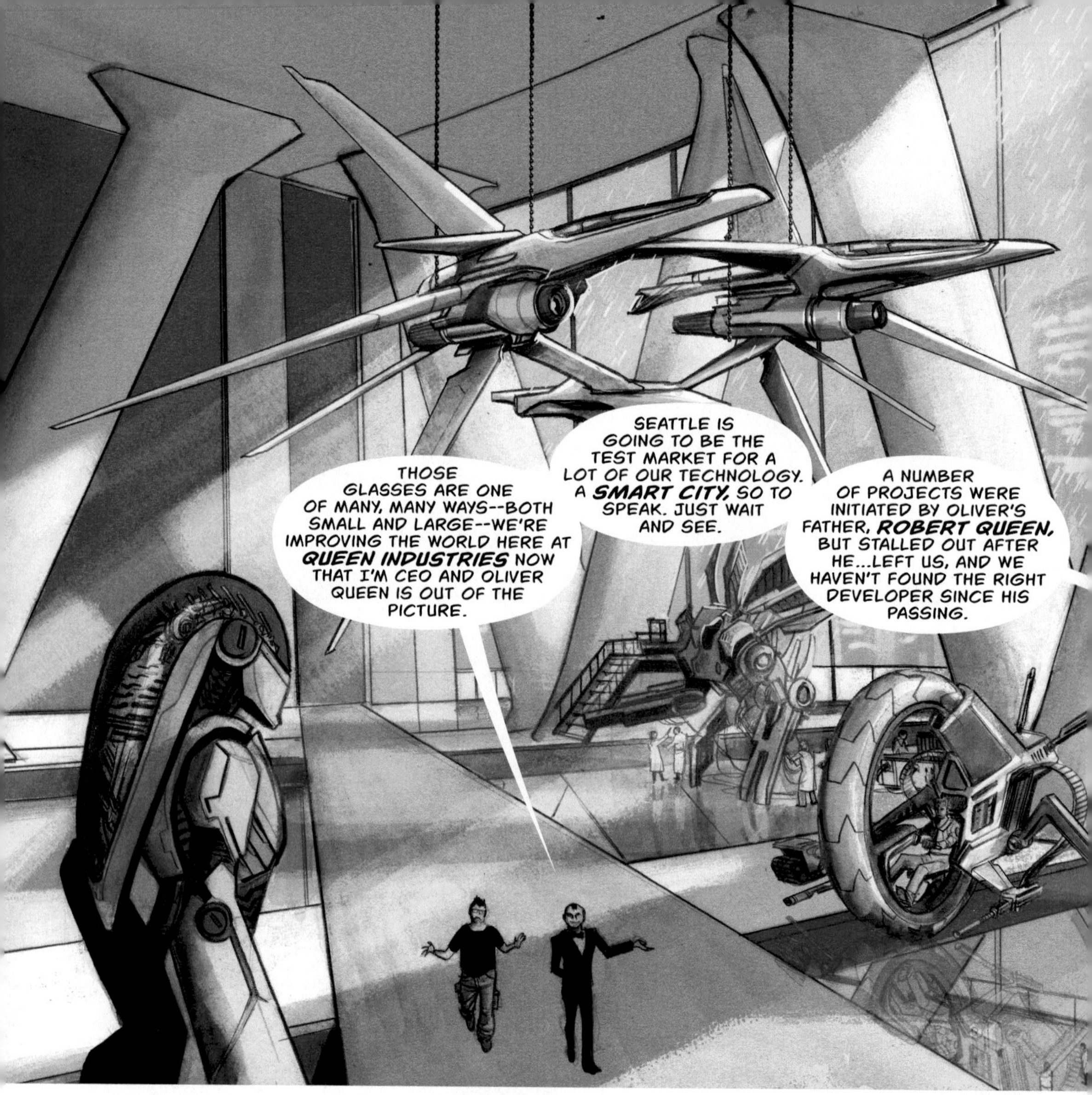
THOSE GLASSES ARE ONE OF MANY, MANY WAYS--BOTH SMALL AND LARGE--WE'RE IMPROVING THE WORLD HERE AT QUEEN INDUSTRIES NOW THAT I'M CEO AND OLIVER QUEEN IS OUT OF THE PICTURE.
SEATTLE IS GOING TO BE THE TEST MARKET FOR A LOT OF OUR TECHNOLOGY. A SMART CITY, SO TO SPEAK. JUST WAIT AND SEE.
A NUMBER OF PROJECTS WERE INITIATED BY OLIVER'S FATHER, ROBERT QUEEN, BUT STALLED OUT AFTER HE...LEFT US, AND WE HAVEN'T FOUND THE RIGHT DEVELOPER SINCE HIS PASSING.

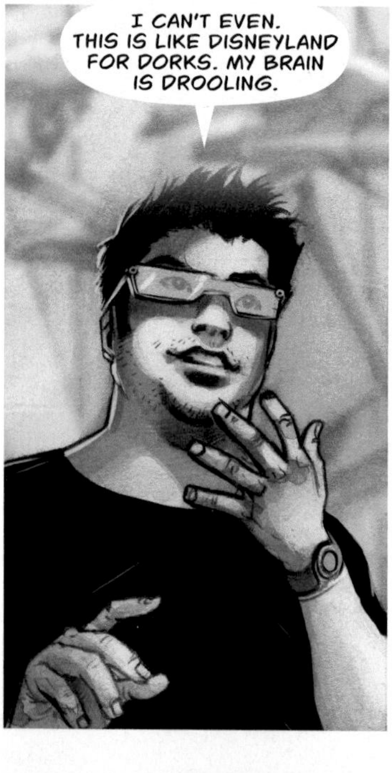
I CAN'T EVEN. THIS IS LIKE DISNEYLAND FOR DORKS. MY BRAIN IS DROOLING.

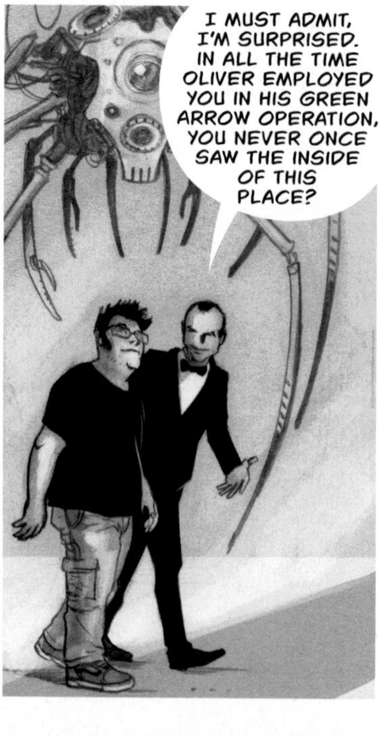
I MUST ADMIT, I'M SURPRISED. IN ALL THE TIME OLIVER EMPLOYED YOU IN HIS GREEN ARROW OPERATION, YOU NEVER ONCE SAW THE INSIDE OF THIS PLACE?

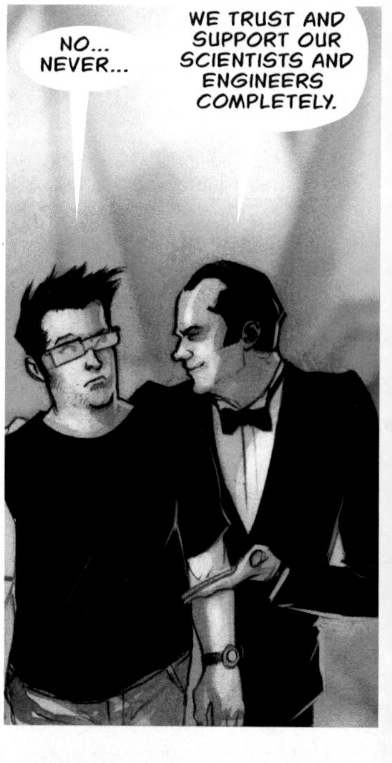
NO... NEVER...
WE TRUST AND SUPPORT OUR SCIENTISTS AND ENGINEERS COMPLETELY.

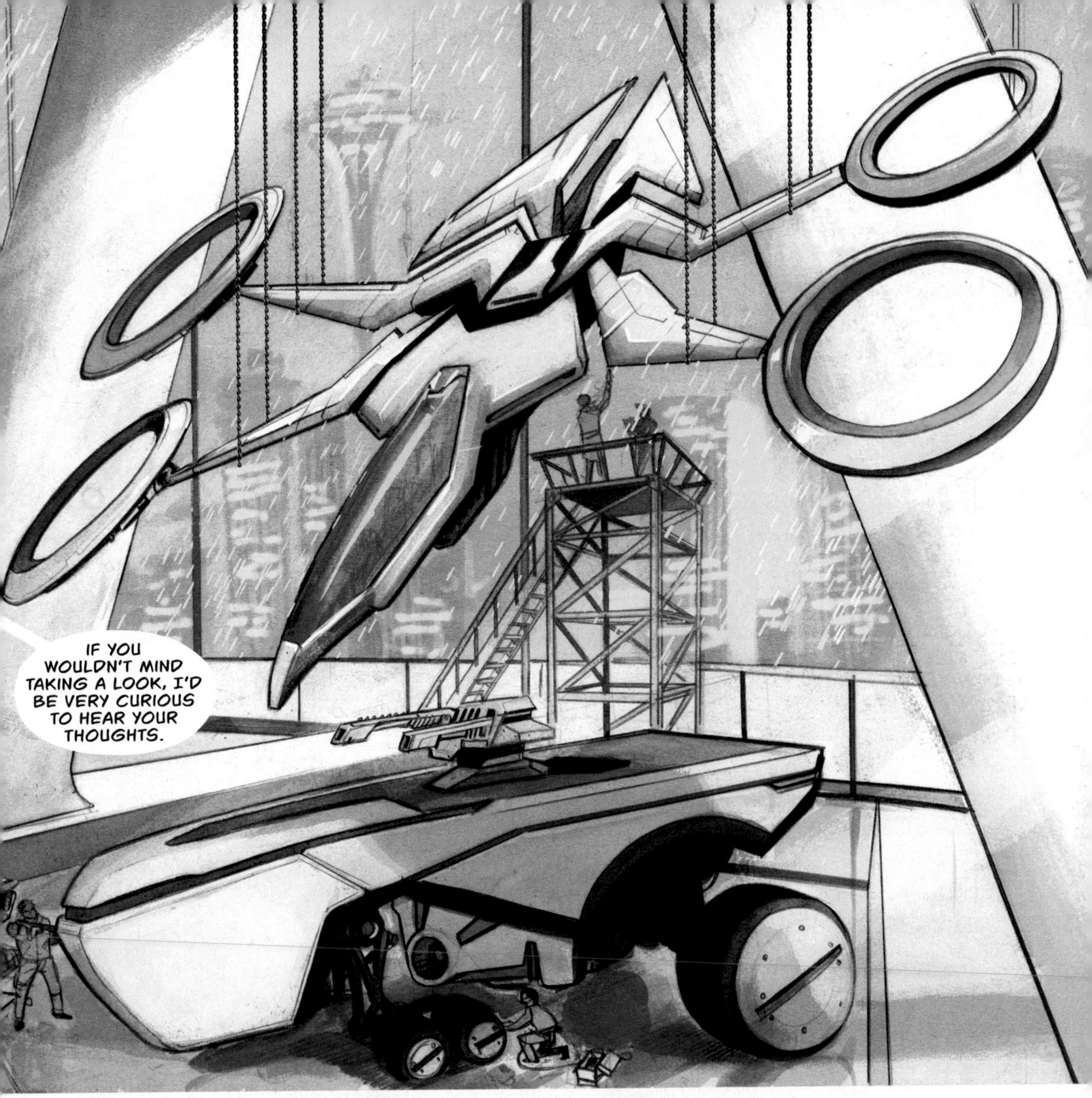
IF YOU WOULDN'T MIND TAKING A LOOK, I'D BE VERY CURIOUS TO HEAR YOUR THOUGHTS.

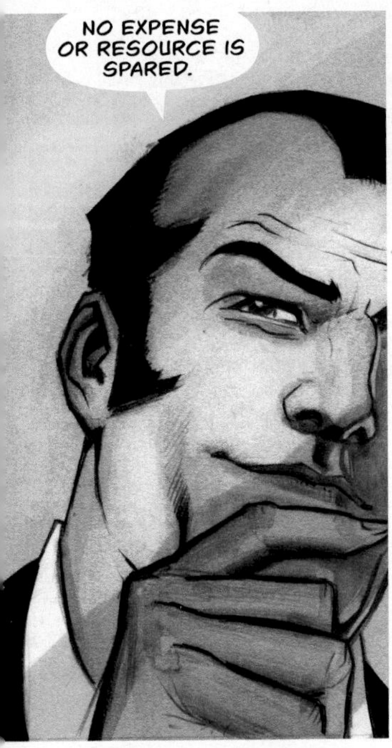
NO EXPENSE OR RESOURCE IS SPARED.

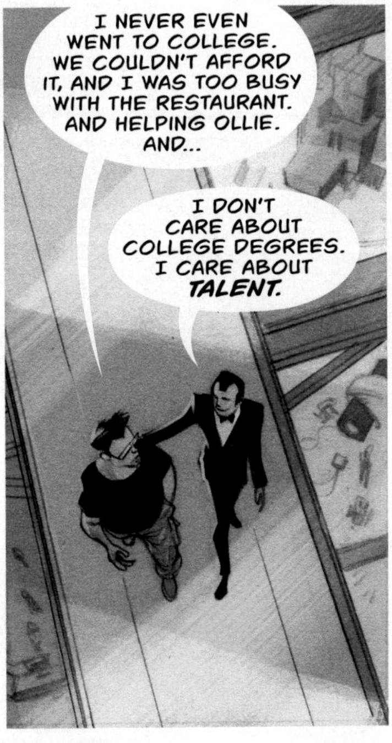
I NEVER EVEN WENT TO COLLEGE. WE COULDN'T AFFORD IT, AND I WAS TOO BUSY WITH THE RESTAURANT. AND HELPING OLLIE. AND...
I DON'T CARE ABOUT COLLEGE DEGREES. I CARE ABOUT *TALENT.*

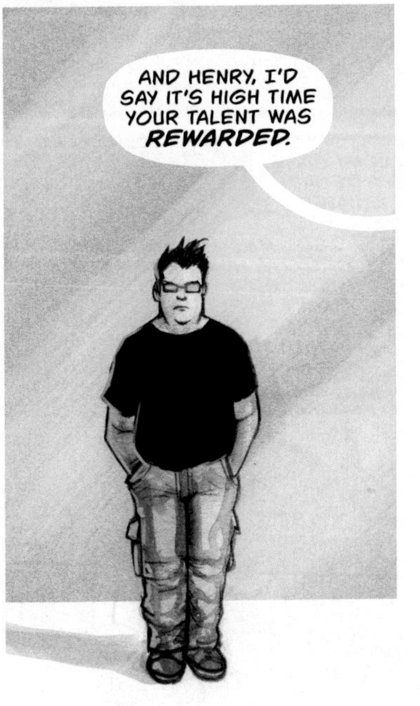
AND HENRY, I'D SAY IT'S HIGH TIME YOUR TALENT WAS ***REWARDED.***

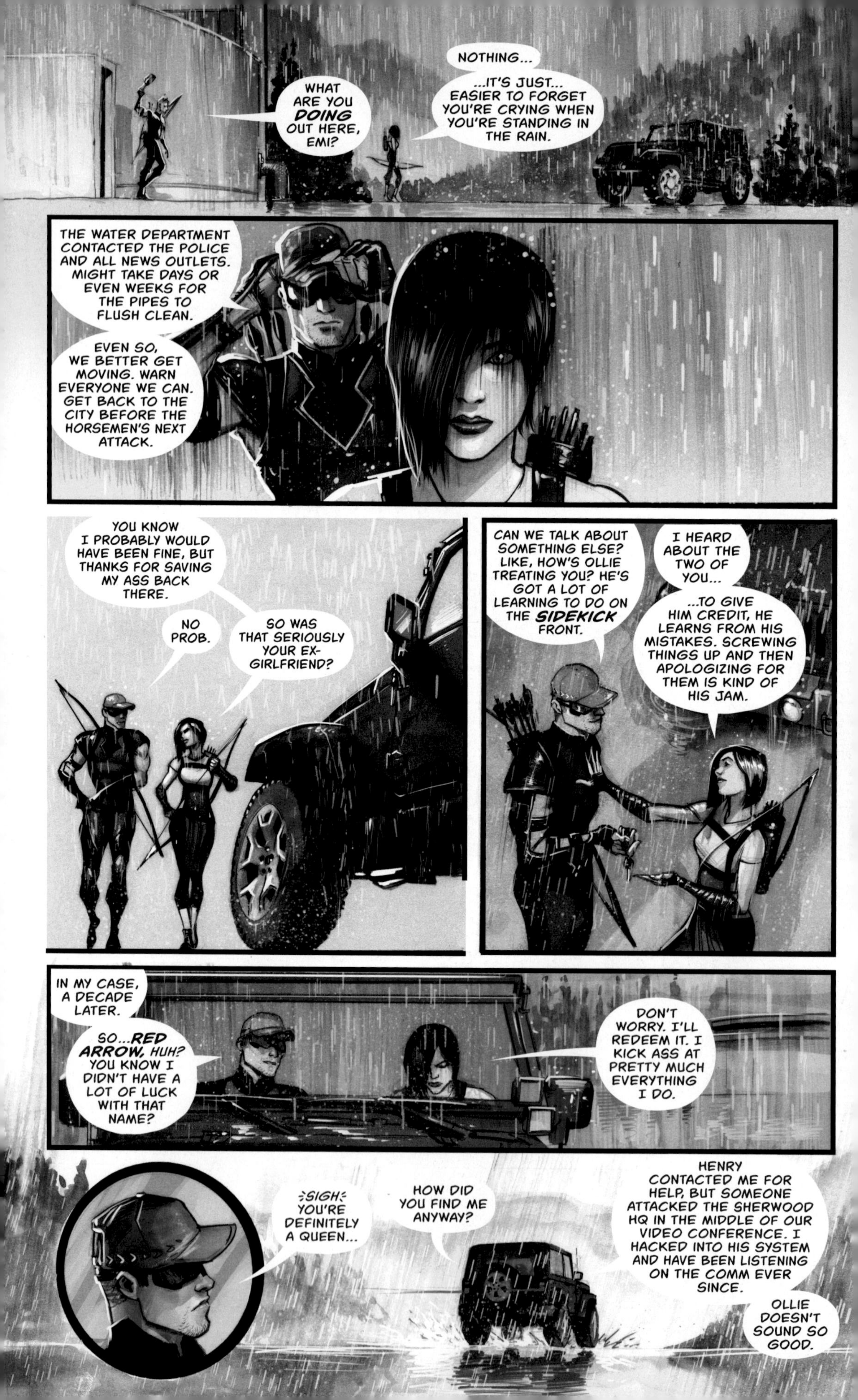
WHAT ARE YOU DOING OUT HERE, EMI?
NOTHING...
...IT'S JUST... EASIER TO FORGET YOU'RE CRYING WHEN YOU'RE STANDING IN THE RAIN.
THE WATER DEPARTMENT CONTACTED THE POLICE AND ALL NEWS OUTLETS. MIGHT TAKE DAYS OR EVEN WEEKS FOR THE PIPES TO FLUSH CLEAN.
EVEN SO, WE BETTER GET MOVING. WARN EVERYONE WE CAN. GET BACK TO THE CITY BEFORE THE HORSEMEN'S NEXT ATTACK.
YOU KNOW I PROBABLY WOULD HAVE BEEN FINE, BUT THANKS FOR SAVING MY ASS BACK THERE.
NO PROB.
SO WAS THAT SERIOUSLY YOUR EX-GIRLFRIEND?
CAN WE TALK ABOUT SOMETHING ELSE? LIKE, HOW'S OLLIE TREATING YOU? HE'S GOT A LOT OF LEARNING TO DO ON THE SIDEKICK FRONT.
I HEARD ABOUT THE TWO OF YOU...
...TO GIVE HIM CREDIT, HE LEARNS FROM HIS MISTAKES. SCREWING THINGS UP AND THEN APOLOGIZING FOR THEM IS KIND OF HIS JAM.
IN MY CASE, A DECADE LATER.
SO...RED ARROW, HUH? YOU KNOW I DIDN'T HAVE A LOT OF LUCK WITH THAT NAME?
DON'T WORRY. I'LL REDEEM IT. I KICK ASS AT PRETTY MUCH EVERYTHING I DO.
SIGH YOU'RE DEFINITELY A QUEEN...
HOW DID YOU FIND ME ANYWAY?
HENRY CONTACTED ME FOR HELP, BUT SOMEONE ATTACKED THE SHERWOOD HQ IN THE MIDDLE OF OUR VIDEO CONFERENCE. I HACKED INTO HIS SYSTEM AND HAVE BEEN LISTENING ON THE COMM EVER SINCE.
OLLIE DOESN'T SOUND SO GOOD.

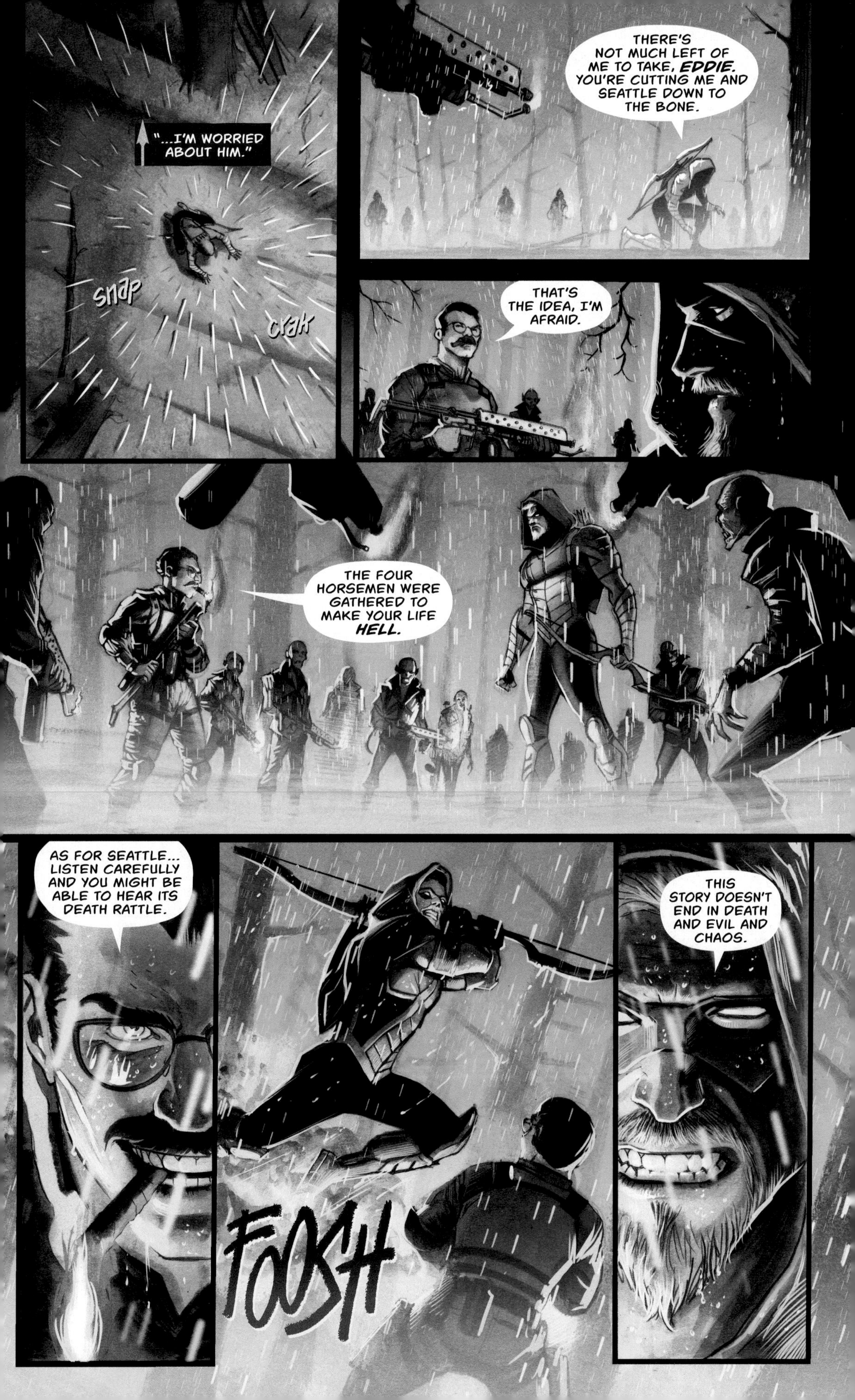
"...I'M WORRIED ABOUT HIM."
SNAP
CRAK
THERE'S NOT MUCH LEFT OF ME TO TAKE, EDDIE. YOU'RE CUTTING ME AND SEATTLE DOWN TO THE BONE.
THAT'S THE IDEA, I'M AFRAID.
THE FOUR HORSEMEN WERE GATHERED TO MAKE YOUR LIFE HELL.
AS FOR SEATTLE... LISTEN CAREFULLY AND YOU MIGHT BE ABLE TO HEAR ITS DEATH RATTLE.
FOOSH
THIS STORY DOESN'T END IN DEATH AND EVIL AND CHAOS.

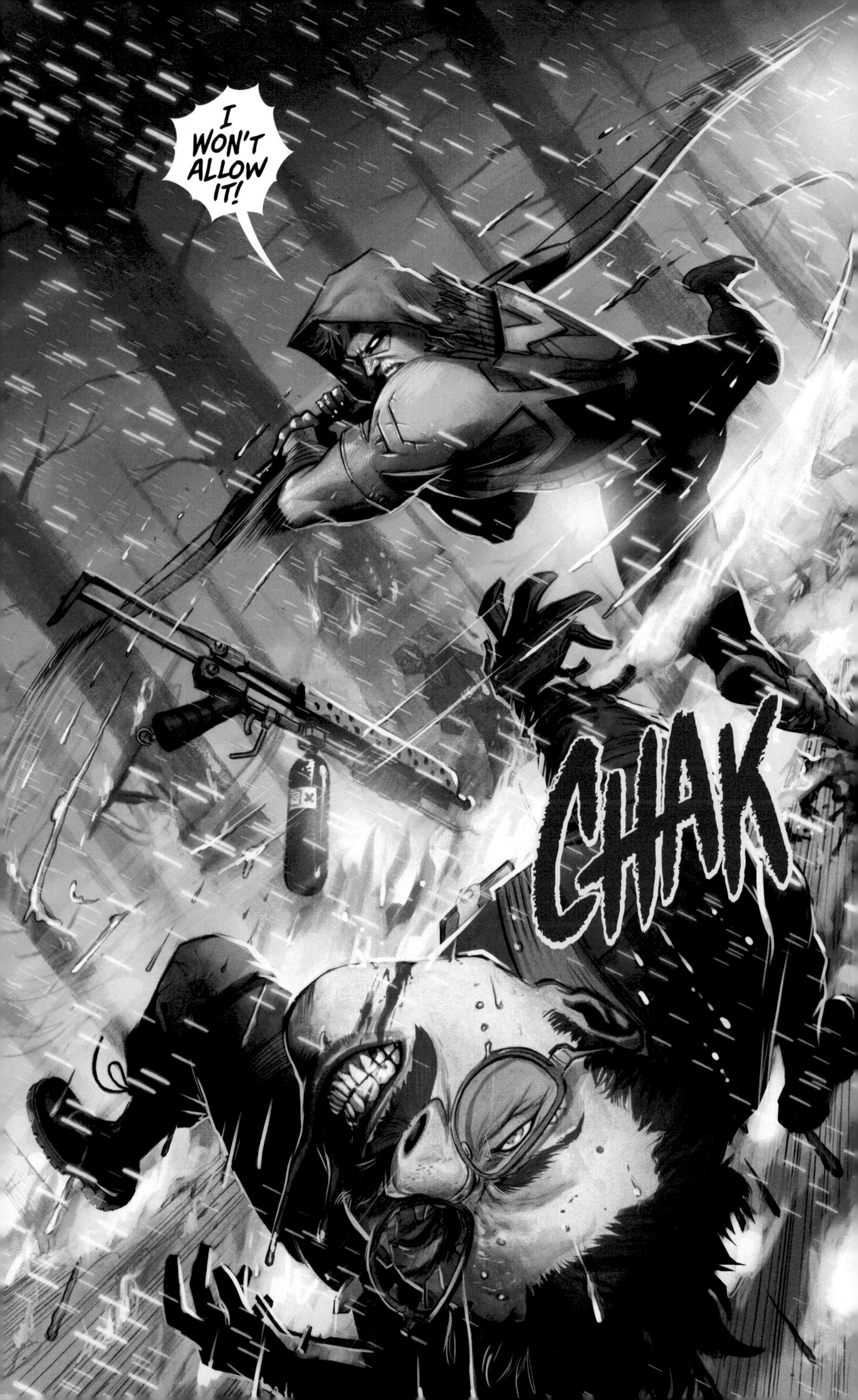
I WON'T ALLOW IT!
CHAK

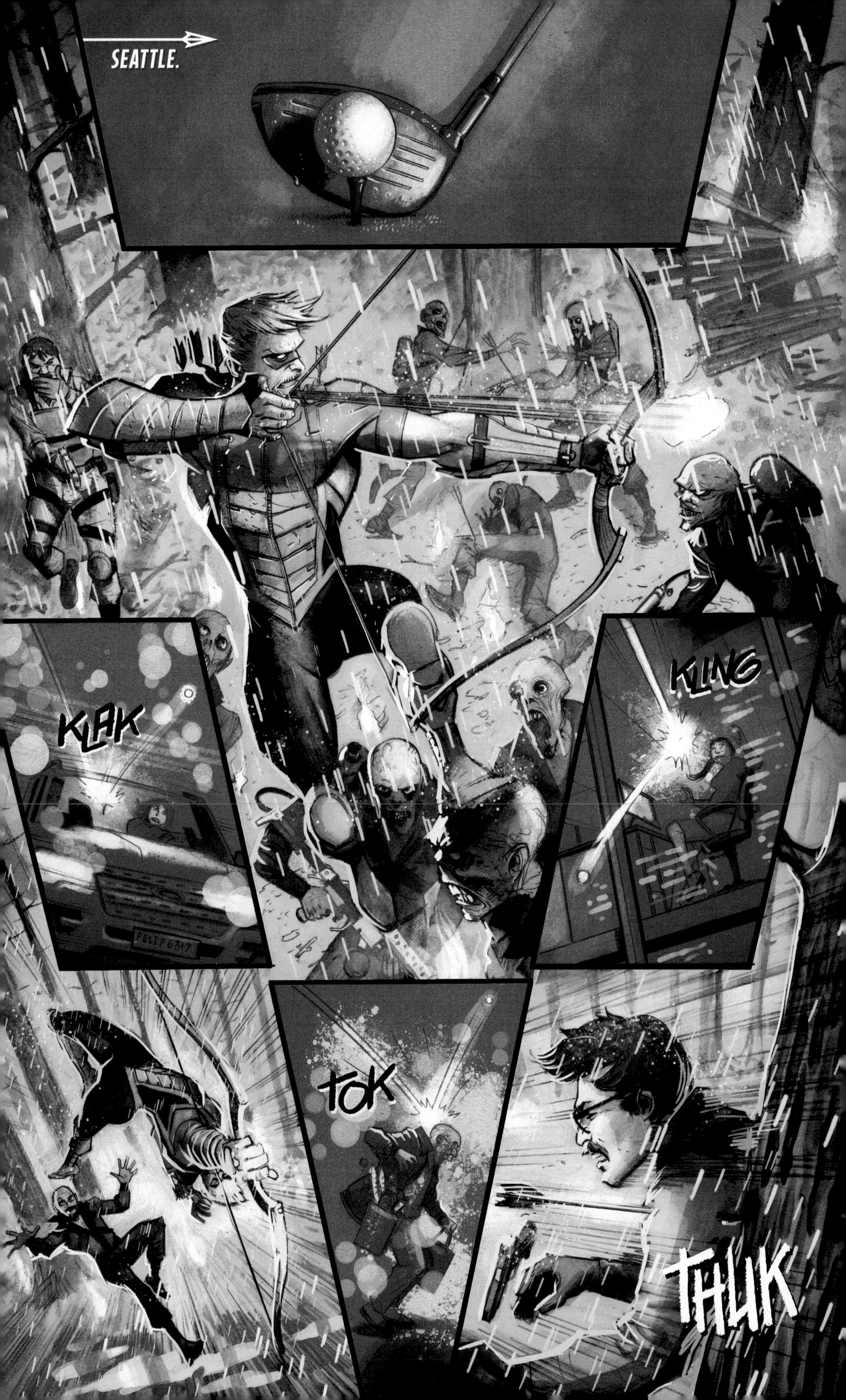

SEATTLE.
KLAK
KLING
TOK
THUK

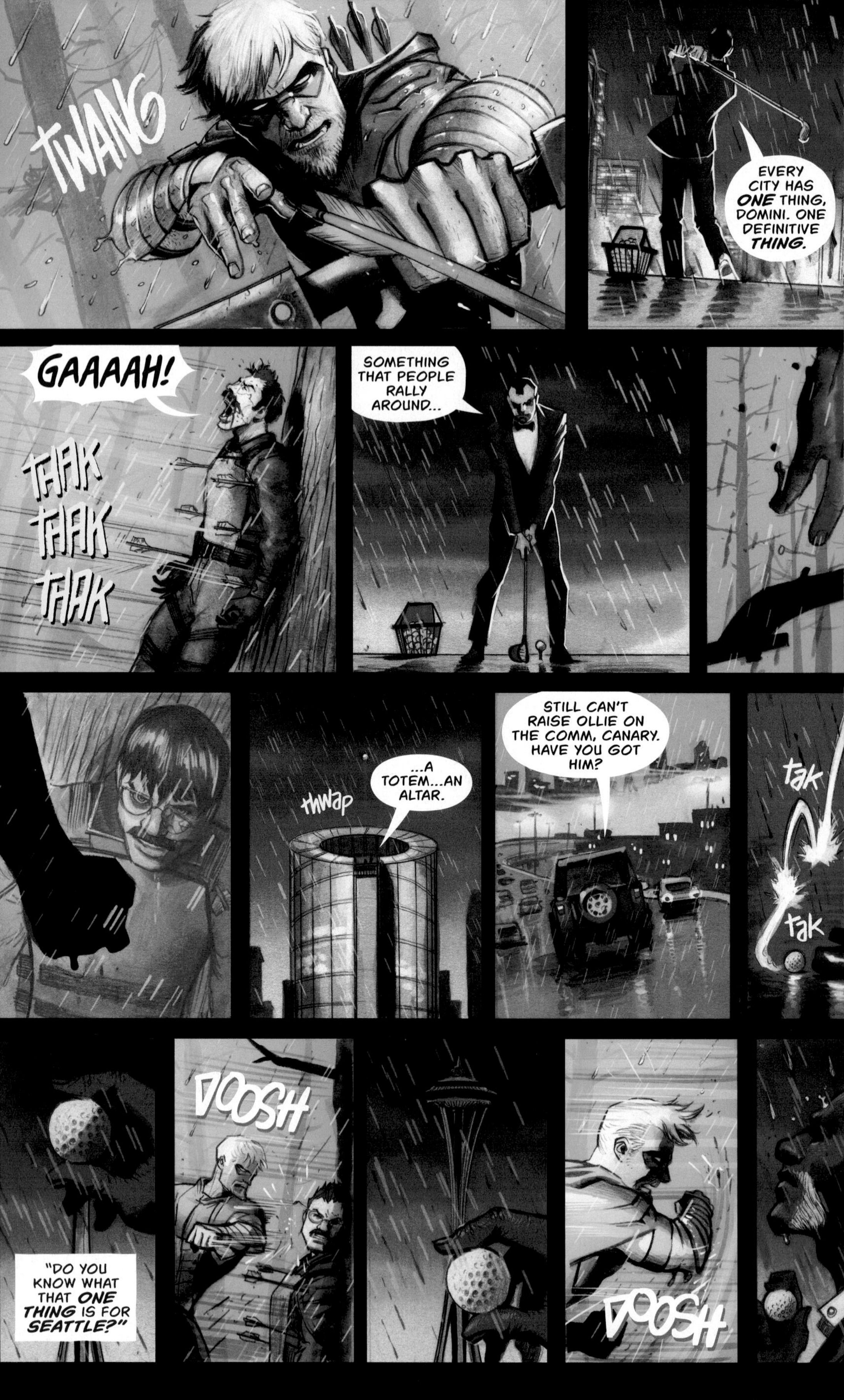
TWANG
EVERY CITY HAS ONE THING, DOMINI. ONE DEFINITIVE THING.
GAAAAH!
THAK THAK THAK
SOMETHING THAT PEOPLE RALLY AROUND...
...A TOTEM...AN ALTAR.
thwap
STILL CAN'T RAISE OLLIE ON THE COMM, CANARY. HAVE YOU GOT HIM?
tak
tak
"DO YOU KNOW WHAT THAT ONE THING IS FOR SEATTLE?"
DOOSH
DOOSH

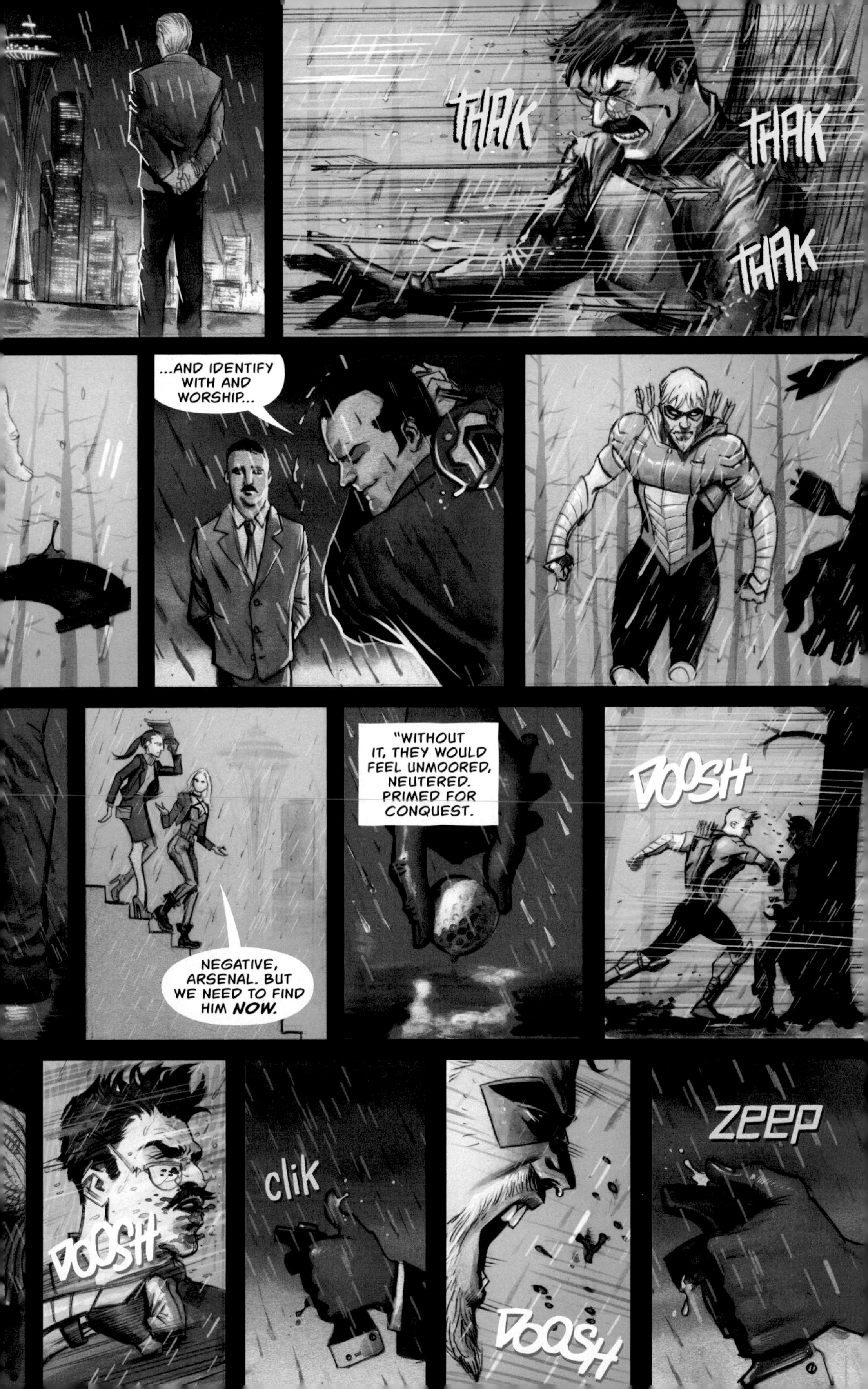

THAK
THAK
THAK
...AND IDENTIFY WITH AND WORSHIP...
NEGATIVE, ARSENAL. BUT WE NEED TO FIND HIM NOW.
"WITHOUT IT, THEY WOULD FEEL UNMOORED, NEUTERED. PRIMED FOR CONQUEST.
DOOSH
DOOSH
clik
DOOSH
ZEEP

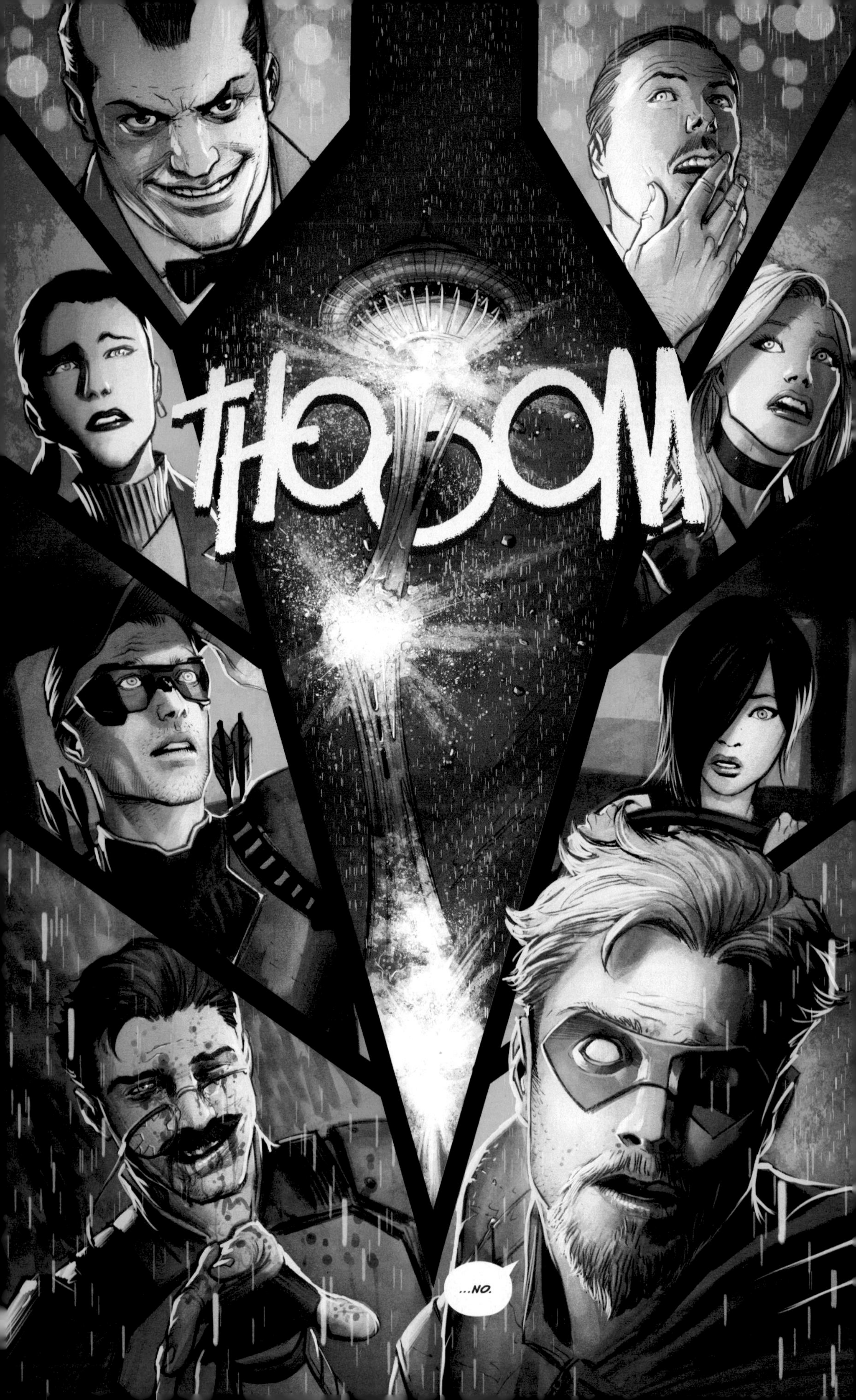
THOOOM
...NO.

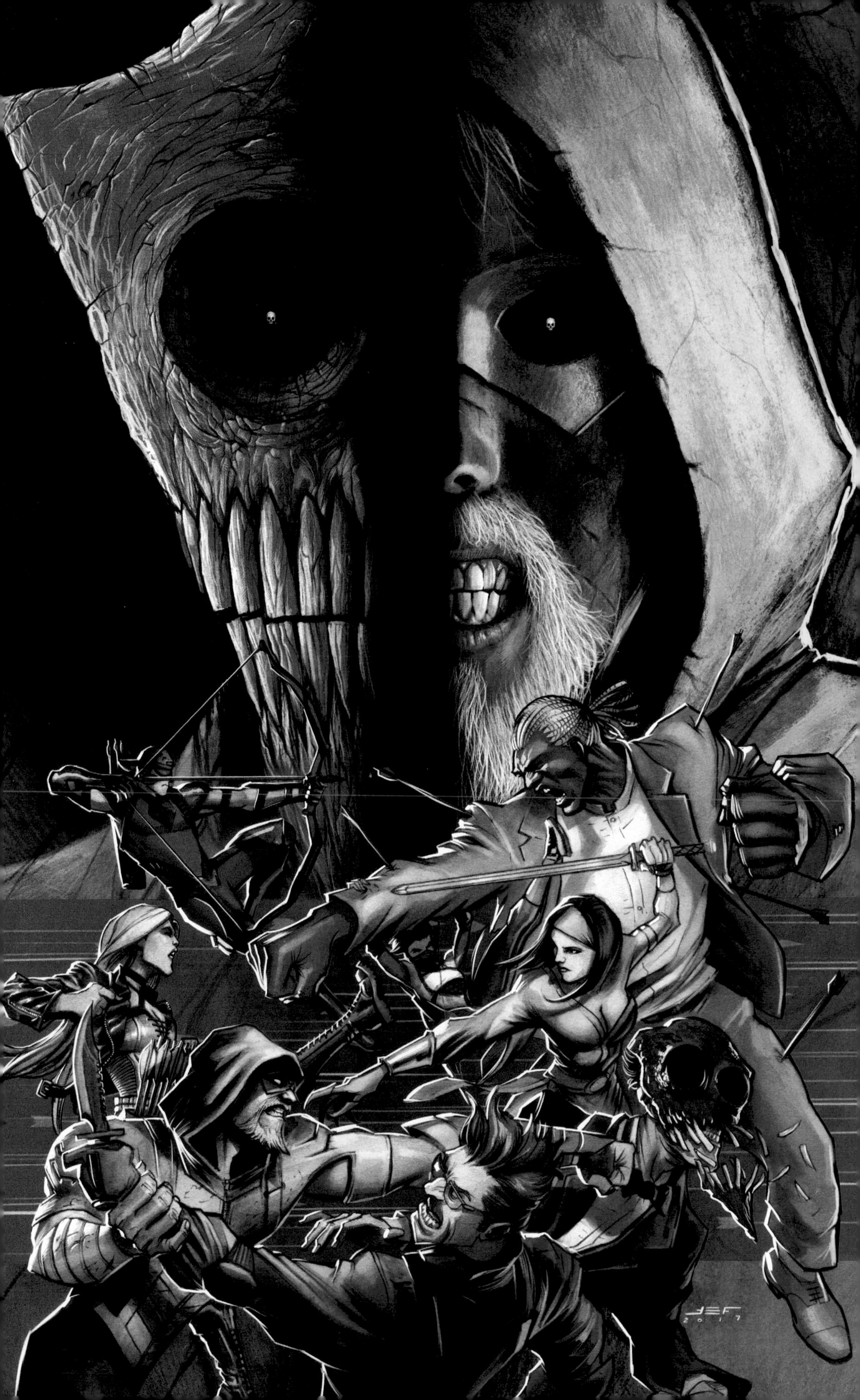

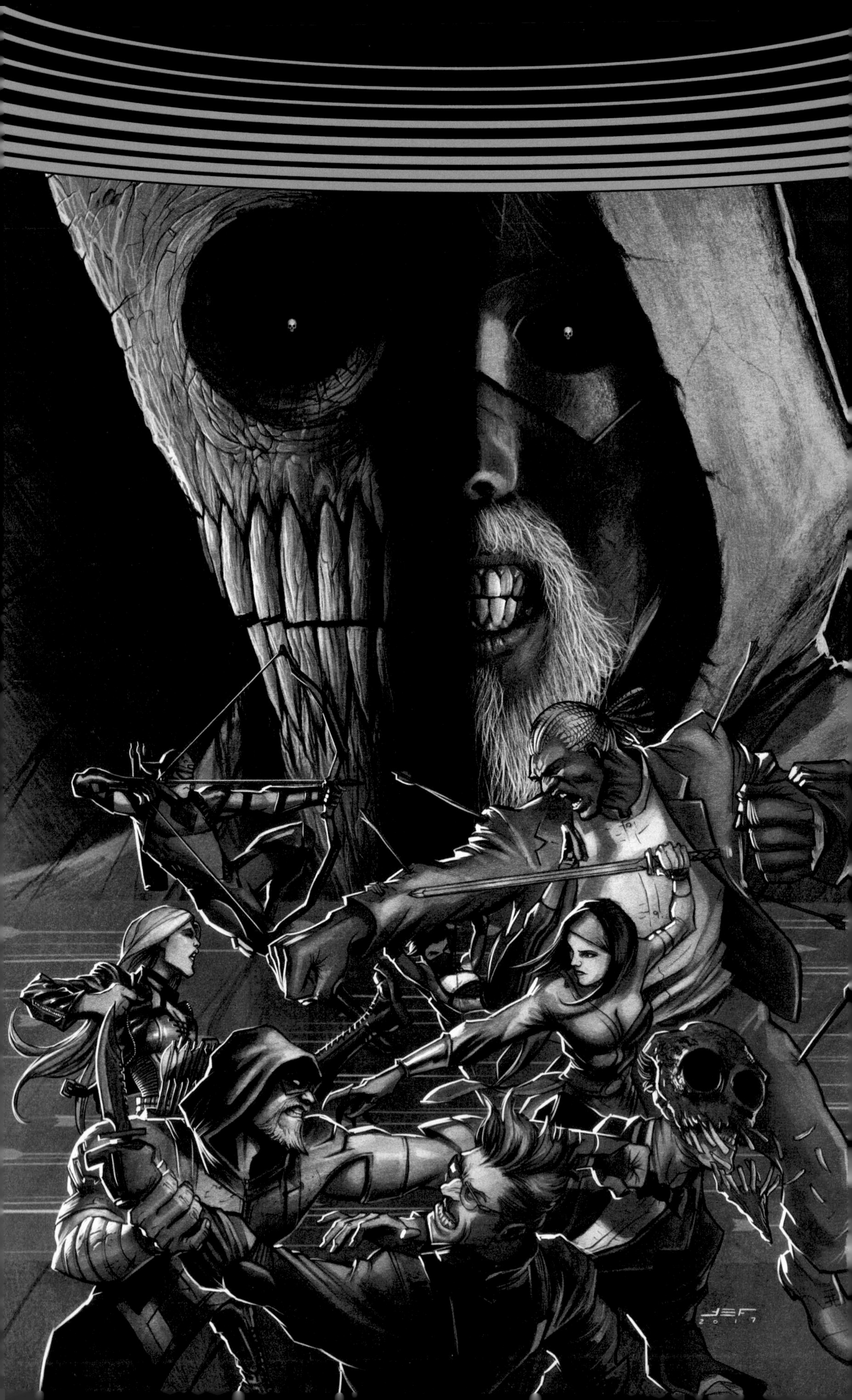

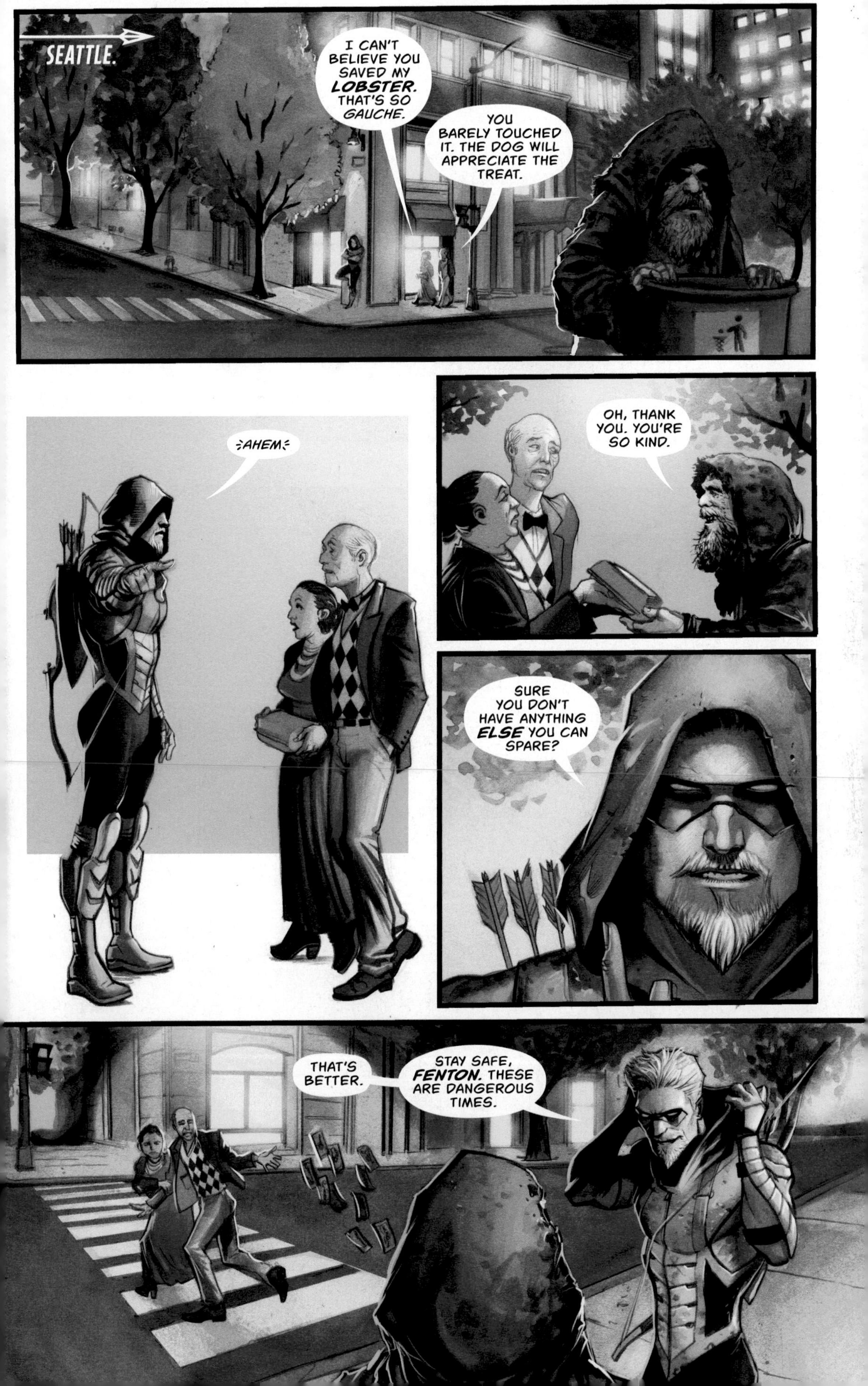
SEATTLE.
I CAN'T BELIEVE YOU SAVED MY LOBSTER. THAT'S SO GAUCHE.
YOU BARELY TOUCHED IT. THE DOG WILL APPRECIATE THE TREAT.
AHEM
OH, THANK YOU. YOU'RE SO KIND.
SURE YOU DON'T HAVE ANYTHING ELSE YOU CAN SPARE?
THAT'S BETTER.
STAY SAFE, FENTON. THESE ARE DANGEROUS TIMES.

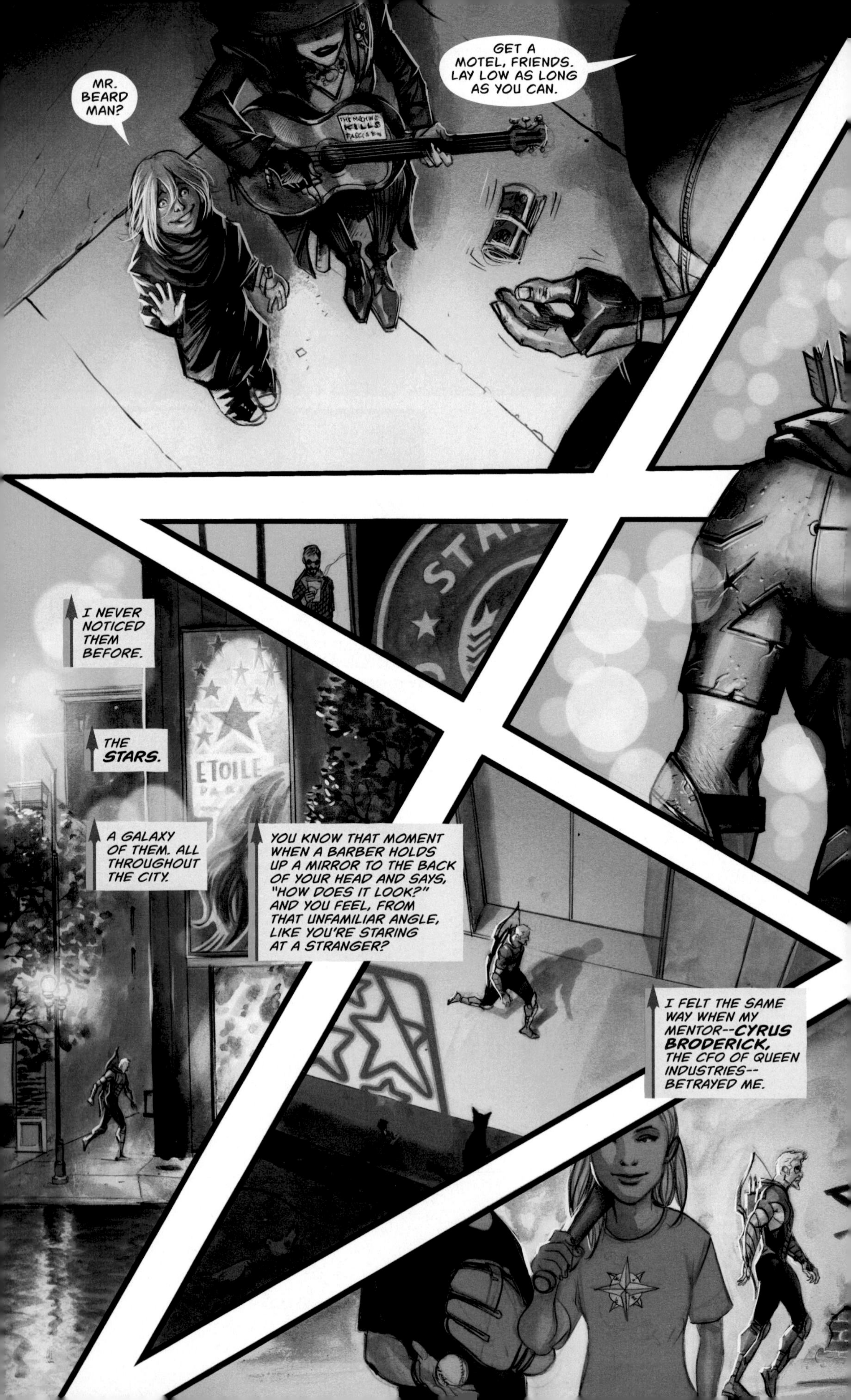
MR. BEARD MAN?
GET A MOTEL, FRIENDS. LAY LOW AS LONG AS YOU CAN.
THE MACHINE KILLS
I NEVER NOTICED THEM BEFORE.
THE STARS.
A GALAXY OF THEM. ALL THROUGHOUT THE CITY.
ETOILE
YOU KNOW THAT MOMENT WHEN A BARBER HOLDS UP A MIRROR TO THE BACK OF YOUR HEAD AND SAYS, "HOW DOES IT LOOK?" AND YOU FEEL, FROM THAT UNFAMILIAR ANGLE, LIKE YOU'RE STARING AT A STRANGER?
I FELT THE SAME WAY WHEN MY MENTOR--CYRUS BRODERICK, THE CFO OF QUEEN INDUSTRIES--BETRAYED ME.

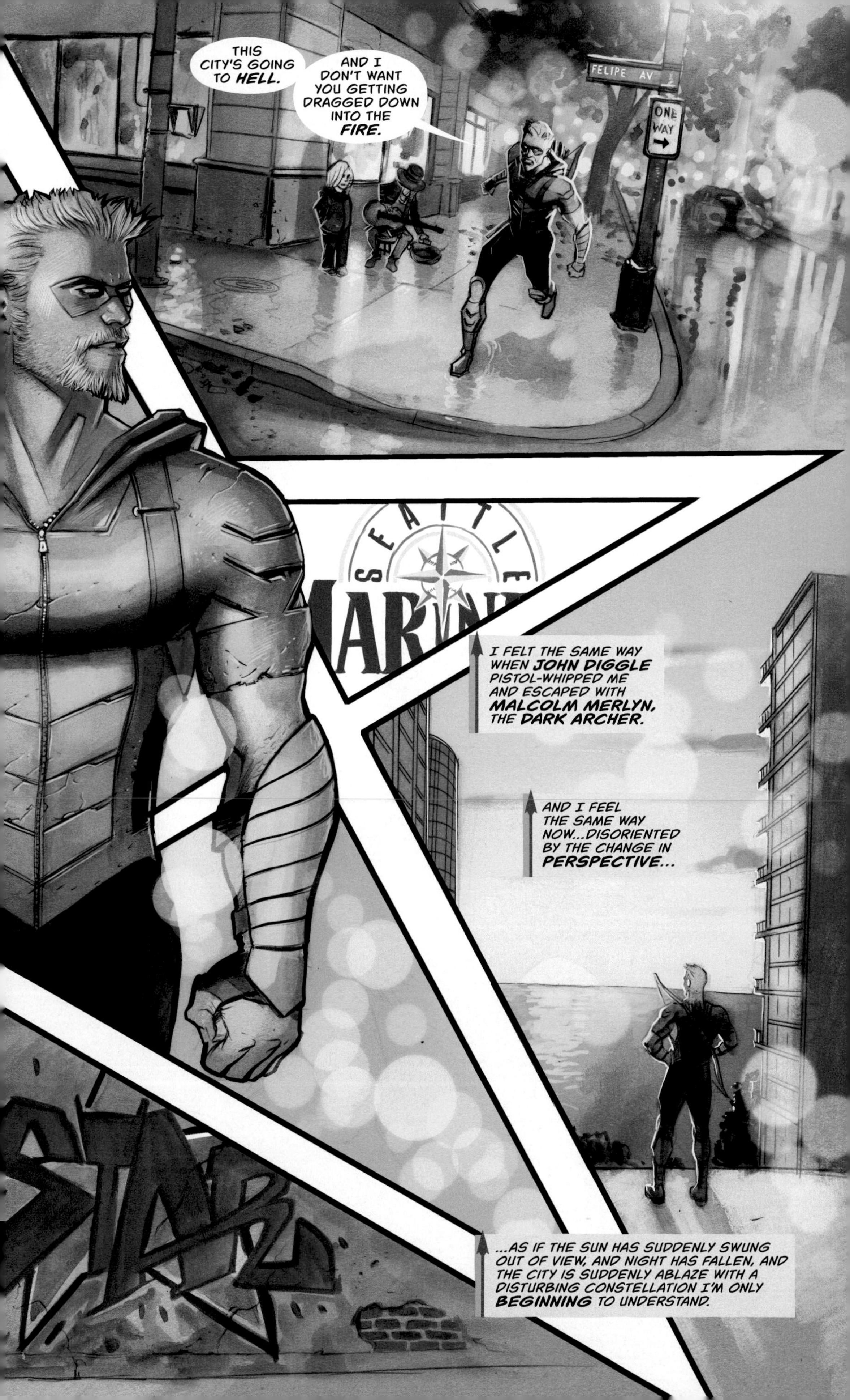

THIS CITY'S GOING TO HELL.
AND I DON'T WANT YOU GETTING DRAGGED DOWN INTO THE FIRE.
FELIPE AV
ONE WAY
SEATTLE
MARINE
I FELT THE SAME WAY WHEN JOHN DIGGLE PISTOL-WHIPPED ME AND ESCAPED WITH MALCOLM MERLYN, THE DARK ARCHER.
AND I FEEL THE SAME WAY NOW...DISORIENTED BY THE CHANGE IN PERSPECTIVE...
...AS IF THE SUN HAS SUDDENLY SWUNG OUT OF VIEW, AND NIGHT HAS FALLEN, AND THE CITY IS SUDDENLY ABLAZE WITH A DISTURBING CONSTELLATION I'M ONLY BEGINNING TO UNDERSTAND.

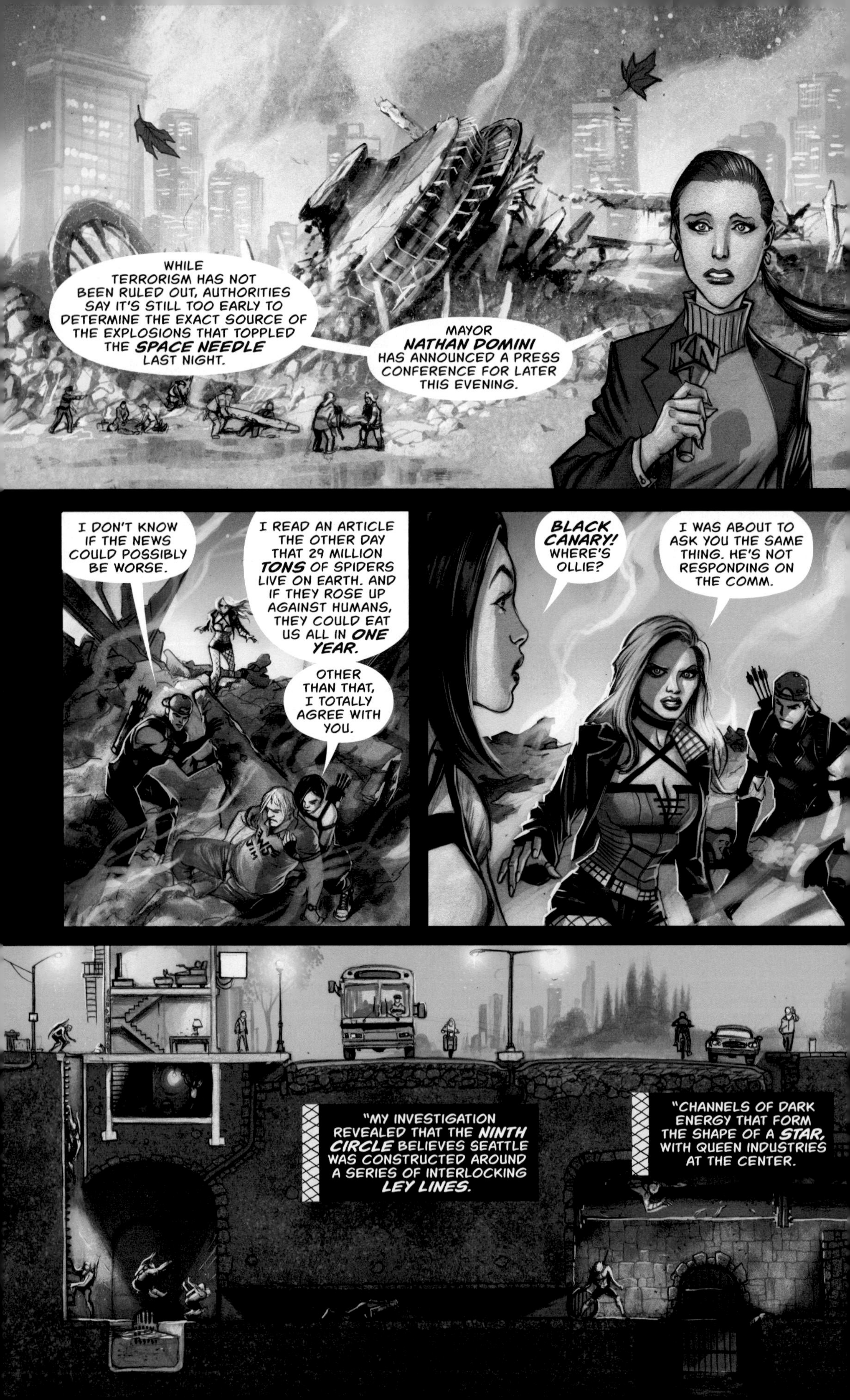
WHILE TERRORISM HAS NOT BEEN RULED OUT, AUTHORITIES SAY IT'S STILL TOO EARLY TO DETERMINE THE EXACT SOURCE OF THE EXPLOSIONS THAT TOPPLED THE SPACE NEEDLE LAST NIGHT.
MAYOR NATHAN DOMINI HAS ANNOUNCED A PRESS CONFERENCE FOR LATER THIS EVENING.
KN
I DON'T KNOW IF THE NEWS COULD POSSIBLY BE WORSE.
I READ AN ARTICLE THE OTHER DAY THAT 29 MILLION TONS OF SPIDERS LIVE ON EARTH. AND IF THEY ROSE UP AGAINST HUMANS, THEY COULD EAT US ALL IN ONE YEAR.
OTHER THAN THAT, I TOTALLY AGREE WITH YOU.
BLACK CANARY! WHERE'S OLLIE?
I WAS ABOUT TO ASK YOU THE SAME THING. HE'S NOT RESPONDING ON THE COMM.
"MY INVESTIGATION REVEALED THAT THE NINTH CIRCLE BELIEVES SEATTLE WAS CONSTRUCTED AROUND A SERIES OF INTERLOCKING LEY LINES.
"CHANNELS OF DARK ENERGY THAT FORM THE SHAPE OF A STAR, WITH QUEEN INDUSTRIES AT THE CENTER.

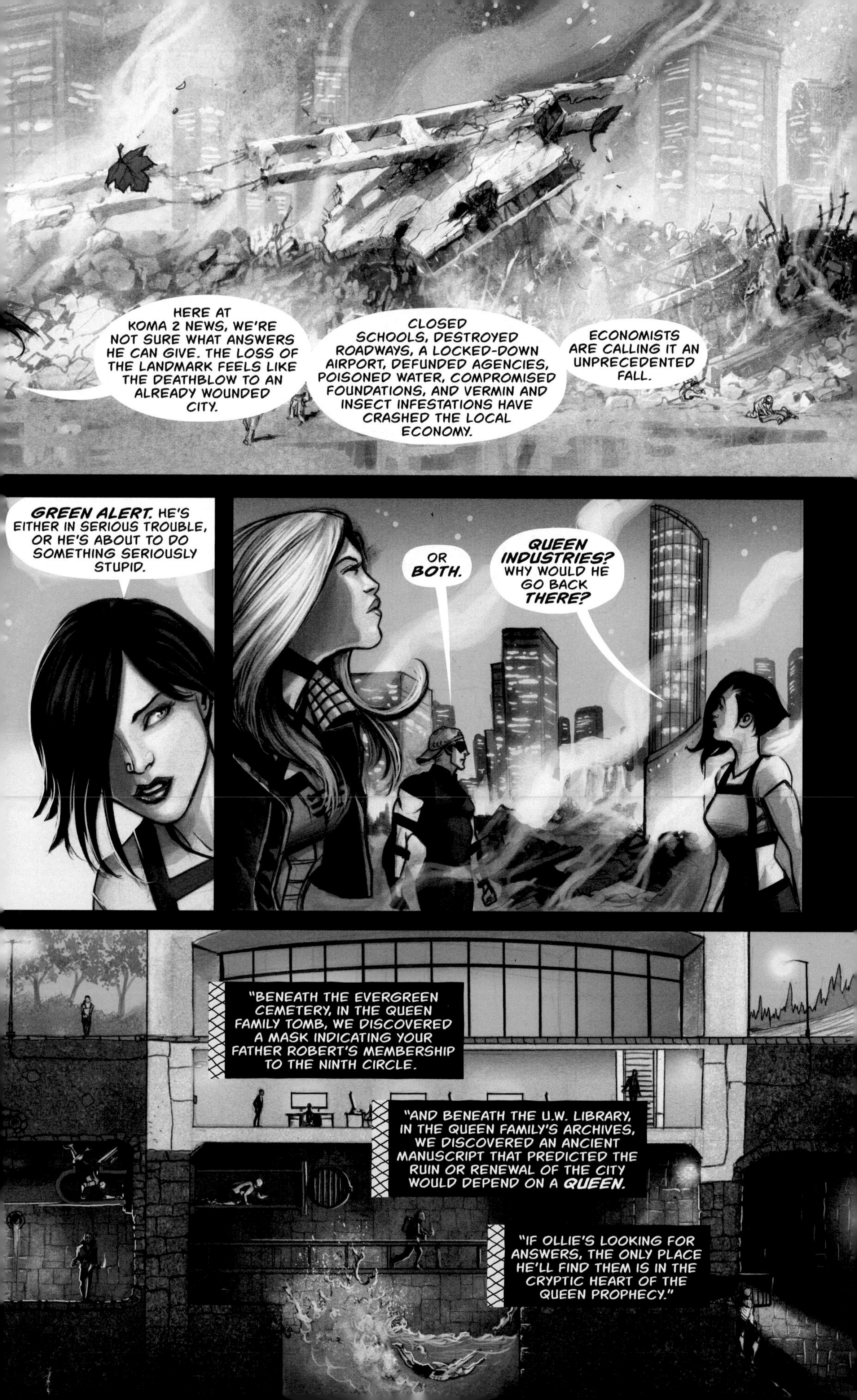
HERE AT KOMA 2 NEWS, WE'RE NOT SURE WHAT ANSWERS HE CAN GIVE. THE LOSS OF THE LANDMARK FEELS LIKE THE DEATHBLOW TO AN ALREADY WOUNDED CITY.
CLOSED SCHOOLS, DESTROYED ROADWAYS, A LOCKED-DOWN AIRPORT, DEFUNDED AGENCIES, POISONED WATER, COMPROMISED FOUNDATIONS, AND VERMIN AND INSECT INFESTATIONS HAVE CRASHED THE LOCAL ECONOMY.
ECONOMISTS ARE CALLING IT AN UNPRECEDENTED FALL.
GREEN ALERT. HE'S EITHER IN SERIOUS TROUBLE, OR HE'S ABOUT TO DO SOMETHING SERIOUSLY STUPID.
OR BOTH.
QUEEN INDUSTRIES? WHY WOULD HE GO BACK THERE?
"BENEATH THE EVERGREEN CEMETERY, IN THE QUEEN FAMILY TOMB, WE DISCOVERED A MASK INDICATING YOUR FATHER ROBERT'S MEMBERSHIP TO THE NINTH CIRCLE.
"AND BENEATH THE U.W. LIBRARY, IN THE QUEEN FAMILY'S ARCHIVES, WE DISCOVERED AN ANCIENT MANUSCRIPT THAT PREDICTED THE RUIN OR RENEWAL OF THE CITY WOULD DEPEND ON A QUEEN.
"IF OLLIE'S LOOKING FOR ANSWERS, THE ONLY PLACE HE'LL FIND THEM IS IN THE CRYPTIC HEART OF THE QUEEN PROPHECY."

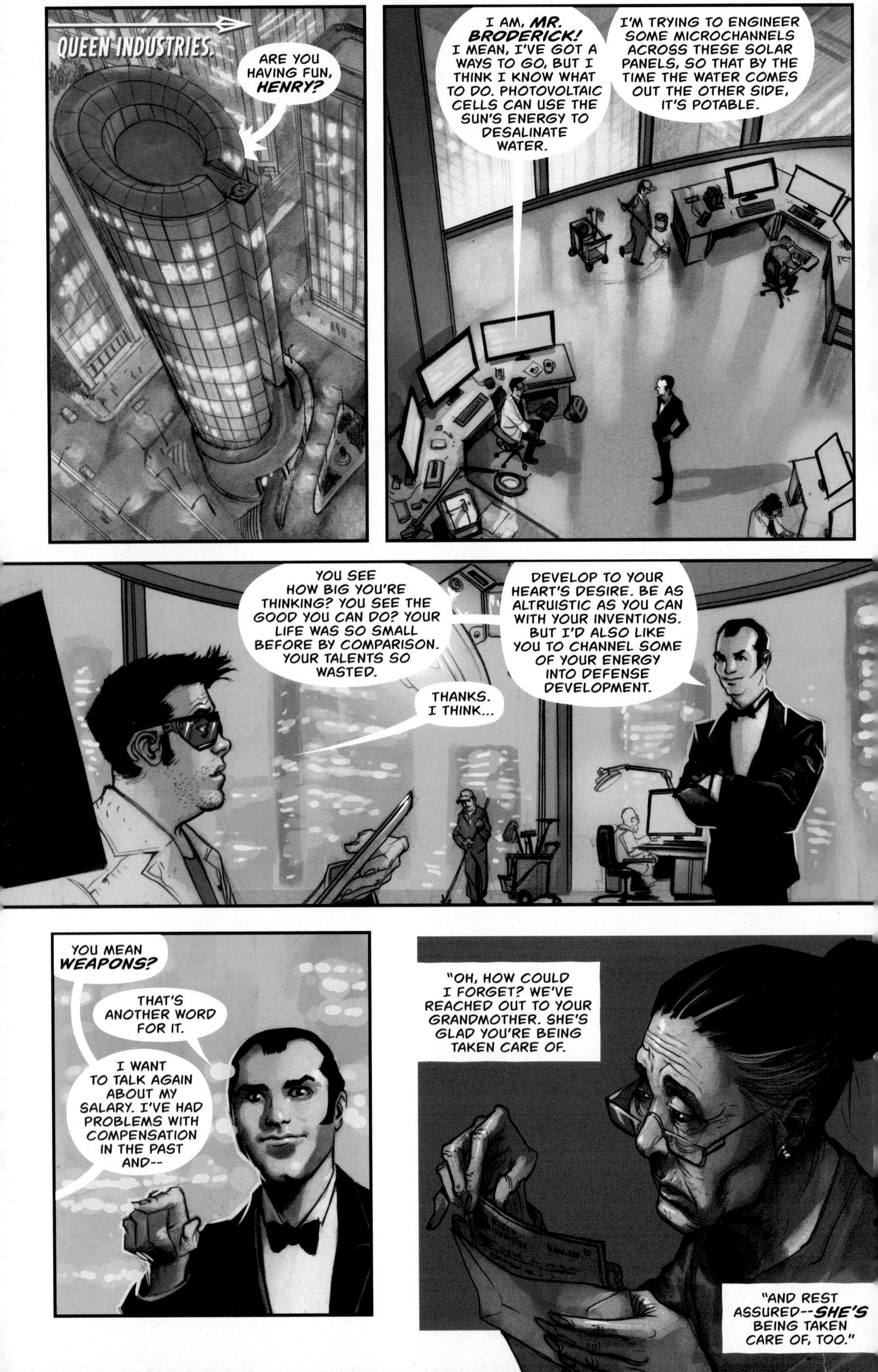
QUEEN INDUSTRIES.
ARE YOU HAVING FUN, HENRY?
I AM, MR. BRODERICK! I MEAN, I'VE GOT A WAYS TO GO, BUT I THINK I KNOW WHAT TO DO. PHOTOVOLTAIC CELLS CAN USE THE SUN'S ENERGY TO DESALINATE WATER.
I'M TRYING TO ENGINEER SOME MICROCHANNELS ACROSS THESE SOLAR PANELS, SO THAT BY THE TIME THE WATER COMES OUT THE OTHER SIDE, IT'S POTABLE.
YOU SEE HOW BIG YOU'RE THINKING? YOU SEE THE GOOD YOU CAN DO? YOUR LIFE WAS SO SMALL BEFORE BY COMPARISON. YOUR TALENTS SO WASTED.
THANKS. I THINK...
DEVELOP TO YOUR HEART'S DESIRE. BE AS ALTRUISTIC AS YOU CAN WITH YOUR INVENTIONS. BUT I'D ALSO LIKE YOU TO CHANNEL SOME OF YOUR ENERGY INTO DEFENSE DEVELOPMENT.
YOU MEAN WEAPONS?
THAT'S ANOTHER WORD FOR IT.
I WANT TO TALK AGAIN ABOUT MY SALARY. I'VE HAD PROBLEMS WITH COMPENSATION IN THE PAST AND--
"OH, HOW COULD I FORGET? WE'VE REACHED OUT TO YOUR GRANDMOTHER. SHE'S GLAD YOU'RE BEING TAKEN CARE OF.
"AND REST ASSURED--SHE'S BEING TAKEN CARE OF, TOO."

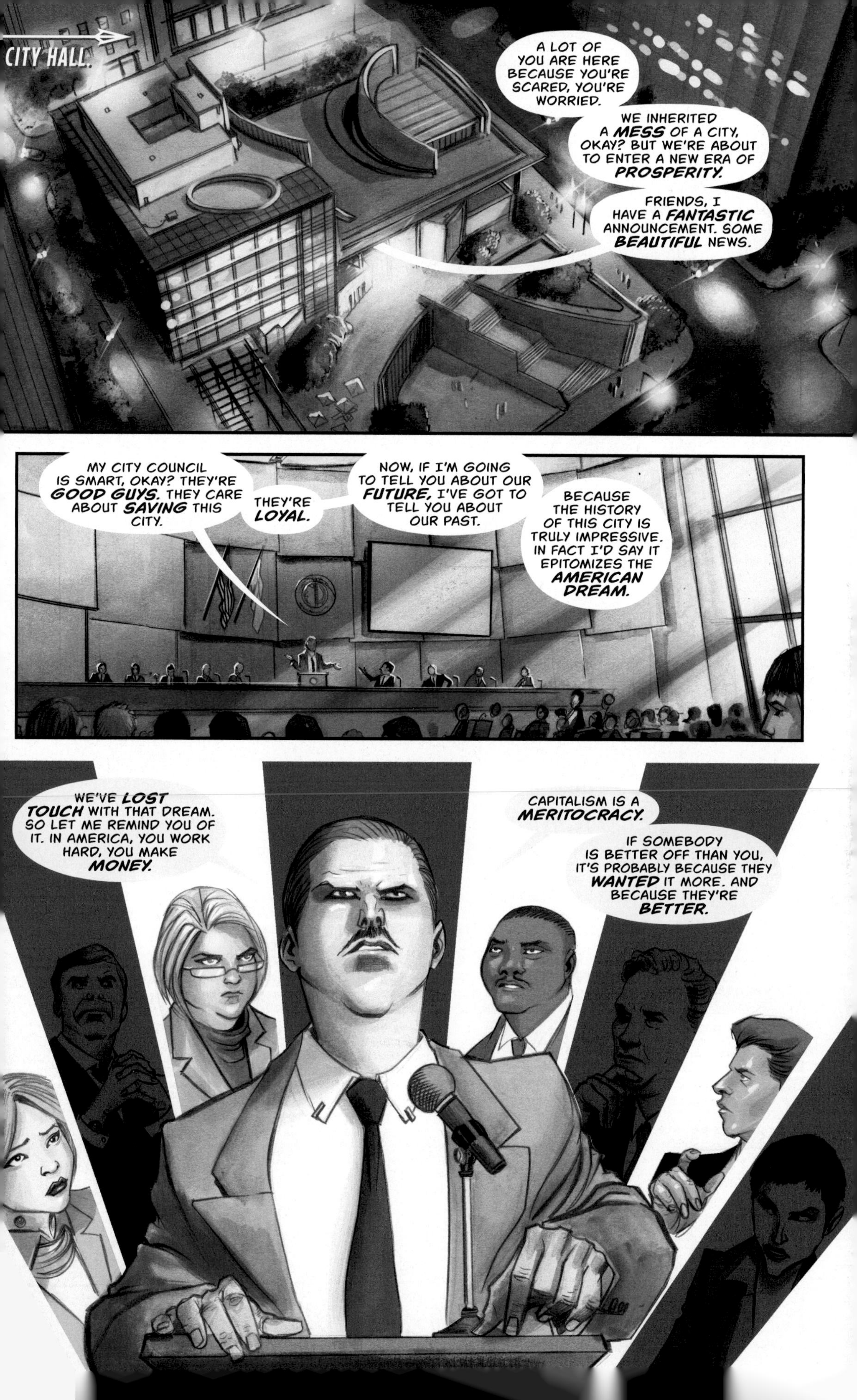
CITY HALL.
A LOT OF YOU ARE HERE BECAUSE YOU'RE SCARED, YOU'RE WORRIED.
WE INHERITED A MESS OF A CITY, OKAY? BUT WE'RE ABOUT TO ENTER A NEW ERA OF PROSPERITY.
FRIENDS, I HAVE A FANTASTIC ANNOUNCEMENT. SOME BEAUTIFUL NEWS.
MY CITY COUNCIL IS SMART, OKAY? THEY'RE GOOD GUYS. THEY CARE ABOUT SAVING THIS CITY.
THEY'RE LOYAL.
NOW, IF I'M GOING TO TELL YOU ABOUT OUR FUTURE, I'VE GOT TO TELL YOU ABOUT OUR PAST.
BECAUSE THE HISTORY OF THIS CITY IS TRULY IMPRESSIVE. IN FACT I'D SAY IT EPITOMIZES THE AMERICAN DREAM.
WE'VE LOST TOUCH WITH THAT DREAM. SO LET ME REMIND YOU OF IT. IN AMERICA, YOU WORK HARD, YOU MAKE MONEY.
CAPITALISM IS A MERITOCRACY.
IF SOMEBODY IS BETTER OFF THAN YOU, IT'S PROBABLY BECAUSE THEY WANTED IT MORE. AND BECAUSE THEY'RE BETTER.

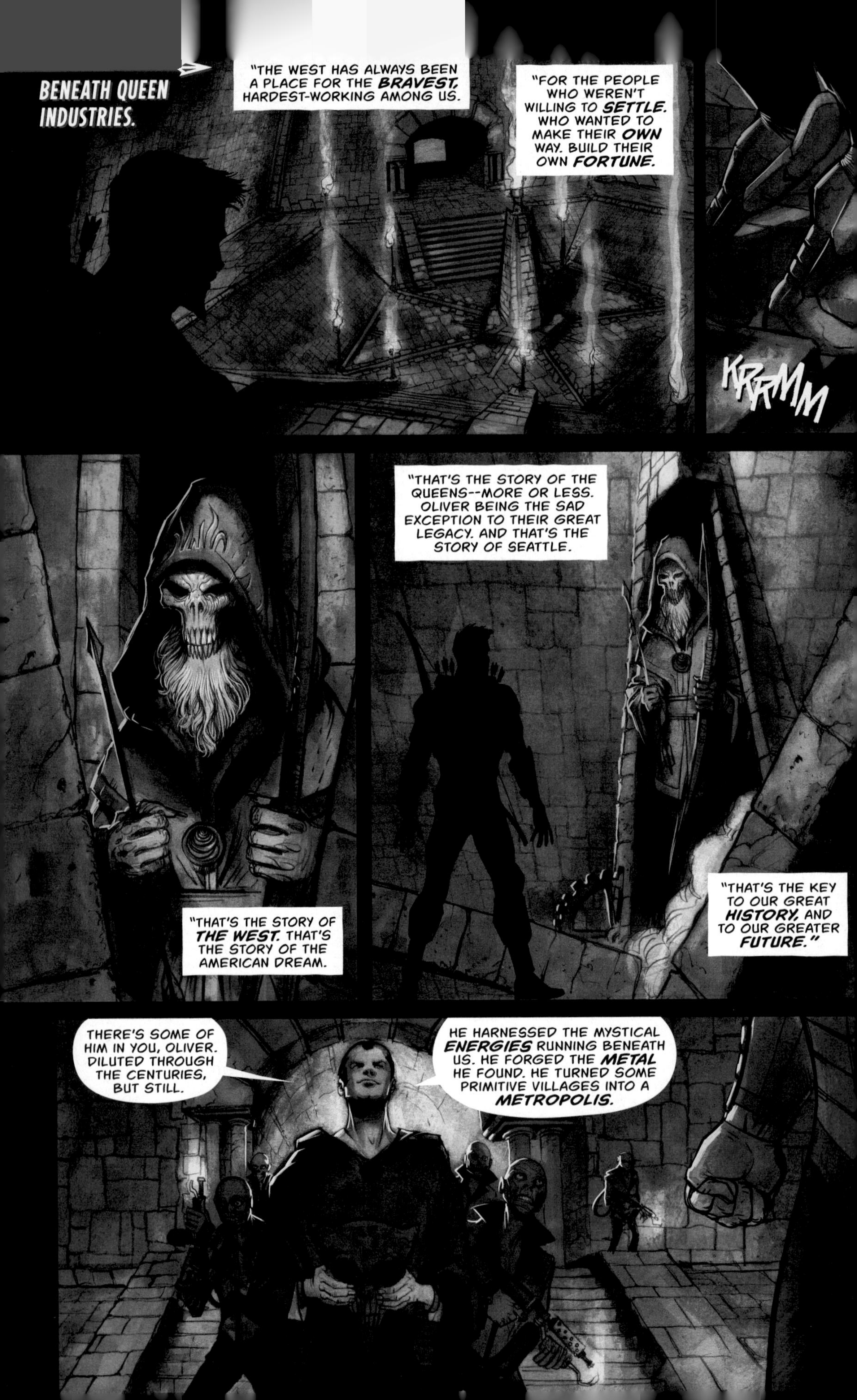
BENEATH QUEEN INDUSTRIES.
"THE WEST HAS ALWAYS BEEN A PLACE FOR THE BRAVEST, HARDEST-WORKING AMONG US.
"FOR THE PEOPLE WHO WEREN'T WILLING TO SETTLE. WHO WANTED TO MAKE THEIR OWN WAY. BUILD THEIR OWN FORTUNE.
KRRMM
"THAT'S THE STORY OF THE WEST. THAT'S THE STORY OF THE AMERICAN DREAM.
"THAT'S THE STORY OF THE QUEENS--MORE OR LESS. OLIVER BEING THE SAD EXCEPTION TO THEIR GREAT LEGACY. AND THAT'S THE STORY OF SEATTLE.
"THAT'S THE KEY TO OUR GREAT HISTORY, AND TO OUR GREATER FUTURE."
THERE'S SOME OF HIM IN YOU, OLIVER. DILUTED THROUGH THE CENTURIES, BUT STILL.
HE HARNESSED THE MYSTICAL ENERGIES RUNNING BENEATH US. HE FORGED THE METAL HE FOUND. HE TURNED SOME PRIMITIVE VILLAGES INTO A METROPOLIS.

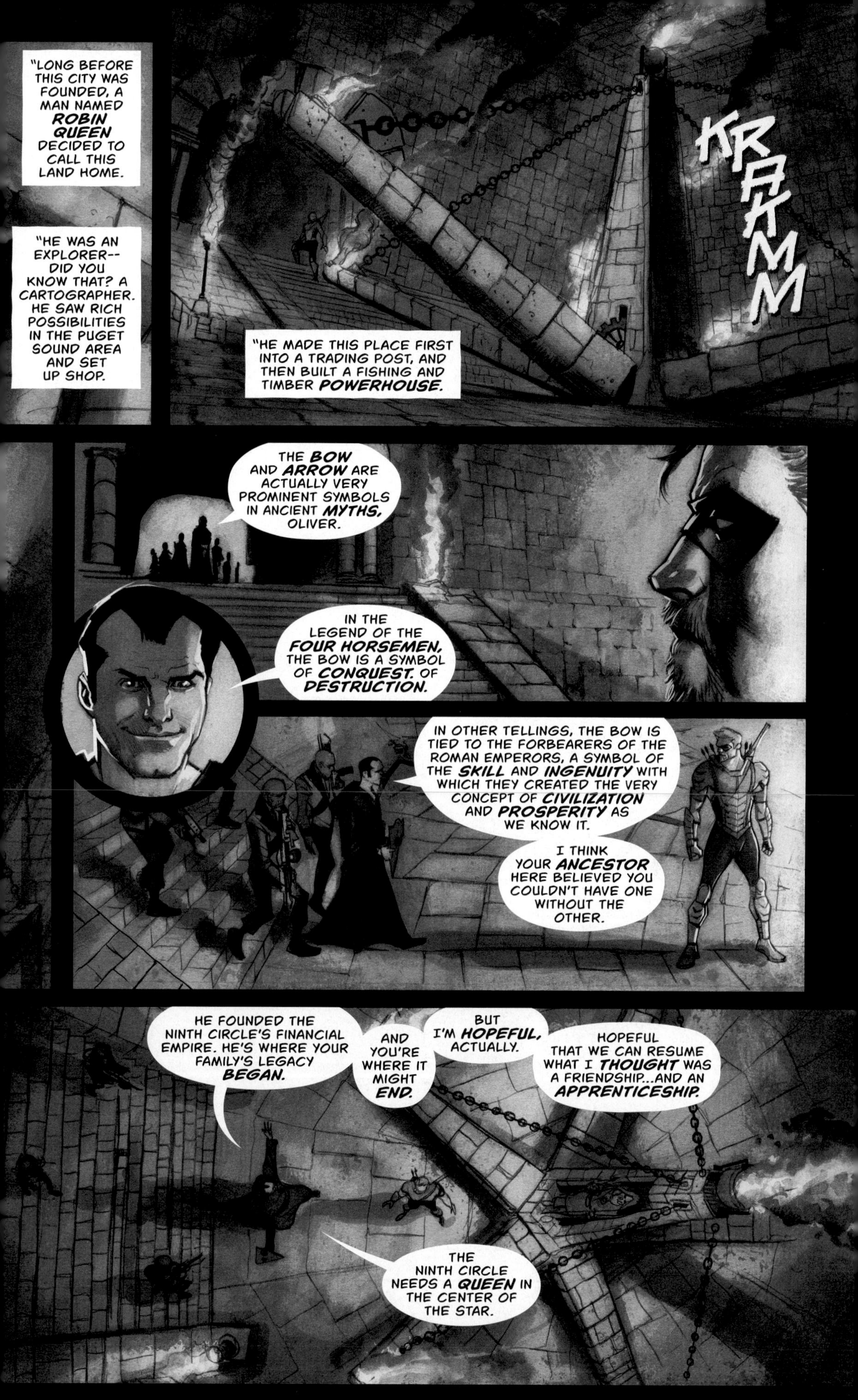
"LONG BEFORE THIS CITY WAS FOUNDED, A MAN NAMED ROBIN QUEEN DECIDED TO CALL THIS LAND HOME.
"HE WAS AN EXPLORER-- DID YOU KNOW THAT? A CARTOGRAPHER. HE SAW RICH POSSIBILITIES IN THE PUGET SOUND AREA AND SET UP SHOP.
"HE MADE THIS PLACE FIRST INTO A TRADING POST, AND THEN BUILT A FISHING AND TIMBER POWERHOUSE.
KRAKMM
THE BOW AND ARROW ARE ACTUALLY VERY PROMINENT SYMBOLS IN ANCIENT MYTHS, OLIVER.
IN THE LEGEND OF THE FOUR HORSEMEN, THE BOW IS A SYMBOL OF CONQUEST. OF DESTRUCTION.
IN OTHER TELLINGS, THE BOW IS TIED TO THE FORBEARERS OF THE ROMAN EMPERORS, A SYMBOL OF THE SKILL AND INGENUITY WITH WHICH THEY CREATED THE VERY CONCEPT OF CIVILIZATION AND PROSPERITY AS WE KNOW IT.
I THINK YOUR ANCESTOR HERE BELIEVED YOU COULDN'T HAVE ONE WITHOUT THE OTHER.
HE FOUNDED THE NINTH CIRCLE'S FINANCIAL EMPIRE. HE'S WHERE YOUR FAMILY'S LEGACY BEGAN.
AND YOU'RE WHERE IT MIGHT END.
BUT I'M HOPEFUL, ACTUALLY.
HOPEFUL THAT WE CAN RESUME WHAT I THOUGHT WAS A FRIENDSHIP...AND AN APPRENTICESHIP.
THE NINTH CIRCLE NEEDS A QUEEN IN THE CENTER OF THE STAR.

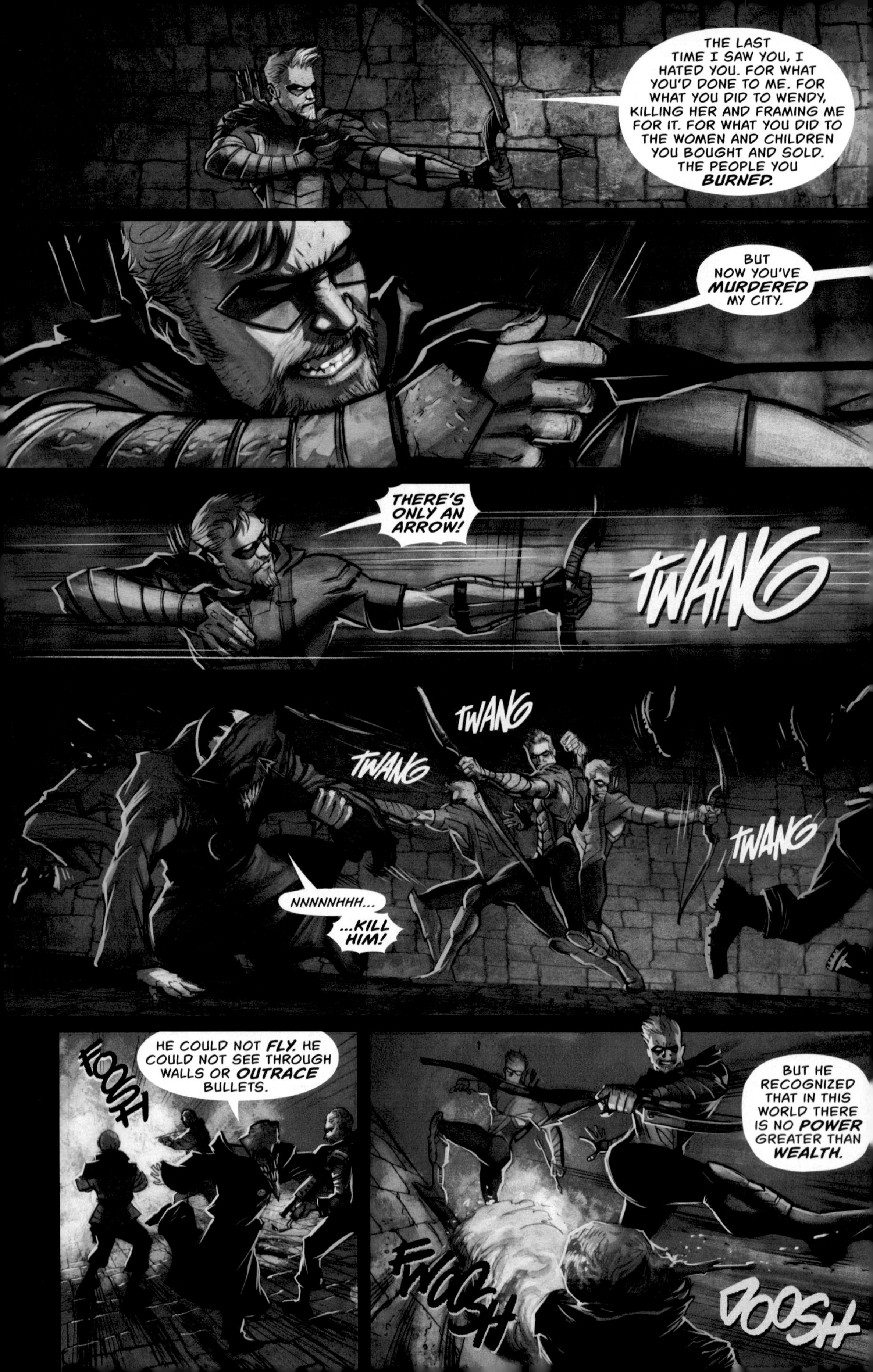
THE LAST TIME I SAW YOU, I HATED YOU. FOR WHAT YOU'D DONE TO ME. FOR WHAT YOU DID TO WENDY, KILLING HER AND FRAMING ME FOR IT. FOR WHAT YOU DID TO THE WOMEN AND CHILDREN YOU BOUGHT AND SOLD. THE PEOPLE YOU **BURNED.**
BUT NOW YOU'VE **MURDERED** MY CITY.
THERE'S ONLY AN ARROW!
TWANG
TWANG
TWANG
TWANG
NNNNNHHH...
...KILL HIM!
FOOSH
HE COULD NOT **FLY.** HE COULD NOT SEE THROUGH WALLS OR **OUTRACE** BULLETS.
BUT HE RECOGNIZED THAT IN THIS WORLD THERE IS NO **POWER** GREATER THAN **WEALTH.**
FWOOSH
DOOSH

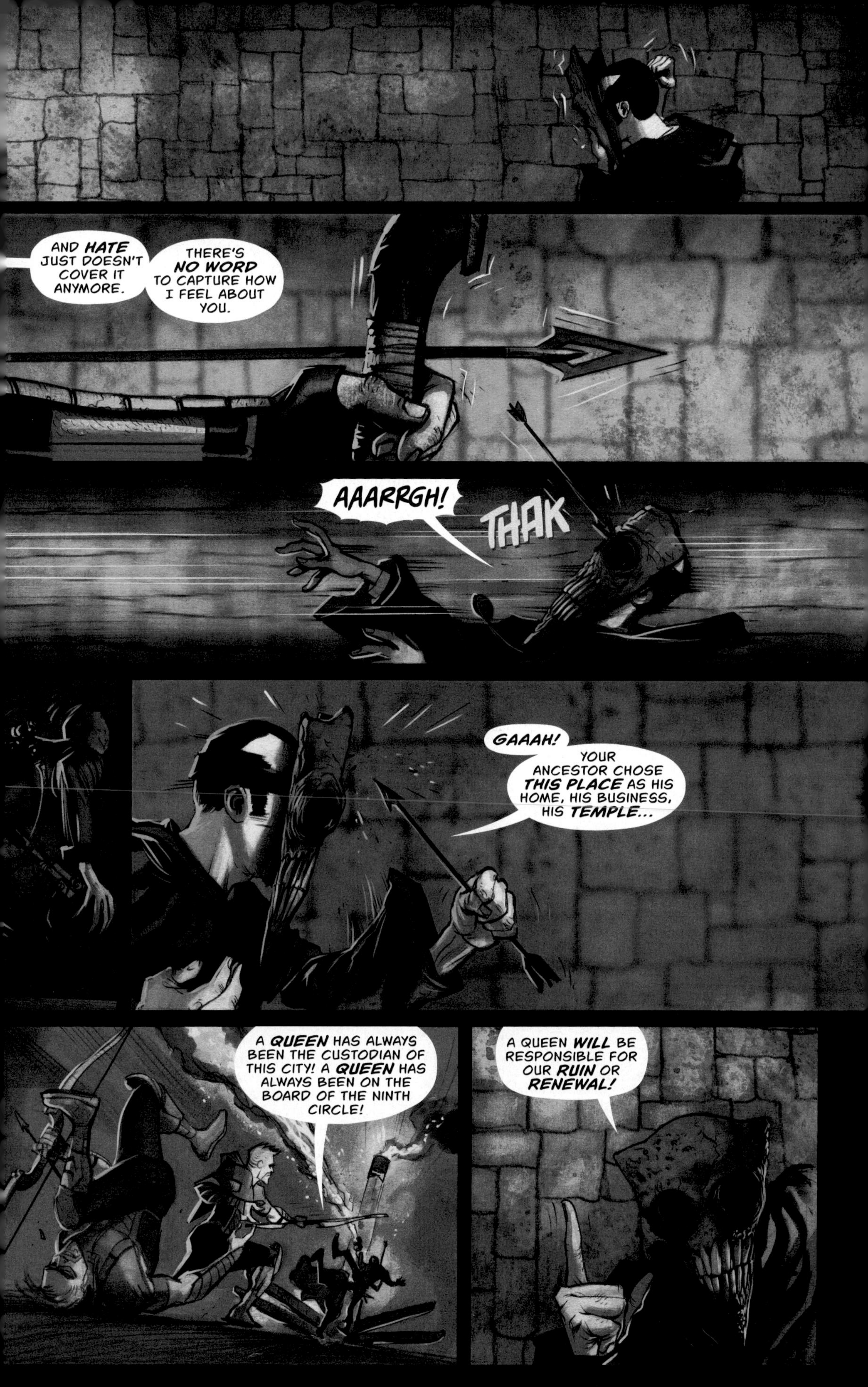
AND HATE JUST DOESN'T COVER IT ANYMORE.
THERE'S NO WORD TO CAPTURE HOW I FEEL ABOUT YOU.
AAARRGH!
THAK
GAAAH!
YOUR ANCESTOR CHOSE THIS PLACE AS HIS HOME, HIS BUSINESS, HIS TEMPLE...
A QUEEN HAS ALWAYS BEEN THE CUSTODIAN OF THIS CITY! A QUEEN HAS ALWAYS BEEN ON THE BOARD OF THE NINTH CIRCLE!
A QUEEN WILL BE RESPONSIBLE FOR OUR RUIN OR RENEWAL!

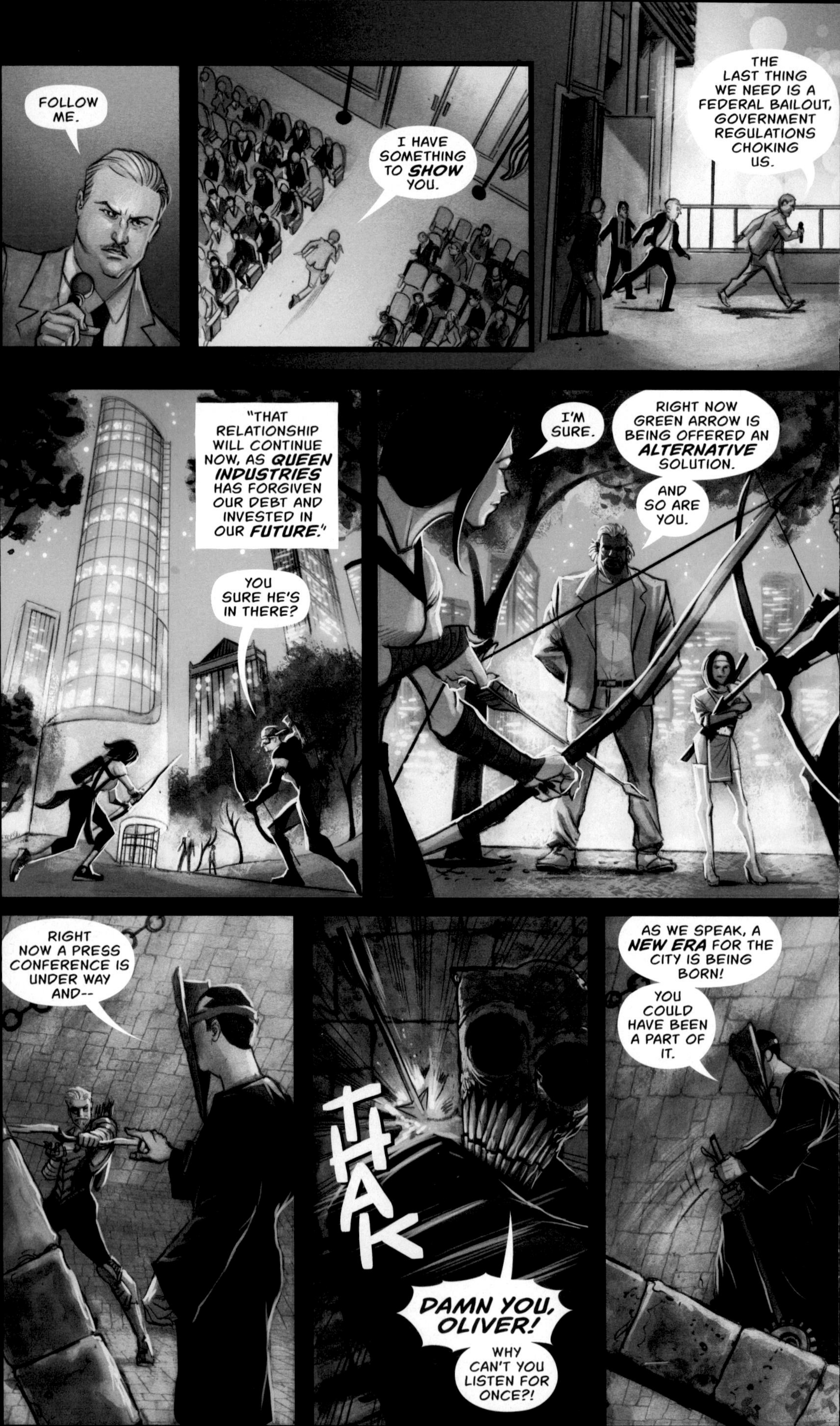
FOLLOW ME.
I HAVE SOMETHING TO SHOW YOU.
THE LAST THING WE NEED IS A FEDERAL BAILOUT, GOVERNMENT REGULATIONS CHOKING US.
"THAT RELATIONSHIP WILL CONTINUE NOW, AS QUEEN INDUSTRIES HAS FORGIVEN OUR DEBT AND INVESTED IN OUR FUTURE."
YOU SURE HE'S IN THERE?
I'M SURE.
RIGHT NOW GREEN ARROW IS BEING OFFERED AN ALTERNATIVE SOLUTION.
AND SO ARE YOU.
RIGHT NOW A PRESS CONFERENCE IS UNDER WAY AND--
THAK
DAMN YOU, OLIVER!
WHY CAN'T YOU LISTEN FOR ONCE?!
AS WE SPEAK, A NEW ERA FOR THE CITY IS BEING BORN!
YOU COULD HAVE BEEN A PART OF IT.

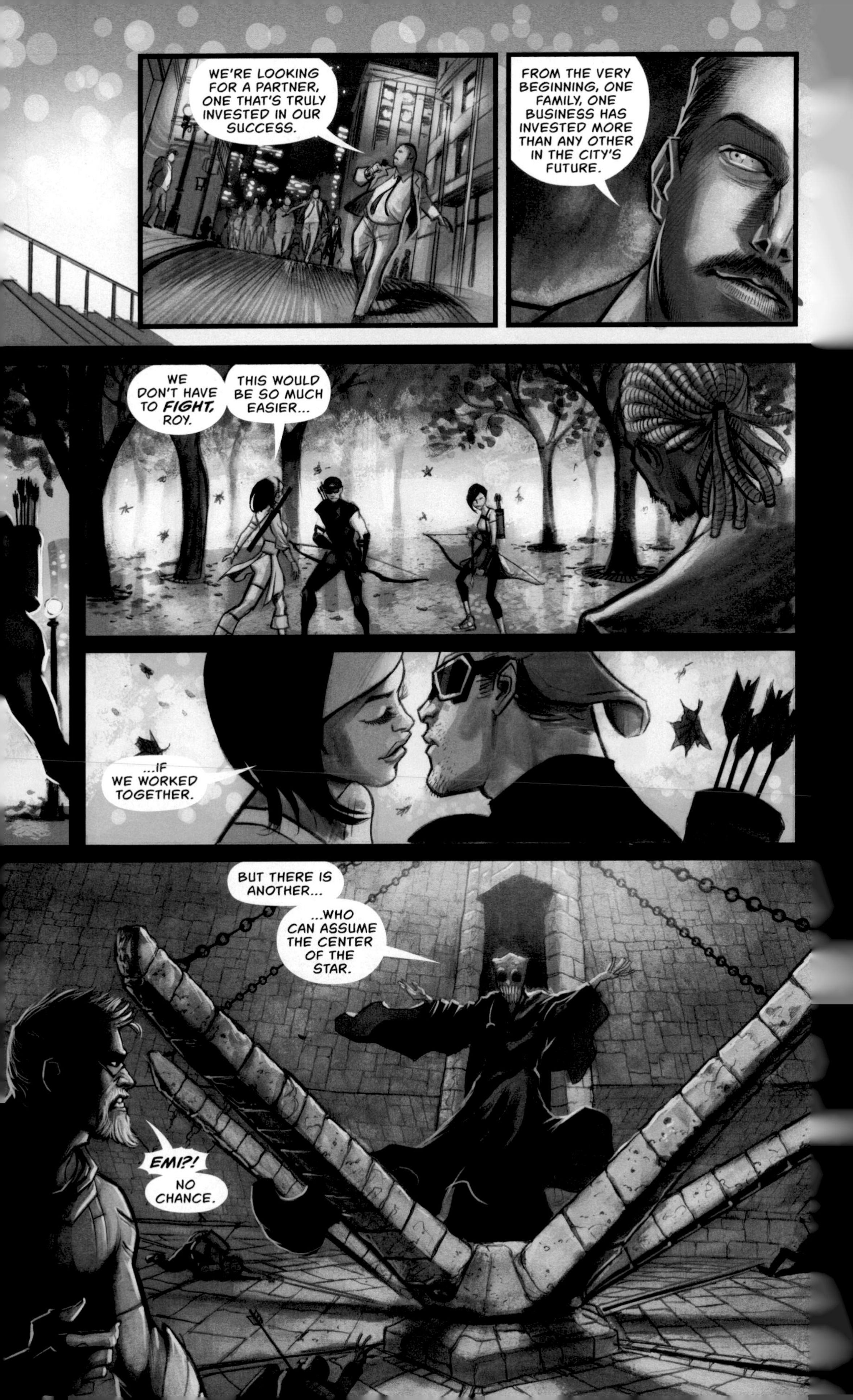
WE'RE LOOKING FOR A PARTNER, ONE THAT'S TRULY INVESTED IN OUR SUCCESS.
FROM THE VERY BEGINNING, ONE FAMILY, ONE BUSINESS HAS INVESTED MORE THAN ANY OTHER IN THE CITY'S FUTURE.
WE DON'T HAVE TO FIGHT, ROY.
THIS WOULD BE SO MUCH EASIER...
...IF WE WORKED TOGETHER.
BUT THERE IS ANOTHER...
...WHO CAN ASSUME THE CENTER OF THE STAR.
EMI?! NO CHANCE.

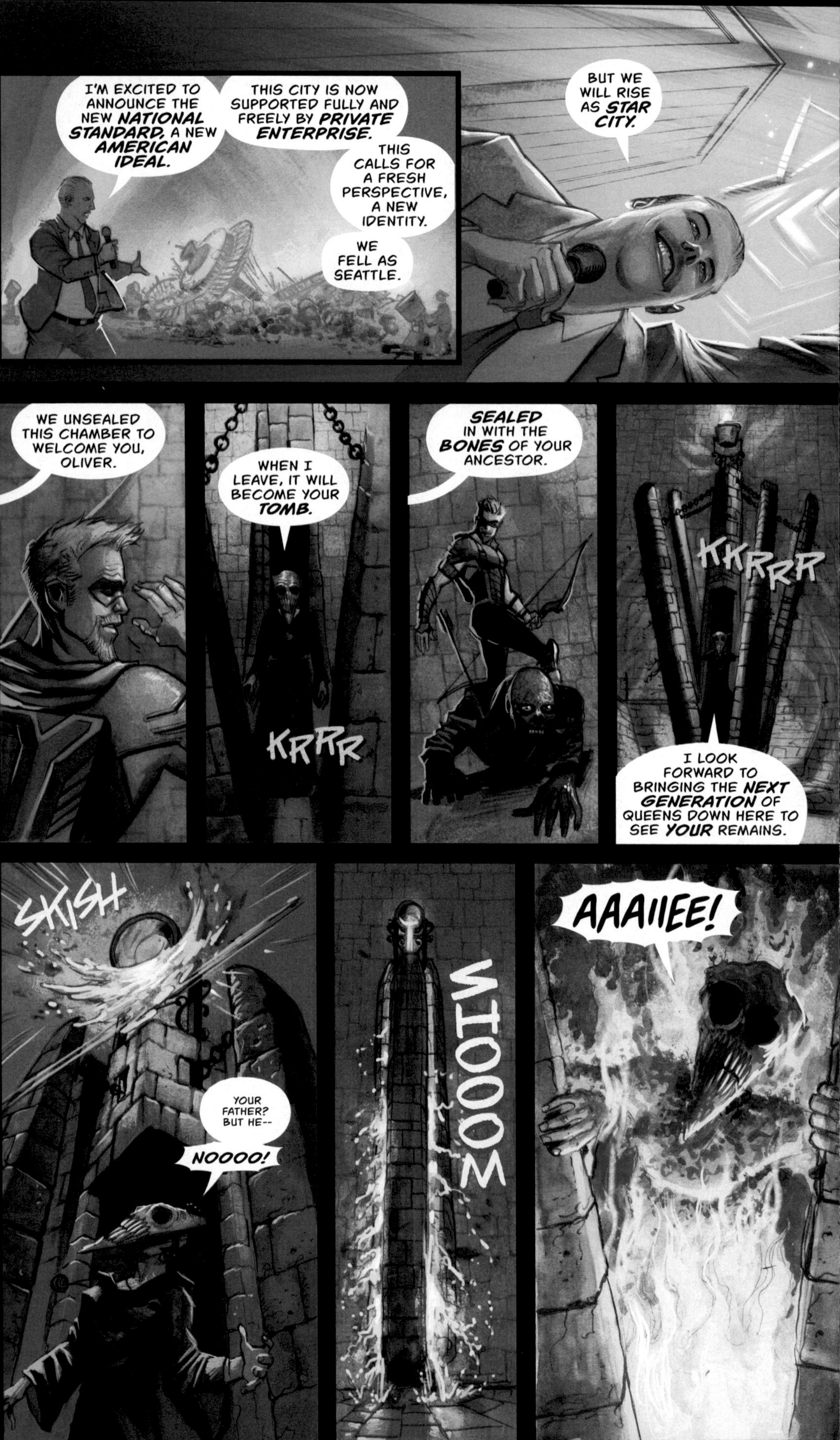
I'M EXCITED TO ANNOUNCE THE NEW NATIONAL STANDARD, A NEW AMERICAN IDEAL.
THIS CITY IS NOW SUPPORTED FULLY AND FREELY BY PRIVATE ENTERPRISE.
THIS CALLS FOR A FRESH PERSPECTIVE, A NEW IDENTITY.
WE FELL AS SEATTLE.
BUT WE WILL RISE AS STAR CITY.
WE UNSEALED THIS CHAMBER TO WELCOME YOU, OLIVER.
WHEN I LEAVE, IT WILL BECOME YOUR TOMB.
KRRR
SEALED IN WITH THE BONES OF YOUR ANCESTOR.
KKRRRR
I LOOK FORWARD TO BRINGING THE NEXT GENERATION OF QUEENS DOWN HERE TO SEE YOUR REMAINS.
SKISH
YOUR FATHER? BUT HE--
NOOOO!
WHOOOM
AAAIIEE!

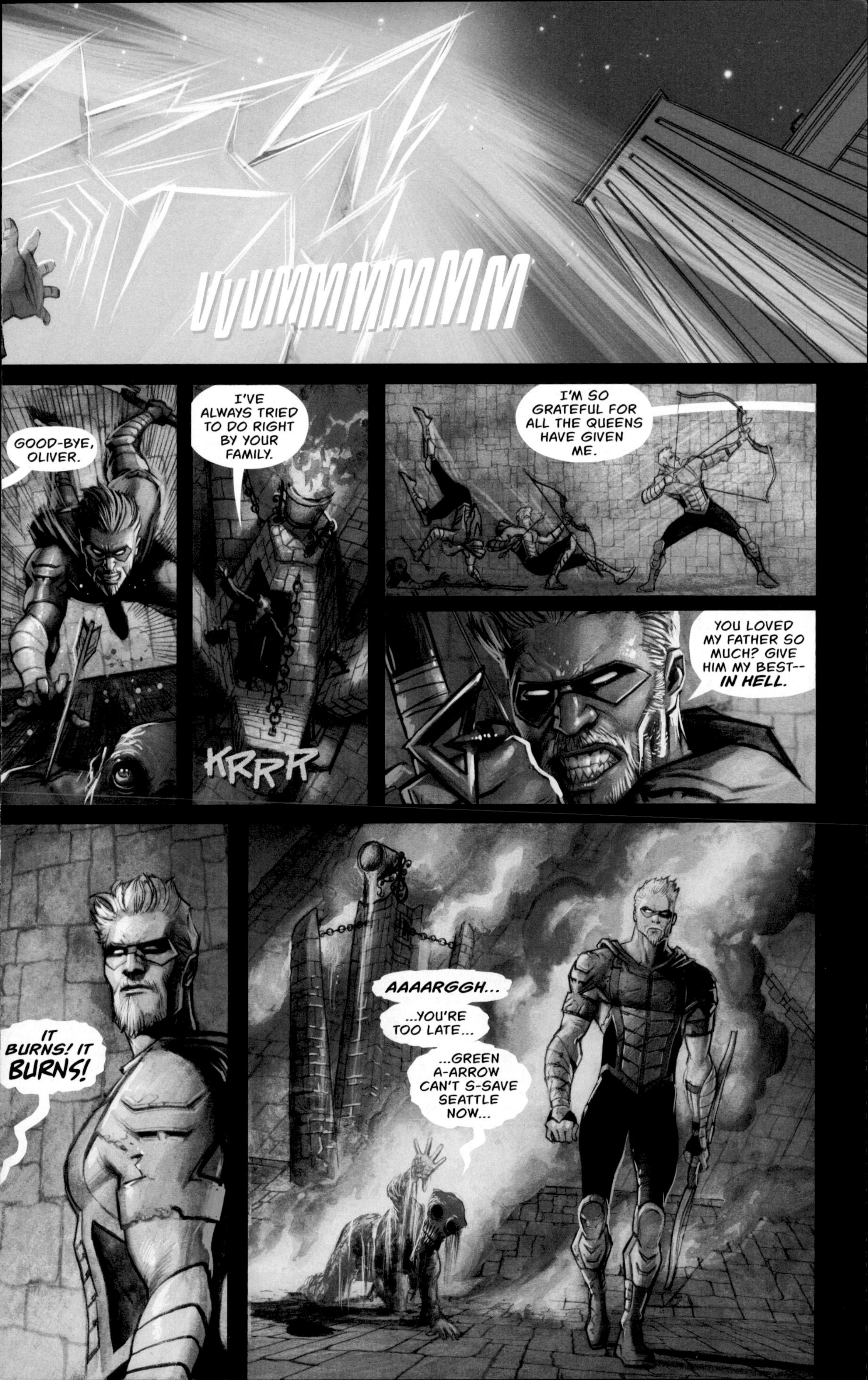
VVVMMMMMMM
GOOD-BYE, OLIVER.
I'VE ALWAYS TRIED TO DO RIGHT BY YOUR FAMILY.
KRRR
I'M SO GRATEFUL FOR ALL THE QUEENS HAVE GIVEN ME.
YOU LOVED MY FATHER SO MUCH? GIVE HIM MY BEST-- IN HELL.
IT BURNS! IT BURNS!
AAAARGGH...
...YOU'RE TOO LATE...
...GREEN A-ARROW CAN'T S-SAVE SEATTLE NOW...

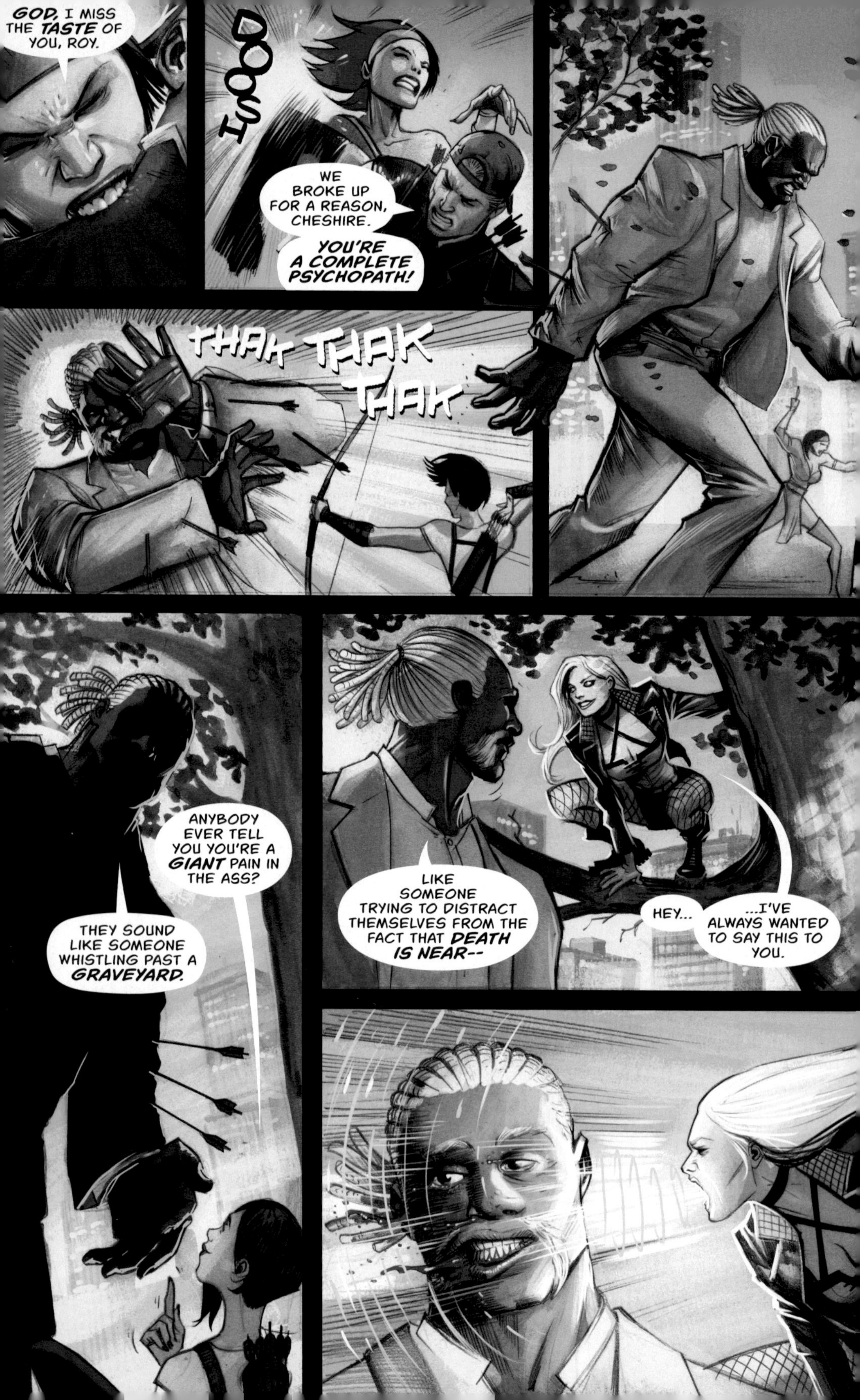
GOD, I MISS THE TASTE OF YOU, ROY.
DOOSH
WE BROKE UP FOR A REASON, CHESHIRE.
YOU'RE A COMPLETE PSYCHOPATH!
THAK THAK THAK
ANYBODY EVER TELL YOU YOU'RE A GIANT PAIN IN THE ASS?
THEY SOUND LIKE SOMEONE WHISTLING PAST A GRAVEYARD.
LIKE SOMEONE TRYING TO DISTRACT THEMSELVES FROM THE FACT THAT DEATH IS NEAR--
HEY...
...I'VE ALWAYS WANTED TO SAY THIS TO YOU.

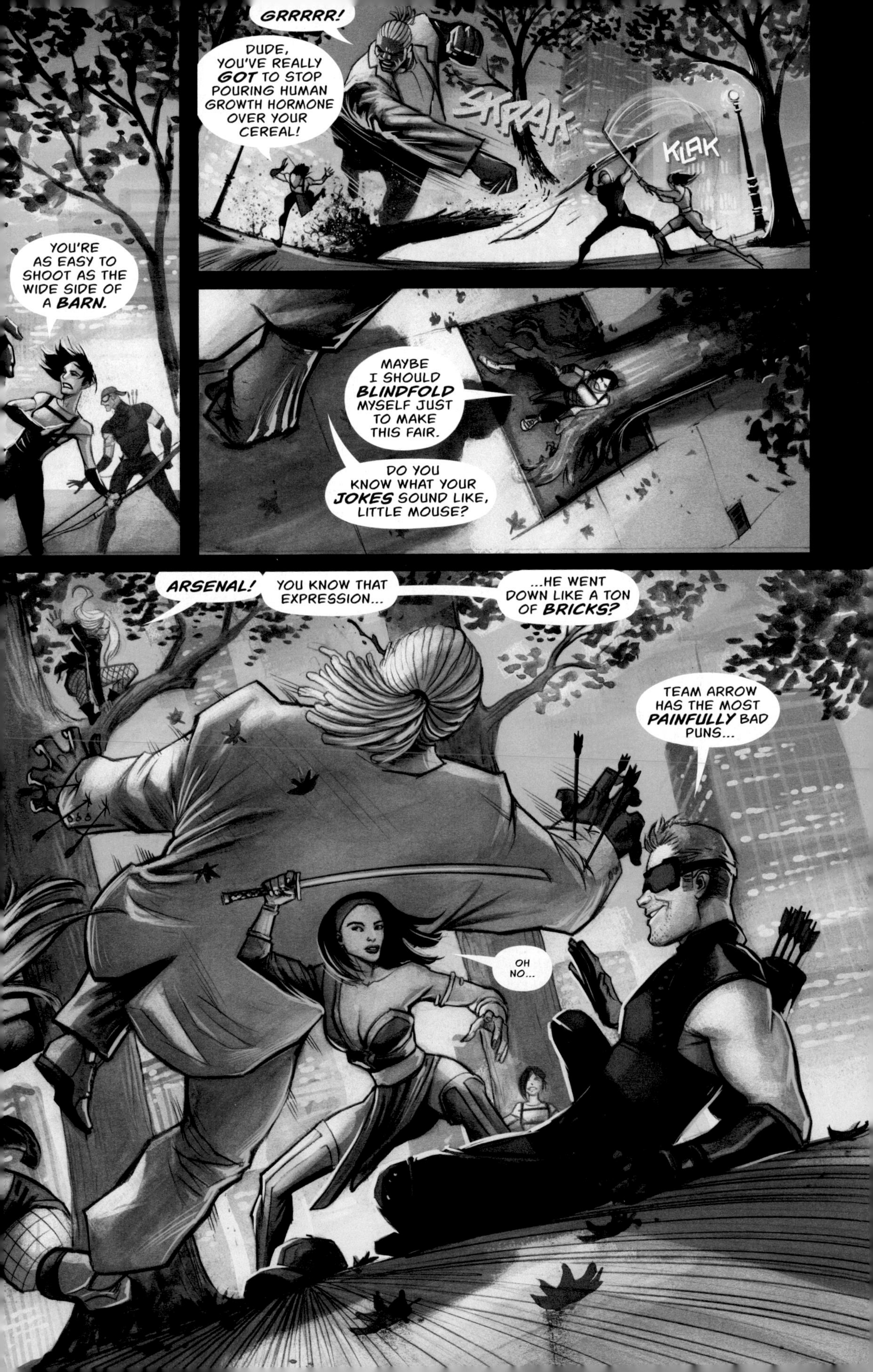
GRRRRR!
DUDE, YOU'VE REALLY GOT TO STOP POURING HUMAN GROWTH HORMONE OVER YOUR CEREAL!
SKRAK
KLAK
YOU'RE AS EASY TO SHOOT AS THE WIDE SIDE OF A BARN.
MAYBE I SHOULD BLINDFOLD MYSELF JUST TO MAKE THIS FAIR.
DO YOU KNOW WHAT YOUR JOKES SOUND LIKE, LITTLE MOUSE?
ARSENAL!
YOU KNOW THAT EXPRESSION...
...HE WENT DOWN LIKE A TON OF BRICKS?
TEAM ARROW HAS THE MOST PAINFULLY BAD PUNS...
OH NO...

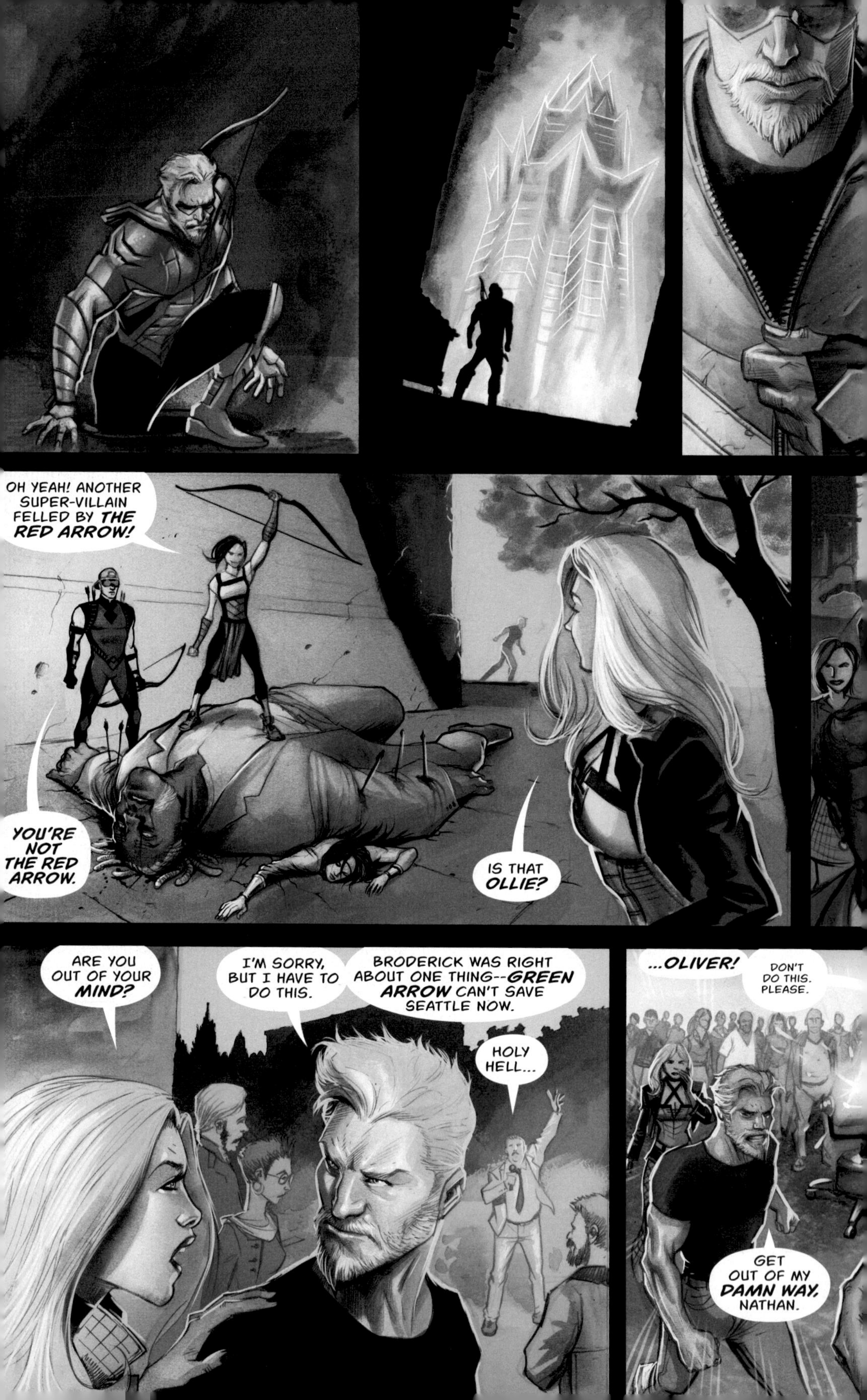
OH YEAH! ANOTHER SUPER-VILLAIN FELLED BY THE RED ARROW!
YOU'RE NOT THE RED ARROW.
IS THAT OLLIE?
ARE YOU OUT OF YOUR MIND?
I'M SORRY, BUT I HAVE TO DO THIS.
BRODERICK WAS RIGHT ABOUT ONE THING--GREEN ARROW CAN'T SAVE SEATTLE NOW.
HOLY HELL...
...OLIVER!
DON'T DO THIS. PLEASE.
GET OUT OF MY DAMN WAY, NATHAN.

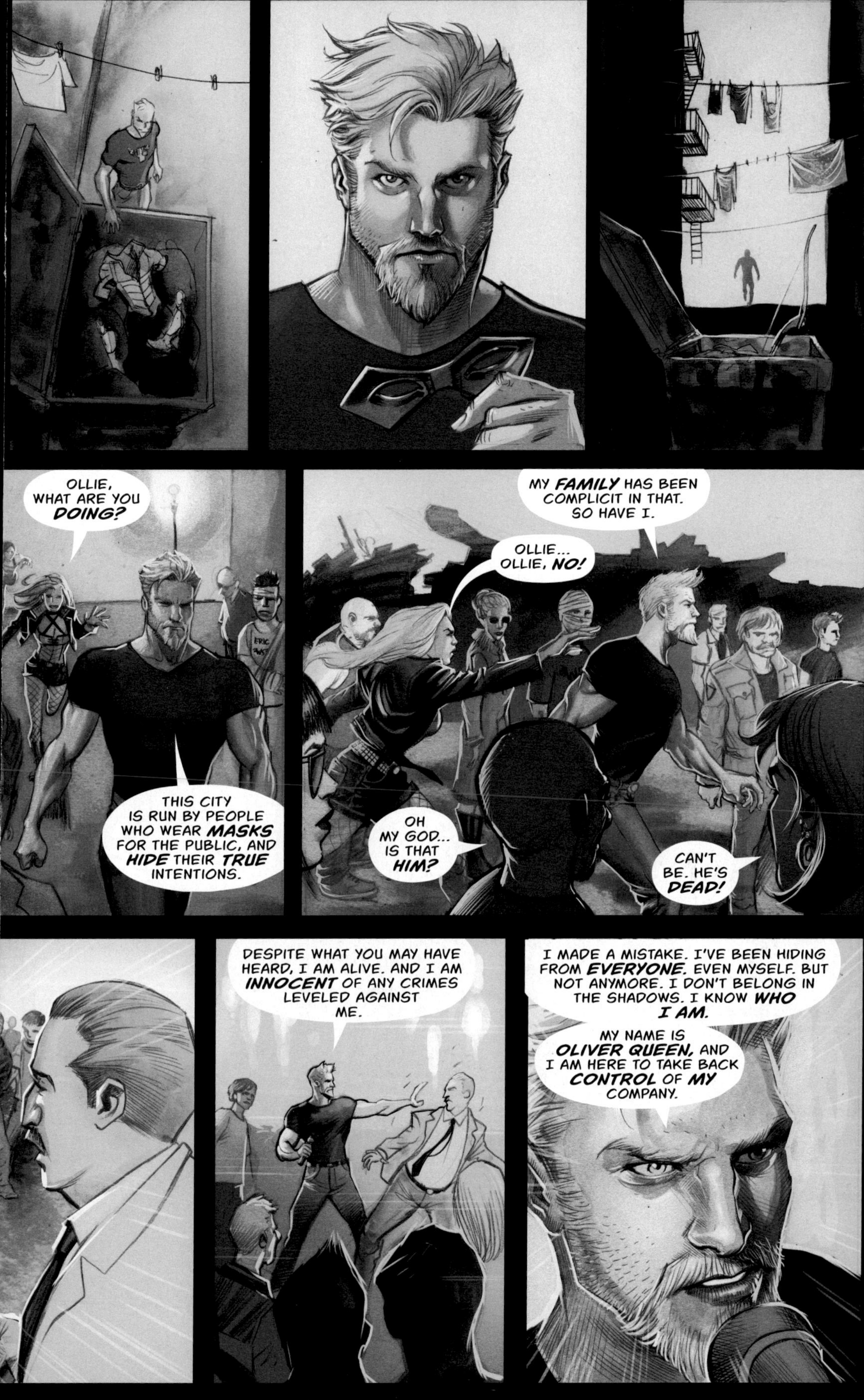

OLLIE, WHAT ARE YOU DOING?
THIS CITY IS RUN BY PEOPLE WHO WEAR MASKS FOR THE PUBLIC, AND HIDE THEIR TRUE INTENTIONS.
MY FAMILY HAS BEEN COMPLICIT IN THAT. SO HAVE I.
OLLIE... OLLIE, NO!
OH MY GOD... IS THAT HIM?
CAN'T BE. HE'S DEAD!
DESPITE WHAT YOU MAY HAVE HEARD, I AM ALIVE. AND I AM INNOCENT OF ANY CRIMES LEVELED AGAINST ME.
I MADE A MISTAKE. I'VE BEEN HIDING FROM EVERYONE. EVEN MYSELF. BUT NOT ANYMORE. I DON'T BELONG IN THE SHADOWS. I KNOW WHO I AM.
MY NAME IS OLIVER QUEEN, AND I AM HERE TO TAKE BACK CONTROL OF MY COMPANY.

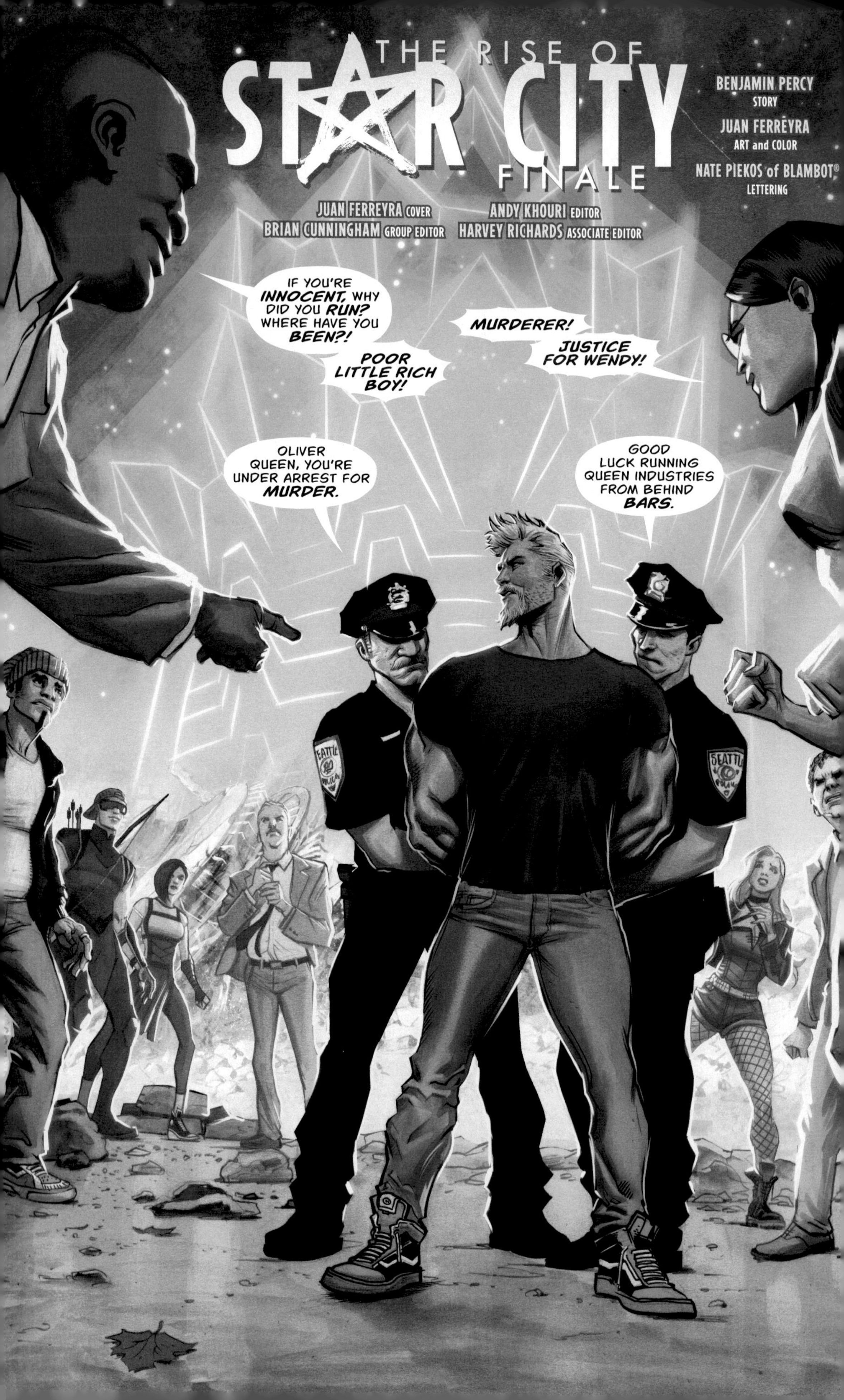
THE RISE OF
STAR CITY
FINALE
BENJAMIN PERCY STORY
JUAN FERREYRA ART and COLOR
NATE PIEKOS of BLAMBOT® LETTERING
JUAN FERREYRA COVER
ANDY KHOURI EDITOR
BRIAN CUNNINGHAM GROUP EDITOR
HARVEY RICHARDS ASSOCIATE EDITOR
IF YOU'RE INNOCENT, WHY DID YOU RUN? WHERE HAVE YOU BEEN?!
POOR LITTLE RICH BOY!
MURDERER!
JUSTICE FOR WENDY!
OLIVER QUEEN, YOU'RE UNDER ARREST FOR MURDER.
GOOD LUCK RUNNING QUEEN INDUSTRIES FROM BEHIND BARS.
SEATTLE
SEATTLE

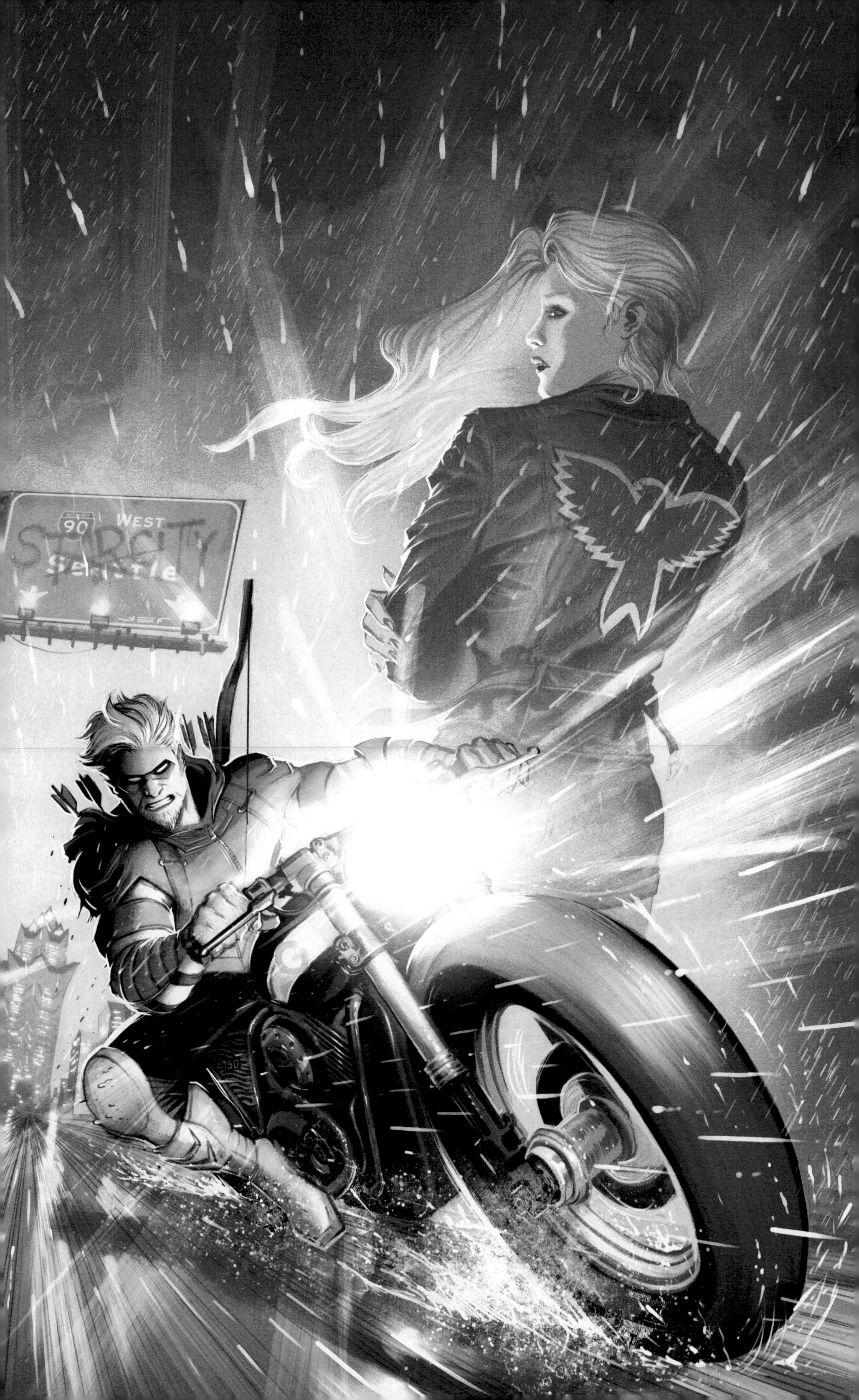
90
WEST
STARCITY
Seattle

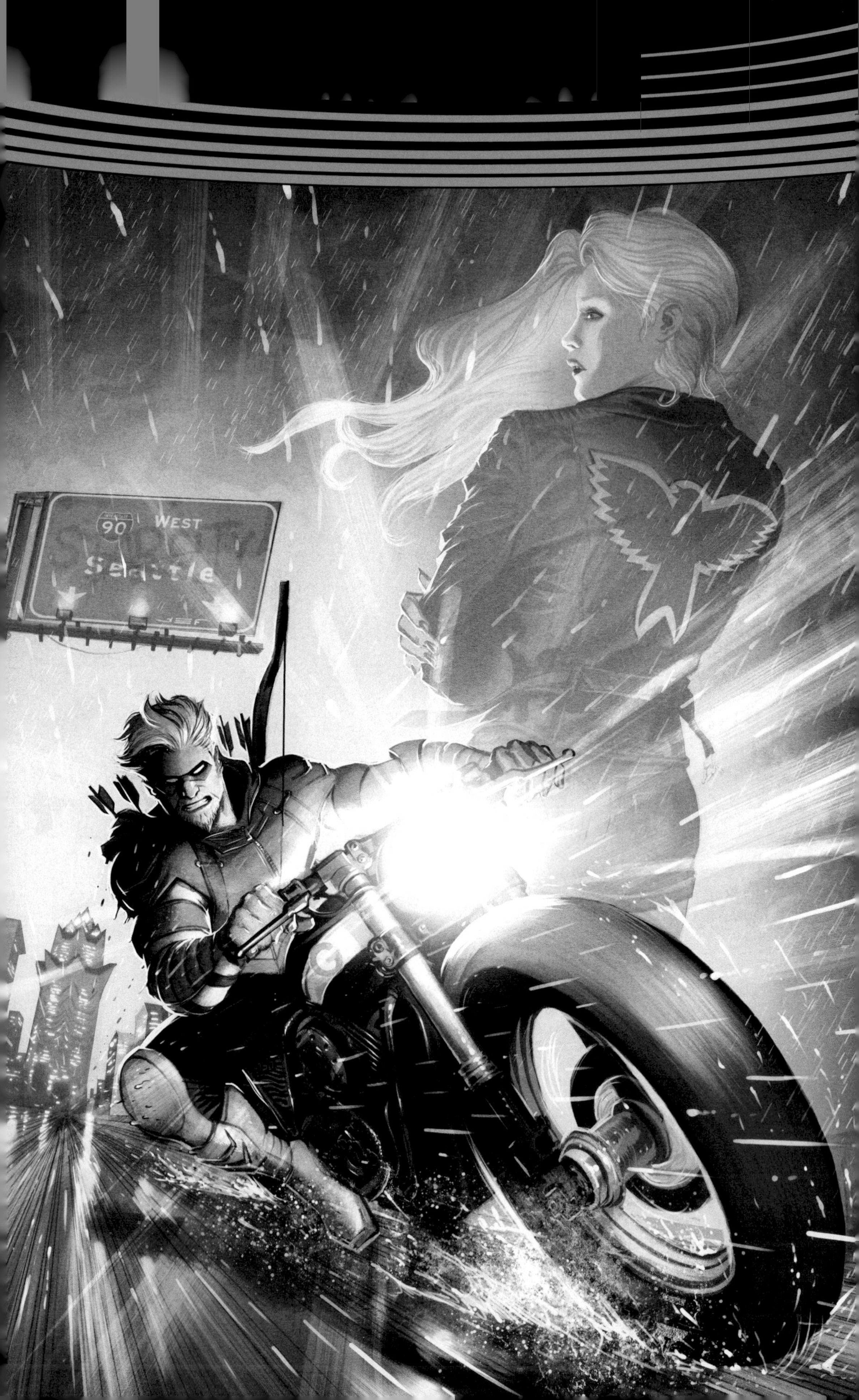
90
WEST
Seattle

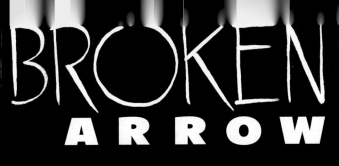

BROKEN ARROW

BENJAMIN PERCY STORY
OTTO SCHMIDT ART AND COLOR
NATE PIEKOS of BLAMBOT® LETTERING
JUAN FERREYRA COVER
BRIAN CUNNINGHAM GROUP EDITOR
HARVEY RICHARDS ASSOCIATE EDITOR
ANDY KHOURI EDITOR

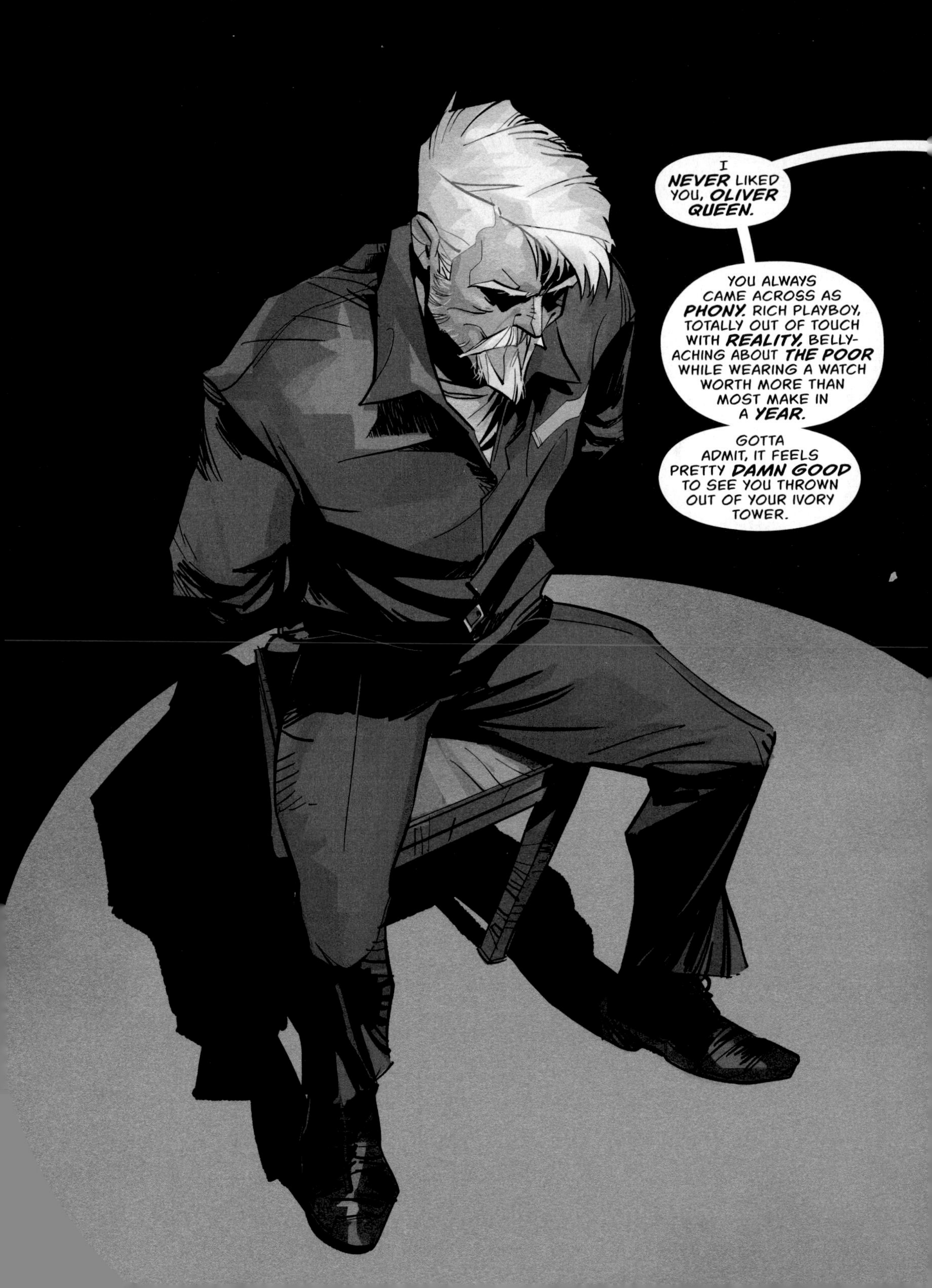

I NEVER LIKED YOU, OLIVER QUEEN.
YOU ALWAYS CAME ACROSS AS PHONY. RICH PLAYBOY, TOTALLY OUT OF TOUCH WITH REALITY, BELLY-ACHING ABOUT THE POOR WHILE WEARING A WATCH WORTH MORE THAN MOST MAKE IN A YEAR.
GOTTA ADMIT, IT FEELS PRETTY DAMN GOOD TO SEE YOU THROWN OUT OF YOUR IVORY TOWER.

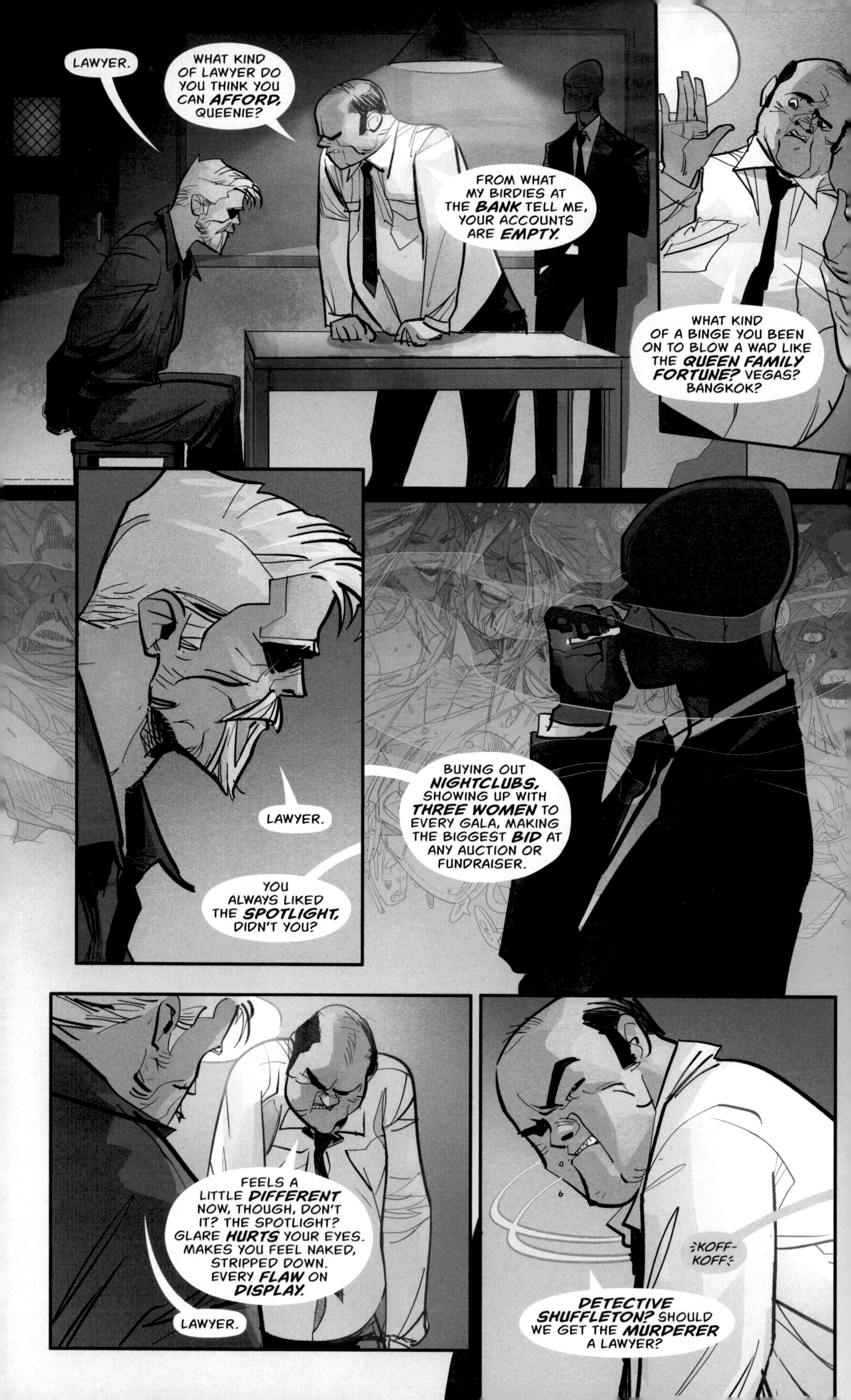
LAWYER.
WHAT KIND OF LAWYER DO YOU THINK YOU CAN AFFORD, QUEENIE?
FROM WHAT MY BIRDIES AT THE BANK TELL ME, YOUR ACCOUNTS ARE EMPTY.
WHAT KIND OF A BINGE YOU BEEN ON TO BLOW A WAD LIKE THE QUEEN FAMILY FORTUNE? VEGAS? BANGKOK?
LAWYER.
BUYING OUT NIGHTCLUBS, SHOWING UP WITH THREE WOMEN TO EVERY GALA, MAKING THE BIGGEST BID AT ANY AUCTION OR FUNDRAISER.
YOU ALWAYS LIKED THE SPOTLIGHT, DIDN'T YOU?
FEELS A LITTLE DIFFERENT NOW, THOUGH, DON'T IT? THE SPOTLIGHT? GLARE HURTS YOUR EYES. MAKES YOU FEEL NAKED, STRIPPED DOWN. EVERY FLAW ON DISPLAY.
LAWYER.
KOFF-KOFF
DETECTIVE SHUFFLETON? SHOULD WE GET THE MURDERER A LAWYER?

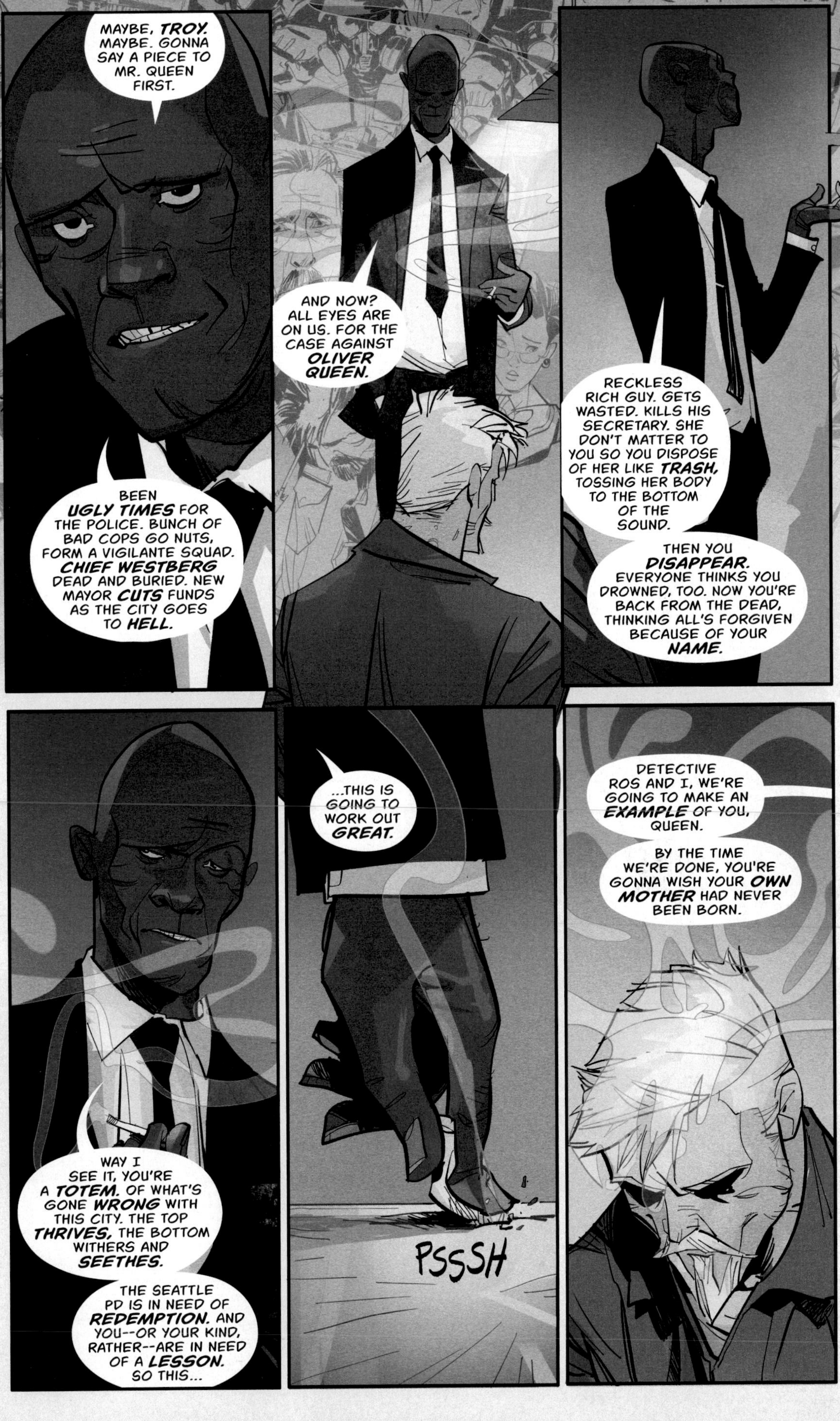
MAYBE, TROY. MAYBE. GONNA SAY A PIECE TO MR. QUEEN FIRST.
BEEN UGLY TIMES FOR THE POLICE. BUNCH OF BAD COPS GO NUTS, FORM A VIGILANTE SQUAD. CHIEF WESTBERG DEAD AND BURIED. NEW MAYOR CUTS FUNDS AS THE CITY GOES TO HELL.
AND NOW? ALL EYES ARE ON US. FOR THE CASE AGAINST OLIVER QUEEN.
RECKLESS RICH GUY. GETS WASTED. KILLS HIS SECRETARY. SHE DON'T MATTER TO YOU SO YOU DISPOSE OF HER LIKE TRASH, TOSSING HER BODY TO THE BOTTOM OF THE SOUND.
THEN YOU DISAPPEAR. EVERYONE THINKS YOU DROWNED, TOO. NOW YOU'RE BACK FROM THE DEAD, THINKING ALL'S FORGIVEN BECAUSE OF YOUR NAME.
WAY I SEE IT, YOU'RE A TOTEM. OF WHAT'S GONE WRONG WITH THIS CITY. THE TOP THRIVES, THE BOTTOM WITHERS AND SEETHES.
THE SEATTLE PD IS IN NEED OF REDEMPTION. AND YOU--OR YOUR KIND, RATHER--ARE IN NEED OF A LESSON. SO THIS...
...THIS IS GOING TO WORK OUT GREAT.
PSSSH
DETECTIVE ROS AND I, WE'RE GOING TO MAKE AN EXAMPLE OF YOU, QUEEN.
BY THE TIME WE'RE DONE, YOU'RE GONNA WISH YOUR OWN MOTHER HAD NEVER BEEN BORN.

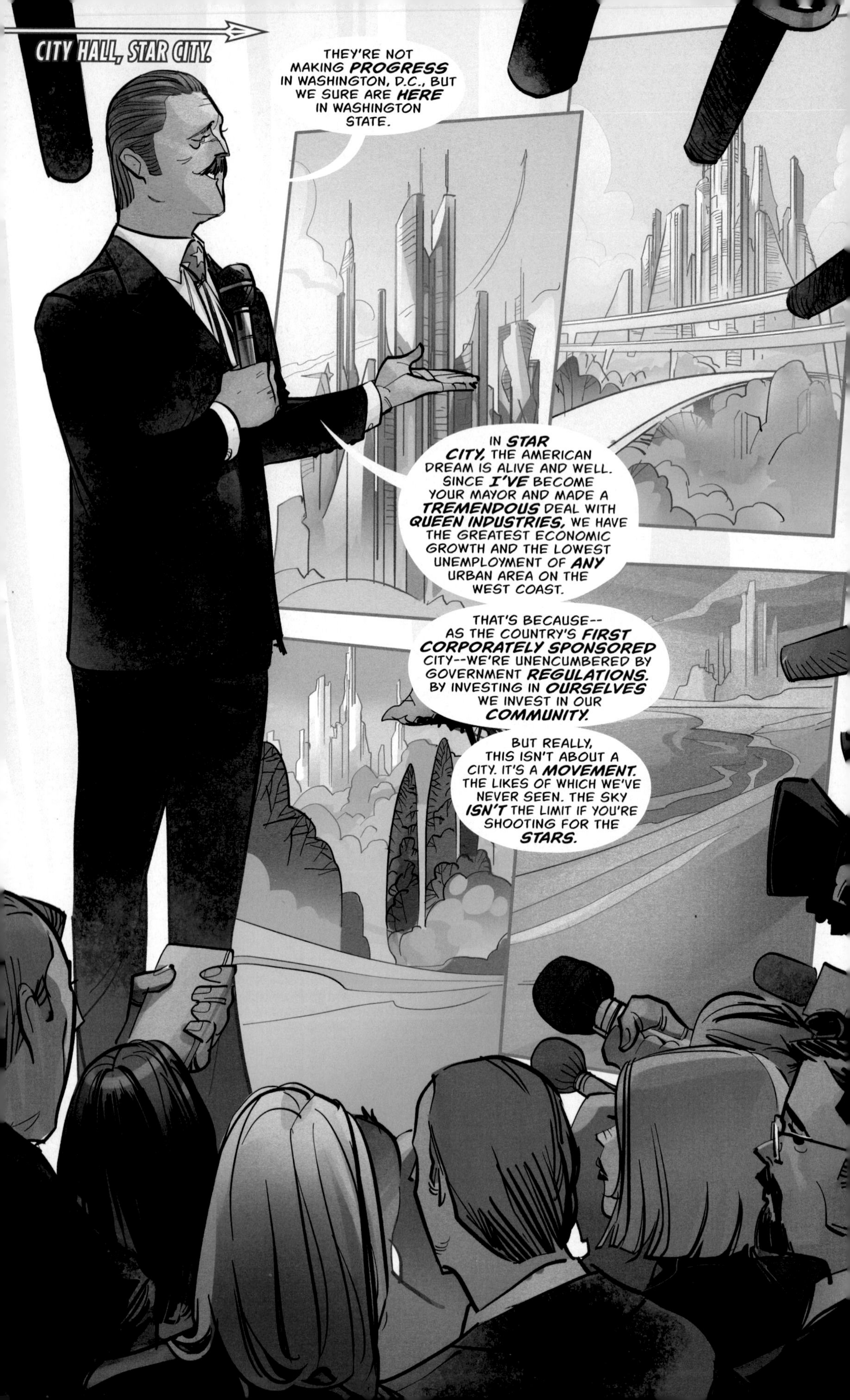
CITY HALL, STAR CITY.
THEY'RE NOT MAKING PROGRESS IN WASHINGTON, D.C., BUT WE SURE ARE HERE IN WASHINGTON STATE.
IN STAR CITY, THE AMERICAN DREAM IS ALIVE AND WELL. SINCE I'VE BECOME YOUR MAYOR AND MADE A TREMENDOUS DEAL WITH QUEEN INDUSTRIES, WE HAVE THE GREATEST ECONOMIC GROWTH AND THE LOWEST UNEMPLOYMENT OF ANY URBAN AREA ON THE WEST COAST.
THAT'S BECAUSE-- AS THE COUNTRY'S FIRST CORPORATELY SPONSORED CITY--WE'RE UNENCUMBERED BY GOVERNMENT REGULATIONS. BY INVESTING IN OURSELVES WE INVEST IN OUR COMMUNITY.
BUT REALLY, THIS ISN'T ABOUT A CITY. IT'S A MOVEMENT. THE LIKES OF WHICH WE'VE NEVER SEEN. THE SKY ISN'T THE LIMIT IF YOU'RE SHOOTING FOR THE STARS.

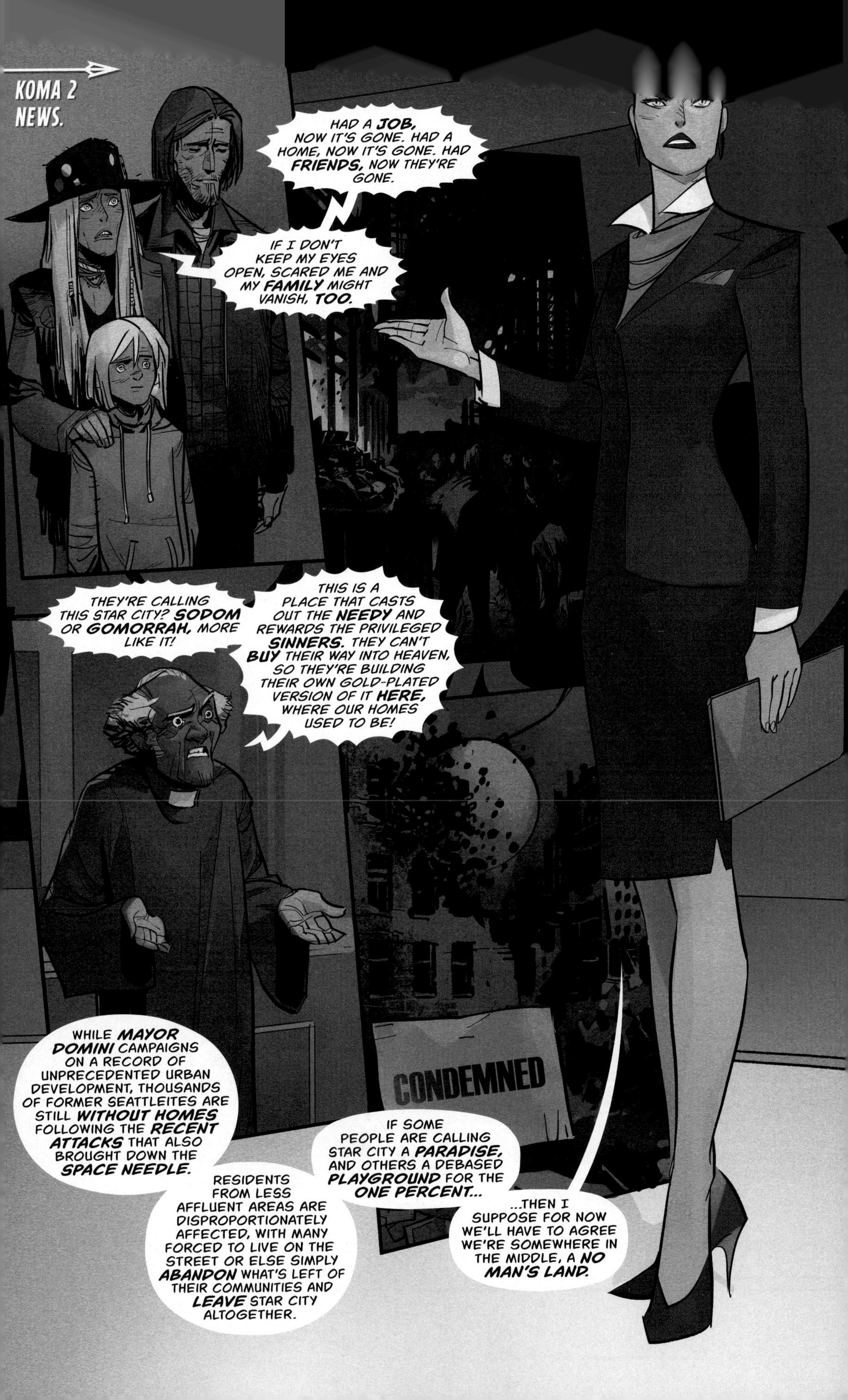
KOMA 2 NEWS.
HAD A JOB, NOW IT'S GONE. HAD A HOME, NOW IT'S GONE. HAD FRIENDS, NOW THEY'RE GONE.
IF I DON'T KEEP MY EYES OPEN, SCARED ME AND MY FAMILY MIGHT VANISH, TOO.
THEY'RE CALLING THIS STAR CITY? SODOM OR GOMORRAH, MORE LIKE IT!
THIS IS A PLACE THAT CASTS OUT THE NEEDY AND REWARDS THE PRIVILEGED SINNERS. THEY CAN'T BUY THEIR WAY INTO HEAVEN, SO THEY'RE BUILDING THEIR OWN GOLD-PLATED VERSION OF IT HERE, WHERE OUR HOMES USED TO BE!
CONDEMNED
WHILE MAYOR DOMINI CAMPAIGNS ON A RECORD OF UNPRECEDENTED URBAN DEVELOPMENT, THOUSANDS OF FORMER SEATTLEITES ARE STILL WITHOUT HOMES FOLLOWING THE RECENT ATTACKS THAT ALSO BROUGHT DOWN THE SPACE NEEDLE.
RESIDENTS FROM LESS AFFLUENT AREAS ARE DISPROPORTIONATELY AFFECTED, WITH MANY FORCED TO LIVE ON THE STREET OR ELSE SIMPLY ABANDON WHAT'S LEFT OF THEIR COMMUNITIES AND LEAVE STAR CITY ALTOGETHER.
IF SOME PEOPLE ARE CALLING STAR CITY A PARADISE, AND OTHERS A DEBASED PLAYGROUND FOR THE ONE PERCENT...
...THEN I SUPPOSE FOR NOW WE'LL HAVE TO AGREE WE'RE SOMEWHERE IN THE MIDDLE, A NO MAN'S LAND.

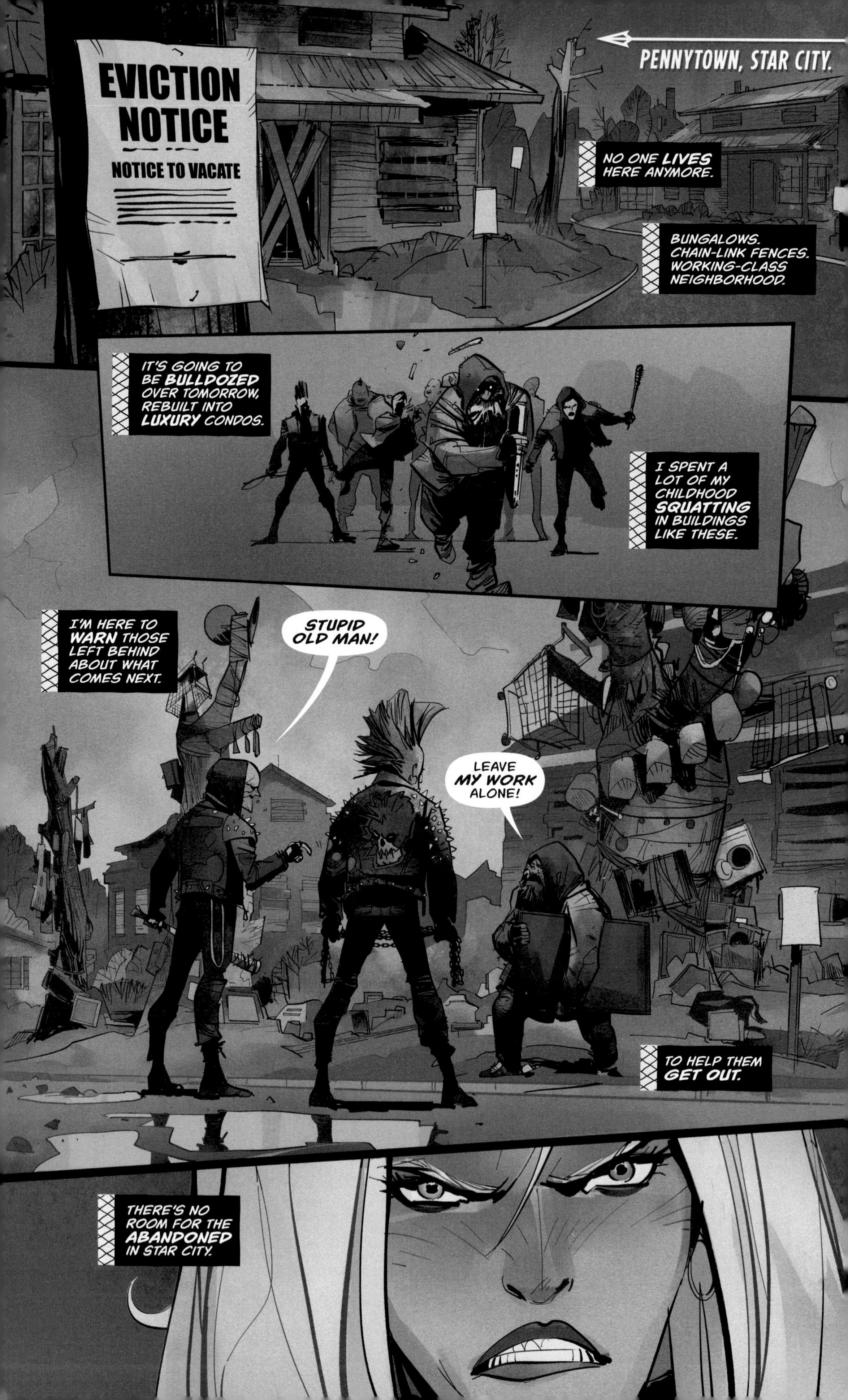
EVICTION NOTICE
NOTICE TO VACATE
PENNYTOWN, STAR CITY.
NO ONE LIVES HERE ANYMORE.
BUNGALOWS. CHAIN-LINK FENCES. WORKING-CLASS NEIGHBORHOOD.
IT'S GOING TO BE BULLDOZED OVER TOMORROW, REBUILT INTO LUXURY CONDOS.
I SPENT A LOT OF MY CHILDHOOD SQUATTING IN BUILDINGS LIKE THESE.
I'M HERE TO WARN THOSE LEFT BEHIND ABOUT WHAT COMES NEXT.
STUPID OLD MAN!
LEAVE MY WORK ALONE!
TO HELP THEM GET OUT.
THERE'S NO ROOM FOR THE ABANDONED IN STAR CITY.

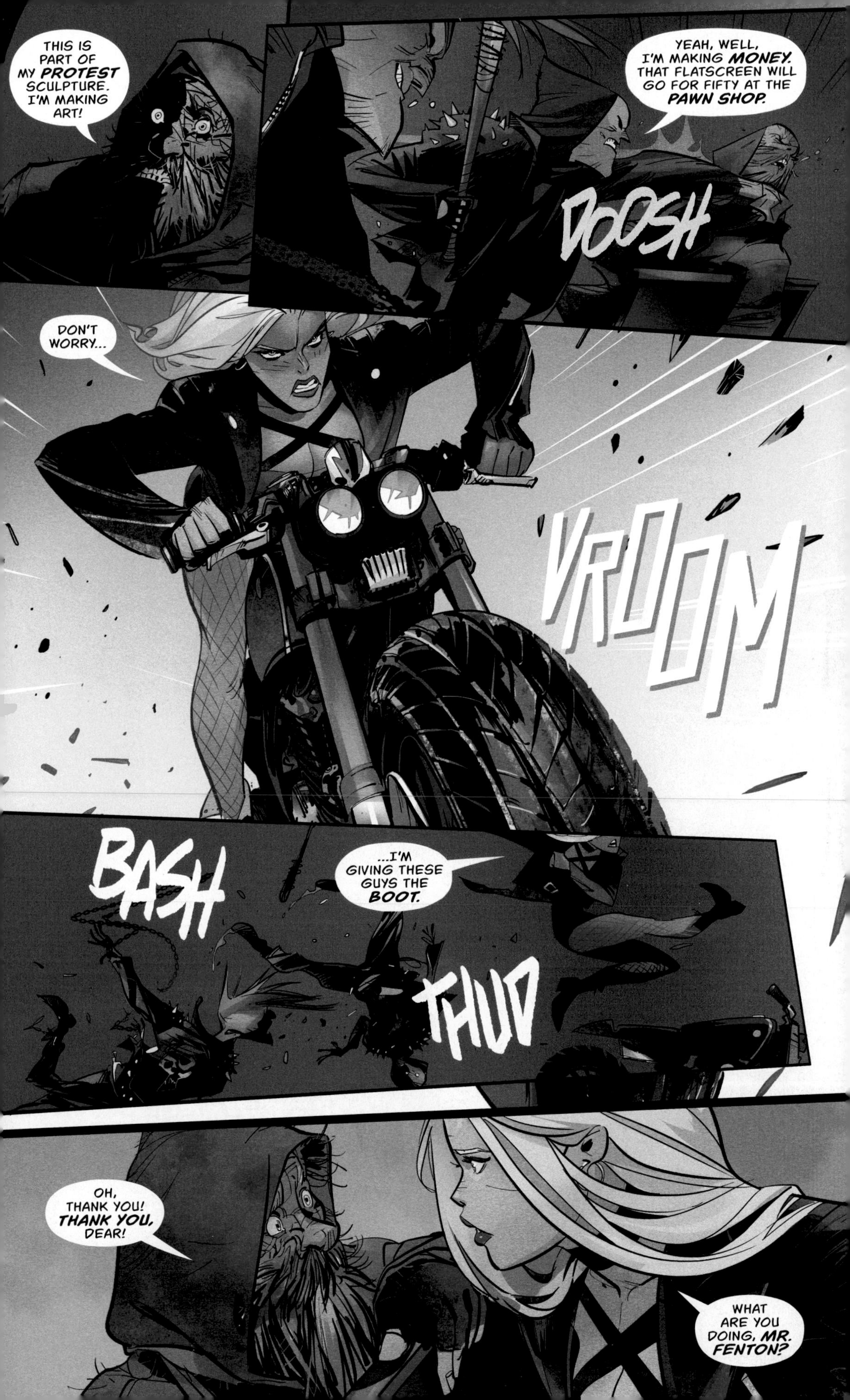
THIS IS PART OF MY PROTEST SCULPTURE. I'M MAKING ART!
YEAH, WELL, I'M MAKING MONEY. THAT FLATSCREEN WILL GO FOR FIFTY AT THE PAWN SHOP.
DOOSH
DON'T WORRY...
VROOOM
BASH
...I'M GIVING THESE GUYS THE BOOT.
THUD
OH, THANK YOU! THANK YOU, DEAR!
WHAT ARE YOU DOING, MR. FENTON?

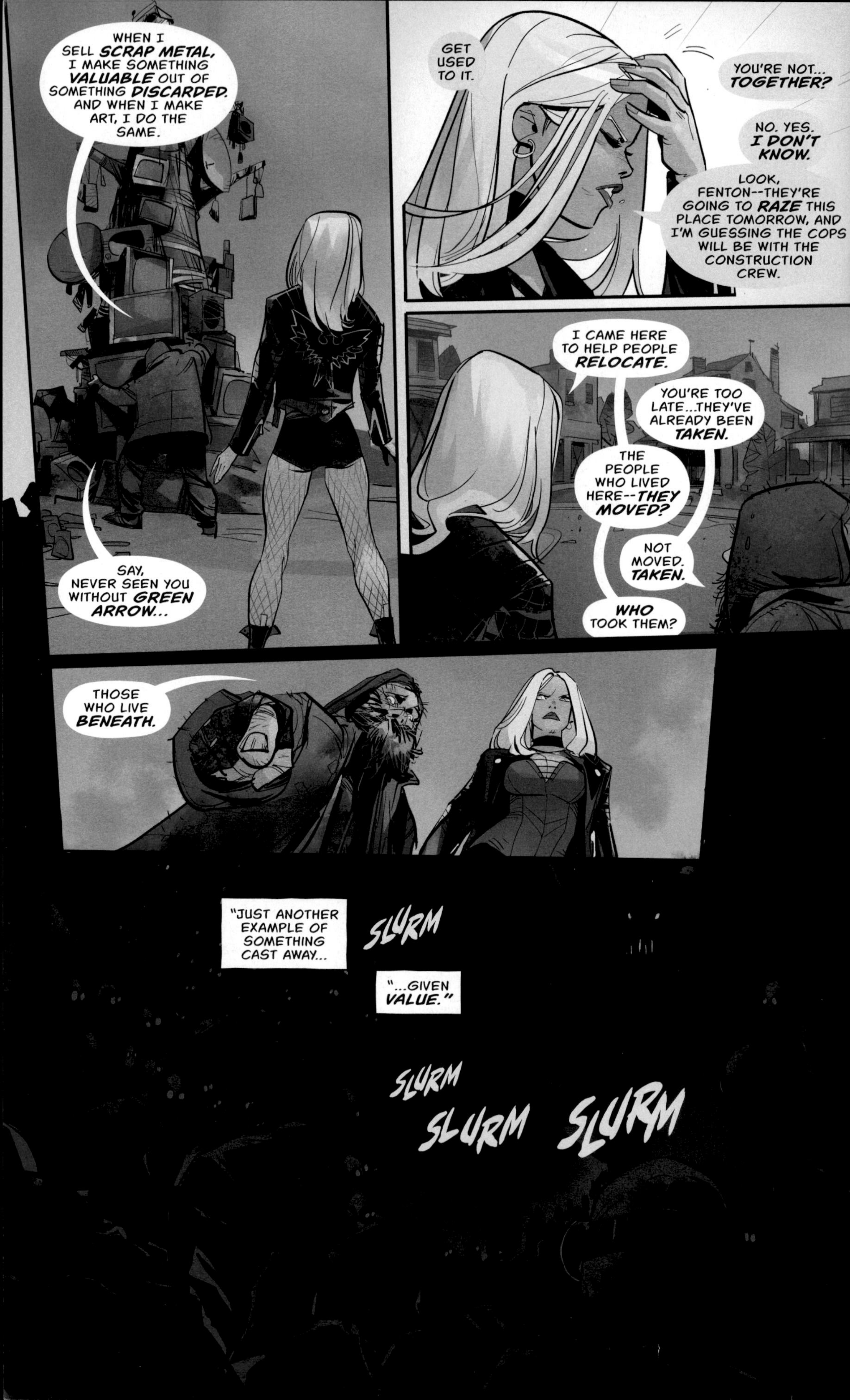
WHEN I SELL SCRAP METAL, I MAKE SOMETHING VALUABLE OUT OF SOMETHING DISCARDED. AND WHEN I MAKE ART, I DO THE SAME.
SAY, NEVER SEEN YOU WITHOUT GREEN ARROW...
GET USED TO IT.
YOU'RE NOT... TOGETHER?
NO. YES. I DON'T KNOW.
LOOK, FENTON--THEY'RE GOING TO RAZE THIS PLACE TOMORROW, AND I'M GUESSING THE COPS WILL BE WITH THE CONSTRUCTION CREW.
I CAME HERE TO HELP PEOPLE RELOCATE.
YOU'RE TOO LATE...THEY'VE ALREADY BEEN TAKEN.
THE PEOPLE WHO LIVED HERE--THEY MOVED?
NOT MOVED. TAKEN.
WHO TOOK THEM?
THOSE WHO LIVE BENEATH.
"JUST ANOTHER EXAMPLE OF SOMETHING CAST AWAY...
SLURM
"...GIVEN VALUE."
SLURM
SLURM SLURM

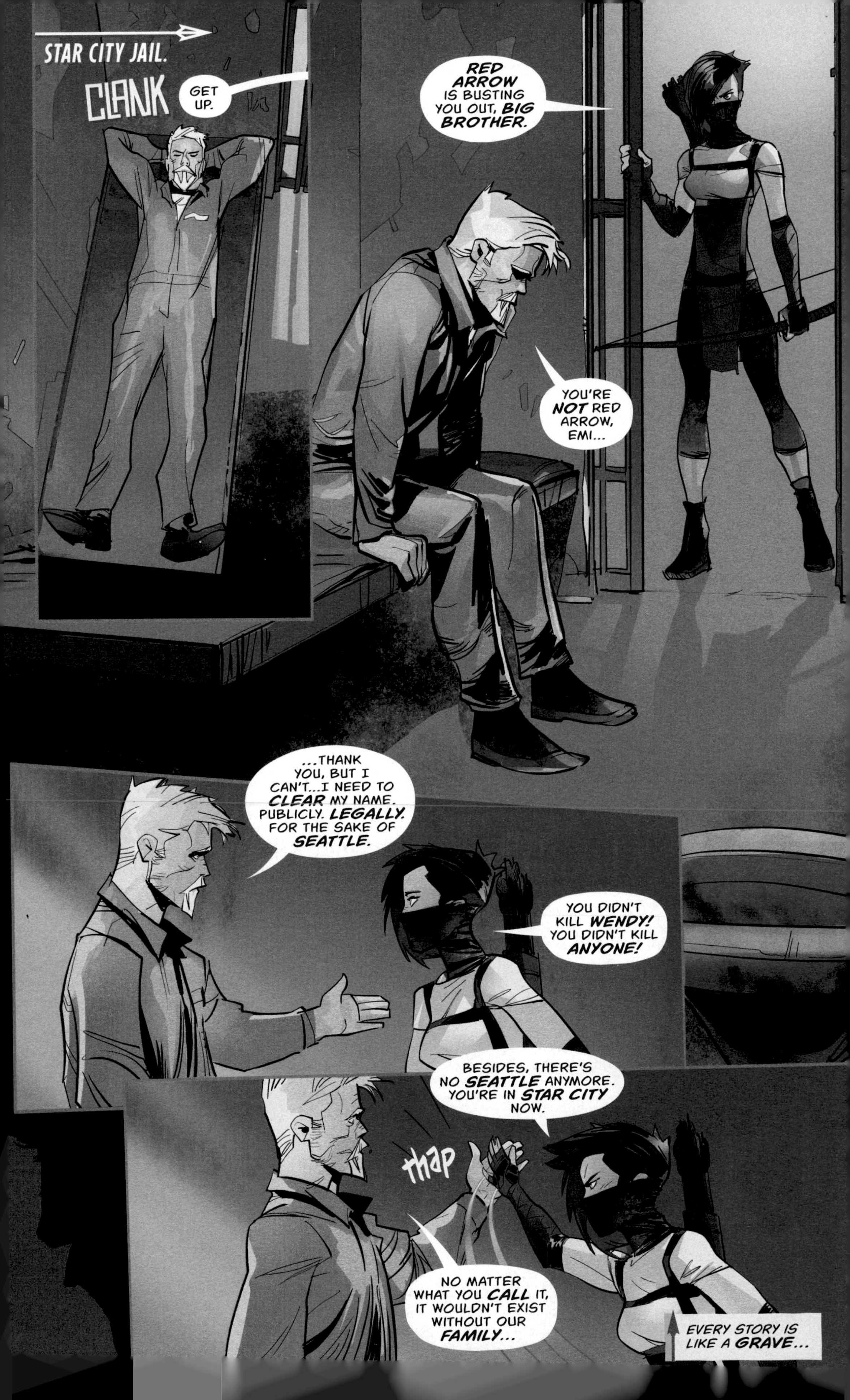
STAR CITY JAIL.
CLANK
GET UP.
RED ARROW IS BUSTING YOU OUT, BIG BROTHER.
YOU'RE NOT RED ARROW, EMI...
...THANK YOU, BUT I CAN'T...I NEED TO CLEAR MY NAME. PUBLICLY. LEGALLY. FOR THE SAKE OF SEATTLE.
YOU DIDN'T KILL WENDY! YOU DIDN'T KILL ANYONE!
BESIDES, THERE'S NO SEATTLE ANYMORE. YOU'RE IN STAR CITY NOW.
thap
NO MATTER WHAT YOU CALL IT, IT WOULDN'T EXIST WITHOUT OUR FAMILY...
EVERY STORY IS LIKE A GRAVE...

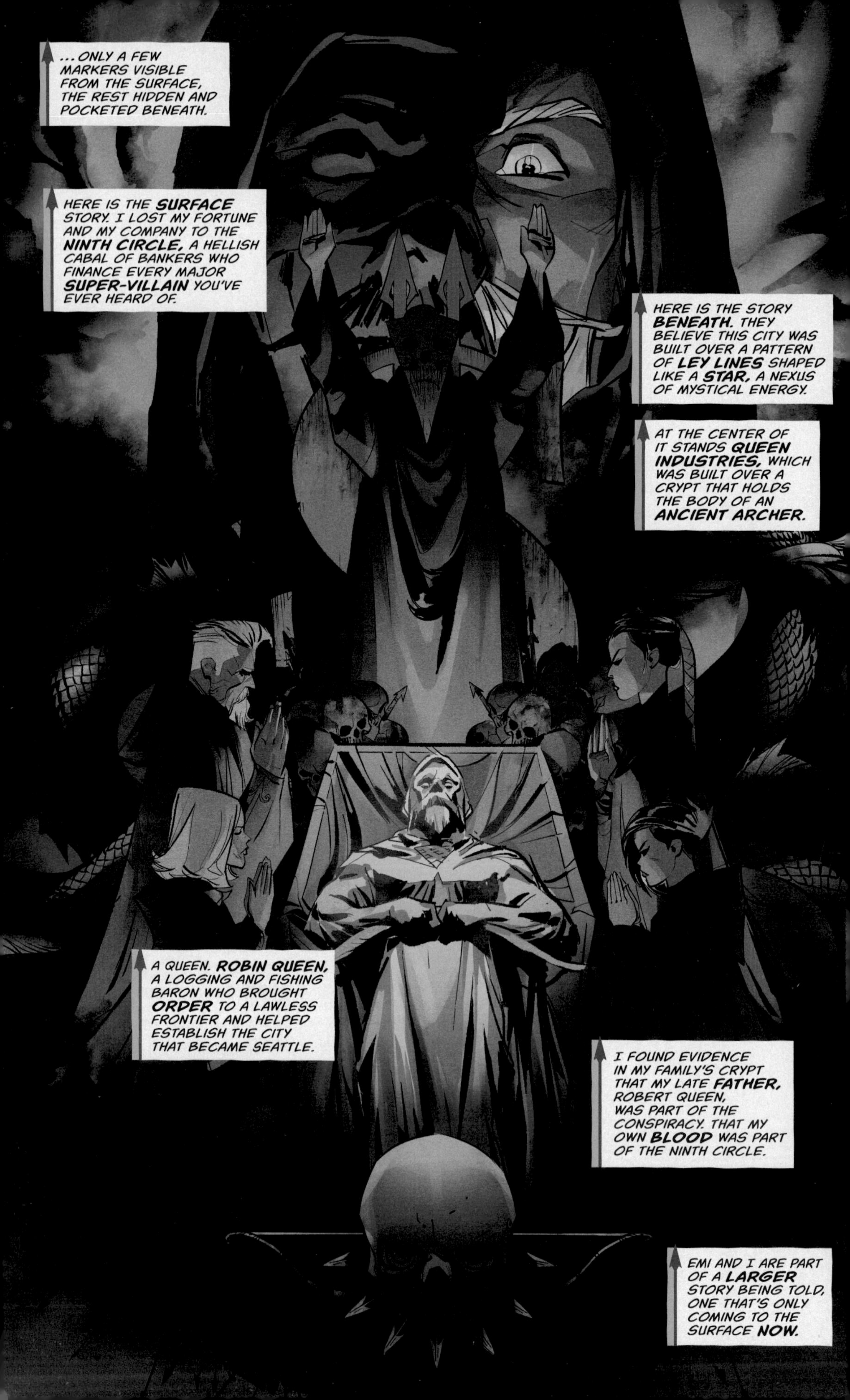
...ONLY A FEW MARKERS VISIBLE FROM THE SURFACE, THE REST HIDDEN AND POCKETED BENEATH.
HERE IS THE SURFACE STORY. I LOST MY FORTUNE AND MY COMPANY TO THE NINTH CIRCLE, A HELLISH CABAL OF BANKERS WHO FINANCE EVERY MAJOR SUPER-VILLAIN YOU'VE EVER HEARD OF.
HERE IS THE STORY BENEATH. THEY BELIEVE THIS CITY WAS BUILT OVER A PATTERN OF LEY LINES SHAPED LIKE A STAR, A NEXUS OF MYSTICAL ENERGY.
AT THE CENTER OF IT STANDS QUEEN INDUSTRIES, WHICH WAS BUILT OVER A CRYPT THAT HOLDS THE BODY OF AN ANCIENT ARCHER.
A QUEEN. ROBIN QUEEN, A LOGGING AND FISHING BARON WHO BROUGHT ORDER TO A LAWLESS FRONTIER AND HELPED ESTABLISH THE CITY THAT BECAME SEATTLE.
I FOUND EVIDENCE IN MY FAMILY'S CRYPT THAT MY LATE FATHER, ROBERT QUEEN, WAS PART OF THE CONSPIRACY. THAT MY OWN BLOOD WAS PART OF THE NINTH CIRCLE.
EMI AND I ARE PART OF A LARGER STORY BEING TOLD, ONE THAT'S ONLY COMING TO THE SURFACE NOW.

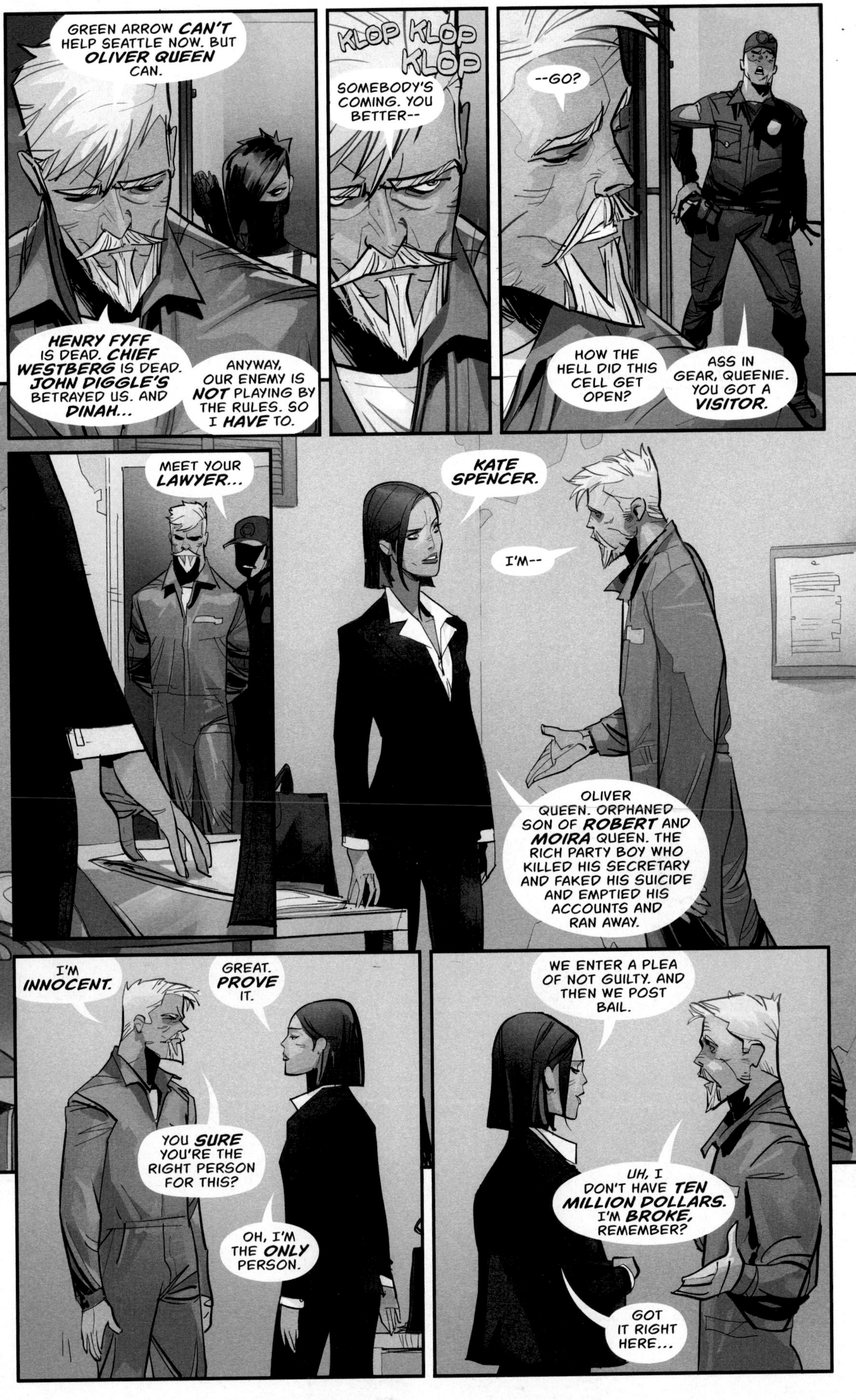

GREEN ARROW CAN'T HELP SEATTLE NOW. BUT OLIVER QUEEN CAN.
HENRY FYFF IS DEAD. CHIEF WESTBERG IS DEAD. JOHN DIGGLE'S BETRAYED US. AND DINAH...
ANYWAY, OUR ENEMY IS NOT PLAYING BY THE RULES. SO I HAVE TO.
KLOP KLOP KLOP
SOMEBODY'S COMING. YOU BETTER--
--GO?
HOW THE HELL DID THIS CELL GET OPEN?
ASS IN GEAR, QUEENIE. YOU GOT A VISITOR.
MEET YOUR LAWYER...
KATE SPENCER.
I'M--
OLIVER QUEEN. ORPHANED SON OF ROBERT AND MOIRA QUEEN. THE RICH PARTY BOY WHO KILLED HIS SECRETARY AND FAKED HIS SUICIDE AND EMPTIED HIS ACCOUNTS AND RAN AWAY.
I'M INNOCENT.
GREAT. PROVE IT.
YOU SURE YOU'RE THE RIGHT PERSON FOR THIS?
OH, I'M THE ONLY PERSON.
WE ENTER A PLEA OF NOT GUILTY. AND THEN WE POST BAIL.
UH, I DON'T HAVE TEN MILLION DOLLARS. I'M BROKE, REMEMBER?
GOT IT RIGHT HERE...

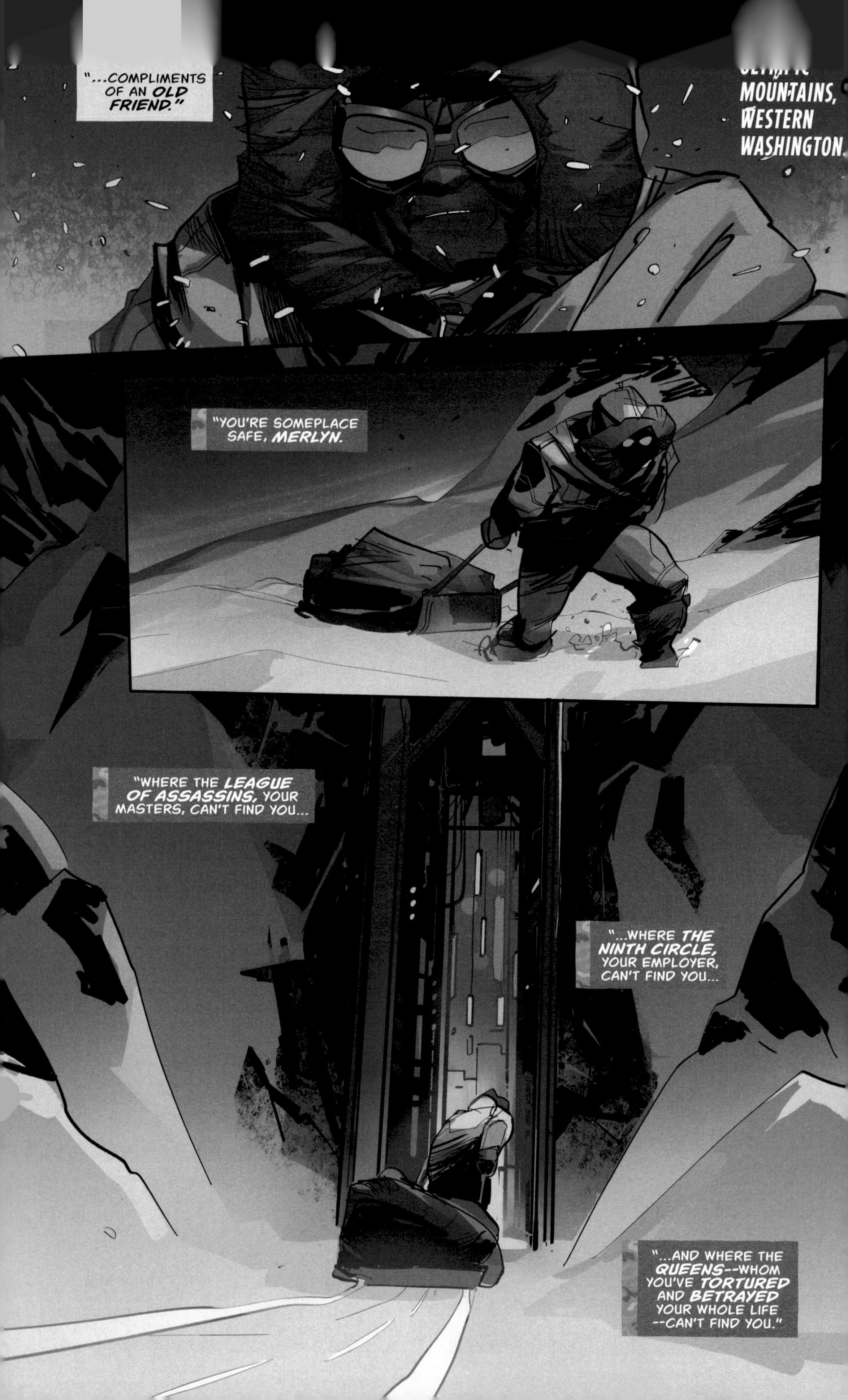
"...COMPLIMENTS OF AN OLD FRIEND."
MOUNTAINS, WESTERN WASHINGTON.
"YOU'RE SOMEPLACE SAFE, MERLYN.
"WHERE THE LEAGUE OF ASSASSINS, YOUR MASTERS, CAN'T FIND YOU...
"...WHERE THE NINTH CIRCLE, YOUR EMPLOYER, CAN'T FIND YOU...
"...AND WHERE THE QUEENS--WHOM YOU'VE TORTURED AND BETRAYED YOUR WHOLE LIFE --CAN'T FIND YOU."

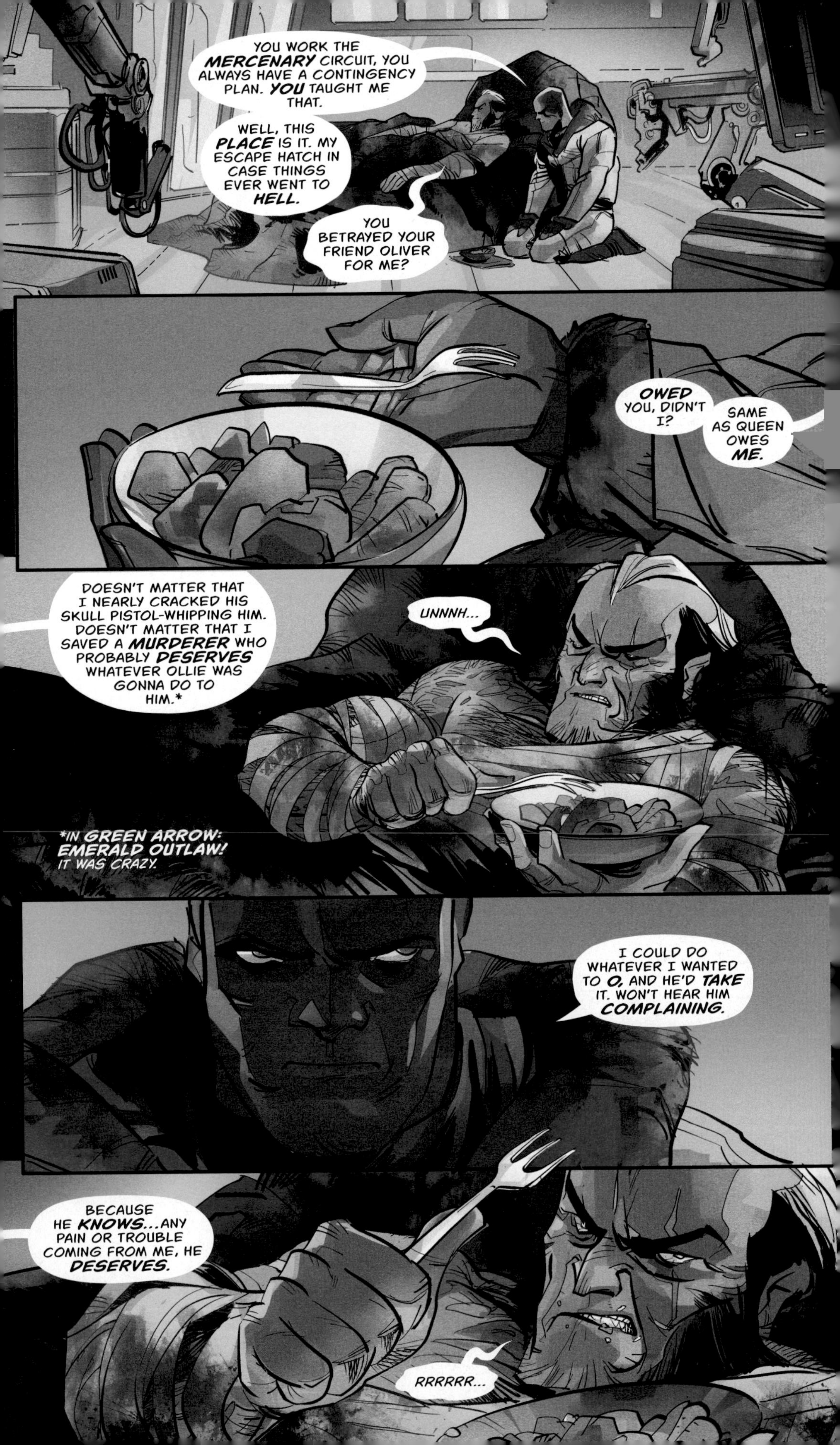
YOU WORK THE MERCENARY CIRCUIT, YOU ALWAYS HAVE A CONTINGENCY PLAN. YOU TAUGHT ME THAT.
WELL, THIS PLACE IS IT. MY ESCAPE HATCH IN CASE THINGS EVER WENT TO HELL.
YOU BETRAYED YOUR FRIEND OLIVER FOR ME?
OWED YOU, DIDN'T I?
SAME AS QUEEN OWES ME.
DOESN'T MATTER THAT I NEARLY CRACKED HIS SKULL PISTOL-WHIPPING HIM. DOESN'T MATTER THAT I SAVED A MURDERER WHO PROBABLY DESERVES WHATEVER OLLIE WAS GONNA DO TO HIM.*
UNNNH...
*IN GREEN ARROW: EMERALD OUTLAW! IT WAS CRAZY.
I COULD DO WHATEVER I WANTED TO O, AND HE'D TAKE IT. WON'T HEAR HIM COMPLAINING.
BECAUSE HE KNOWS...ANY PAIN OR TROUBLE COMING FROM ME, HE DESERVES.
RRRRRR...

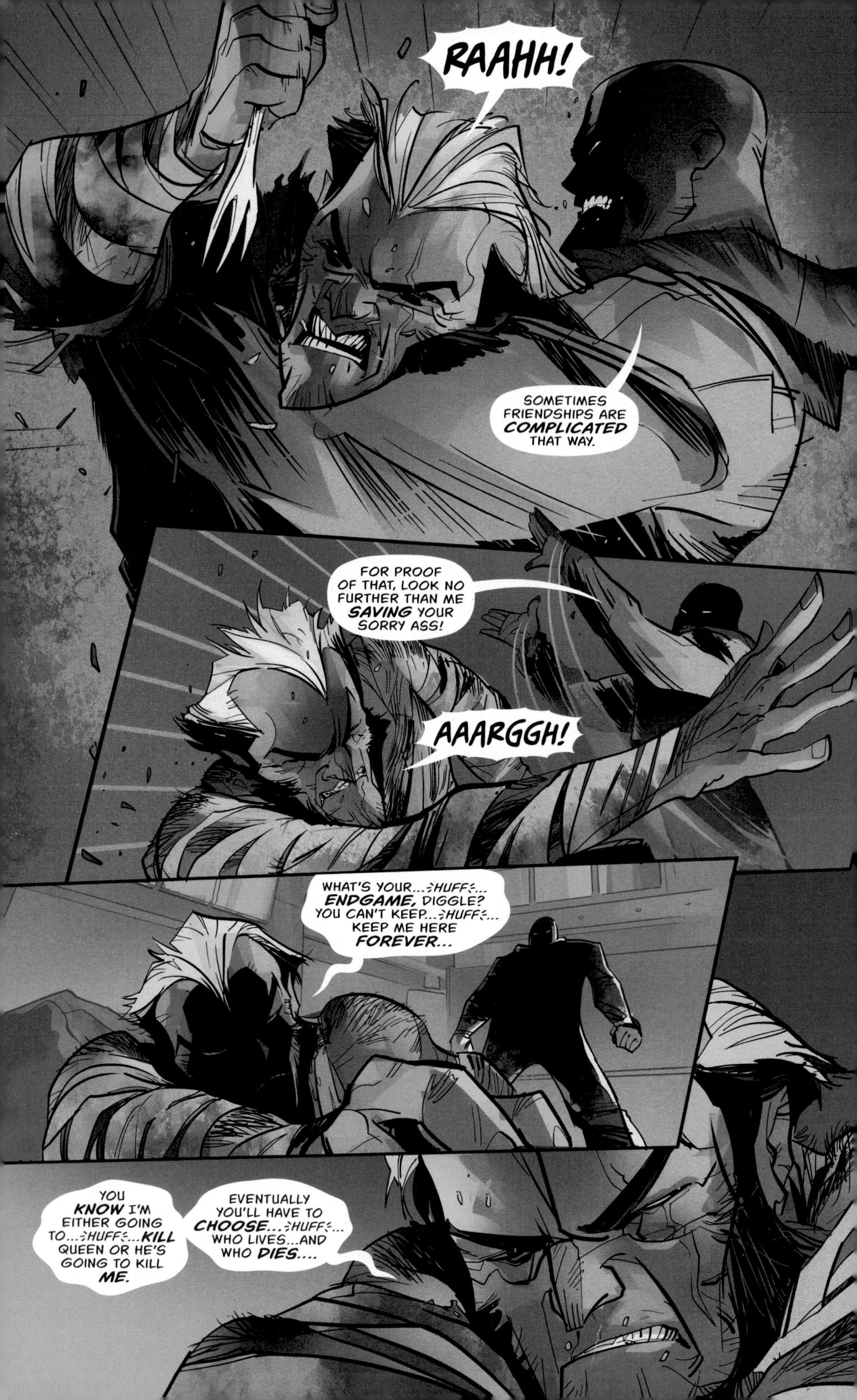
RAAHH!
SOMETIMES FRIENDSHIPS ARE COMPLICATED THAT WAY.
FOR PROOF OF THAT, LOOK NO FURTHER THAN ME SAVING YOUR SORRY ASS!
AAARGGH!
WHAT'S YOUR...HUFF... ENDGAME, DIGGLE? YOU CAN'T KEEP...HUFF... KEEP ME HERE FOREVER...
YOU KNOW I'M EITHER GOING TO...HUFF...KILL QUEEN OR HE'S GOING TO KILL ME.
EVENTUALLY YOU'LL HAVE TO CHOOSE...HUFF... WHO LIVES...AND WHO DIES....

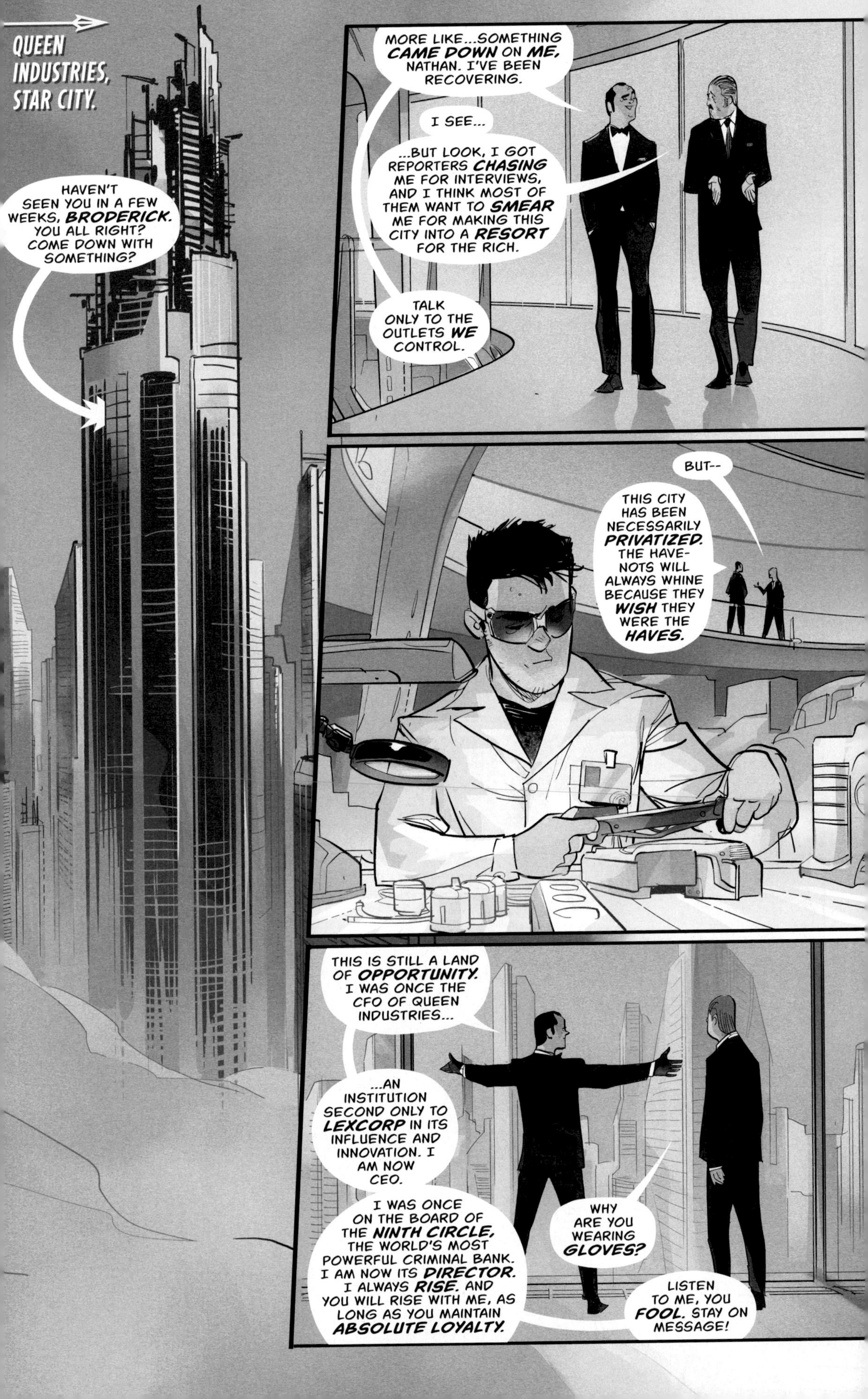
QUEEN INDUSTRIES, STAR CITY.
HAVEN'T SEEN YOU IN A FEW WEEKS, BRODERICK. YOU ALL RIGHT? COME DOWN WITH SOMETHING?
MORE LIKE...SOMETHING CAME DOWN ON ME, NATHAN. I'VE BEEN RECOVERING.
I SEE...
...BUT LOOK, I GOT REPORTERS CHASING ME FOR INTERVIEWS, AND I THINK MOST OF THEM WANT TO SMEAR ME FOR MAKING THIS CITY INTO A RESORT FOR THE RICH.
TALK ONLY TO THE OUTLETS WE CONTROL.
BUT--
THIS CITY HAS BEEN NECESSARILY PRIVATIZED. THE HAVE-NOTS WILL ALWAYS WHINE BECAUSE THEY WISH THEY WERE THE HAVES.
THIS IS STILL A LAND OF OPPORTUNITY. I WAS ONCE THE CFO OF QUEEN INDUSTRIES...
...AN INSTITUTION SECOND ONLY TO LEXCORP IN ITS INFLUENCE AND INNOVATION. I AM NOW CEO.
I WAS ONCE ON THE BOARD OF THE NINTH CIRCLE, THE WORLD'S MOST POWERFUL CRIMINAL BANK. I AM NOW ITS DIRECTOR. I ALWAYS RISE. AND YOU WILL RISE WITH ME, AS LONG AS YOU MAINTAIN ABSOLUTE LOYALTY.
WHY ARE YOU WEARING GLOVES?
LISTEN TO ME, YOU FOOL. STAY ON MESSAGE!

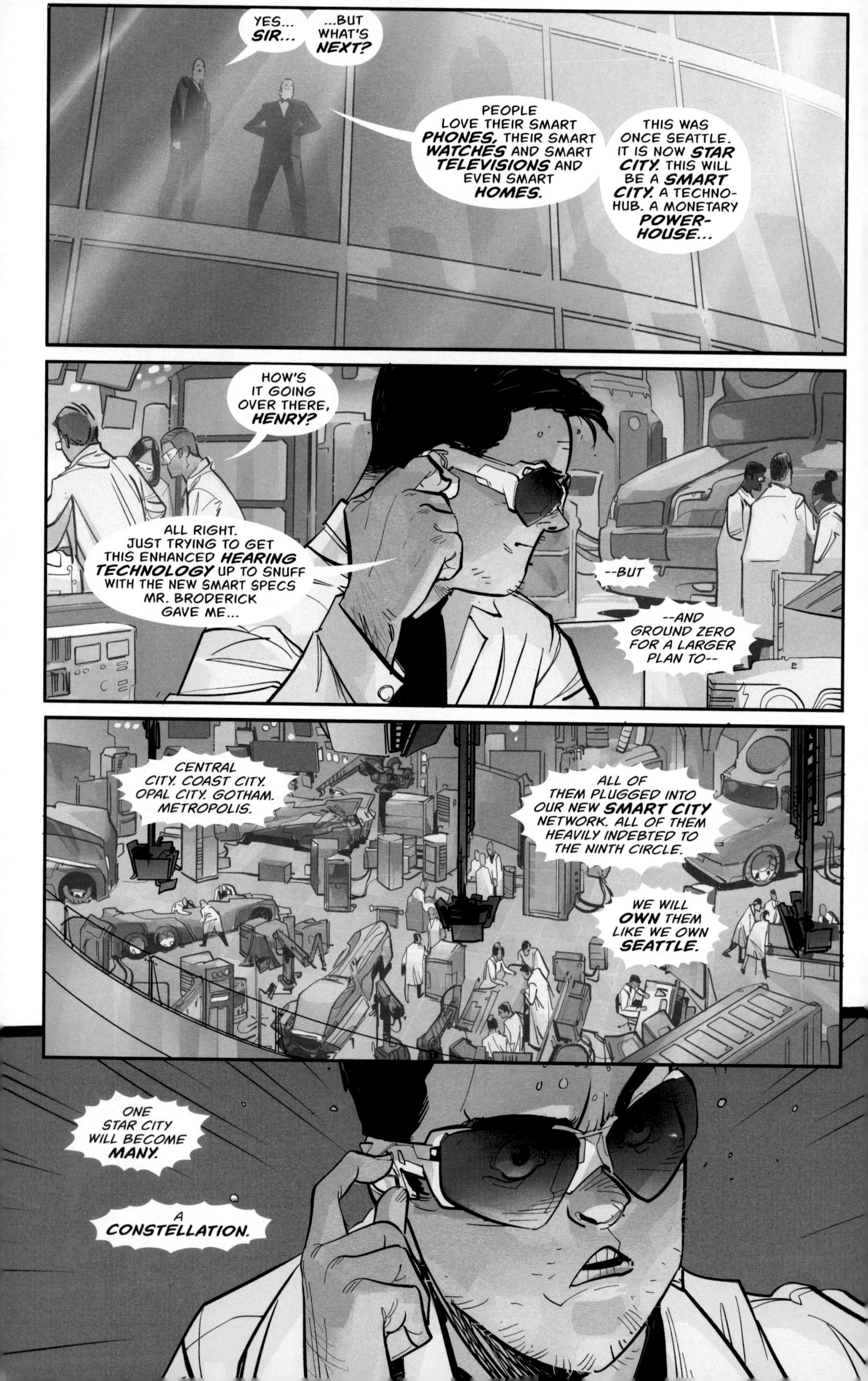
YES... SIR...
...BUT WHAT'S NEXT?
PEOPLE LOVE THEIR SMART PHONES, THEIR SMART WATCHES AND SMART TELEVISIONS AND EVEN SMART HOMES.
THIS WAS ONCE SEATTLE. IT IS NOW STAR CITY. THIS WILL BE A SMART CITY. A TECHNO-HUB. A MONETARY POWER-HOUSE...
HOW'S IT GOING OVER THERE, HENRY?
ALL RIGHT. JUST TRYING TO GET THIS ENHANCED HEARING TECHNOLOGY UP TO SNUFF WITH THE NEW SMART SPECS MR. BRODERICK GAVE ME...
--BUT
--AND GROUND ZERO FOR A LARGER PLAN TO--
CENTRAL CITY. COAST CITY. OPAL CITY. GOTHAM. METROPOLIS.
ALL OF THEM PLUGGED INTO OUR NEW SMART CITY NETWORK. ALL OF THEM HEAVILY INDEBTED TO THE NINTH CIRCLE.
WE WILL OWN THEM LIKE WE OWN SEATTLE.
ONE STAR CITY WILL BECOME MANY.
A CONSTELLATION.

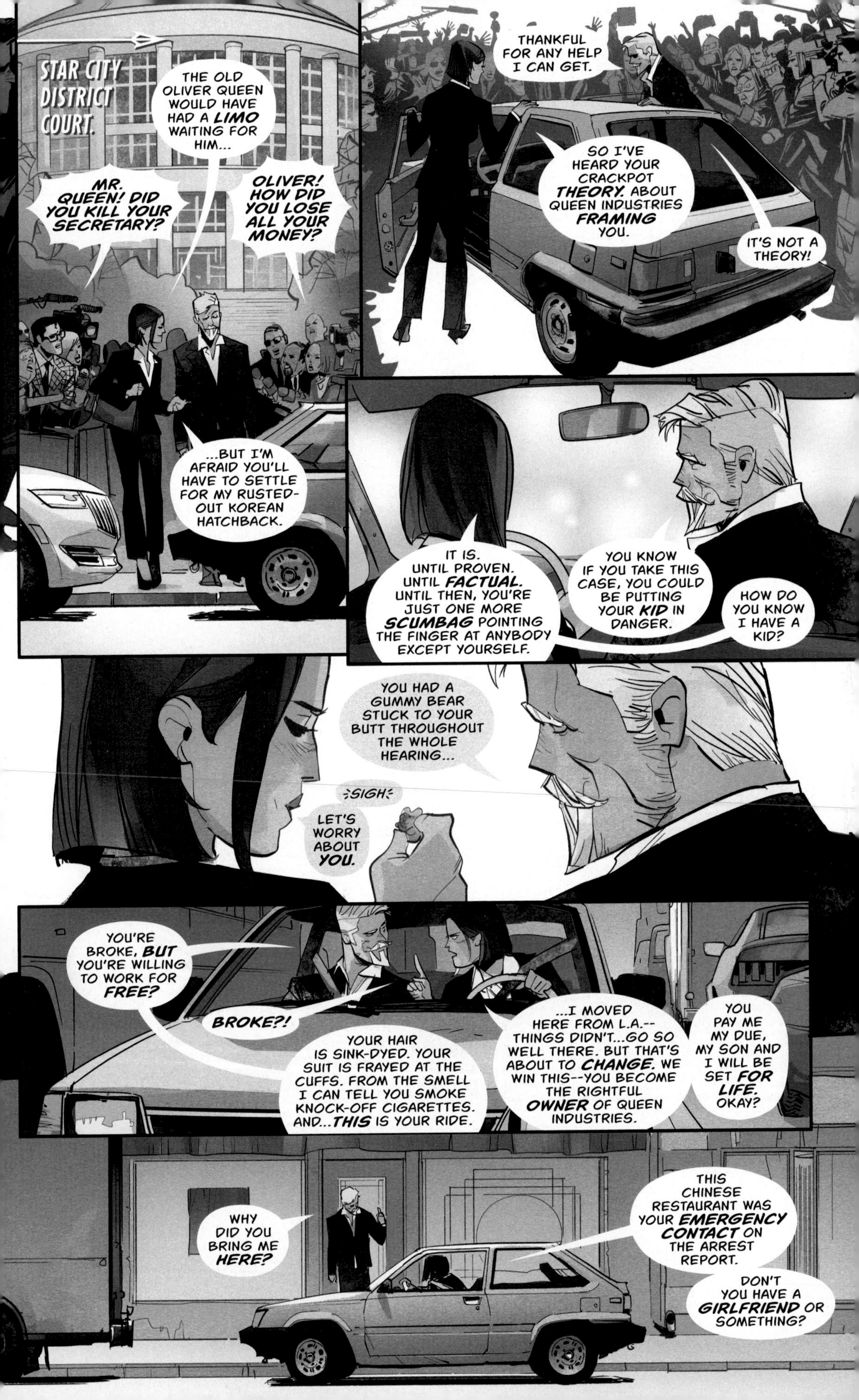
STAR CITY DISTRICT COURT.
THE OLD OLIVER QUEEN WOULD HAVE HAD A LIMO WAITING FOR HIM...
MR. QUEEN! DID YOU KILL YOUR SECRETARY?
OLIVER! HOW DID YOU LOSE ALL YOUR MONEY?
...BUT I'M AFRAID YOU'LL HAVE TO SETTLE FOR MY RUSTED-OUT KOREAN HATCHBACK.
THANKFUL FOR ANY HELP I CAN GET.
SO I'VE HEARD YOUR CRACKPOT THEORY. ABOUT QUEEN INDUSTRIES FRAMING YOU.
IT'S NOT A THEORY!
IT IS. UNTIL PROVEN. UNTIL FACTUAL. UNTIL THEN, YOU'RE JUST ONE MORE SCUMBAG POINTING THE FINGER AT ANYBODY EXCEPT YOURSELF.
YOU KNOW IF YOU TAKE THIS CASE, YOU COULD BE PUTTING YOUR KID IN DANGER.
HOW DO YOU KNOW I HAVE A KID?
YOU HAD A GUMMY BEAR STUCK TO YOUR BUTT THROUGHOUT THE WHOLE HEARING...
SIGH
LET'S WORRY ABOUT YOU.
YOU'RE BROKE, BUT YOU'RE WILLING TO WORK FOR FREE?
BROKE?!
YOUR HAIR IS SINK-DYED. YOUR SUIT IS FRAYED AT THE CUFFS. FROM THE SMELL I CAN TELL YOU SMOKE KNOCK-OFF CIGARETTES. AND...THIS IS YOUR RIDE.
...I MOVED HERE FROM L.A.--THINGS DIDN'T...GO SO WELL THERE. BUT THAT'S ABOUT TO CHANGE. WE WIN THIS--YOU BECOME THE RIGHTFUL OWNER OF QUEEN INDUSTRIES.
YOU PAY ME MY DUE, MY SON AND I WILL BE SET FOR LIFE. OKAY?
WHY DID YOU BRING ME HERE?
THIS CHINESE RESTAURANT WAS YOUR EMERGENCY CONTACT ON THE ARREST REPORT.
DON'T YOU HAVE A GIRLFRIEND OR SOMETHING?

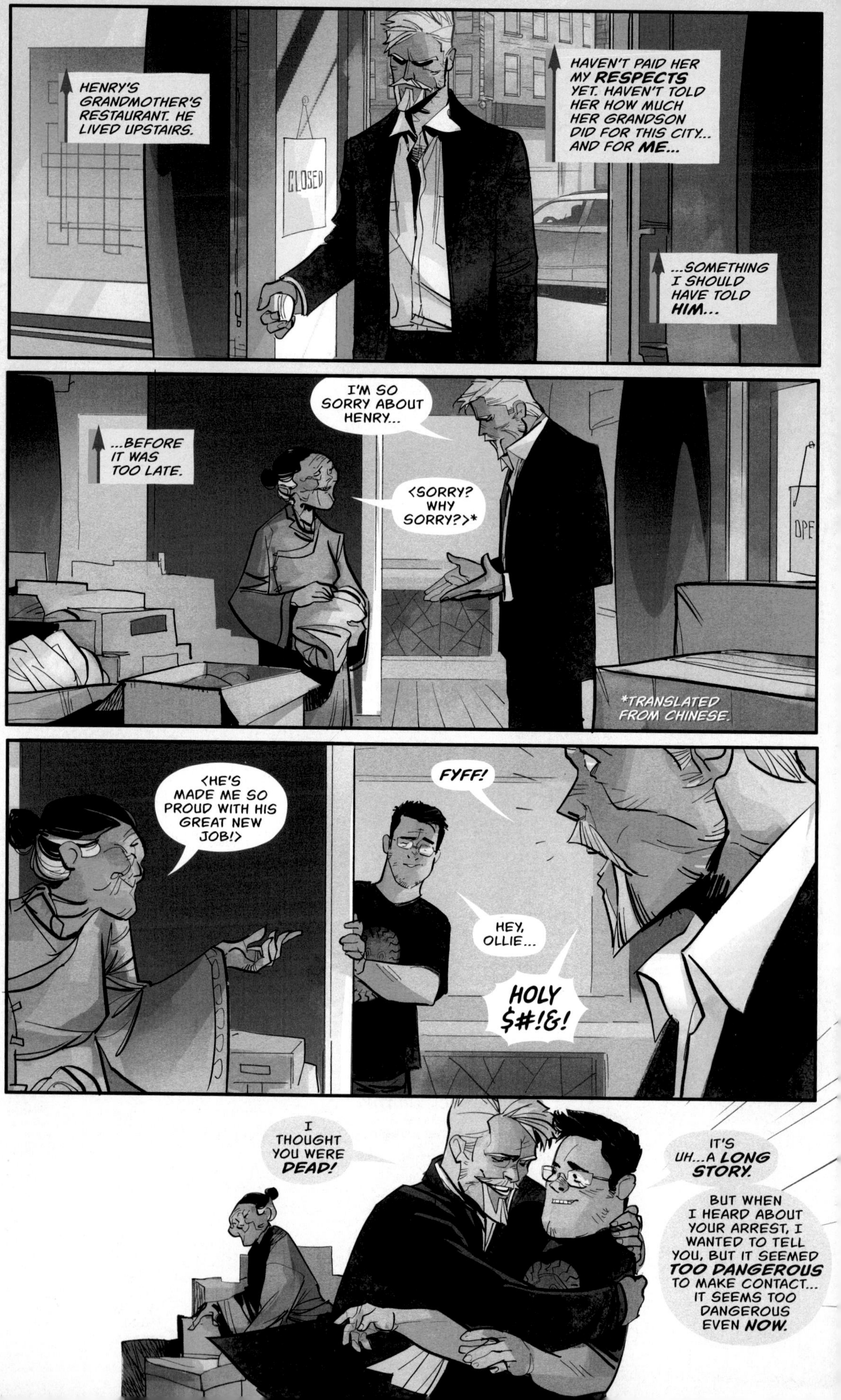
HENRY'S GRANDMOTHER'S RESTAURANT. HE LIVED UPSTAIRS.
HAVEN'T PAID HER MY RESPECTS YET. HAVEN'T TOLD HER HOW MUCH HER GRANDSON DID FOR THIS CITY... AND FOR ME...
CLOSED
...SOMETHING I SHOULD HAVE TOLD HIM...
...BEFORE IT WAS TOO LATE.
I'M SO SORRY ABOUT HENRY...
<SORRY? WHY SORRY?>*
*TRANSLATED FROM CHINESE.
<HE'S MADE ME SO PROUD WITH HIS GREAT NEW JOB!>
FYFF!
HEY, OLLIE...
HOLY $#!&!
I THOUGHT YOU WERE DEAD!
IT'S UH...A LONG STORY.
BUT WHEN I HEARD ABOUT YOUR ARREST, I WANTED TO TELL YOU, BUT IT SEEMED TOO DANGEROUS TO MAKE CONTACT... IT SEEMS TOO DANGEROUS EVEN NOW.

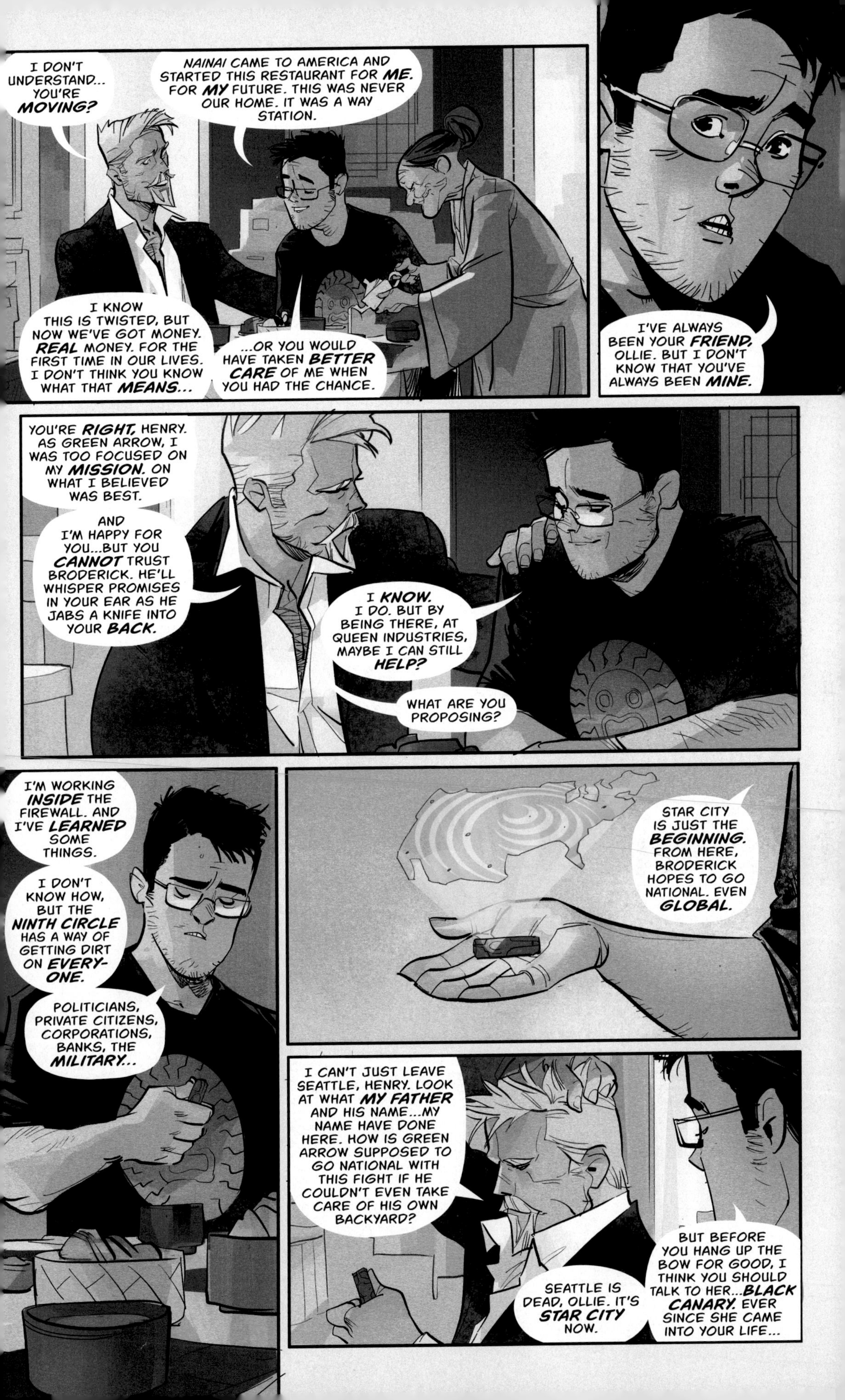
I DON'T UNDERSTAND... YOU'RE MOVING?
NAINAI CAME TO AMERICA AND STARTED THIS RESTAURANT FOR ME. FOR MY FUTURE. THIS WAS NEVER OUR HOME. IT WAS A WAY STATION.
I KNOW THIS IS TWISTED, BUT NOW WE'VE GOT MONEY. REAL MONEY. FOR THE FIRST TIME IN OUR LIVES. I DON'T THINK YOU KNOW WHAT THAT MEANS...
...OR YOU WOULD HAVE TAKEN BETTER CARE OF ME WHEN YOU HAD THE CHANCE.
I'VE ALWAYS BEEN YOUR FRIEND, OLLIE. BUT I DON'T KNOW THAT YOU'VE ALWAYS BEEN MINE.
YOU'RE RIGHT, HENRY. AS GREEN ARROW, I WAS TOO FOCUSED ON MY MISSION. ON WHAT I BELIEVED WAS BEST.
AND I'M HAPPY FOR YOU...BUT YOU CANNOT TRUST BRODERICK. HE'LL WHISPER PROMISES IN YOUR EAR AS HE JABS A KNIFE INTO YOUR BACK.
I KNOW. I DO. BUT BY BEING THERE, AT QUEEN INDUSTRIES, MAYBE I CAN STILL HELP?
WHAT ARE YOU PROPOSING?
I'M WORKING INSIDE THE FIREWALL. AND I'VE LEARNED SOME THINGS.
I DON'T KNOW HOW, BUT THE NINTH CIRCLE HAS A WAY OF GETTING DIRT ON EVERY-ONE.
POLITICIANS, PRIVATE CITIZENS, CORPORATIONS, BANKS, THE MILITARY...
STAR CITY IS JUST THE BEGINNING. FROM HERE, BRODERICK HOPES TO GO NATIONAL. EVEN GLOBAL.
I CAN'T JUST LEAVE SEATTLE, HENRY. LOOK AT WHAT MY FATHER AND HIS NAME...MY NAME HAVE DONE HERE. HOW IS GREEN ARROW SUPPOSED TO GO NATIONAL WITH THIS FIGHT IF HE COULDN'T EVEN TAKE CARE OF HIS OWN BACKYARD?
SEATTLE IS DEAD, OLLIE. IT'S STAR CITY NOW.
BUT BEFORE YOU HANG UP THE BOW FOR GOOD, I THINK YOU SHOULD TALK TO HER...BLACK CANARY. EVER SINCE SHE CAME INTO YOUR LIFE...

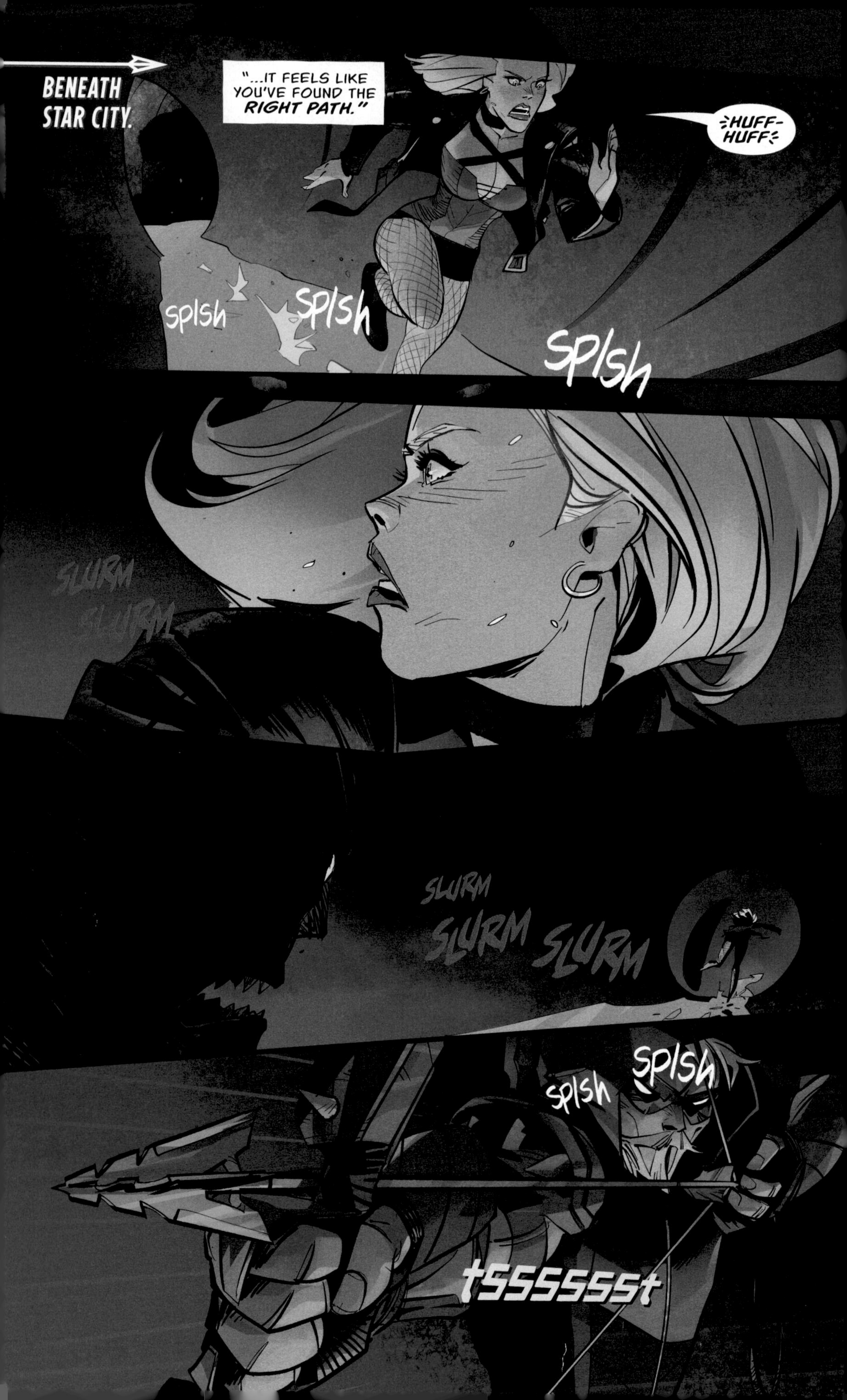
BENEATH STAR CITY.
"...IT FEELS LIKE YOU'VE FOUND THE RIGHT PATH."
HUFF-HUFF
SPISH
SPISH
SPISH
SLURM
SLURM
SLURM
SLURM
SLURM
SPISH
SPISH
tSSSSSSt

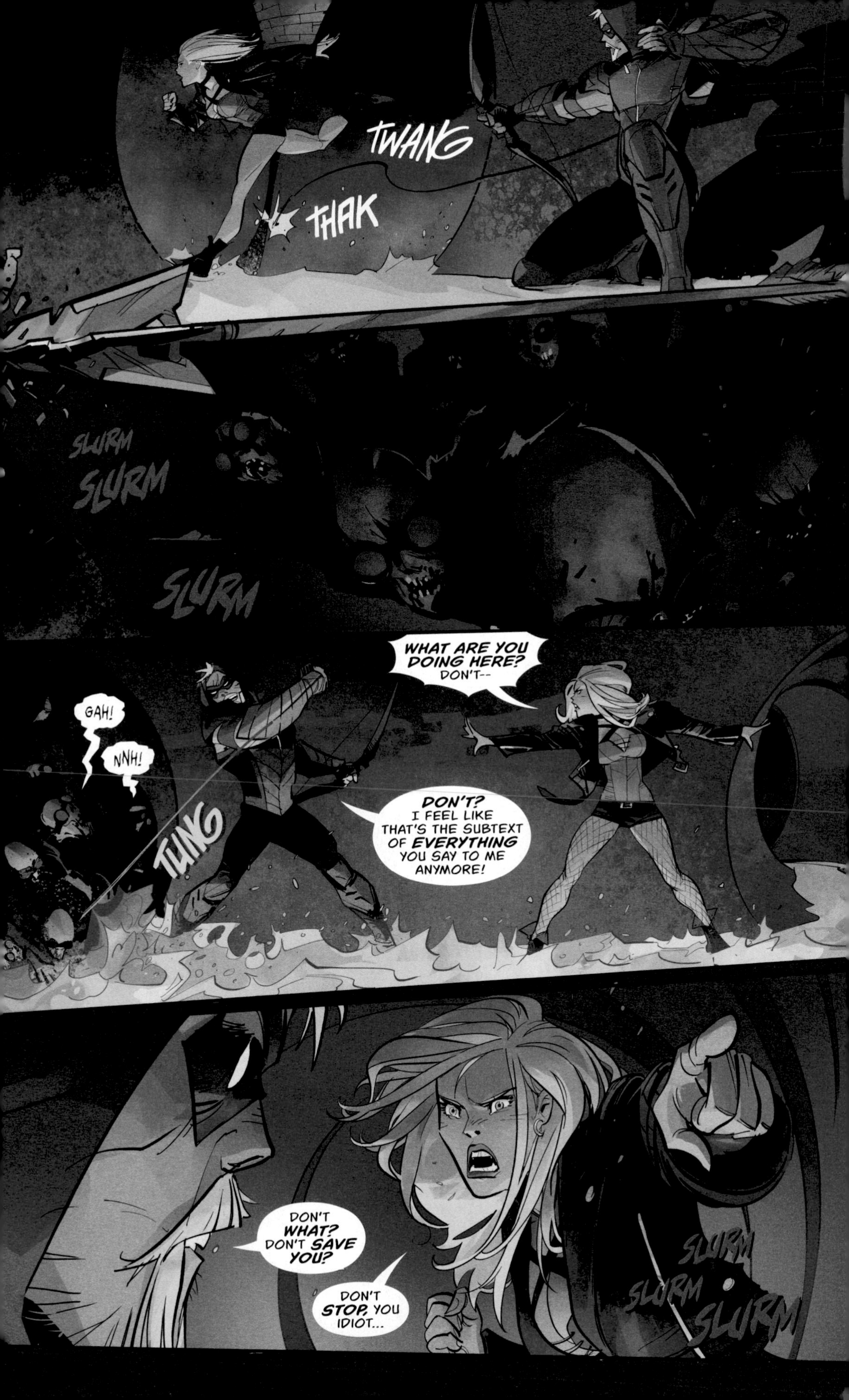
TWANG
THAK
SLURM
SLURM
SLURM
WHAT ARE YOU DOING HERE? DON'T--
GAH!
NNH!
TUNG
DON'T? I FEEL LIKE THAT'S THE SUBTEXT OF EVERYTHING YOU SAY TO ME ANYMORE!
DON'T WHAT? DON'T SAVE YOU?
DON'T STOP, YOU IDIOT...
SLURM
SLURM
SLURM

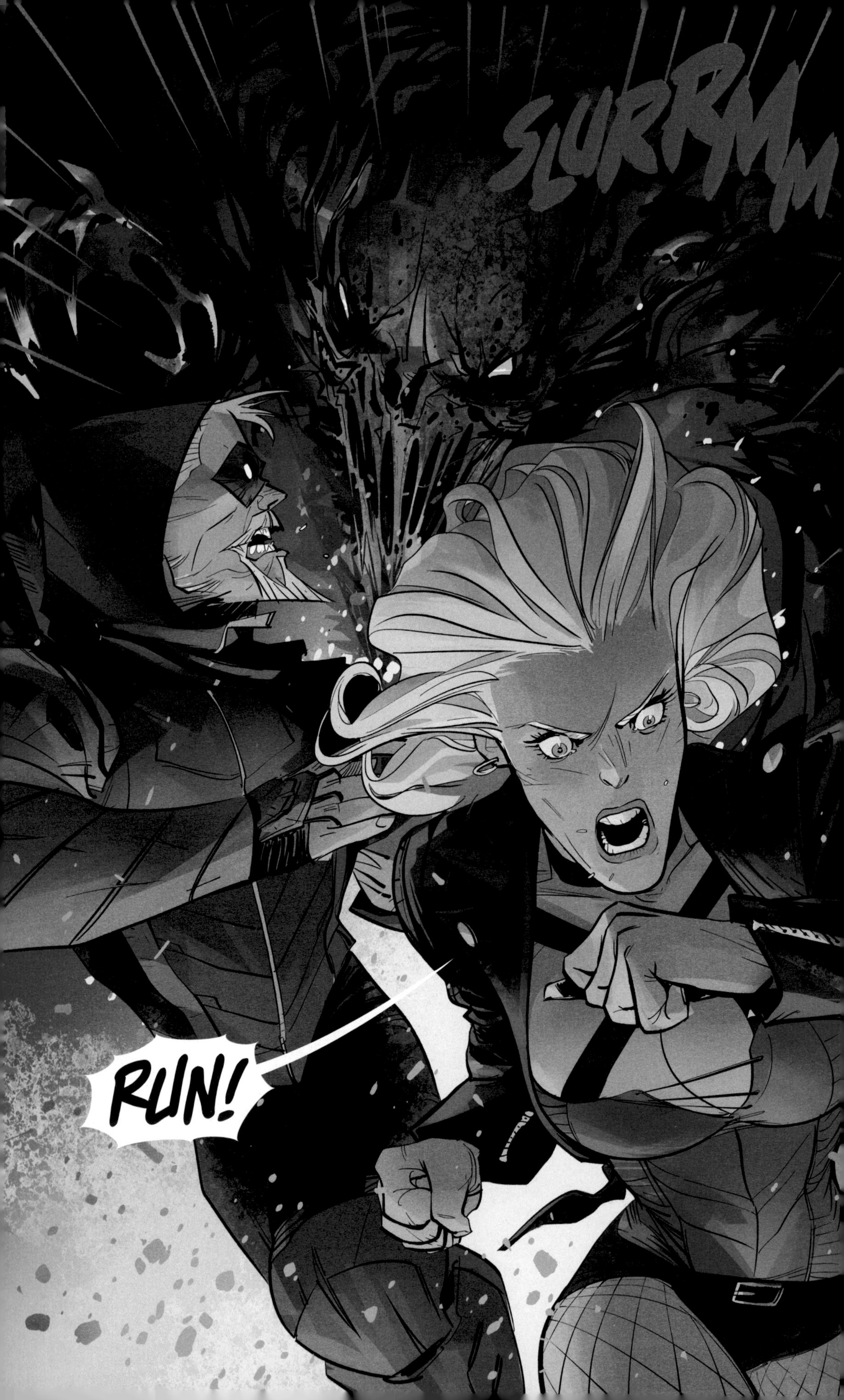
SLURRMMM
RUN!

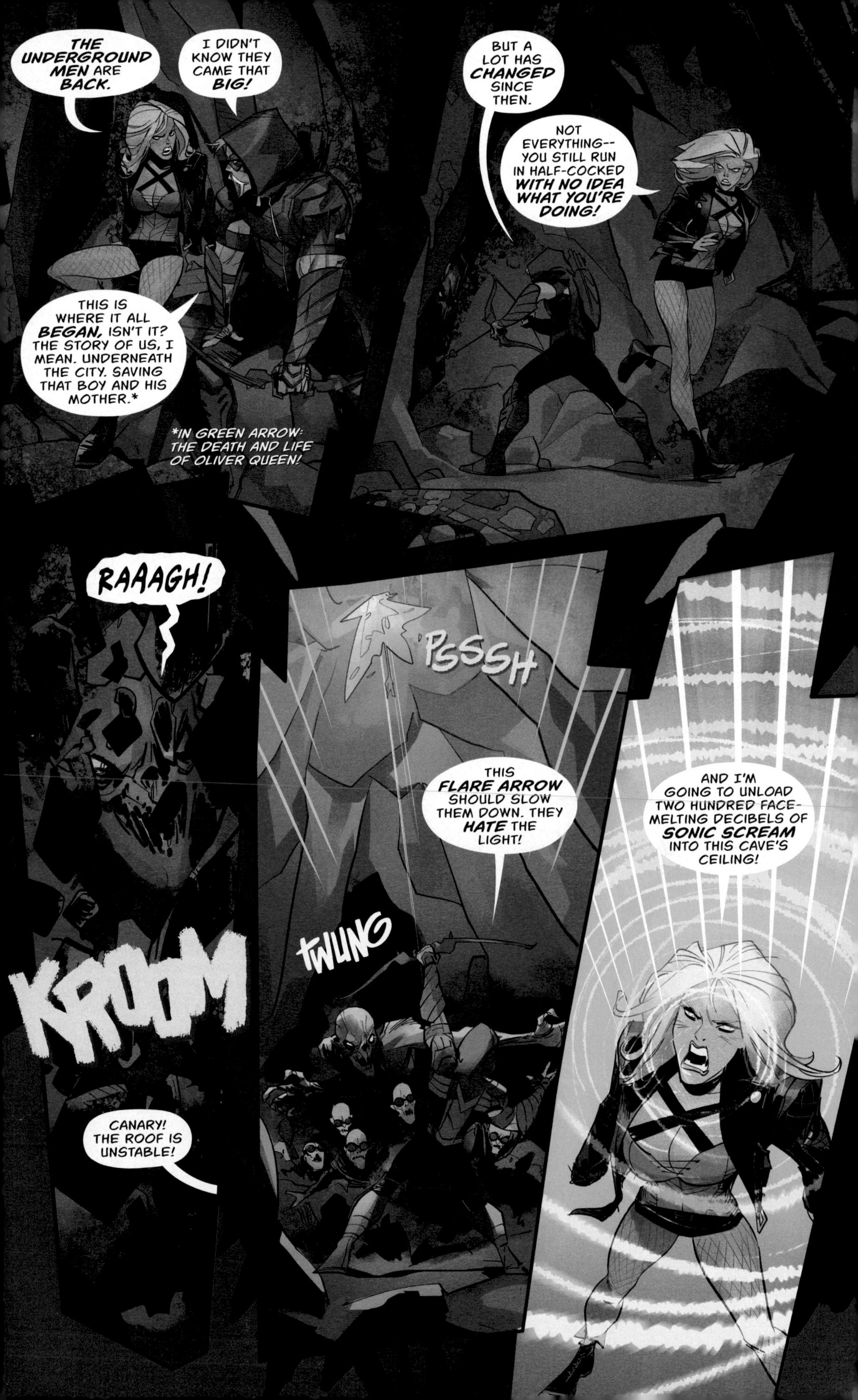

THE UNDERGROUND MEN ARE BACK.
I DIDN'T KNOW THEY CAME THAT BIG!
THIS IS WHERE IT ALL BEGAN, ISN'T IT? THE STORY OF US, I MEAN. UNDERNEATH THE CITY. SAVING THAT BOY AND HIS MOTHER.*
*IN GREEN ARROW: THE DEATH AND LIFE OF OLIVER QUEEN!
BUT A LOT HAS CHANGED SINCE THEN.
NOT EVERYTHING--YOU STILL RUN IN HALF-COCKED WITH NO IDEA WHAT YOU'RE DOING!
RAAAGH!
KROOM
CANARY! THE ROOF IS UNSTABLE!
PSSSH
THIS FLARE ARROW SHOULD SLOW THEM DOWN. THEY HATE THE LIGHT!
TWUNG
AND I'M GOING TO UNLOAD TWO HUNDRED FACE-MELTING DECIBELS OF SONIC SCREAM INTO THIS CAVE'S CEILING!

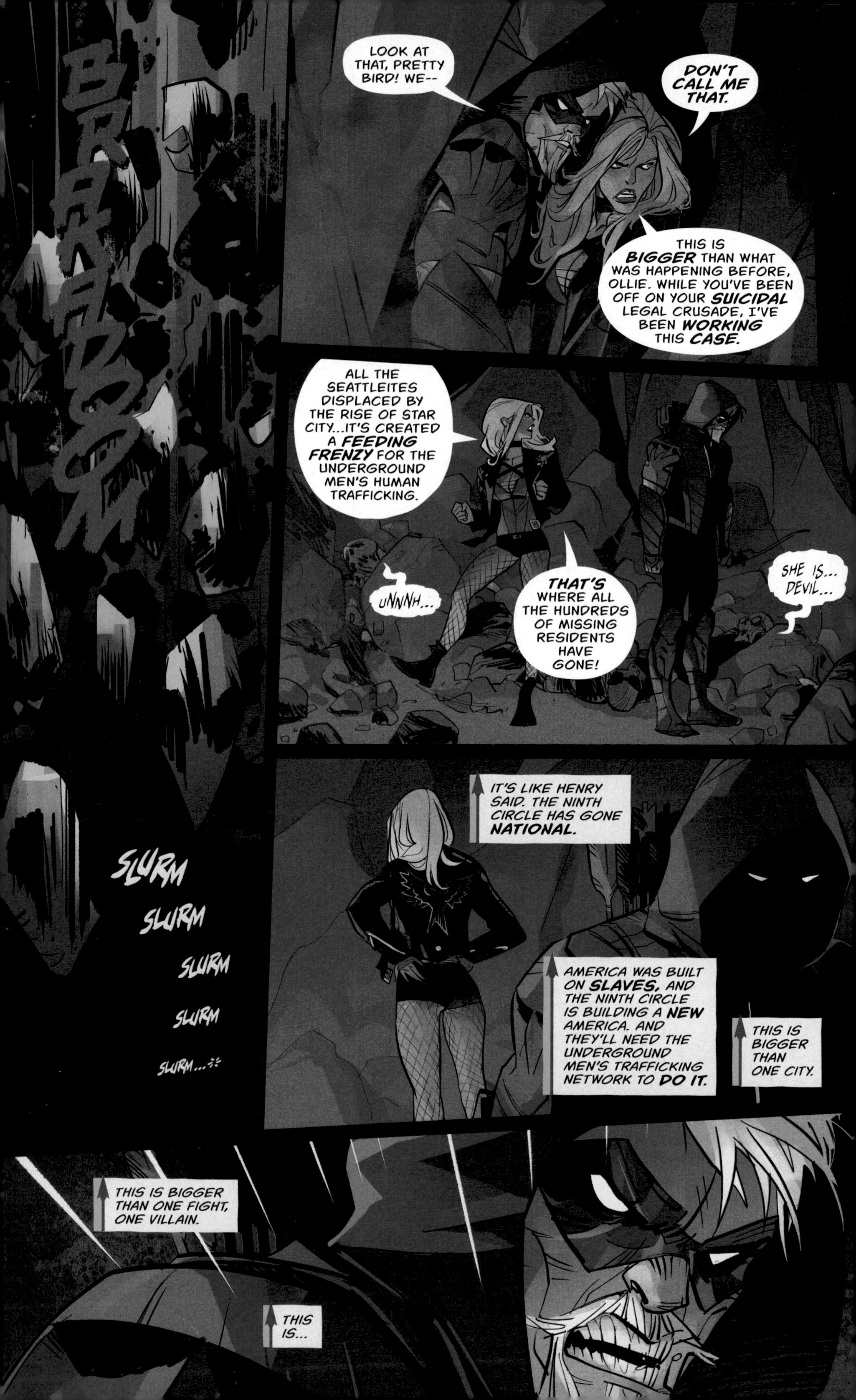
LOOK AT THAT, PRETTY BIRD! WE--
DON'T CALL ME THAT.
THIS IS BIGGER THAN WHAT WAS HAPPENING BEFORE, OLLIE. WHILE YOU'VE BEEN OFF ON YOUR SUICIDAL LEGAL CRUSADE, I'VE BEEN WORKING THIS CASE.
ALL THE SEATTLEITES DISPLACED BY THE RISE OF STAR CITY...IT'S CREATED A FEEDING FRENZY FOR THE UNDERGROUND MEN'S HUMAN TRAFFICKING.
UNNNH...
THAT'S WHERE ALL THE HUNDREDS OF MISSING RESIDENTS HAVE GONE!
SHE IS... DEVIL...
IT'S LIKE HENRY SAID. THE NINTH CIRCLE HAS GONE NATIONAL.
SLURM
SLURM
SLURM
SLURM
SLURM...
AMERICA WAS BUILT ON SLAVES, AND THE NINTH CIRCLE IS BUILDING A NEW AMERICA. AND THEY'LL NEED THE UNDERGROUND MEN'S TRAFFICKING NETWORK TO DO IT.
THIS IS BIGGER THAN ONE CITY.
THIS IS BIGGER THAN ONE FIGHT, ONE VILLAIN.
THIS IS...

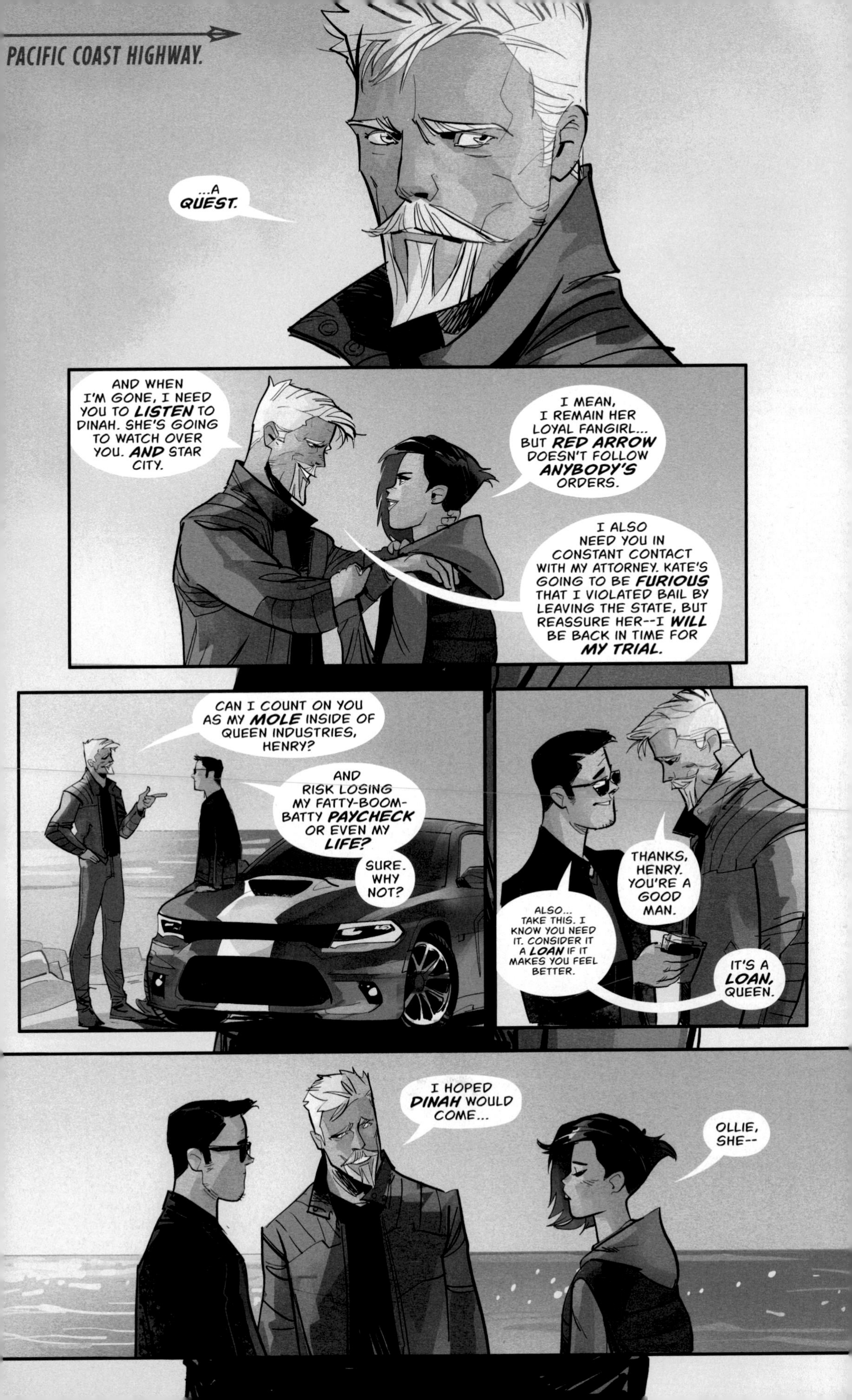
PACIFIC COAST HIGHWAY.
...A QUEST.
AND WHEN I'M GONE, I NEED YOU TO LISTEN TO DINAH. SHE'S GOING TO WATCH OVER YOU. AND STAR CITY.
I MEAN, I REMAIN HER LOYAL FANGIRL... BUT RED ARROW DOESN'T FOLLOW ANYBODY'S ORDERS.
I ALSO NEED YOU IN CONSTANT CONTACT WITH MY ATTORNEY. KATE'S GOING TO BE FURIOUS THAT I VIOLATED BAIL BY LEAVING THE STATE, BUT REASSURE HER--I WILL BE BACK IN TIME FOR MY TRIAL.
CAN I COUNT ON YOU AS MY MOLE INSIDE OF QUEEN INDUSTRIES, HENRY?
AND RISK LOSING MY FATTY-BOOM-BATTY PAYCHECK OR EVEN MY LIFE?
SURE. WHY NOT?
THANKS, HENRY. YOU'RE A GOOD MAN.
ALSO... TAKE THIS. I KNOW YOU NEED IT. CONSIDER IT A LOAN IF IT MAKES YOU FEEL BETTER.
IT'S A LOAN, QUEEN.
I HOPED DINAH WOULD COME...
OLLIE, SHE--

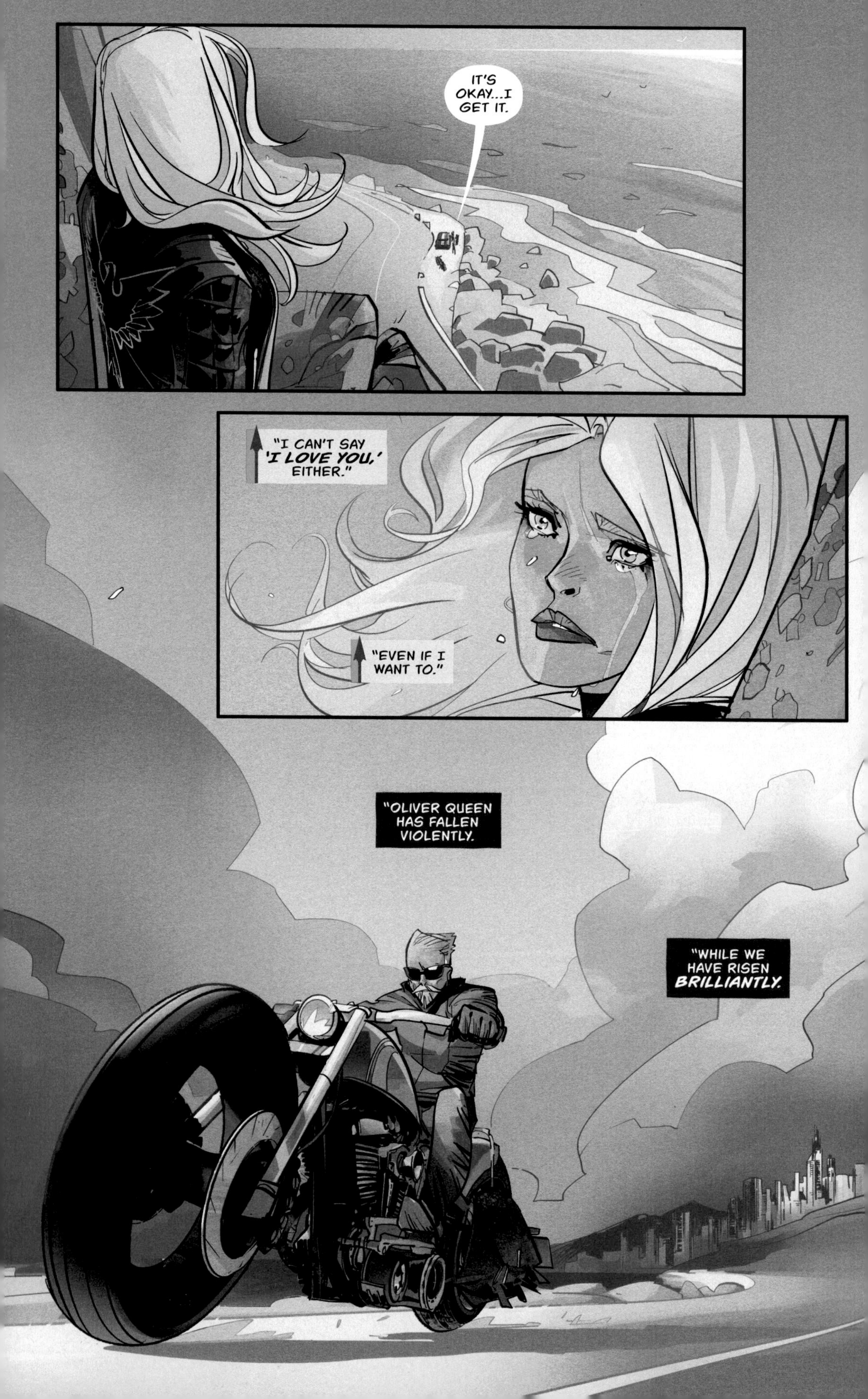
IT'S OKAY...I GET IT.
"I CAN'T SAY 'I LOVE YOU,' EITHER."
"EVEN IF I WANT TO."
"OLIVER QUEEN HAS FALLEN VIOLENTLY.
"WHILE WE HAVE RISEN BRILLIANTLY.

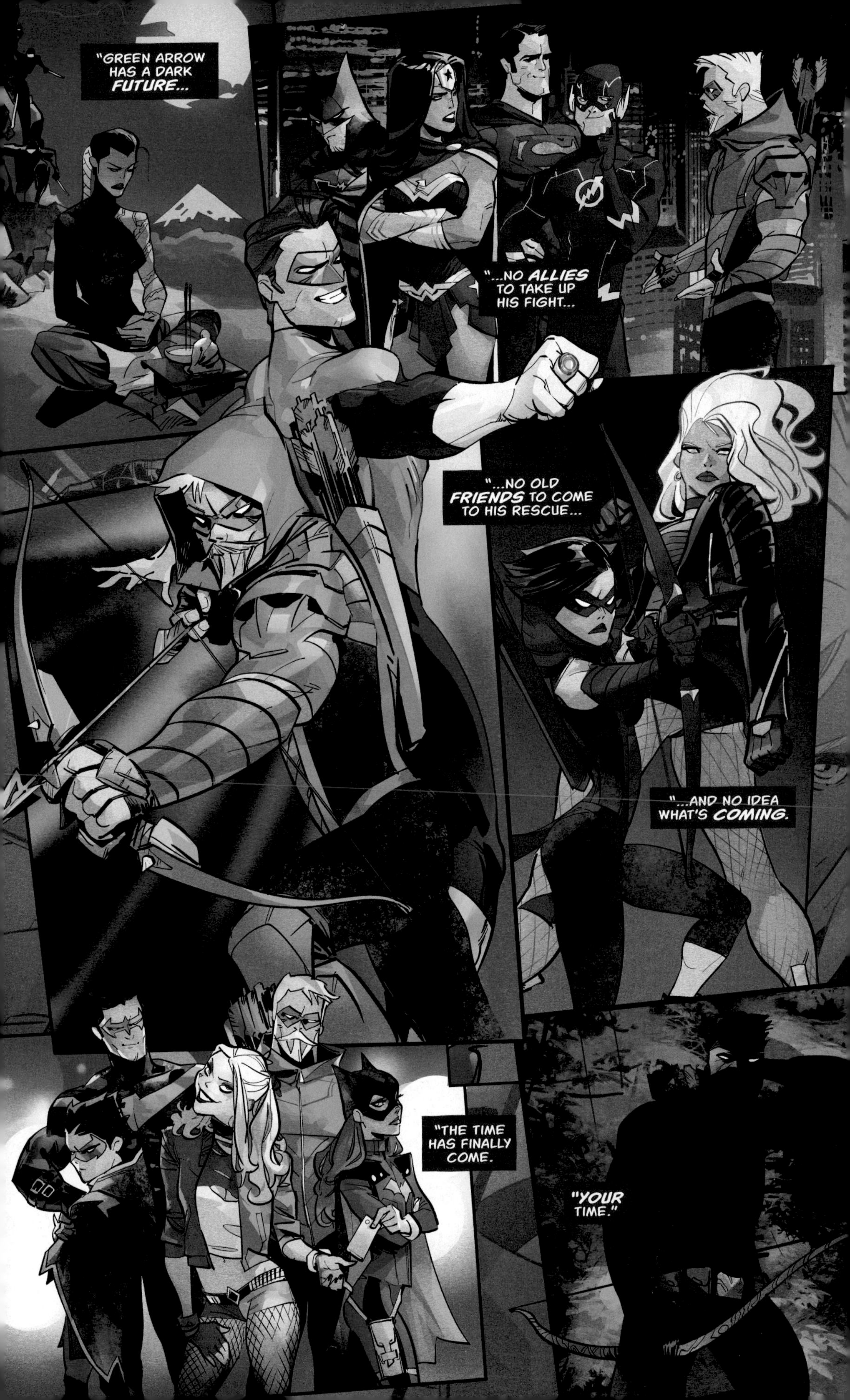
"GREEN ARROW HAS A DARK FUTURE...
"...NO ALLIES TO TAKE UP HIS FIGHT...
"...NO OLD FRIENDS TO COME TO HIS RESCUE...
"...AND NO IDEA WHAT'S COMING.
"THE TIME HAS FINALLY COME.
"YOUR TIME."

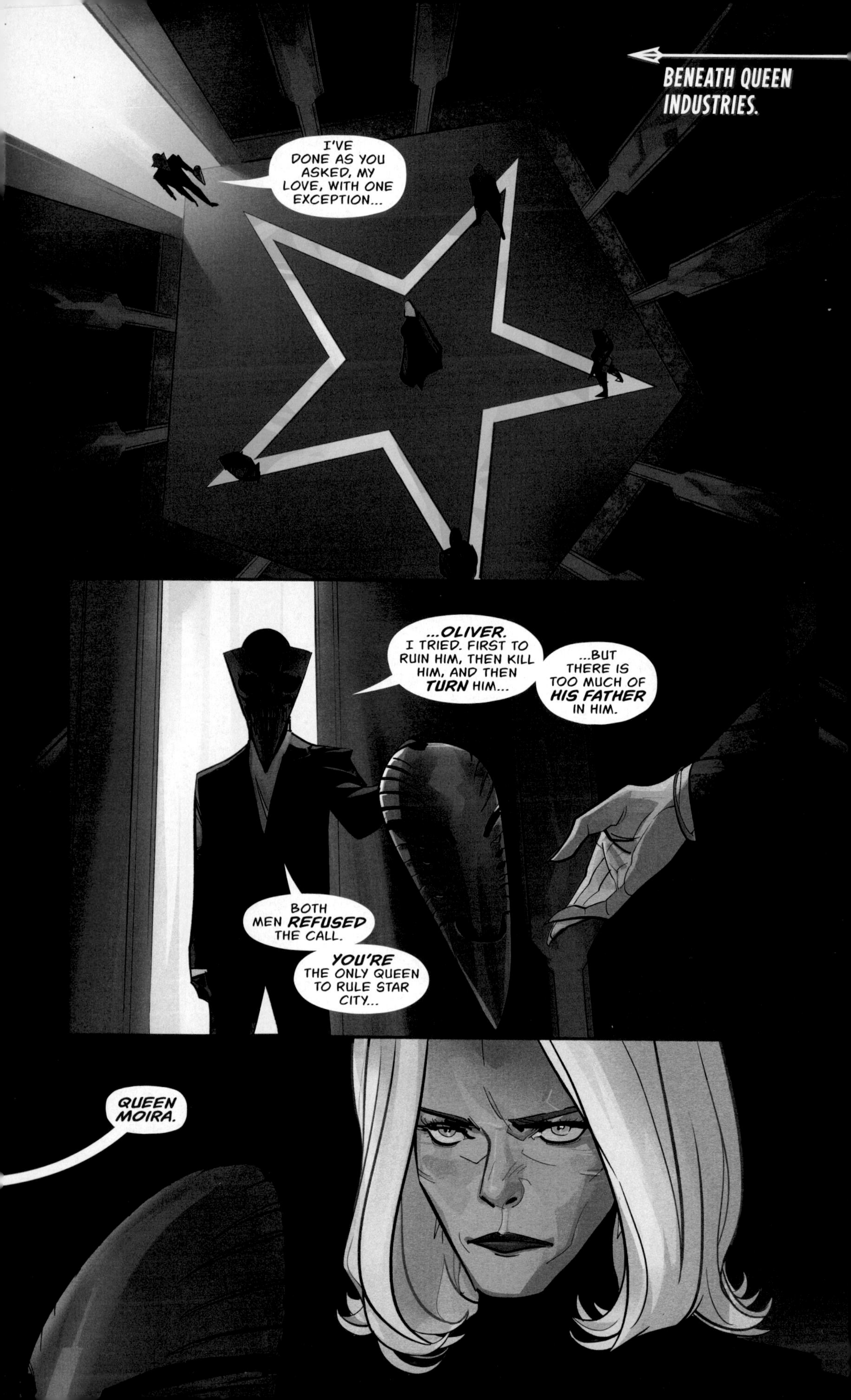

BENEATH QUEEN INDUSTRIES.
I'VE DONE AS YOU ASKED, MY LOVE, WITH ONE EXCEPTION...
...OLIVER. I TRIED. FIRST TO RUIN HIM, THEN KILL HIM, AND THEN TURN HIM...
...BUT THERE IS TOO MUCH OF HIS FATHER IN HIM.
BOTH MEN REFUSED THE CALL.
YOU'RE THE ONLY QUEEN TO RULE STAR CITY...
QUEEN MOIRA.

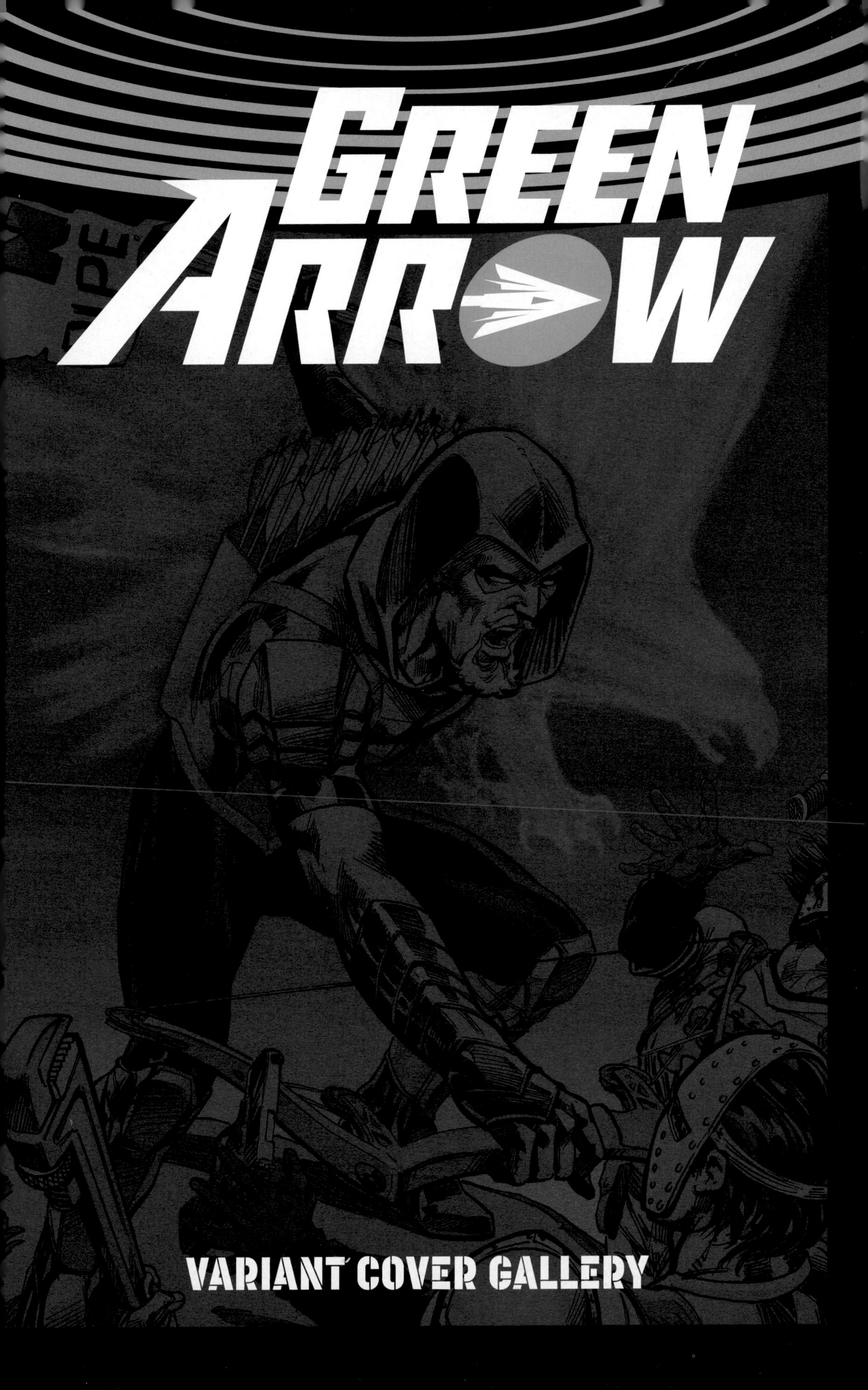
GREEN ARROW
VARIANT COVER GALLERY

GREEN ARROW #18 variant cover by MIKE GRELL with LOVERN KINDZIERSKI

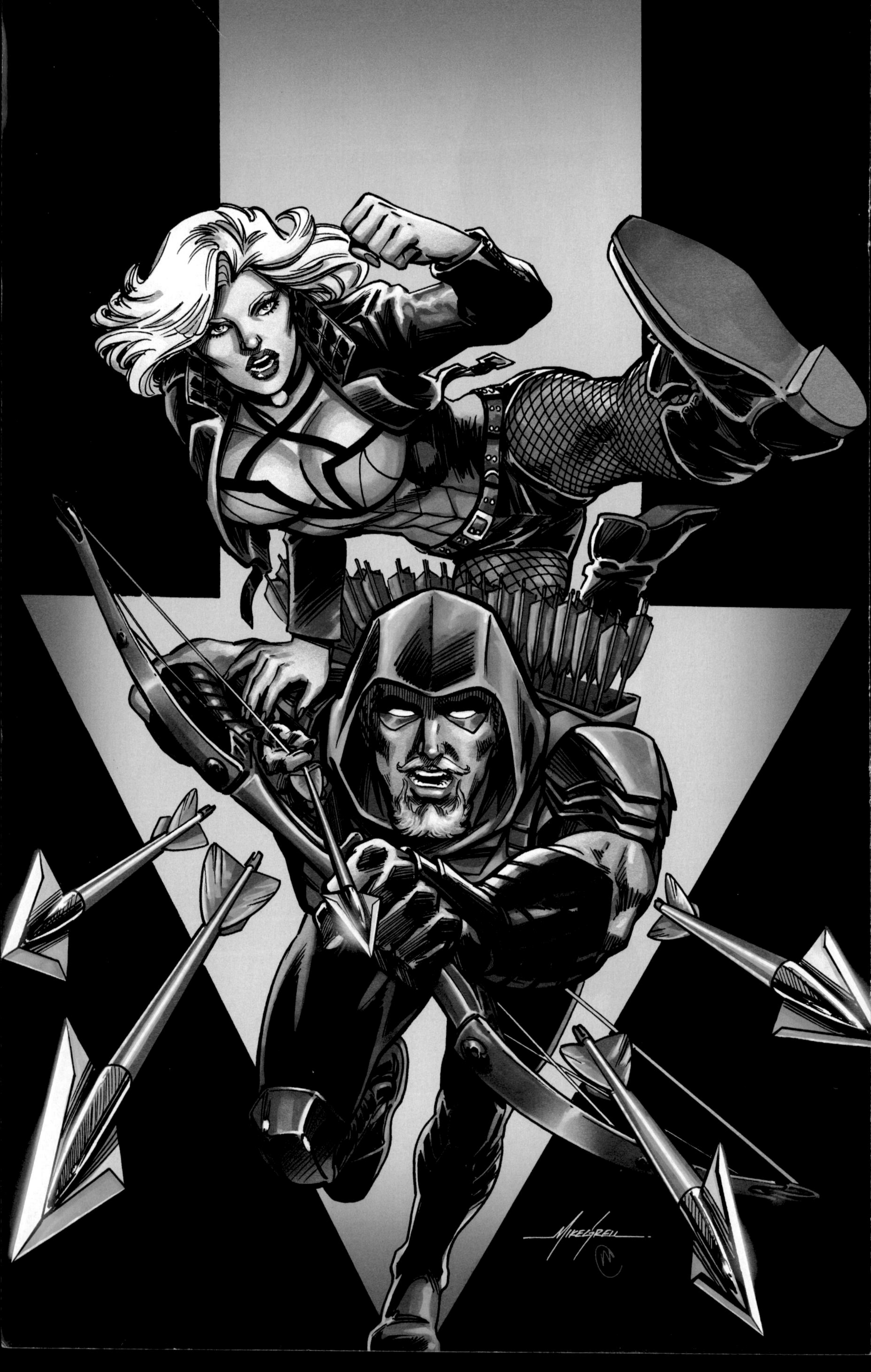

GREEN ARROW #19 variant cover by MIKE GRELL with LOVERN KINDZIERSKI

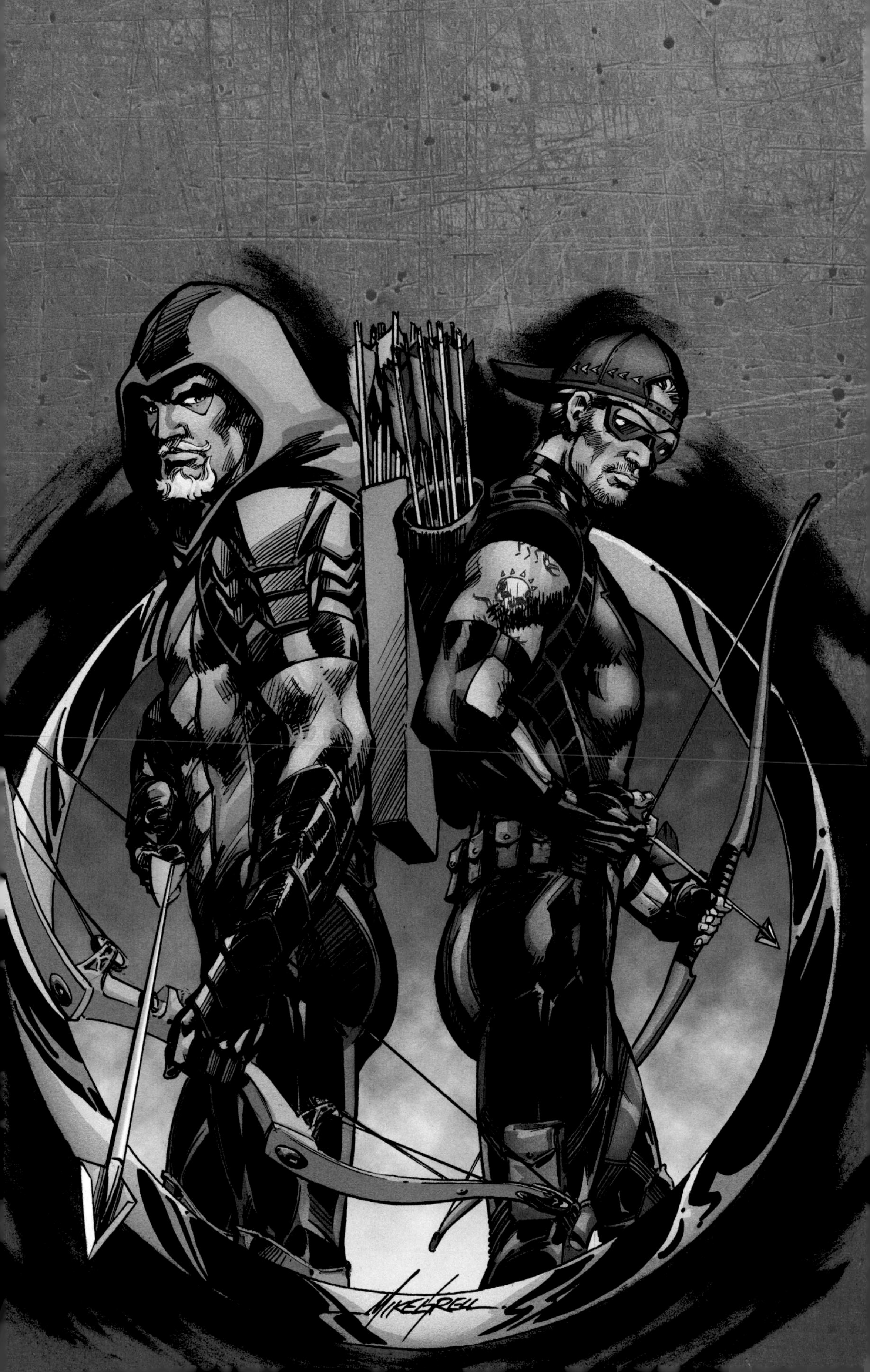

GREEN ARROW #20 variant cover by MIKE GRELL with LOVERN KINDZIERSKI

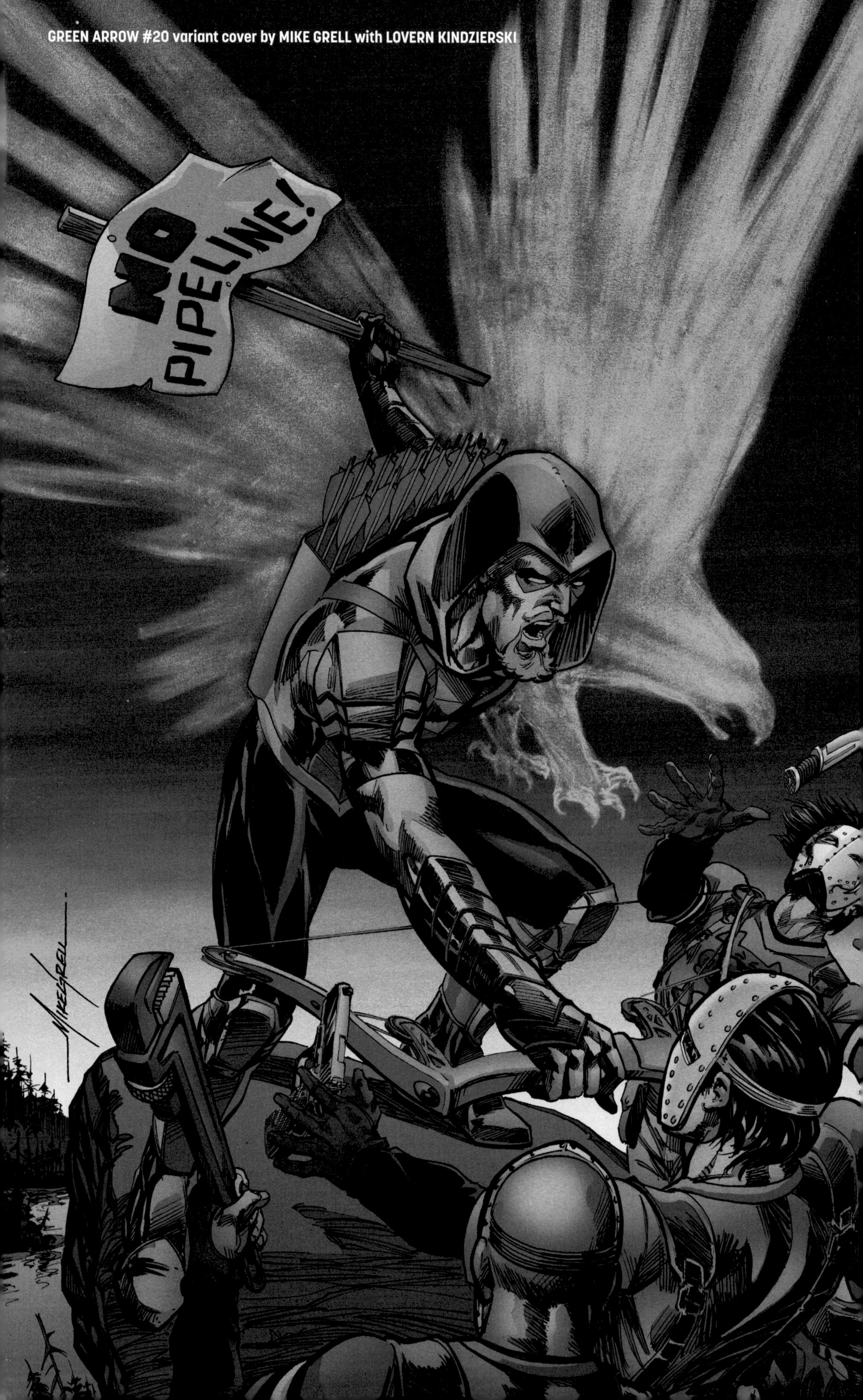

GREEN ARROW #21 variant cover by MIKE GRELL with LOVERN KINDZIERSKI

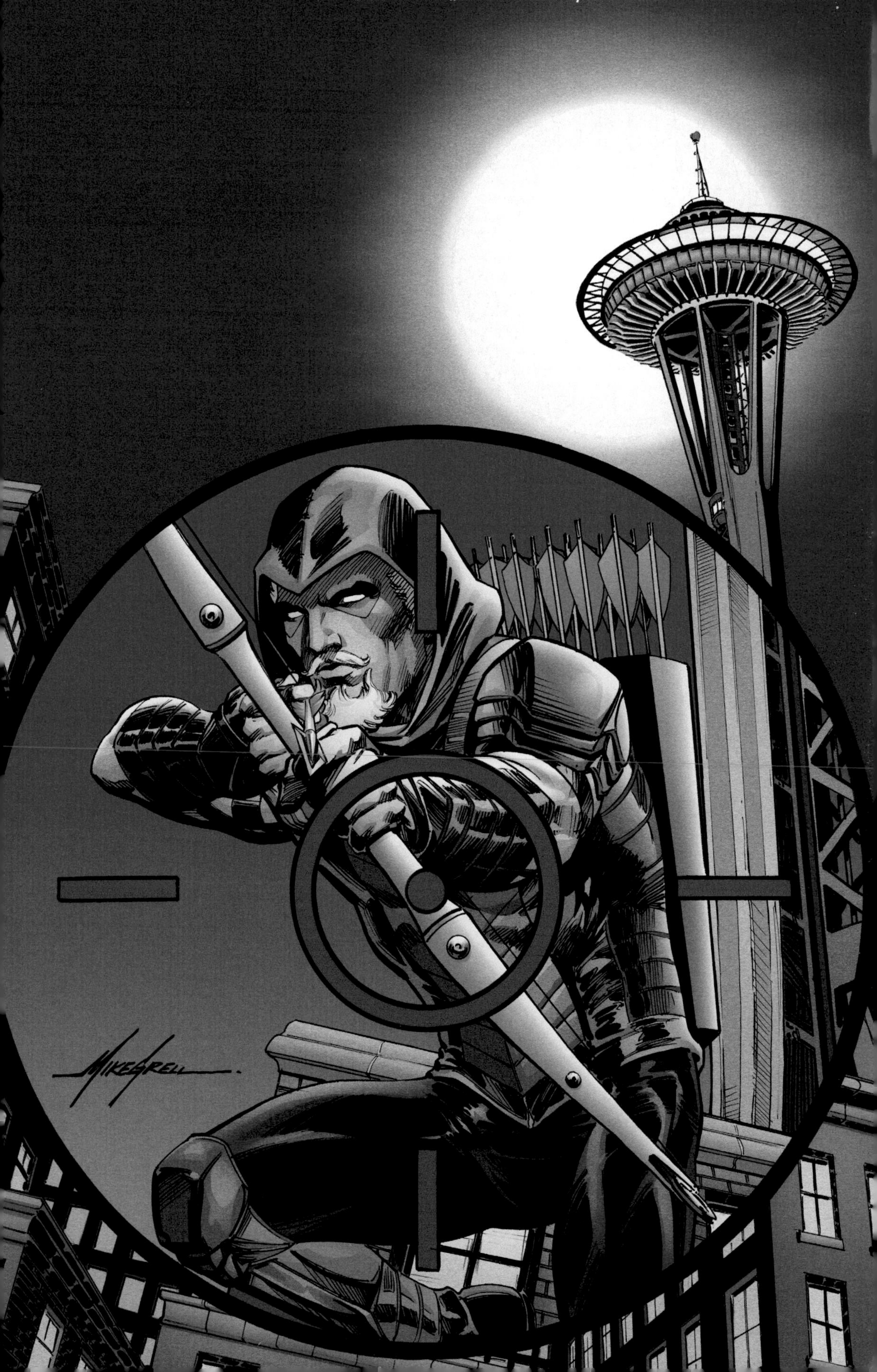
MIKE GRELL

GREEN ARROW #22 variant cover by MIKE GRELL with LOVERN KINDZIERSKI

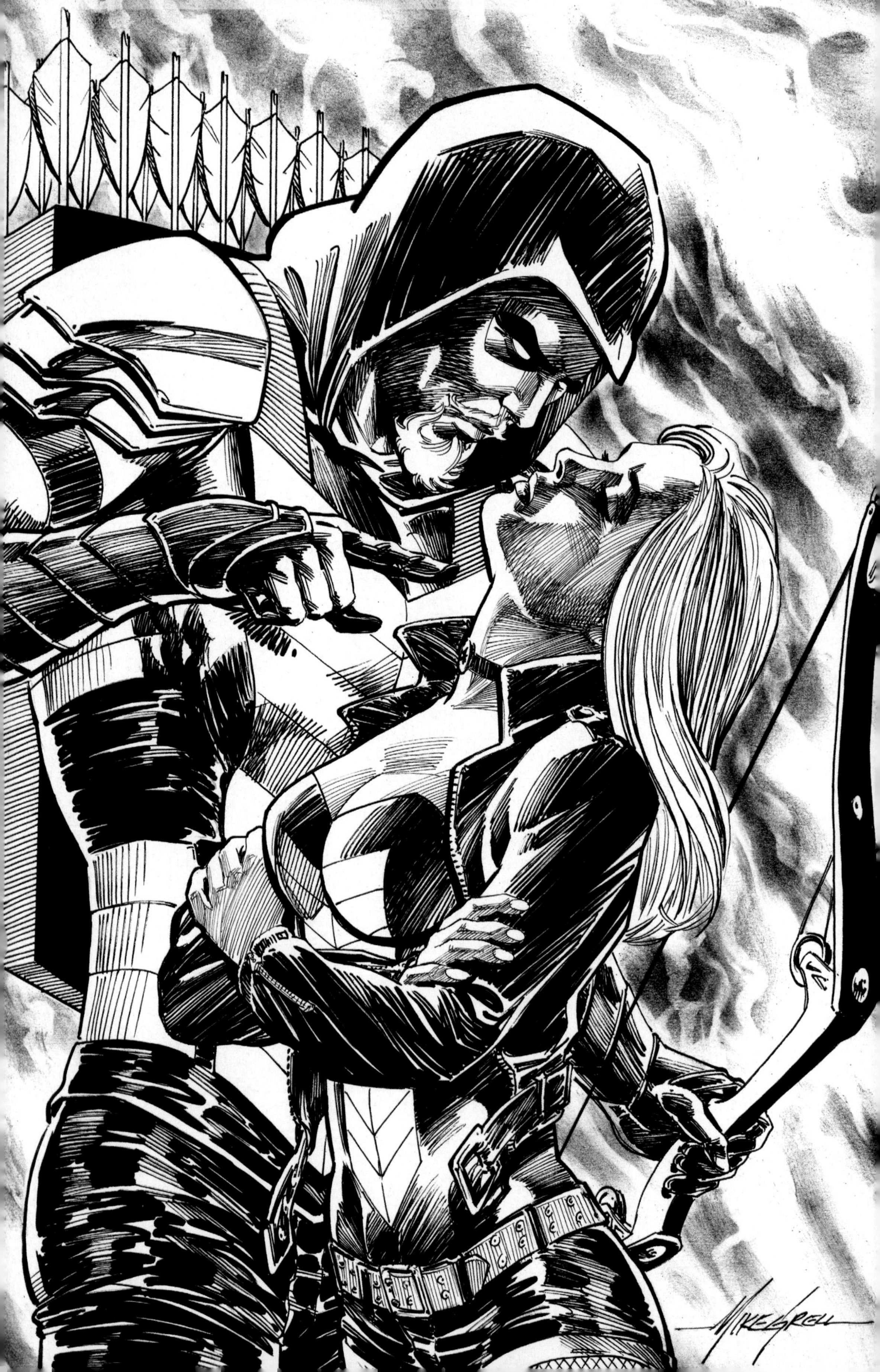

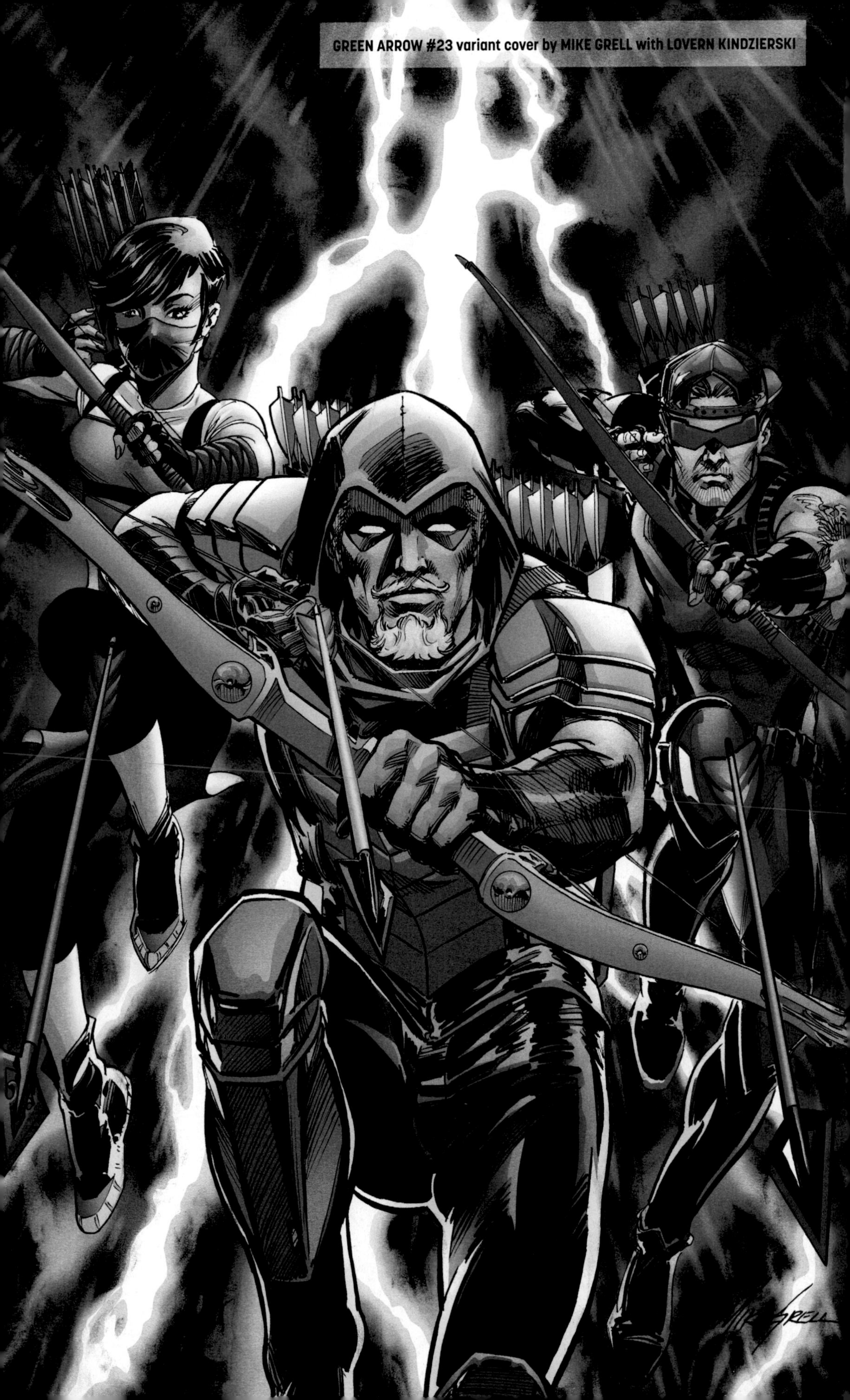

GREEN ARROW #23 variant cover by MIKE GRELL with LOVERN KINDZIERSKI

GREEN ARROW #24 variant cover by MIKE GRELL with LOVERN KINDZIERSKI

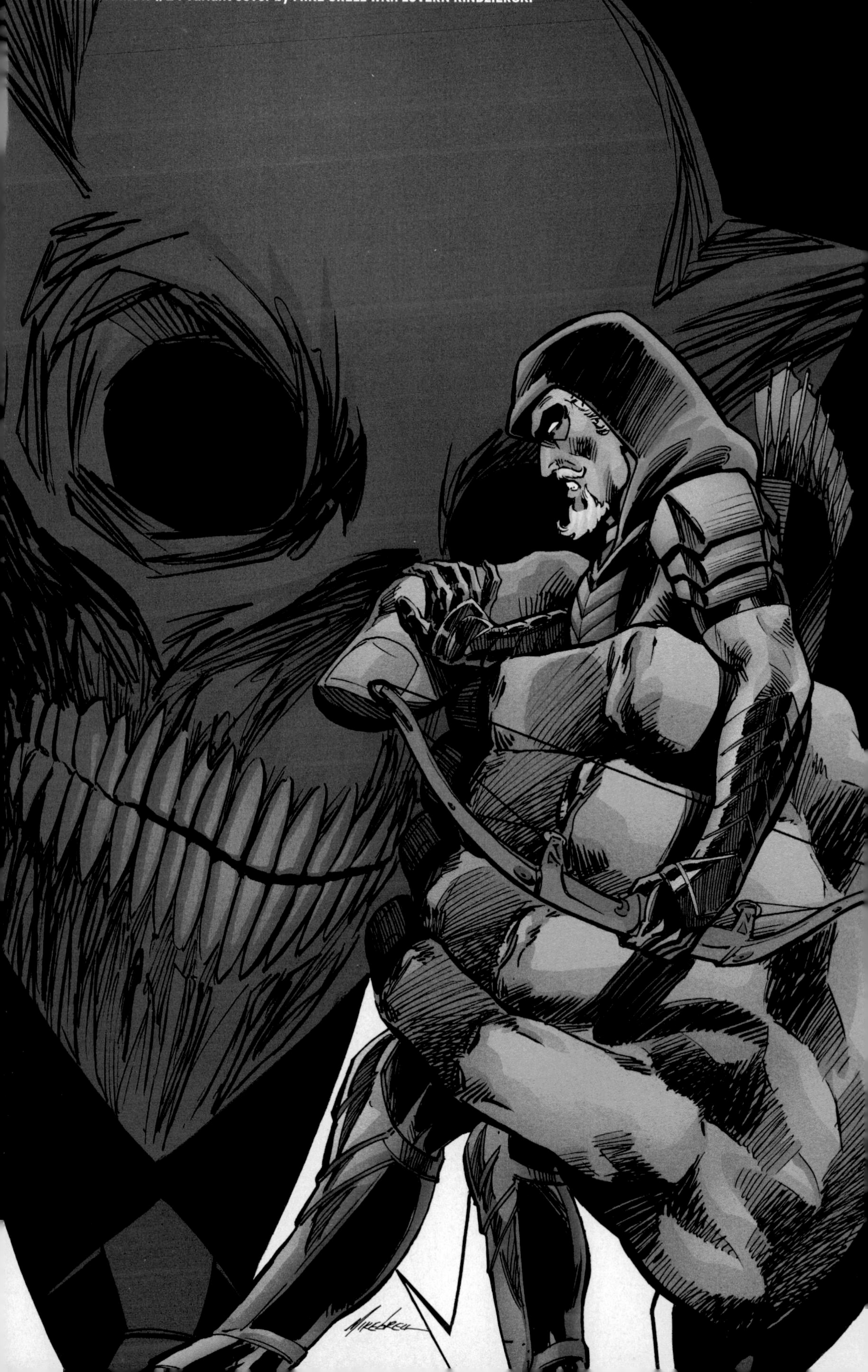

GREEN ARROW #25 variant cover by MIKE GRELL with LOVERN KINDZIERSKI

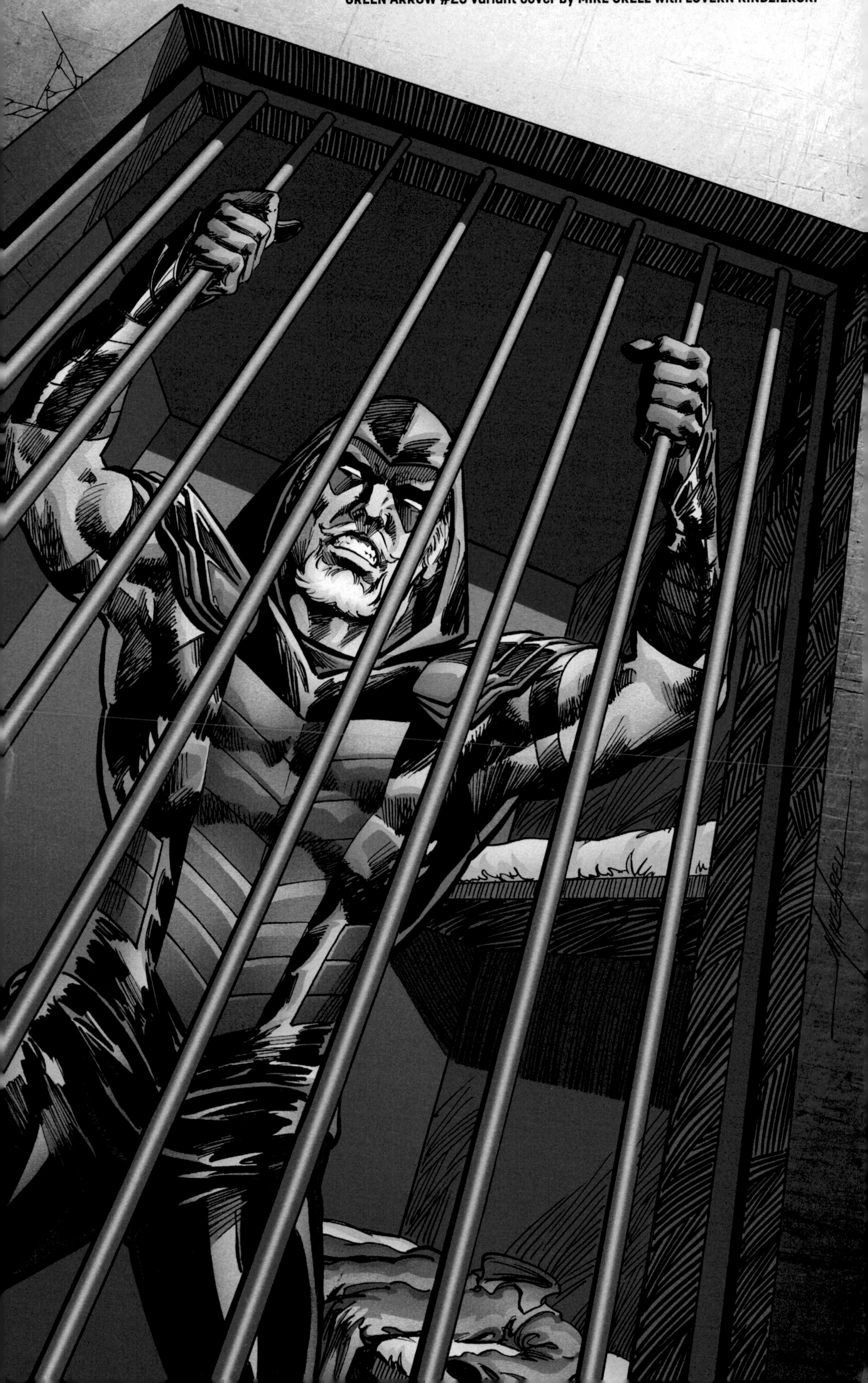

COUNT VERTIGO SKETCHES

BY ELEONORA CARLINI and OTTO SCHMIDT
BASED ON CONCEPTS BY JIM LEE

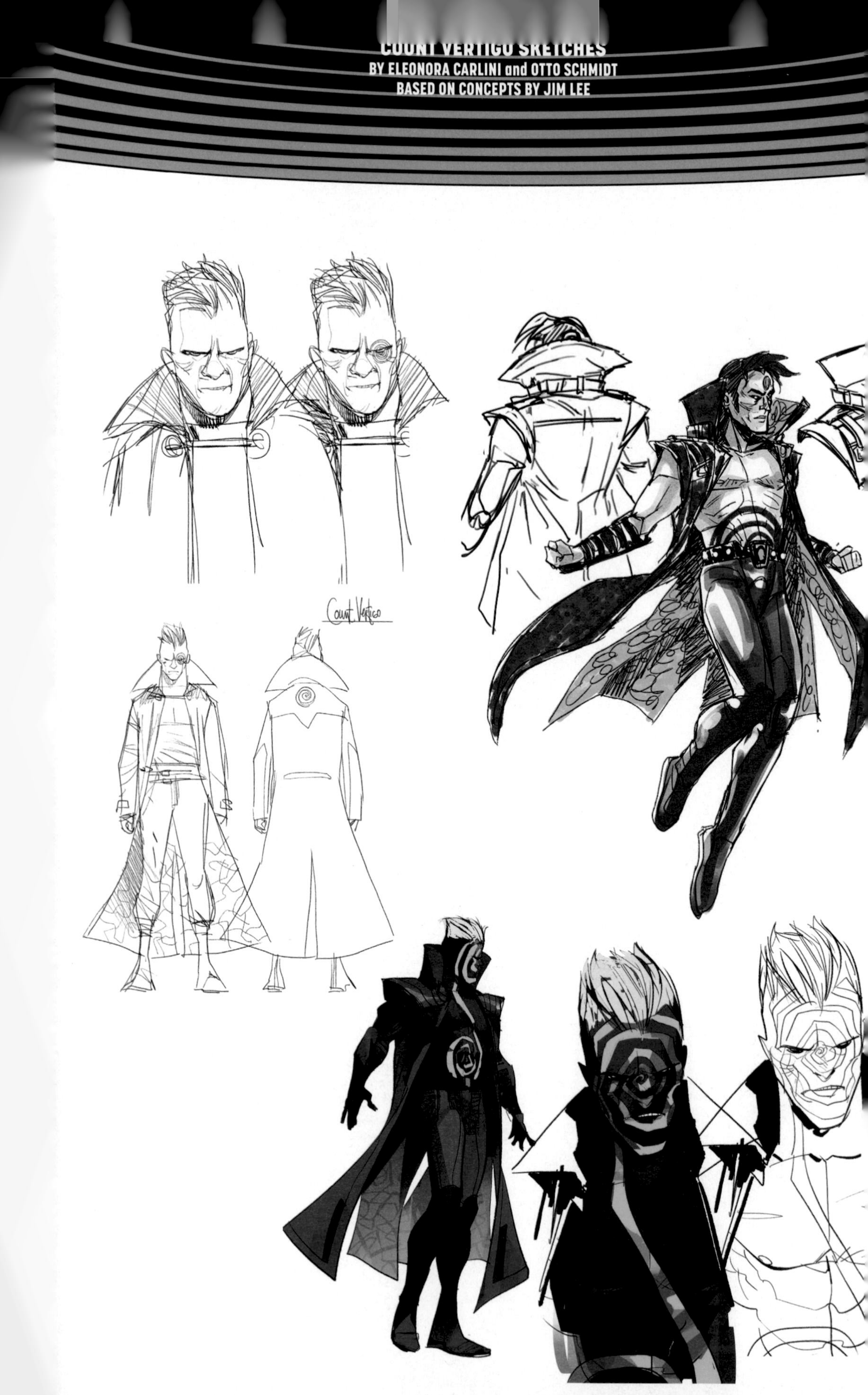
Count Vertigo

GREEN ARROW #21 PAGES 6-7 SKETCH-TO-COLOR PROGRESSIONS
BY JUAN FERREYRA

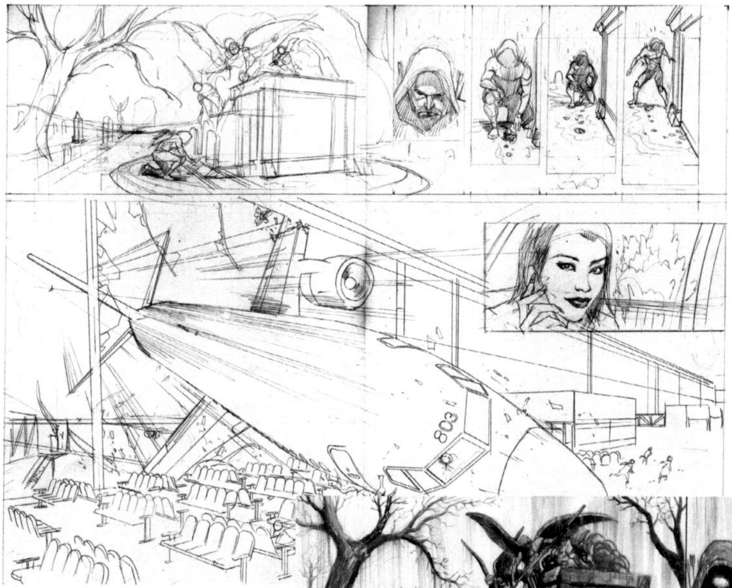
803

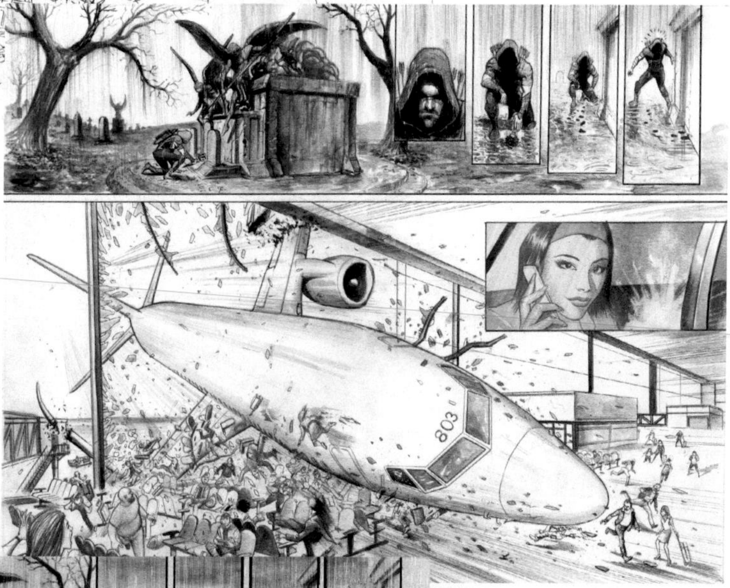
803

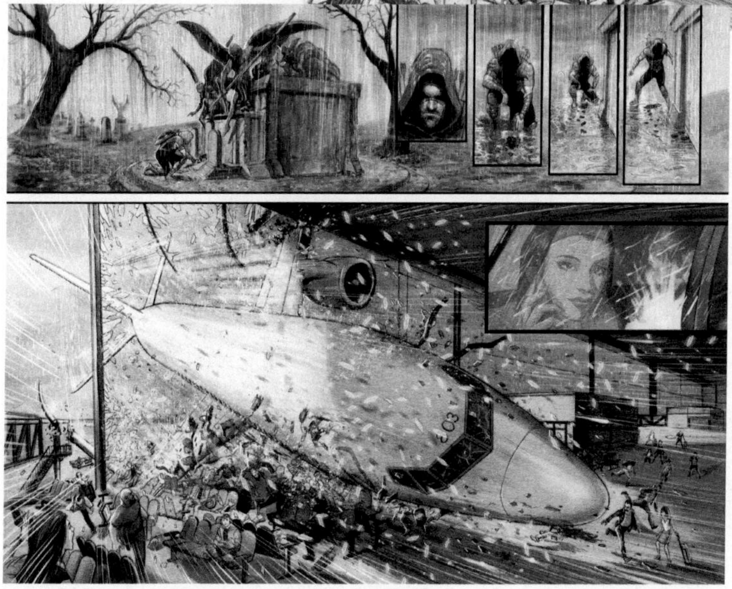

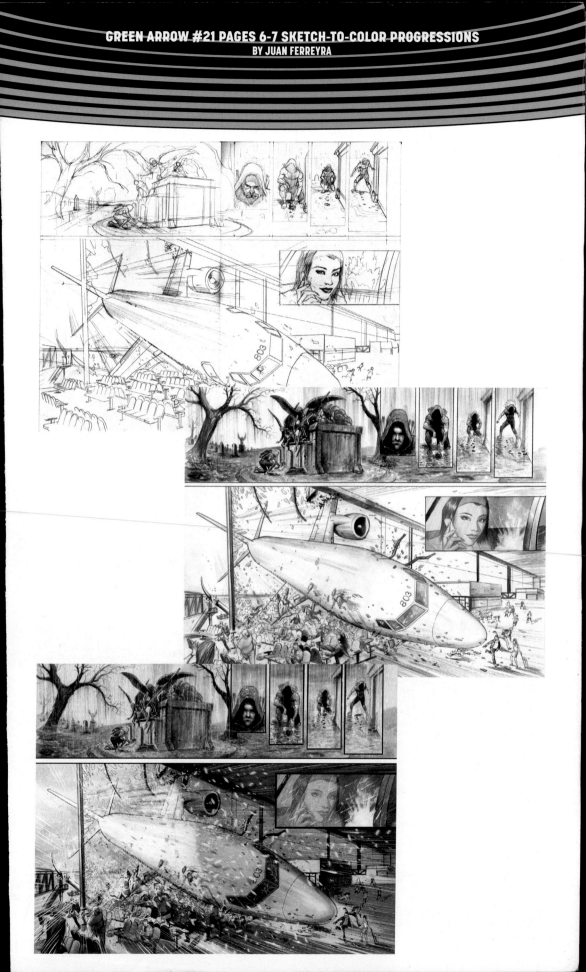

GREEN ARROW #23 PAGES 18-19 SKETCH-TO-COLOR PROGRESSIONS
BY JUAN FERREYRA

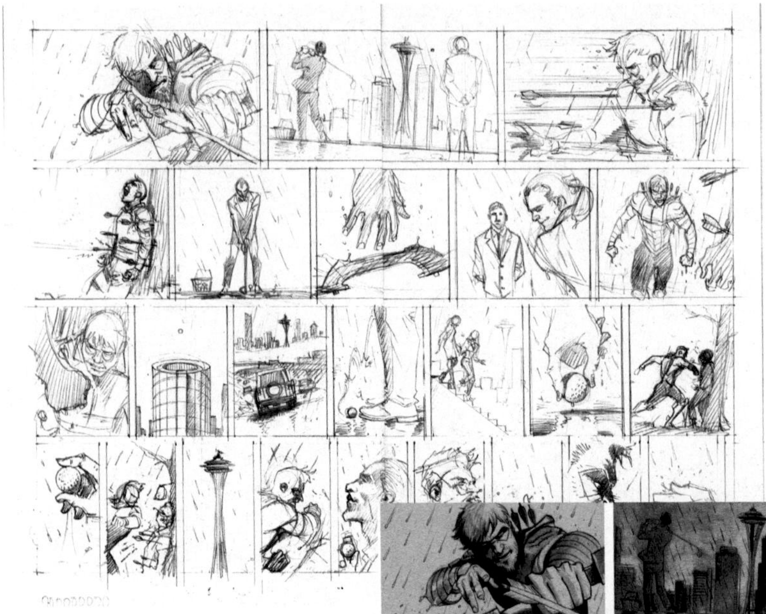

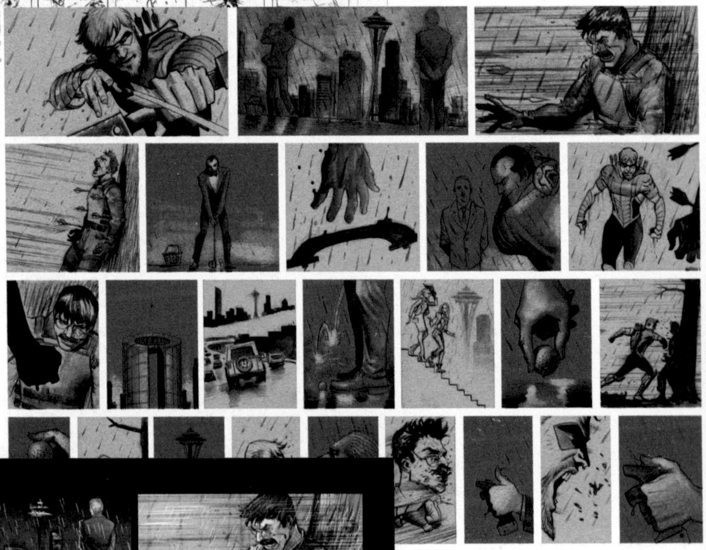

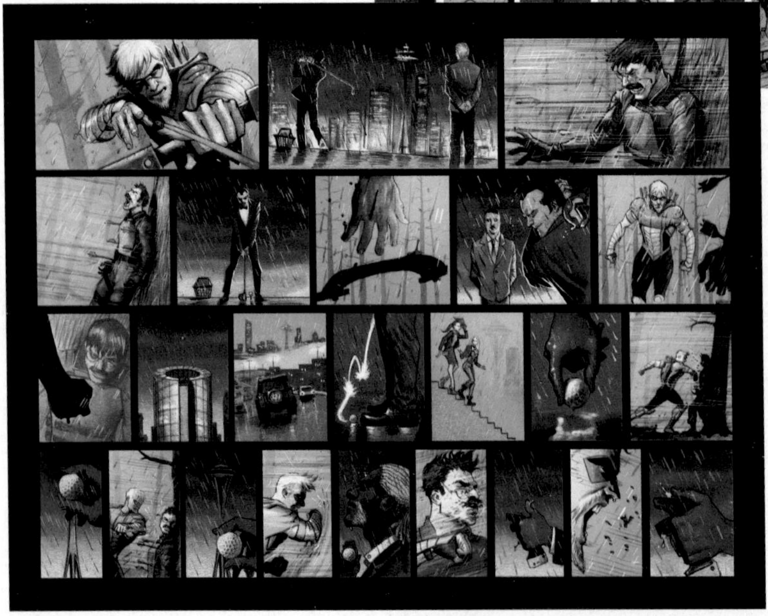

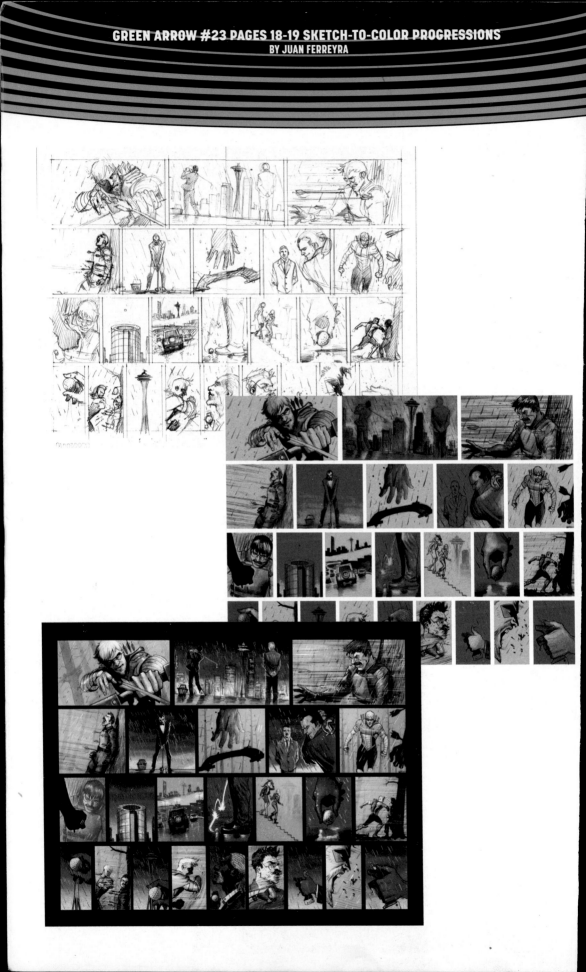